# SPEECHES OF THE EARL OF SHAFTESBURY

The Development of Industrial Society Series

Anthony A. Cooper
Earl of Shaftesbury

# SPEECHES OF THE EARL OF SHAFTESBURY

## upon Subjects Relating to the Claims and Interests of the Labouring Class

IRISH UNIVERSITY PRESS
Shannon   Ireland

First edition London 1868

This I U P reprint is a photolithographic facsimile of the first edition and is unabridged, retaining the original printer's imprint.

ⓒ *1971 Irish University Press Shannon Ireland*

*All forms of micropublishing*
ⓒ *Irish University Microforms Shannon Ireland*

ISBN 0 7165 1765 5

*T M MacGlinchey Publisher*
*Irish University Press Shannon Ireland*

PRINTED IN THE REPUBLIC OF IRELAND BY
ROBERT HOGG PRINTER TO IRISH UNIVERSITY PRESS

# The Development of Industrial Society Series

This series comprises reprints of contemporary documents and commentaries on the social, political and economic upheavals in nineteenth-century England.

England, as the first industrial nation, was also the first country to experience the tremendous social and cultural impact consequent on the alienation of people in industrialized countries from their rural ancestry. The Industrial Revolution which had begun to intensify in the mid-eighteenth century, spread swiftly from England to Europe and America. Its effects have been far-reaching: the growth of cities with their urgent social and physical problems; greater social mobility; mass education; increasingly complex administration requirements in both local and central government; the growth of democracy and the development of new theories in economics; agricultural reform and the transformation of a way of life.

While it would be pretentious to claim for a series such as this an in-depth coverage of all these aspects of the new society, the works selected range in content from *The Hungry Forties* (1904), a collection of letters by ordinary working people describing their living conditions and the effects of mechanization on their day-to-day lives, to such analytical studies as Leone Levi's *History of British Commerce* (1880) and *Wages and Earnings of the Working Classes* (1885); M. T. Sadler's *The Law of Population* (1830); John Wade's radical documentation of government corruption, *The Extraordinary Black Book* (1831); C. Edward Lester's trenchant social investigation, *The Glory and Shame of England* (1866); and many other influential books and pamphlets.

The editor's intention has been to make available important contemporary accounts, studies and records, written or compiled by men and women of integrity and scholarship whose reactions to the growth of a new kind of society are valid touchstones for today's reader. Each title (and the particular edition used) has been chosen on a twofold basis (1) its intrinsic worth as a record or commentary, and (2) its contribution to the development of an industrial society. It is hoped that this collection will help to increase our understanding of a people and an epoch.

The Editor
Irish University Press

# SPEECHES

OF THE

# EARL OF SHAFTESBURY, K.G.

UPON SUBJECTS HAVING RELATION CHIEFLY TO THE
CLAIMS AND INTERESTS OF

## THE LABOURING CLASS.

*WITH A PREFACE.*

LONDON:
CHAPMAN AND HALL, 193, PICCADILLY.
1868.

LONDON: PRINTED BY WILLIAM CLOWES AND SONS, STAMFORD STREET
AND CHARING CROSS.

# PREFACE.

THE idea of giving to the world a volume of speeches originated with my friends, and not with myself; and it is only in reluctant obedience to their wishes that I now venture to offer this selection to the notice of the public.

The object is to show the movement, by legislation and other means, towards the regulation of industrial labour for children and young persons, in the interest of their moral and physical condition. It purposes also to give some statements of other efforts made, with the same view, for the improvement of special classes, and of large masses of aggregated populations.

The first Sir Robert Peel, in 1802, after a long experience and use of the system, carried a measure to provide for the care and education of apprentices, who were sent down by barge-loads into Lancashire from the workhouses in London.

It had little or no effect. Sir John Hobhouse, now Lord Broughton, passed a bill, in 1825, for certain regulations in cotton mills; one in particular, for the prohibition of night-work in specified departments; and, at a much earlier period, Mr. Nathaniel Gould, whose name will ever be cherished in the manufacturing districts, had pressed the state of the children on the consideration of the mill-owners.

But the great movement which sought the reduction of the

hours of work did not begin until 1830, when Mr. Oastler, the Rev. Mr. Bull, Mr. Walker, and, above all, Mr. John Wood, worsted-spinner, of Bradford, whose zeal was only equalled by his munificence, appeared in the field. Michael Thomas Sadler at that time maintained the cause in Parliament with unrivalled eloquence and energy. The evidence of the Committee which he obtained, revealed to the world at large all the physical and moral evils of the system. He lost, however, his seat in 1833. It was then that, at the request of a deputation, the duty passed into my hands; and I desire to record the invaluable services of the remarkable men who preceded me. Had they not gone before, and borne such an amount of responsibility and toil, I do not believe that it would have been in my power to have achieved anything at all.

Nor can I, in justice to the operatives of the counties of Chester, Lancaster, and York, withhold an explanation of the principles on which the agitation was conducted. They agreed from the outset that all should be carried on in the most conciliatory manner; that there should be a careful abstinence from all approach to questions of wages and capital; that the labour of children and young persons should alone be touched; that there should be no strikes, no intimidation, and no strong language against their employers, either within or without the walls of Parliament. The movement was closed in the spirit in which it began. The great principle of the ten hours limit having been affirmed by the legislature, there arose no noisy and affronting exultation. Both parties, in the interest of peace, had made moderate concessions to each other. The men embraced the act with gratitude; the employers accepted it with cheerfulness; and to this we may ascribe the unbroken harmony between them that has subsisted to the present day. The great and terrible trial of the cotton famine may also be adduced in proof of the beneficial character of these remedial measures. The heroism and resignation, then manifested, called forth universal sympathy and admiration; and though I readily concede to the repeal of the Corn Laws the principal share in producing that marvellous tranquillity, I claim (and this on the authority of the operatives themselves) a part for the "Ten Hours Act;" because it showed unanswerably that the legislature had done for them, all that it could do, in the way of justice and humanity.

It was in no invidious spirit that the textile fabrics were the first selected for legislative operation. Everything could not be done at once; the prominence of these fabrics, with the vast numbers engaged in them, had attracted the attention of every one—and it was manifest, besides, that their order and discipline, the multitudes gathered under a single roof, whose toil was governed by the precision and publicity of steam-power, offered, for the enactment of legal restrictions, facilities which could not be found in employments of a less symmetrical and more widely spread character.

Very little was said on the introduction of my bill in 1833. It was allowed to go to a second reading without opposition, the government being determined to issue thereupon a Commission for further inquiry. The Commission being carried on a division, and having reported, after the delay of a few months, the House went into committee on the bill; but the first and important clause having been rejected, I threw the whole into the hands of the ministry. The clauses underwent, in consequence, very serious modifications; but though the measure fell far short of what I desired, it contained, nevertheless, some humane and highly useful provisions, and established, for the first time, the great principle that labour and education should be combined. In order to give the act a fair trial, little was done, for a few years in Parliament (though much out of it), beyond repeated remonstrances to the government, and an anxious observation of its working. It was not until 1838 that, in consequence of official negligences and delays, I actively resumed the question. From that time it was frequently before the House, and passed through many vicissitudes of success and defeat. It survived the powerful opposition of the government of Sir Robert Peel, who threatened, in 1844, to break up his administration unless the House of Commons rescinded the vote it had passed in favour of the ten hours principle. That vote was rescinded accordingly.

Throughout the whole of its parliamentary career two gentlemen, Mr. Fielden, the great manufacturer of Todmorden, and Mr. Brotherton, the member for Salford, rendered it the most important—in truth, indispensable services. The House of Commons felt the full weight of the singular experience, zeal, and disinterestedness of Mr. Fielden;—and the warm-hearted resolution and perseverance of Mr. Brotherton, who had himself been a factory lad, have left an impression on the minds of many, and specially on my own, that can never be effaced.

In 1845, having resigned my seat for Dorset, being unwilling any longer to resist the abolition of the Corn Laws, I gave the conduct of the amending bill I had introduced for fixing the limit of ten hours, to the care of Mr. Fielden. That bill was defeated by a majority of ten.

In 1847, Sir R. Peel having quitted office, another amending bill to the same effect was brought in by Mr. Fielden, carried successfully through the House, and sent to the Lords, where, under the able management of the first Lord Ellesmere, it passed, after an interesting debate, by a large majority. The bill became law; but its operation was greatly impeded by legal intricacies and every form of ingenious difficulty.

In 1848 I was enabled to resume the charge of the measure; and in 1850, emerging from many struggles, it was reduced to good working order. One provision alone was wanting, the provision for confining the labour of children of tender years within the hours between six and six. This was effected in 1853 by Lord Palmerston, when Secretary of State for the Home Department; and since that day the act has required neither impulse nor amendment.

In 1840, the ten hours question being fairly afloat, acknowledged in principle, and defying hostility, it seemed that a favourable hour had arrived for entering on the second part of the undertaking.

A Royal Commission, therefore, was moved for and granted, to "Inquire into the state of children in trades not protected by the Factory Acts." The Report having been made in 1842, became the basis of two bills, one for the removal of females from the mines and collieries, the other for the care and education of children in calico print-works. No more was done at that time; for, although the ability and diligence of the Commissioners had collected a vast amount of evidence showing the fearful condition of some one hundred and fifty trades, public opinion was not sufficiently ripe for so many extensive changes.

In the year 1862 I ventured to propose a renewal of the Commission, stating that since the issue of the first reports many trades had disappeared, and that others of a dangerous nature had started into existence. It was obtained; and on its voluminous evidence and wise recommendations was founded the legislation of 1864 and 1867. The bills were introduced by the governments of the day, by Mr. Bruce in 1864, and by Mr. Walpole in 1867. To the zeal and ability of the Commissioner Tremenheere, and Mr. Thring, the standing counsel to the Home Office, the public is indebted for the admirable arrangements of these measures. These bills were referred to a Select Committee; and perhaps I may be allowed to mention with gratitude the readiness of many of the great employers of labour to place themselves under restrictions for the benefit of the community.

The agricultural part of the question was reserved to the last, first, because it presented the greatest difficulties; and, secondly, because it required all the sympathy and experience to be derived from the proofs of success, furnished by the factories, to obtain for it a favourable reception. The subject of agricultural gangs I introduced to the House of Lords, on 11th April 1867, who referred it for farther inquiry to the Employment Commissioners. I shortly afterwards, on 18th June, presented a bill with provisions for the education, and, in some instances, for the regulation of the time of the youngest workers engaged in field-labour. The principle of it was affirmed by a second reading; and there seems to be no doubt that these children, like their fellows in the towns, will, so soon as the Commissioners have made a further report, be placed within the reach of the benefits and blessings of education.

It is most desirable that means should be instituted for bringing the rural children in larger numbers, and more regularly, into the elementary schools; that their education should, if possible, be prolonged beyond the present scanty term; and that, by the instrumentality of night-schools and other appliances, opportunity should be afforded of retaining, and refreshing, the knowledge which so many have acquired at nine years of age, but which they have totally lost at the age of seventeen. Nevertheless, with all these deficiencies, which the wisdom of Parliament will endeavour to supply, I cannot refrain from making, on behalf of the first-rate agricultural labourer, a larger claim than is usually admitted, to be considered a man of education. That he is "a skilled artisan" will any one deny? Look at him engaged with the plough; see the the length and straightness of each furrow, its mathematical precision, the steadiness of his hand and eye, and his masterly calculation of distance and force. Observe a hedger in all the various branches of that part of labour, and admit the accuracy of judgment that is required for a calling so apparently humble. No spinner could do what he does, any more than he could do what is done by the spinner. His talk, too, may be of bullocks; it may be also of sheep; it may be of every parochial matter; but then it is talk upon his special vocation; and oftentimes how sound and sensible it is! He has not, of course, the acquirements and acuteness of the urban operative; his labour is passed in comparative solitude, and he returns to his home at night, in a remote cottage or a small village, without the resource of clubs, mechanics' institutes, and the friction of his fellow-men. Still, he may say, with the most scientific, that he is master of the profession to which he is called; and every one will rejoice to add, to this honourable and useful career, whatever is possible to comfort and adorn it.

Among the improvements of agricultural life, I cannot omit

to mention one, which, whatever rebuke it may excite from some, has the approval of many experienced and thoughtful landowners.

The exclusion of girls of tender years from field labour (the periods of harvest, of course, excepted) would tend greatly to the moral, physical, and financial, advancement of the rural population. They go to their work under no supervision, or control, and are exposed (most injuriously to the female constitution, as every medical man will testify) to all the vicissitudes and inclemencies of the seasons. One of the main difficulties would lie, no doubt, in the strong antipathy of the girls themselves to the restraints of domestic service. They prefer the freedom, it may be the license, of out-door, or associated, labour. The taste may be seen, to a large extent, in the localities where the factory system prevails; it may be seen in many of our country districts, and I have very lately seen it in the south of France. The alteration might cause some trouble, and, perhaps, for a time, a little inconvenience; but I venture to think that it is indispensable to the real and permanent welfare of our race of husbandmen. The truth must be plainly stated; we require, in many classes of society, a new generation of wives and mothers.

The speeches on Lunatics and Lunatic Asylums are in harmony with the purpose of all the others, dealing, as they do, with the condition, mental and physical, of many thousands of the poorer sort. The address to the young men in houses of business in Manchester is equally applicable to the young men in similar establishments in all our great cities. They may be numbered by tens of thousands. The speech on Irrigation in India touches a matter which is of vital importance to millions of our fellow-subjects. And that on Religious Liberty in Turkey (religious liberty being the basis of civil liberty) concerns the freedom and progress of some fourteen millions of Christians, in whose independence and welfare none are more interested than the people of Great Britain.

In the direction of labour, very little now remains to be done. The legislature has covered nearly the whole of the industrial occupations; and the limit which, in their caution, they imposed of not extending the Factory Acts, at first, lower than to such establishments as contained fifty work-people, will hardly outlive the next session. The acts, if brought into operation with sagacity and zeal, will remove many of the abuses which have shocked the public mind by their cruel character and their defiance of all amendment.

But in other directions there is much room for personal and legislative effort. The Poor Laws, though vastly improved, are still much in arrear. It is more than probable that a better administration of them, in all their departments, would produce a greater amount of good at one half of the expense.

In all the large towns of the United Empire, and specially in London, there are myriads of vagrant children of both sexes; the seed-plot of every mischief, if left to themselves, but easily reclaimable, if taken in time. For these are provided the valuable, though, of course, temporary, institutions of ragged schools, training-ships, refuges, reformatories, and the like. But, while effective so far as they go, they are inadequate to the extent of the demand. If we have thirty thousand children in the ragged schools of the metropolis, we find full the same amount beyond their pale; and we could rapidly fill a dozen school-vessels, were the funds at hand for the maintenance of the lads.

It must, too, be borne in mind that these wandering tribes elude all permanent or systematic treatment. If forty thousand people, as it is estimated, flow into London every year, as many flow out; and there is within the circle of the town itself an enormous migratory mass, perpetually on the move, and giving rarely a three months' residence to any locality on which they may drop down. No one will fancy that such stragglers as these can ever be met by any of the ordinary appliances.

But it is to sanitary and domiciliary improvements, without which all schemes for education will be nearly fruitless, that the public must look for the most beneficial and lasting results; and it is to the neglect of them that it must look for the most disastrous issues, physically and morally. I trust I shall not be regarded as speaking in too dogmatic a spirit, when I assert, after more than thirty years of anxious and constant inquiry, that the horrible state of our towns, and the condition of the dwellings of many of our people, lie at the root of two thirds of the disorders that afflict our land. Good drainage, good ventilation, good and healthy houses, and an ample supply of good water, would, by their effects, abate the demands on private charity, and the public rates; would go far to extinguish epidemics, and largely reduce fevers; would lessen mortality, and increase the length of man's working-life. There would be fewer young widows, and fewer orphans. New habits would be formed, and the spirit of vagrancy much suppressed; and, with it, a fruitful means of the spread of disease. The magistrates would have more leisure, and the police less trouble. Intemperance, also, the great curse of our country, the cause and consequence of innumerable evils, would bend before their influence. Much legislation, now necessary, would become needless; even Sunday-trading, and liquor-bills, would be superseded by the self-imposed restrictions of the people themselves.

The people will shortly be in the possession of absolute power. It will be for them to preserve these benefits that they have attained. They will no longer require any advocates, though doubtless many would be at hand, should the necessity arise. The twofold object of those who undertook these movements has received, in one part, an accomplishment, while the other is yet wrapped in the future. The first object was the happiness, honour, and prosperity of the Working-People themselves. That this end has been attained, is attested by the united voice of the operatives, the employers, the inspectors, and all who are conversant with industrial life, and especially by the generous avowals of the late Sir James Graham and of Mr. Roebuck, who had given, during many years, the hottest opposition to all factory legislation.

The second contemplated the interest of the State, in the probability of the event which has just consigned to the people at large the government of this great empire. Though an

*

issue so sudden and extensive had not been foreseen, it was manifest that serious changes could not be very far distant. Whether these humble efforts have contributed, in any measure, however small, to render the revolution less dangerous, and more gentle, is yet to be developed.

S.

*May,* 1868.

---

NOTE. In 1862, the last account made up, the number of children at school daily, between the ages of eight and thirteen, employed in the textile fabrics, originally protected by the Factory Act, was 64,411.

In 1833, a few attended Sunday school. Perhaps not fifty would have been found in day schools.

When the Factory Acts Extension shall be in full operation over the additional surface of fourteen hundred thousand women, children, and young persons, engaged in trades, and when the principle of them shall have been applied to the agricultural districts, it may safely be calculated that the number, combining education and labour, will be six-fold what it is at present.

I subjoin some passages from a statement sent to me a few days ago by Mr. Baker, now Chief Inspector of Factories, who for thirty-four years has devoted the greatest ability and most consummate judgment to this department of the public service.

"Remembering as I do when there was no Factory Act, except that of 1802—when the little secular education that factory-workers obtained was almost wholly in the Sunday-school—when children of the tenderest years were employed fourteen or fifteen hours a-day, and often, all night—when factory cripples were a specific class of deformities constantly to be seen in the manufacturing districts, and when human life indeed was held in small comparison with commercial profits—I cannot but regard every movement towards reasonable legislative restriction of labour, as providential in every sense, whether nationally, locally, or individually. What should we have been as a people, morally and socially, but for the means which this has afforded to the workers for instruction both in domestic and general acquirements? . . . Its value is already manifest in the improved character of the people amongst whom the law has been longest extant: similar results are following in districts where it has even been but recently introduced; and everywhere, both at home and abroad, the great principles of the Factory Acts are recognized as the readiest and most politic method of bringing all labour within the scope of education, which, however variously carried out, cannot fail to be productive of the happiest effects on the people."

# TABLE OF CONTENTS.

## Table of Contents.

## ERRATUM.

Page 403, for " viz." *read* " in."

*Children in Factories.*

# HOUSE OF COMMONS,

## Friday, July 20, 1838.*

On the question that the House do resolve itself into a Committee of Supply,

Lord Ashley rose and said that he felt exceedingly sorry to interfere with the order of the day, and he felt himself most reluctantly driven to adopt that course; he had made every effort to avoid it, but the House must be aware that those efforts had been made in vain. Nothing, then, remained for him but to bring the question forward on the present occasion. In doing this, he felt that at least his was a perfectly constitutional course, and from that course he had resolved not to swerve until he should obtain from the Queen's Government a full, final, and decisive answer. Were he to do otherwise, his sincerity might reasonably be suspected after the many pledges he had given on the subject, and after the many ministerial promises and infringements of them; and he trusted that in discharging this important duty, he should prove how unfair it was to designate the excitement which prevailed on the subject as unjust agitation.

According to returns made up to the year 1835—returns even then confessedly imperfect—it appeared that the number of persons manually engaged in cotton and other mills amounted to 354,684. Of course the numbers directly and indirectly interested in these trades greatly exceeded that amount. From the able pamphlet of Mr. Greg, he learned that not fewer than 4,000,000 men, women, and children, were interested in the various branches

* From "Hansard."

of these manufactures. From the statement which he intended to lay before the House he hoped to be able to show that the question was one not only of importance to the manufacturing districts, but of great moment to the country at large. Of the 354,684 persons manually engaged in cotton mills, 196,385 were females, being about 55 per cent. drawn in this way from their domestic duties and occupations to the unsuitable labour of the mills. Since the year 1816, 80 surgeons and physicians had deposed to the cruel and alarming oppression to which factory children were exposed. This evidence he need hardly add was confirmed by the medical commissioners appointed in 1833. In 1815 it appeared that the length which a child travelled in a single day in the performance of its labour was 8¼ miles. In the year 1832 the distance they travelled daily was 20, often 25 miles. This was stated with respect to the mill of the hon. member for Oldham, from observations made by himself, a mill which did not work at such high speed as others of the same class. In some the length travelled per day amounted to 30 miles, being a severity of labour exceeding that imposed upon soldiers in forced marches, or under arms before the enemy, a fact established by the evidence of the eminent surgeon, Mr. Guthrie.

The consequences of this cruel labour were apparent in the returns relating to mortality in the manufacturing districts. This was an issue as to matters of fact, and he had spared no pains to establish his facts on grounds which could not be shaken. His calculations he had submitted to the most careful investigation; they had been examined by one of the first actuaries in England, or perhaps in Europe, who had gone through them with the greatest accuracy and patience. The result on which he staked his credit was, that in those districts where the factory system extensively prevailed as many persons died under 20 years of age as under 40 in any other part of England.

Not many days ago a document was transmitted to him from Mr. William Pare, the superintendent registrar in Birmingham, which drew a comparison between the mortality of that town and Manchester. He (Lord Ashley) had submitted it, lest there should be some mistake, to the same actuary, and the result was, that in Birmingham one half of the population attained their 16th year, while in Manchester one half died within the first three years. From the several comparisons which had been instituted, it appeared that the value of human life was much greater in Birmingham than in Manchester, arising in part, no doubt, from the superiority of its geographical position, but mainly from the superior nature of the employment, and the better habits of the working people. So much for their bodies; but what was their moral state? Since 1816 no less than 60 clergymen, either by documents or in person, had exhibited the vicious and awful condition of those districts, and the utter hopelessness of any efforts to impart to people engaged in factory labour anything like moral or religious instruction. In 1835 a petition was presented from 200 Sunday-school teachers, declaring that it was quite impossible, even on the Sabbath-day, to convey to their minds, wearied and exhausted as they were, any beneficial instruction whatever.

The noble lord then read several extracts from the evidence given before the committee on combination by Mr. Sheriff Alison, of Glasgow. Mr. Sheriff Alison said—" I would recommend that the hours of employment of workmen should be peremptorily fixed at 10 hours a day. I am quite sure that this would have the best possible effect, both upon the spinners, and in particular upon the piecers and the factory children; and I am quite sure it is the only thing that can possibly be done which will ever remedy the evils to which the inferior class of labourers connected with cotton factories are exposed." When asked whether he considered " this mitigation of labour as a *sine quâ non* with respect to any improvement of the manufacturing population?" "I think," he said, " it is, decidedly; I am quite sure that all attempts to improve the condition of the factory children would be nugatory without it ;" and he added, in answer to this question: " Do you see any means whatever of securing the peace and the happiness of those people, and the peace and happiness of the empire, except by giving to the children both the time and the means of a moral and religious education?" " I think not; unless they can get the means of moral and religious education, and time for it, and unless the habits of moral depravity which now overspread the skilled classes from the operation of those combinations are removed, I am perfectly certain that the existence of the British empire will be overthrown, that the moral pestilence will overturn entirely the social state of the country, and I see already around me every day in Glasgow that we are just to be considered as standing at the gate of the great pest-house. I see the labouring classes depraving to an extent under my eyes which I cannot find language sufficiently strong to impress the committee with." This was neither more nor less than an ample fulfilment of the prophecy uttered before a committee of the House of Commons in 1816 by the late Sir Robert Peel, when giving evidence in support of a bill to limit the hours of factory labour. " Such indiscriminate and unlimited employment of the poor will be attended with effects to the rising generation so serious and alarming, that I cannot contemplate them without dismay; and thus that great effort of British ingenuity, whereby the machinery of our manufactures has been brought to such perfection, instead of being a blessing to the nation, will be converted into the bitterest curse."

Did the noble lord opposite, then, think that this question was to be evaded? Did he believe matters of this kind could be forgotten by the people because they were not listened to with attention in that House? It was utterly impossible. The evil was increasing daily and hourly; and unless they addressed themselves to it speedily and effectively, it would assume a magnitude which they would never be able to master. It was not his business, at that moment, to enter into any statement of the comparative merits of the 10 or 12 hours bill; but, looking to the measure which had been introduced and passed by the present Government, he did require a full and final answer as to their intentions with respect to their own law. If it were good, let them enforce it; if bad, let them mend it; if it were unnecessary or dangerous, let them repeal it. But to leave the law in its present condition was equally unwise and absurd. It not only withheld just protection from the factory children, but, by pretending to give protection, deprived them of the sympathy of a deluded public.

The noble lord then alluded to the history of the Factory Bill in so far as he had been identified with it. In 1833 he introduced a measure nominally called the Ten Hours Bill; it met with great support in the country, upwards of 200,000 having signed petitions in its favour. The Government then felt something must be done, and they introduced a bill which was substituted for his on the ground of its superior humanity and higher moral pretensions. In particular, it enacted that no children under nine should be employed in factories (making exceptions, however, with respect to *silk* and *lace* mills), and that those above that age and under 13 should be worked only 48 hours a week. Those who employed the children were also compelled to give them two hours of instruction every week. Such were the provisions by which the sympathy of the public and the support of that House had been obtained to the defeat of his own bill; but those were the very clauses that were the first to be violated, and violated they had been to the present day. The noble lord and his colleagues were perfectly aware of those violations of the law, and yet they connived at them. (*No, no*, from Lord J. Russell.) Would the noble lord say that he was not aware that the educational clauses of his own bill had been set at nought in almost every factory in the country? Had the Government been left in ignorance of the operation of their own bill? Had they been left in the belief that it was carried into effect, and generally, or even partially, obeyed throughout the populous districts? Why, in August, 1834, seven months after it came into operation, Mr. Rickards, who had charge of the great manufacturing district in Lancashire, reported that unless an effective system of check and control were adopted, the execution of the law must depend on the will of individual millowners, the grossest abuses must prevail, the act itself become a standing jest, and the situation of inspector perfectly useless.

The noble lord then read several extracts from the inspectors' reports. He was anxious to state the whole of his case, not from private documents, not from individual reasonings, but from the official statements of inspectors appointed by the Government to carry the act into operation, and who made their reports to the noble lord the Secretary of State for the Home Department four times every year. He would undertake to show from those reports, and from them exclusively, that the act had been systematically violated from the time when it passed till the present day, and that, notwithstanding the urgent representations and remonstrances of their own inspectors, the Government had done nothing whatever to assist them in the discharge of their duties. Mr. Rickards said, " The utter impracticability of the education clauses is so obvious that should this matter be hereafter called in question, I trust I shall stand excused for dispensing with it altogether." Such was the fate of the principal of those clauses, on the strength of which ministers had been enabled to reject the bill of 1833. In a joint report of the inspectors in the same year it was stated that, unless the superintendents had power to enter the mills whenever they pleased, the act itself would become a dead letter. In 1835, Mr. Rickards said, " I have repeatedly urged in former reports, and still beg to repeat to your lordship, that it is essential to the efficiency of the act that the superintendents should be empowered to enter the mills from time to time, as they may think proper." Yet nothing whatever had been done to assist the inspectors in that respect. Delay was the most convenient course of policy which the noble lord could follow, and delay was therefore preferred to justice.

Had the act in 1836 and 1837 been better observed? Did the inspectors discover any further inherent power in the act to enable them to carry it into effect without the interference of the Legislature? During the whole of that time Mr. Horner and Mr.

Howell were still loud in their remonstrances. The former, in 1837, said, with great emphasis, at the end of his report—" I cannot omit to lay again before your lordship (the Secretary for the Home Department) my firm conviction that an alteration in the law as regards the age of the children is absolutely necessary, in order to carry into effect the intention of the Legislature—that no child under 13 shall work more than 48 hours a week. In many instances," continued the inspector, " children under 11 work 12 hours a day." In 1838, Mr. Horner reported—" I must again state that the protection afforded to children under 13 is very incomplete, owing to the defective nature of the act." The noble lord might perhaps say, that within the last two or three weeks he had received communications from the manufacturing districts which proved that the law was now better observed; but was this a state of things to be endured, that, the act itself being totally inoperative, we should be content with the voluntary conformity of a few? If that House were to sit for 12 months, and if he were allowed to bring the matter forward every week, he had no doubt that the law would be observed; but whenever Parliament was prorogued, every abuse and license would recommence. He was not to be supposed to say anything in disparagement of the inspectors, whose zeal and diligence were certainly greater than their powers, and who no doubt had great difficulties to contend with; and least of all should he say anything against the superintendents, so long as they could allege their insufficient authority.

Now let the House hear the operation of the Bill in a few of its details. By Clause 31 magistrates had the power to mitigate the penalties which were imposed on convictions under the act, and to what extent had this power been carried? Absolutely to neutralise the force of the law. What was the forcible language of Mr. Horner, upon this part of the subject, in the report of October last? He said—" The extent to which those mitigations had been carried would tend rather to increase than check the future violations of the law. The disreputable millowner, who is regardless of the discredit of a prosecution for violating the law, solely made for the protection of helpless children, looks only to the amount of the penalty imposed on his neighbours, and finds, on casting up the account, that it is far more profitable to disobey than to observe the Act." After these representations of the state of the law made by his own inspectors, how could the noble lord opposite reconcile it with his conscience as an individual, and with his public duty as a Minister of the Crown, during the whole course of his administration never to have brought forward any measure for the removal of so tremendous an evil? From a return now made periodically to that House, it appeared that between the 1st of May, 1836, and the 1st of January, 1837, there were 822 convictions, more than one-half of which were for the grievous offence of overworking the children, and working them without surgeons' certificates, which was tantamount to overworking. The average amount of penalties was 2*l.* 5*s.* Between the years 1837 and 1838, the number of convictions was 800; and, whilst on this subject, he would, just in passing, say a word or two in reply to an observation which had been made to him by the Under Secretary of State for the Home Department the last time it was discussed—namely, that there had been an abatement of the number of convictions during the last year. It was true that during the first quarter of the year there was some abatement; but the aggregate for the whole year was 800, being only an abatement of 20. " I cannot ascribe this," said one of the inspectors, " to any increased willingness to obey, or any increased alacrity to enforce, the law; but I ascribe it to the difficulty of the times, and to the inclination which the mill-owners in consequence feel to throw a number of children out of work." What did the House think was the average amount of penalties during the last year? He had already stated that in the year 1836 the average amount was 2*l.* 5*s.* Last year the average amount was only 1*l.* 10*s.*

Could the House, then, doubt that it was far more profitable for a millowner to disobey than to obey the law, when he (Lord Ashley) told them that a millowner had only to pay a penalty of 1*l.* 10*s.* for a gross violation of it, although he gained far more than that sum by the hours during which he overworked a child, and when, in the almost certain case of his over working 100 children at once, it was only considered as a single offence, and then the highest penalty that could be inflicted on him for it would not amount to more than 2*s.* 6*d.* a-head for each child? He had no hesitation in affirming that a merciless griping ruffian would gain more than 500 times the amount of such a penalty during the hours he overworked these unfortunate children. Now, the amount of these convictions was taken from the returns for England only; but was it to be supposed that this statement showed the full amount of offences committed against this Act in Great Britain, because we read that the inspector for Scotland, Mr. Stuart, contrary to the evidence of the sheriff of Lanarkshire, contrary to the evidence of many respectable gentlemen, and contrary even to common sense, had sent in a return of " *nil* " for Scotland, or, in other words, had stated that through all Scotland not one offence had been committed against this Bill? Let it be observed, too, that the number of convictions was no index of the number of offences committed. First of all, there was the difficulty of detecting the offences; next there was the difficulty of procuring evidence; then no offence could be prosecuted to conviction unless it were brought to the notice of the inspector within 14 days of its commission. How, then, could one-third of the offences against this Act ever be brought to light? The inspectors themselves declared the thing to be impossible. The House might perhaps be desirous to see after what fashion these penalties had been remitted and adjudicated upon. Before, however, he came to that part of the subject, let him state the reasons why the spirit of this law had evaporated until it had become a mere *corpus mortuum*. The fact was, that the millowners sat on the bench, and adjudicated in their own cases. There were, undoubtedly, exceptions to that position, bright and honourable exceptions, some of them members of that House, who did not concur with him in opinion upon the question of factory legislation. It was only right to state, that he had heard nothing but commendation of the manner in which the mills of the honourable member for Derby, Mr. Strutt, were managed. But that he might not be considered as accusing a large class of men without cause, and on his own responsibility alone, he begged to read a few extracts from the valuable report which he then held in his hand. Mr. Howell, the inspector, having said that the magistrates gave certificates in a mass, proceeded to add, " As if to exemplify the futility of the countersigning of the magistrates as a check on the certificates of the surgeon, cases have in my district occurred in which the manufacturer, being a magistrate, has countersigned the certificates for his own factory, and two magistrates, being both millowners in the same town, have reciprocated civilities in this manner for each other to a considerable extent." The noble lord next proceeded to read an extract from a report of Mr. Horner. " I have had," said Mr. Horner, " in my district, millowners trying cases as magistrates against other millowners residing in the same town with themselves. I had one instance of a millowner sitting as a magistrate on an information presented against his own sons, as tenants of a mill of which he was the proprietor." Mr. Horner also added, that another millowner had adjudicated upon an information filed against his own brother; and that, in all these cases, the magistrates had awarded the lowest penalties which the law enabled them to impose, and this too in cases where the penalties were inflicted for a second and even a third offence.

And now let the House bear in mind that all this sad state of things had arisen from the measures proposed and carried by her Majesty's Government; for, by Sir John Hobhouse's Act, which the existing Act repealed, it was enacted that no magistrate being concerned by himself or his relatives in mills should be allowed to adjudicate on points of factory law. As the House might wish to see by an instance how the existing law operated, he would mention a case which he had taken out of the report, and which, if quoted incorrectly, could be immediately set right by honourable gentlemen then present, and who were qualified to contradict him. On the 10th of December, 1836, an information was laid against a millowner. The resistance to that information, and the manner in which the magistrates dealt with it, appeared to Mr. Horner to be so flagrant as to require him to make a special report upon it to Government. He had selected three out of the many charges which were preferred against this millowner. The first was for employing 29 young children more than nine hours a-day. The second was for employing 24 children without surgeons' certificates, which was, in point of fact, a confession that they were overworked. The third was for employing 22 children more than 12 hours a day. Now, before whom was this information tried? Why, before three magistrates all interested in mills. What was the amount of the penalties which the magistrates could have imposed on this millowner, had they awarded them to the full extent of the law? The full amount would have been 160*l*. What was the amount of penalties actually awarded? Would the House believe him when he stated that, notwithstanding this was a most flagrant case, and notwithstanding the great profits which the magistrates knew that the millowner must have derived by his merciless conduct to these poor children, the penalties, which might have been extended to 160*l*., had the magistrates put the law fully into execution, were reduced down to 17*l*., which was not more than the result of ten minutes' labour of those children whom he had unmercifully overworked for several hours? And this was the way in which, with the knowledge of the Government, the present Act was carried into effect.

Now, let the House see whether there was the same caution exhibited with respect to other parts of this Bill. Since the time this Act was brought into operation the whole amount of the penalties levied was 4,422*l*.; but in consequence of certain regulations made by the inspectors themselves, every child taking out a certificate was obliged to pay 6*d*. for it as a sort of remuneration for the trouble of writing it. Now, what sum did the House think had been levied in this manner upon the wages of all children under 14 years of age since the passing of the Factory Act? A sum not much under 12,000*l*. And this for a certificate which, so far from giving protection to the child, only gave impunity to the aggressor upon its hours of comfort and repose. If this certificate gave any protection to the child, he should not complain of the tax levied upon it; but when this certificate— for which the child was compelled to pay—was put into the master's hand, and was used by him as a shield to protect himself from any conviction under this Act, he must say that the law was at once ridiculous and tyrannical.

Was it then surprising that there should be discontent and dissatisfaction among the operatives in the manufacturing districts, when they saw that the law which had been passed for the protection of young children was daily violated, not only with impunity, but also with advantage to the rich, and with tremendous consequences to the poor? Could the House be surprised that these men thought that its members were inclined to legislate for the richer in opposition to the poorer classes, and that, as a necessary consequence, they held in equal contempt the makers of the law, the administrators of the law, and the law itself? With respect to the education clauses, he would say but little; for it was universally confessed that they were not observed in one mill out of 50, and where they were observed, "there," said Mr. Horner, "the schooling given is a mere mockery of instruction." And yet would the noble lord opposite venture to say that the education of the manufacturing classes was a matter of indifference to the country at large? Would he refuse to attend to the language of his own inspector, Mr. Horner, who said that vice and ignorance, and their natural consequences, misery and suffering, were rife among the population of these districts? The Bill which the noble lord had himself introduced, and had afterwards withdrawn, on this subject, acknowledged the defects of the existing law. *Habes confitentem reum.* If, then, the noble lord admitted the existence of these defects, it was unnecessary for him to point out where the new law, had it passed through Parliament, would have amended the defects of the old. He (Lord Ashley) was anxious that that Bill should have become law, because, if it had had no other effect, it would have given force to the Act now in the statute-book; and though it was not by any means all that he desired, yet it would have conferred great benefit on the younger classes in the manufacturing districts. The learned Solicitor-General had twitted him with his desire for a Bill which was short of all he sought for; he had asserted that the interests of humanity were not concerned in the passing of that measure. Why, would it not have given life and activity to what was now a dead and sapless trunk? It would have limited the hours for their labour, it would have provided education for them, and it would have given them a knowledge of their rights as men, and of their duties as Christians. But the noble lord opposite had thought right to withdraw it. Had the Bill been converted into law they might have straitened a few millowners, but they would have given liberty and joy to thousands of helpless children, and the year of delay, which was now to be passed in vice, ignorance, and suffering, might have been devoted to mercy, and to moral and religious education. The noble lord, however, had his reasons for leaving the law as it stood at present. For his own part, he (Lord Ashley) thought that to leave the law in its present state was unjust by the children, whom they consigned by it to oppression; by the honest millowner, who was anxious to conform to it, and who was defrauded by those who did not; by the dishonest millowner, whom they tempted and encouraged to violate its enactments; by the law itself, which they knew will be violated, and violated with impunity; and by the executive government, which ought to demand and deserve respect.

Some time ago he had brought before the House the course which her Majesty's Ministers had thought fit to adopt. He would not weary the House by repeating what he had then said; but there was one point to which he must briefly advert, as showing the *animus* by which they were influenced, and the lamentable perplexity of the law. In the year 1836 the Government brought in a Bill, not to amend the existing law, but to repeal one of its best provisions, which secured to the child of not more than 12 years of age immunity from 12 hours' labour. That Bill, having been carried on the second reading by a majority of two only, was withdrawn by the Government in deference to the sense then expressed by the House, the Government giving at the same time, both by speech and in writing, a most solemn pledge that the existing Act should be rigorously and speedily enforced. How had the Government redeemed that most solemn pledge? By an immediate and monstrous violation of the law. (*Hear, hear, and a smile from Lord John Russell.*) The noble lord laughed. [*Lord John Russell, " It is so absurd."*] The noble lord might think so, but he fancied that the House would be disposed to agree with him when they heard the statement which he was about to make to them. Shortly after that pledge was given, there came out a letter from Mr. Inspector Horner, *verbosa et grandis epistola*, addressed to all the surgeons in his district. Here let him explain that, before a child could be allowed to work 12 hours a day, a certificate from a surgeon must be given in proof that the child had attained 13 years of age; and therefore, when the noble lord stated that the Act would be rigorously enforced for the future, the country expected that it would be immediately carried out. Here the noble lord stated the substance of Mr. Horner's letter. It contained instructions to the different surgeons how they were to grant certificates, and what they were to consider as fitness for 12 hours' labour. The surgeons were told that they were not to ask a question as to the age. " If you find," said the letter-writer, " a child not more than 12 years of age with such an unusual degree of development as to have the appearance of 13 years of age, you will be justified in inserting the word 'thirteen' in the certificate." So that, although they knew the child to be 12, yet if they found an unusual degree of development, they would be justified in inserting the word thirteen. The document then proceeded to define the writer's notion of this unusual degree of development, which was, that no child who had attained the height of 4 feet 3½ inches should be considered less than 13 years of age. The surgeon was then to give the child a certificate in proof of its having attained the age of 13, for so the Act required.

Lord J. Russell.—Read the clause.

Lord Ashley might have made a legal mistake as to the technicalities of the Act, but the language of the clause was, " That no young person or child shall be allowed to work more than 12 hours a day, without first requiring and receiving from such person a certificate in proof that such child is above the age of 13." Then was formed, to meet and almost nullify this clause, the regulation he had mentioned, that any child who had attained the height of 4 feet 3½ inches should be held to be 13. Was it possible the noble lord could think that this regulation carried out the spirit of the Act? Was he not aware that such an order must have the effect of setting completely at naught its provisions? If he wanted any motive to assign for it, he could find it in certain facts that he would lay before the House. When the order in question was issued, his hon. friend the member for Oldham had taken the measurements of all the children in his own mill, and what was the result? That out of 103 children then in his service between the ages of 9 and 13, 57 were found to be at or to exceed the height of 4 feet 3½ inches. He (Lord Ashley) also procured the measurements of the children in another mill, and found that out of 318 between the ages of 9 and 13, 71 were at the height of 4 feet 3½ inches, or above it, 2 of whom were between 9 and 10 years of age, 15 between 10 and 11, 45 between 11 and 12, and 9 between 12 and 13. It was unnecessary to inquire further. By this regulation, 40, or perhaps nearly 50 per cent. of the children who enjoyed the benefit of the Act passed for their protection, in working only eight hours a day, according to its merciful provisions, were at once transferred to a servitude of 12 hours' duration.

Thus had the considerate intentions of the House for the protection of these children of 10 years of age been carried out. Thus had the pledge of the Government been accomplished. What remedy had been applied? Had the noble lord the moment he heard of this great grievance proceeded instantly to remove it? Representations on the subject were made to him, memorials were transmitted to him, but nothing was done. When the House met, indeed, and he gave notice of his intention to bring the subject before it, then, and not till then, as usual, was there shown an ample profession of readiness to investigate the complaints. November, December, January, and February passed away without anything being done to cancel the regulation or give effect to the spirit of the Act. But when he had given notice of a motion, he received a letter from the noble lord opposite, stating that he had submitted the regulation to the law officers of the Crown, who declared that it did not come within the provisions of the Act, and that it must be cancelled. Cancelled accordingly it was, but could they cancel the effects of it? That result the noble lord must know to be impossible till an Act was passed to remedy the abuses at present perpetrated. Could a single instance be named in which a child transferred under this regulation from a labour of eight hours' duration to one of 12 was brought back to its former condition when it was cancelled? Mr. Howell, the inspector, a gentleman whose fidelity and diligence in the discharge of his duties were most commendable, stated, that on inspecting several of the cotton mills, he found children working as 13 years old who not only were, but were admitted to be, under that age, and the cause was that the surgeons had looked to the *height*, and not to the *ages* of the children. The order was made in 1836; it was cancelled in March, 1837, but not till it had produced the most frightful abuses. Mr. Horner, writing in March, 1837, stated, that from the great imperfection of the Act in all that related to the determination of the age of the children, it was impossible for the inspectors to check the most palpable frauds. He was fully persuaded that one-half of the children now working under a surgeon's certificate that they were 13 years old, were, in fact not more than 12, and many not more than 11. Mr. Horner, added, "that until the defects inherent in this part of the law were remedied, the object of the law would, to a great extent, be defeated." Yet the opinion of Mr. Horner, a man of great ability and experience, was treated with supreme contempt. He (Lord Ashley) thought it would have been more becoming if the noble lord, fortified by this opinion, had called for additional powers for the protection of the children, or had at least introduced a Bill for the amendment of details, either a Bill for increasing the amount of the penalties leviable, or for preventing interested magistrates from sitting on the bench. One Bill had been laid aside, under one pretence, among others, of the indisposition of the Under Secretary for the Home Department; but the House had been sitting for eight months, and during all the time, from November till the 7th of May, which was the day fixed for the second reading, that hon. gentleman was in his place, and perfectly able to attend to the progress of the measure. The excuse of illness, therefore, would not do, and it was, besides, inadmissible on another ground, for it was not to be tolerated that the passing of a useful measure should be impeded by the illness of any functionary, however efficiently he might discharge his duty.

Thus had a great measure, closely affecting the temporal and eternal welfare of so vast a portion of the population, been set aside and treated like a turnpike bill. But the noble lord might be assured that the people of this country had too much humanity, and that he (Lord Ashley) who had humbly undertaken the subject was too strongly determined to obtain justice, to allow the matter to rest in its present state. Did he really think that he could stifle public sympathy, or silence him (Lord Ashley) by such devices? "Though he should hold his peace, the very stones would immediately cry out." The interest which this question excited was not confined to England; it had extended to France, where it had been discussed in the Chamber of Deputies, and had engaged the eloquent pens of some of the ablest writers of the country, M. Sismondi and others, who had not disdained to support the cause of the helpless children in France and Switzerland. He had received within the last fortnight a communication from France, requesting him to join in a general society to wipe out this blot from the civilization of Christian Europe, in the propriety of which he heartily concurred. He had hoped that this country would have been the first to set the example of such an association, and he felt ashamed that another country, possessing advantages so much inferior, should have anticipated it in setting on foot a general scheme for the amelioration of the condition of infant labourers. This was an evil that was daily on the increase, and was yet unremedied, though one-fifth part of the time the House had given to the settlement of the question of negro slavery would have been sufficient to provide a remedy. When that House in its wisdom and mercy decided that 45 hours in a week was a term of labour long enough for an adult negro, he thought it would not have been unbecoming that spirit of lenity if they had considered whether 69 hours a-week were not too many for the children of the British empire. In the appeal he had now made he had asked nothing unreasonable, he had merely asked for an affirmation of a principle they had already recognised. He wanted them to decide whether they would amend, or repeal, or enforce, the Act now in existence. But if they would do none of these things, if they continued idly indifferent, and obstinately shut their eyes to this great and growing evil, if they would give no heed to that fierce and rapid cancer that was gnawing the very vitals of the social system, if they were careless of the growth of an immense population, plunged in ignorance and vice, which neither feared God nor regarded man, then he warned them that they must be prepared for the very worst results that could befal an empire. The noble lord concluded by moving a resolution : " That this House deeply regrets that the law affecting the regulation of the labour of children in factories, having been found imperfect and ineffective to the purposes for which it was passed, has been suffered to continue so long without any amendment."

## *Children not protected by the Factory Acts.*

---

# HOUSE OF COMMONS,

### TUESDAY, AUGUST 4, 1840.

---

MR. SPEAKER,

It is, Sir, with feelings somewhat akin to despair that I now rise to bring before the House the motion of which I have given notice. When I consider the period of the session, the long discussions that have already taken place to-day, the scanty attendance of members, and the power which any member possesses of stopping me midway in my career, I cannot but entertain misgivings that I shall not be able to bring under the attention of the House this subject, which has now occupied so large a portion of my public life, and in which is now concentrated, in one hour, the labour of years. Sir, I must assure the House that this motion has not been conceived, nor will it be introduced, in any hostile spirit towards her Majesty's Ministers; quite the reverse. I do indeed trust, nay more, I have reason to believe, that I shall obtain their hearty and effectual support.

I know well that I owe an apology and an explanation to the House for trespassing on their patience at so late a period— my explanation is this: I have long been taunted with narrow and exclusive attention to the children in the factories alone; I have been told, in language and writing, that there were other cases fully as grievous, and not less numerous; that I was unjust and inconsiderate in my denouncement of the one, and my omission of the other. I have, however, long contemplated this effort which I am now making; I had long resolved that, so soon as I could see the factory children, as it were, safe in harbour, I would undertake a new task. The Committee of this session on Mills and Factories having fully substantiated the necessity, and rendered certain the amendment of the law, I am now endeavouring to obtain an inquiry into the actual circumstances and condition of another large part of our juvenile population.

I hardly know whether any argument is necessary to prove

that the future hopes of a country must, under God, be laid in the character and condition of its children; however right it may be to attempt, it is almost fruitless to expect, the reformation of its adults: as the sapling has been bent so will it grow. To ensure a vigorous and moral manhood, we must train them aright from their earliest years, and so reserve the full development of their moral and physical energies for the services hereafter of our common country.

Now, whatever may be done or proposed in time to come, we have, I think, a right to know the state of our juvenile population; the House has a right, the country has a right. How is it possible to address ourselves to the remedies of evils which we all feel, unless we have previously ascertained both the nature and the cause of them? the first step towards a cure is a knowledge of the disorder. We have asserted these truths in our factory legislation; and I have on my side the authority of all civilized nations of modern times; the practice of this House; the common sense of the thing; and the justice of the principle.

Sir, I may say with Tacitus, " opus adgredior, opimum casibus . . . ipsâ etiam pace sævum." To give but an outline of all the undertaking would occupy too much of your time and patience; few persons, perhaps, have an idea of the number and variety of the employments which demand and exhaust the physical energies of young children, or of the extent of suffering to which they are exposed. It is right, Sir, that the country should know at what a cost its pre-eminence is purchased, and how

" Petty rogues submit to fate,
   That great ones may enjoy their state."

The number I cannot give with any degree of accuracy, though I may venture to place them as manifold the numbers of those engaged in the factories—the suffering I can exhibit, to a certain degree, in the documents before me.

I will just read a list of some of these occupations, as many as I have been able to collect; but I will abstain from entering into detail upon every one of them: I will select a few instances, and leave the House to judge of the mass by the form and taste of the sample. Now, this is a list of some of the occupations in which I find them engaged (I have not, by any means, a full statement); and in which the employment is both irksome and unhealthy :—

"Earthenware, porcelain, hosiery, pin-making, needle-making, manufacture of arms, nail-making, card-setting, draw-boy-weaving, iron-works, forges, &c., iron foundries, glass trade, collieries, calico-printing, tobacco manufacture, button factories, bleaching and paper-mills."

Now, will the House allow me to set before them, in a few cases, the evidence I have been able to obtain illustrative of the nature and effects of these several departments of industry?

The first I shall take is the manufacture of tobacco, a business of which, perhaps, but little is generally known; in this I find that " children are employed 12 hours a day. They go as early as seven years of age. The smell in the room is very strong and offensive; they are employed in spinning the twist tobacco; in the country, the children work more hours in the day, being frequently until 9 and 10 o'clock at night. Their opportunities for education are almost none, and their appearance altogether sickly."

The next department I shall take is that of bleaching. In bleaching, "children are employed at 11, and oftentimes younger. They go to work at any time of the day or night, when they have a deal of work. The same children labour all night for two or three nights in a week. Their opportunities for education are very few, except in a Sunday-school."

Now, here let the House observe the extent of toil and of watchfulness oftentimes imposed on children of very tender years. During two or three nights in a week they are deprived altogether of their natural rest; a demand so severe on the bodily powers, that, when exacted of the police and soldiery of this metropolis, it has been found most pernicious to their physical constitution. From the Potteries, Mr. Spencer (a factory commissioner) reported, in 1833, " The plate-makers of most works employ boys, often their own, to be their assistants; their occupation is to remove the plates to the drying-houses, which are heated to 120 degrees; and in this occupation, in which the boy is kept on the run, he is laboriously employed from 6 o'clock in the morning till 7 in the evening, excepting the intervals of breakfast and dinner." Again, " In other works some of the children, called cutters, in attendance upon the printer, appear to me to suffer from a prolonged attendance at the factory. They are compelled to attend in the morning an hour before the printer, to light fires and prepare his apartment, and often wait in the evening for some time after the rest have departed to prepare for the ensuing day." Again, " When there is a fair demand, the plate-makers and their assistants work three or four nights per week till 10, and sometimes as late as 11."

Sir, I will proceed. On the subject of draw-boy-weaving, Mr. Horner and Mr. Woolriche reported from Kidderminster in 1833:—" Every weaver of Brussels carpeting must have an assistant, called a drawer, who is usually a boy or girl; few are taken under 10 years of age; the working hours are extremely irregular; this irregularity tells very severely on the drawers, who must attend the weaver at whatever time he is at work; they are often called up at 3 and 4 o'clock in the morning, and kept on for 16 or 18 hours."

With respect to the iron foundries I have not obtained any evidence; though much, I am sure, would be derived from an investigation of this department. As to iron mines, it will be unnecessary to do much more than simply refer the House to a report from the mining districts of South Wales, by Mr. Seymour Tremenheere, the government inspector, dated February, 1840, and published in the extracts from the Proceedings of the Board of Privy Council on the matter of Education. I will, however, take the liberty to read one or two extracts. "Parents," says the inspector, "if they send their children at all to school, seldom do so for many months at a time. They are liable to be away whenever the father has not earned as much as usual, or has spent more. They think instruction of any kind very little necessary for the girls. The boys are taken into the coal or iron mine at 8 or 9 years old." Elsewhere he says, "Hence the custom of taking their children of 7 years old to sit for 8 and 10 hours a day in a mine; it is certain from the time he (the child) enters the mine, he learns nothing more there than to be a miner." Now let the House hear the consequences of this defect of education—the result of this overwork in the first years of life:—"They leave their homes at an early age, and they spend the surplus of their wages in smoking, drinking, and quarrelling. Boys of 13 will not unfrequently boast that they have taken to smoking before they were 12. Early marriages are very frequent. They take their wives from the coke-hearths, the mine, and coal-yard, having had no opportunities of acquiring any better principles or improved habits of domestic economy, and being in all other respects less instructed than their husbands."

As to the frame-work-knitters, a department of the lace trade, nothing can be worse or more distressing. Mr. Power, a factory commissioner, wrote from Nottingham, 1833—"A great proportion of the population of the county of Leicester is employed in the frame-work-knitting: of this number more than one-half, probably two-thirds, are young persons between the ages of 6 and 18; that they work an inordinate number of hours daily; that the hours of work of the young persons are for the most part commensurate with those of the older class; that the occupation is pursued in very low and confined shops and rooms, and that the hours of labour are 16 in the day. With regard to the state of health of men, women, and children employed, their habits of work and subsistence are more destructive of health, comfort, cleanliness, and general well-being, than any state of employment into which I have had at present an opportunity of inquiring. Mr. Macaulay, a surgeon of great talent and experience at Leicester, observed to me, that scarcely any of them of long-standing in the trade were quite sound in constitution."

There is another department of industry called card-setting, in which children are employed to make part of the machinery of the cotton-mills. In answer to some questions I put to a gentleman resident in the neighbourhood of some card-setting establishments, he says—"Children are employed from 5 years old and upwards; their length of labour extends from 5 or 6 o'clock in the morning to 8 at night."

I will now exhibit the state of the collieries, and I cannot well imagine anything worse than these painful disclosures. In reference to this, I will read an abstract of evidence collected from three witnesses by Mr. Tuffnell in 1833:—"Labour very hard, 9 hours a day regularly, sometimes 12, sometimes above 13 hours; stop two or three minutes to eat; some days nothing at all to eat, sometimes work and eat together; have worked a whole day together without stopping to eat; a good many children in the mines, some under 6 years of age; sometimes can't eat, owing to the dust, and damp, and badness of the air; sometimes it is as hot as an oven; sometimes so hot as to melt a candle. A vast many girls in the pits go down just the same as the boys, by ladders or baskets; the girls wear breeches; beaten the same as the boys; many bastards produced in the pits; a good deal of fighting among them; much crookedness caused by the labour; work by candlelight; exposed to terrible accidents: work in very contracted spaces; children are plagued with sore feet and gatherings." "I cannot but think," says one witness, "that many nights they do not sleep with a whole skin, for their backs get cut and bruised with knocking against the mine, it is so low. It is wet under foot; the water oftentimes runs down from the roof; many lives lost in various ways; and many severely injured by burning; workers knocked up after 50." "I cannot much err," says Mr. Commissioner Tuffnell, "in coming to the conclusion, both from what I saw, and the evidence of witnesses given on oath above, that it must appear to every impartial judge of the two occupations, that the hardest labour, in the worst room in the worst-conducted factory, is less hard, less cruel, and less demoralizing, than the labour of the best of coal mines."

Now, the next is a trade to which I must request the particular attention of the House. The scenes it discloses are really horrible: and all who hear me will join in one loud and common condemnation. I speak of the business of pin-making. Several witnesses in 1833 stated, that "it is very unwholesome work; we do it near the wire-works, and the smell of the aquafortis, through which the wire passes, is a very great nuisance. Children go at a very early age, at 5 years old, and work from 6 in the morning till 8 at night. There are as many girls as boys." One witness, a pin-header, aged 12, said, "I have seen the children much beaten ten times a-day, so that with some the blood comes, many a time; none of the children where I work can either read or write." Another witness said, "It is a sedentary employment, requiring great stress upon the eyes, and a constant motion of the foot, finger, and eyes." This is fully confirmed in a letter I have just received; there it is stated, eyesight is much affected; the overseers of the poor have sent many cases of this nature to the Eye Institution of Manchester. "Each child," reports Mr. Commissioner Tuffnell, "is in a position continually bent in the form of the letter C, its head being about 8 inches from the table. My inquiries," he adds, "fully corroborated the account of its being the practice of parents to borrow sums of money on the credit of their children's labour, and then let them out to pin-heading till it is paid. One woman had let out both her children for ten months, and another had sold hers for a year."

Here I must entreat the attention of honourable members to this system of legalised slavery; and I cannot better invite it, than by reading an extract from a letter which I have lately received. "You also know," says my informant, "the practice of the masters in securing the services of these little slaves. One man in this town employs from four to five hundred of them. A very ordinary practice is, for the master to send for the parents or guardians, offer them an advance of money, an irresistible temptation, and then extract a bond,* *which the magistrates enforce*, that the repayment of the loan shall be effected through the labour of the child. A child of tender age can rarely earn more than from ninepence to one shilling a week. Thus the master becomes bodily possessor of the children as his *boná fide* slaves, and works them according to his pleasure." And now mark this: "If he continues with the employment to pay wages, and keep the loan hanging over the head of the parents, who do not refuse to take the wages, yet cannot repay the loan, the master may

* For specimens see note (B) at p. 29.

keep possession of the child as his slave for an indefinite time. This is done to a great extent; the relieving-officer has tried in vain to break through the iniquitous practice; but it seems that the magistrates have not power to do it."

Now, may I ask, is this not a system of legalised slavery? Is not this a state of things which demands the interposition of Parliament, or at least an investigation, that we may know to what an extent these horrid practices have been carried? Surely the House will not now be astonished at the concluding remark of Mr. Tuffnell's report: "Knowing," says he, "the cruelties that are sometimes practised, in order to keep those infants at work, I was not surprised at being told by a manufacturer that he had left the trade, owing to the disgust he felt at this part of the business." Let me conclude this branch of the subject by an extract from a letter descriptive of these works : "These children are collected in rooms varying in size, height, and ventilation ; the filthy state and foul atmosphere of some of these places is very injurious to the health of the children—they are filled to a most unwholesome extent. No education during the week, and very few go to a Sunday-school. I can only tell you, that from my own observation of the effect of the trade as now carried on, I do not hesitate to say that it is the cause of utter ruin, temporal and spiritual, to eight out of every ten children that are employed in it." This, Sir, is the language of a gentleman of great experience, and very conversant, too, with the temporal and spiritual condition of the poorer classes of whom he is speaking.

The next and last trade which I shall now describe is the calico-printing; a business which demands the labour of several thousand children. Mr. Horner, in an admirable pamphlet,* which he has recently published, on the subject of infant labour, both at home and abroad, says—"It is by no means uncommon for children to work as teer-boys as early as 6 and 7 years of age; and sometimes as young as 5. Children of 6, 7, and 8 years old, may be seen going to work at "—What hour will the House think? at what hour of a winter's night? or at what hour of the night at all? Why, he proceeds—"at 12 o'clock of a winter's night, in large numbers, sometimes having to walk a mile or two to the works. When they are twelving, the first set goes at 12 o'clock in the day, and works till 12 at night. Sometimes they do not send away those who have worked from

* On the Employment of Children in Factories and other Works, in the United Kingdom, and in some Foreign Countries; by Leonard Horner, Inspector of Factories. London, 8vo, 1840.

12 in the day to 12 at night, but let them sleep a few hours in the works, and then set them on again. There is no interval for meals in the night set, except breakfast, the children taking something with them; and even their breakfast is taken at the works. The custom of taking their meals in the works is very injurious, for they do not wash their hands, and they consequently sometimes swallow deleterious colouring matter." A person, whose name is not given, states, that "being frequently detained in his counting-house late at night, till 12 or 1 o'clock, he has often, in going home in the depth of winter, met mothers taking their children to the neighbouring print-works, the children crying." All this I can confirm and exceed, by the statements of a letter I hold in my hand, from a medical gentleman, living in the very centre of print-works. I wish there were time to read the whole of it, but I fear I have already fatigued the House by the number of my extracts. " Many children," he writes, "are only 6 years of age: one-half of them, he believes, are under 9; the labour of children is not only harder, but of longer duration. During night-work the men are obliged to shake their teerers to keep them awake, and they are not seldom roused by blows. This work is very fatiguing to the eyes; their sight consequently fails at a very early age. They have to clean the blocks; this is done at the margin of the brook on which the works stand. I often see these little creatures standing up to the calves of their legs in the water, and this, even in the severest weather, after being kept all day in rooms heated to a most oppressive degree. The injurious effect of this close and heated atmosphere is much aggravated by the effluvia of the colours; these are in most cases metallic salts, and . . . . very noxious. The atmosphere of the room is consequently continually loaded with poisonous gases of different kinds."

Sir, these are a few facts, and only a few, of the many that I could adduce for your consideration, were I not afraid of being wearisome to the House. But I think I have sufficiently proved that there prevails a system of slavery under the sanction of law; the parents sell the services of their children, even of the tenderest years, for periods of long and most afflicting duration; that, in many instances, children of not more than 5 or 6 years old are employed in these trades from 12 to 16 hours a-day, of course deprived of all means of education, while their health is under-mined, or utterly destroyed. If the inquiry I move for be granted, it will develop, I am sure, cases far more numerous, and quite as painful, as those I have been able to produce.

I may here, perhaps, be called upon to suggest a remedy. Sir, I am not yet prepared to do so, but I will state my objects, and the motives of my proposition.

My first and great object is to place, if possible, the children of this land in such a position, and under such circumstances, as to lay them open to what Dr. Chalmers would call " an aggressive movement" for education; to reserve and cherish their physical energies, to cultivate and improve their moral part, both of which, be they taken separately or conjointly, are essential to the peace, security, and progress of the empire. Sir, we have had the honour of setting the example in these things, and other nations of the world have begun to follow that example; we must not now fall back into the rear, and become the last where once we were first. I have here a most valuable document, for which I am indebted to the kindness of that distinguished Frenchman, the Baron Charles Dupin; it is the Report of a Commission of the Chamber of Peers, dated February, 1840, on the propriety, nay, the necessity, of extending the protection of the laws to the young and helpless workers in all departments of industry. " What is the state of morality," says the document, " among the young children employed in the workshops?—None at all; everywhere there is want. It is a curious fact," the reporter adds, " that the immorality seems to be greatest in those very places where the children are admitted into the workshops at the earliest ages." Now let the House pay attention to what follows: " We were desirous of ascertaining the amount of difference in force and physical power between parties which had respectively attained the age of manhood in the parts of France most devoted to agriculture, and those where manufacturing industry is more generally diffused. The councils of revision in the recruiting department exhibited the following facts:—For 10,000 young men capable of military service, there were rejected as infirm or otherwise unfit in body, 4,029 in the departments most agricultural; for 10,000 in the departments most manufacturing, there were rejected 9,930." The reporter then proceeds to speak in detail: " There were found," he says, " for 10,000 capable of military service, in Marne 10,309 incapable; in the Lower Seine 11,990 incapable; in L'Eure 14,451 incapable." After such a statement as this, will not the House be prepared to concur in his closing observation? " These deformities cannot allow the Legislature to remain indifferent; they attest the deep and painful mischiefs, they reveal the intolerable nature of individual suffering, they enfeeble the country in respect of its capacity for military operations, and impoverish it in regard to the works of peace. We should blush for agriculture, if in her operations she brought, at the age adapted to labour, so small a proportion of horses or oxen in a fit state for toil, compared with so large a number of infirm or misshapen."

Doubtless, if we could conduct the same investigation (which, I fear, we have not the means of doing), we should obtain, in respect of the greater extent and longer prevalence of these trades among us, far most distressing results. This report, I must say, is most honourable to the Chamber of Peers, most honourable to the Baron Dupin, and it will be honourable to the French nation, if they adopt the advice and enact the provisions suggested by these wise and excellent statesmen.

I next desire to remove these spectacles of suffering and oppression from the eyes of the poorer classes, or at least to ascertain if we can do so: these things perplex the peaceable, and exasperate the discontented; they have a tendency to render capital odious, for wealth is known to them only by its oppressions; they judge of it by what they see immediately around them, they know but little beyond their own narrow sphere; they do not extend their view over the whole surface of the land, and so perceive and understand the compensating advantages that wealth and property bestow on the community at large. Sir, with so much ignorance on one side, and so much oppression on the other, I have never wondered that perilous errors and bitter hatreds have prevailed; but I have wondered much, and been very thankful that they have prevailed so little.

Again, this inquiry is due also to the other branches of trade and manufacture, which are already restricted in their employment of children by the acts of the Legislature—it is requisite we should know how far the exception operates unfavourably on the restricted trades, and how far it impedes the full development of the protective principles of existing laws. Manufacturers, I know, loudly complain, and I think with some reason. A respectable millowner in the West Riding of Yorkshire writes to me,—" When the cotton trade is brisk, we find the demand for young persons to set cards so great, that hands are with difficulty obtained for woollen-mills in this neighbourhood." The House will with difficulty believe for how minute an addition to the daily wages parents will doom their children to excessive labour. " The proprietor of a large cotton-mill told me," says Mr. Horner, " that they suffer severely from the neighbouring print-works carrying off the children under 13 years of age, where they employ them at any age and any number of hours; that they would gladly employ two sets of children, each working half a day, both for the sake of their work, and for the sake of the children themselves, that they might be more at school, and have more play, but that they cannot get them as the print-works carry them off."

No doubt, provisions still more beneficial to the children, and more convenient to the millowners, might be introduced under a more wide-spread system of restriction—the supply of hands for moderate toil would be increased, and more work would be done, at far less expense of health and happiness.

I next propose by this inquiry, and the remedy which .may follow, to enlarge the sphere of safe and useful employments. How many are there now, to which no one of principle or common humanity would consign the children! by this excessive toil, moreover, one unhappy infant does the work of two; redress this grievance, and you will have opened a comparatively safe and healthy career to twice as many children as can now be employed. I have heard, on the authority of the Poor-Law Commissioners, that they have now under their guardianship more then 30,000 children, for whom they must provide a calling; they hesitate, and most laudable is their hesitation, to consign these helpless infants to such a destiny; why, will the House listen to a statement I received only a few mornings ago? it is well worthy of your attention, as showing how this system has proceeded to so frightful an extent, that even persons, whose interest it is to get rid of the children, shrink from the responsibility of exposing them to its horrors. "I have now," says my informant, "made more minute inquiry into this business of wholesale demoralization. I have examined the relieving-officer of the Board of Guardians. He assures me, that he has rarely known an instance of children in a family turning out respectable members of society, who have been brought up in pin-shops; that the Board of Guardians have been obliged to give up the sending children from the poor-house to the pin-works, on account of the invariable consequences of it—the entire corruption of the children; and that children, once contaminated in these works, very rarely are found worth having in factories or elsewhere." Now, Sir, if this be the case; if the children be thus contaminated by the employment of their earliest years; if they really become not worth having in factories or elsewhere, what kind of citizens will they make in after-life? what has this country to hope for in their peaceful obedience or beneficial activity?

Next, I hope to trace some of the secret and efficient causes of crime and pauperism; and by learning the causes, to ascertain the remedy. It is very curious and very instructive to observe how we compel, as it were, vice and misery with one hand, and endeavour to repress them with the other; but the whole course of our manufacturing system tends to these results : you engage children from their earliest and tenderest years in these long, painful, and destructive occupations; when they have approached to manhood, they have outgrown their employments, and they are turned upon the world without moral, without professional education; the business they have learned avails them nothing; to what can they turn their hands for a maintenance? the children, for instance, who have been taught to make pins, having reached 14 or 15 years of age, are unfit to make pins any longer; to procure an honest livelihood then becomes to them almost impossible; the governors of prisons will tell you, the relieving-officers will tell you, that the vicious resort to plunder and prostitution; the rest sink down into a hopeless pauperism.

Again, intemperance, the besetting sin of England, and the cause of many of its woes, is itself the result, in many cases, of our system of labour : just hear the effects of it in one department. The letter I shall quote refers, it is true, to calico-printing only; it furnishes, nevertheless, · a very good example of the effects of that unhealthy and prolonged toil I have endeavoured to describe.

" The most prominent evil," says the writer, "is the excitement to habits of intoxication. The heated atmosphere in which they work, and the profuse perspiration, occasion a burning thirst; and the mouth and throat are often so parched, as to cause a very distressing sensation; they drink excessively; on leaving their highly-heated workshops, they feel disagreeably chilled, and relieve it by taking spirits. A tendency to drunkenness is thus produced; the drunkenness, gambling, and vicious habits of the men are imitated by too many of the children."

Imitated by the children, to be sure they are—but such is our system ; we not only withdraw them, when young and pliable, from the opportunities, at least, of doing good, but we thrust them, unwatched and uncared for, into dens of vice, and misery, and crime.—I should indeed be glad to read the whole of this admirable letter, but I have already transgressed too long on the indulgence of the House.

These things, Mr. Speaker, at all times worthy of deep and anxious consideration, are now tenfold so, when we remember the vast and rapid tendency there is in the present day to multiply infant labour, to the exclusion of that of adults : the House is, perhaps, but little aware of the mighty progress that has been made during the last fifteen years towards the substitution of the sinews of the merest children for the sinews of their parents.

Lastly, my object is to appeal to, and excite the public opinion:

where we cannot legislate, we can exhort, and laws may fail
where example will succeed.  I must appeal to the bishops and
ministers of the Church of England, nay, more, to the ministers of every denomination, to urge on the hearts of their
hearers the mischief and the danger of these covetous and cruel
practices.  I trust they will not fall short of the zeal and eloquence
of a distinguished prelate in a neighbouring country, who, in these
beautiful and emphatic words, exhorted his hearers to justice and
mercy :

" Open your eyes," says the Prince Archbishop, " and behold !
parents and masters demand of these young plants to produce
fruit in the season of blossoms.  By excessive and prolonged
labour they exhaust the rising sap, caring but little that they
leave them to vegetate and perish on a withered and tottering
stem.  Poor little children ! may the laws hasten to extend their
protection over your existence, and may posterity read with
astonishment, on the front of this age, so satisfied with itself,
that in these days of progress and discovery there was needed an
iron law to forbid the murder of children by excessive labour."
This is language worthy of the compatriot of Massillon and Féné-
lon.  It is the language of the primate of Normandy, uttered in
the Cathedral of Rouen, " that country of France," says M. Dupin,
"in which the early labour of children has produced the greatest
evils."  Sir, I must say, from the bottom of my heart, that it is
not a little agreeable, amid all our differences of opinion and religious strifes, to find one common point, on which we can feel a
mutual sympathy, and join together in harmonious action.

And now, to conclude this long, and, I fear, wearisome address—my first grand object, as I have already said, is to bring
these children within the reach of education ; it will then be time
enough to fight about the mode.   Only let us exhibit these evils—
there is wit enough, experience enough, activity enough, and
principle enough in the country, to devise some remedy.   I am
sure that the exhibition of the peril will terrify even the most
sluggish, and the most reluctant, into some attempt at amendment; but I hope for far better motives.   For my own part I will
say, though possibly I may be charged with cant and hypocrisy,
that I have been bold enough to undertake this task, because I
must regard the objects of it as beings created, as ourselves, by
the same Maker, redeemed by the same Saviour, and destined to
the same immortality ; and it is, therefore, in this spirit, and
with these sentiments, which, I am sure, are participated in by all
who hear me, that I now venture to entreat the countenance of
this House, and the co-operation of her Majesty's Ministers; first

to investigate, and ultimately to remove, these sad evils, which press so deeply and so extensively on such a large and such an interesting portion of the human race.

I will therefore, Sir, with very sincere thanks to the House, for the patience with which they have heard me, now move—

"That an humble Address be presented to her Majesty, praying that her Majesty will be graciously pleased to direct an inquiry to be made into the employment of the children of the poorer classes in Mines and Collieries, and in the various branches of trade and manufacture in which numbers of children work together, not being included in the provisions of the Acts for regulating the employment of children and young persons in mills and factories; and to collect information as to the ages at which they are employed, the number of hours they are engaged in work, the time allowed each day for meals, and as to the actual state, condition, and treatment of such children, and as to the effects of such employment, both with regard to their morals and their bodily health."

---

NOTE (A). The Commission was granted, and the reports of it, conjointly with those of that granted in 1862, form the basis of the Factory Acts Extension Acts.

NOTE (B). *Specimens of Contracts entered into by Parents, taken from actual Documents.*

I, Sarah H——, do hereby hire and engage my daughter, Martha H——, to work for S. E——, at sheeting pins, for and during the term of 51 weeks, from this 29th day of June, 1831. As witnesseth my hand,
    Witness, R. E———.                 SARAH H———,
                                           + her mark.

---

I, Thomas H——, do hereby hire and engage my daughter, Sarah H——, to work for I—— and K—— at heading of pins, for and during the term of 51 weeks, from this 25th day of November, 1835.
                        As witness my hand and name,
    Witness, L. M———.                 T. H———,
                                             + his mark.

---

I, R. O——, do hereby hire and engage my daughter, A. O——, to work for P—— and Q——, at sheeting of pins, for and during the term of 51 weeks, from this 27th day of November, 1835.
                        As witness my hand and name,
    Witness, R. S——.                    R. O———,
                                           + his mark.

I, Ann E——, do hereby hire and engage my son W. E——, to work for F—— and G——, at heading of pins, for and during the term of 51 weeks, from this 4th day of December, 1835.

As witness my hand and name,

Witness, H. I. D——.

Ann E——,
+ her mark.

---

I, F. G——, do hereby hire and engage my daughter, M. A. G——, to work for H—— and O——, at sheeting of pins, for and during the term of 51 weeks, from this 4th day of December, 1835.

As witness my hand and name,

Witness, W. S——.

F. G——,
+ his mark.

---

I, B. C——, do hereby hire and engage my son, D. C——, to work for E—— and F——, at heading of pins, for and during the term of 51 weeks, from this 8th day of January, 1836.

As witness my hand and name,

Witness, G. M——.

B. C——.

---

I, Mary U——, do hereby hire and engage my daughter, B. U——, to work for V—— and W——, for the term of TWO YEARS, Sundays excepted, at sheeting of pins, from this 5th day of January, 1836.

As witness my hand and name,

Witness, V. W——.

Mary U——,
+ her mark.

## Children in Mines and Collieries.

# HOUSE OF COMMONS,

### Tuesday, June 7, 1842.

Speech on moving for leave to bring in a bill to make regulations respecting the age and sex of children and young persons employed in the mines and collieries of the United Kingdom.

Sir,

It will not, I hope, be deemed presumptuous on my part when I rise to propound my motion to the House, and when I ask for its sympathy and patient hearing, if I add at the same time that I feel quite certain of obtaining their indulgence. The novelty of the subject, its magnitude, the deep and solemn interest which is felt throughout the country, the consideration of its vital influence on the welfare of so large a portion of our fellow-subjects, will, of themselves, be sufficient to obtain your indulgence; nor can I forget, Sir, how often and how undeservedly I have experienced forbearance at the hands both of yourself and of the House.

Perhaps, Sir, I may be allowed just so far to speak of myself as to say, that there is some little reason why I should be thus forward in bringing this matter under the notice of Parliament. The Report on your table is the First Report of a Commission for which I had the honour to move, in August, 1840. The prayer of that motion was granted by the then Administration; and I shall avail myself of this opportunity, and of every other fitting opportunity, to express my sincere and heartfelt thanks to the members of the late Government, and more especially to my Honourable Friend the Member for Perth,* at that time Under-Secretary of State, and to my Noble Friend† in the other House, then at the head of the Home Department, not only for the Commission which they gave, but for the Commissioners whom they appointed, gentlemen who have discharged the duties assigned to them with unrivalled skill, fidelity, and zeal.

* Hon. Fox Maule, now Earl of Dalhousie.      † Marquis of Normanby.

Sir, it is not possible for any man, whatever be his station, if he have but a heart within his bosom, to read the details of this awful document without a combined feeling of shame, terror, and indignation.   But I will endeavour to dwell upon the evil itself, rather than on the parties that might be accused as, in great measure, the authors of it.   An enormous mischief is discovered, and an immediate remedy is proposed; and sure I am that if those who have the power will be as ready to abate oppression as those who have suffered will be to forgive the sense of it, we may hope to see the revival of such a good understanding between master and man, between wealth and poverty, between ruler and ruled, as will, under God's good providence, conduce to the restoration of social comfort, and to the permanent security of the empire.

Sir, when I moved for the Commission, I ventured to state the manifold and important information that I thought would be obtained by the country from its extended investigations—that expectation has been fulfilled—other Reports will develop more amply the whole length and breadth of our perilous position : but, *ex pede Herculem;* it has shown you the ignorance and neglect of many of those who have property, and the consequent vice and suffering of those who have none; it has shown you many sad causes of pauperism; it has shown you the physical disorders which our system has engendered, and the inevitable deterioration of the British race; it has shown you in part our condition, moral, social, and religious.   We know not what a day may bring forth. I know it will be said, " Vice is not new—danger is not new; this has occurred before, and will occur again."   That is true; but I maintain that our danger is absolute, not comparative—our forefathers had to deal with thousands, we with millions; we must address ourselves to the evil boldly and faithfully, or it will soon acquire so enormous a magnitude, as to be insuperable by any effort either of genius or principle.

I shall now proceed to the statement I have undertaken respecting the condition of the working classes in our mines and collieries, and the measures requisite to ameliorate that condition.   I am sorry to detain the House by reading documents; I shall often have occasion to trespass on their patience; but the subject demands it.   I think that the points I wish to establish should be made out by statements and evidence, rather than by any attempts at declamation.   In the first place, I shall present the House with the result of the evidence respecting the age and sex of persons employed in the mines and collieries.   The extent to which the employment of females prevails varies very much in different districts—in some parts of the country none but males are em-

ployed, in other places a great number of females. With respect
to the age at which children are worked in mines and collieries
in South Staffordshire, it is common to begin at 7 years old;
in Shropshire some begin as early as 6 years of age; in Warwickshire the same; in Leicestershire nearly the same. In
Derbyshire many begin at 5, many between 5 and 6 years,
many at 7. In the West Riding of Yorkshire it is not uncommon for infants even of 5 years old to be sent to the pit.
About Halifax and the neighbourhood children are sometimes
brought to the pits at the age of 6 years, and are taken out of
their beds at 4 o'clock. Bradford and Leeds, the same; in Lancashire and Cheshire, from 5 to 6. Near Oldham children are
worked as low "as 4 years old, and in the small collieries towards
the hills some are so young they are brought to work in their
bed-gowns." In Cumberland, many at 7; in South Durham, as
early as 5 years of age, and by no means uncommonly at 6. In
reference to this I may quote a remark of Dr. Mitchell, one of the
Commissioners: he says, "Though the very young children are
not many in proportion, there are still such a number as is painful
to contemplate, and which the great coal-owners will perhaps now
learn for the first time, and I feel a firm belief that they will do
so with sorrow and regret." Now, in justice to the great coal-
owners of the North, I must say, that if they had been the only
parties with whom we had to deal, the necessity for this Bill
would perhaps not have existed: they have exhibited, in many
respects, care and kindness towards their people. Many children,
the Report goes on to state, are employed in North Durham and
Northumberland at 5, and between 5 and 6: "The instances in
which children begin to work at 7, and between 7 and 8, are so
numerous, that it would be tedious to recite them." In the east
of Scotland it is more common for children to begin work at 5
and 6 than in any part of England. In the west of Scotland
children are taken down into the pits at a very early age, often
when 8 years old, and even earlier. In North Wales the cases are
rare of children being employed at 5 or 6—they are very common
at 7. In South Wales more cases are recorded of the employment
of children in the pits at very early ages than in any other district. It is not unusual to take them into the pits at 4 years.
Many are absolutely carried to the work. In South Gloucestershire cases are recorded of children employed at 6 years, the
general age is about 9. In North Somersetshire many begin to
work between 6 and 7. In the south of Ireland no children at all
are employed. All the underground work, which in the coal-
mines of England, Scotland, and Wales, is done by young chil-

dren, appears in Ireland to be done by young persons between the ages of 13 and 18. Now, with respect to sex, the report states that in South Staffordshire no females are employed in underground work, nor in North Staffordshire. In Shropshire, Warwickshire, Leicestershire, and Derbyshire, the same. In the West Riding of Yorkshire the practice of employing females underground is universal. About Halifax and the neighbourhood girls from 5 years old and upwards regularly perform the same work as boys. At Bradford and Leeds,. far from uncommon. In Lancashire and Cheshire it is the general custom for girls and women to be employed. In North Lancashire, throughout the whole of the district, girls and women are regularly employed underground. In Cumberland there are none, excepting in one old colliery, nor in Durham, nor in Northumberland.. In the east of Scotland the employment of females is general, but in the west of Scotland extremely rare. In North Wales, some on the surface, none underground. In South Wales it is not uncommon. In Gloucestershire and Somersetshire there are none. In none of the collieries in the coal-fields of Ireland was a single instance found of a female child, nor a female of any age, being employed in any kind of work. I must observe that, with respect to that country, neither children of tender years nor females are employed in underground operations. I have often, Sir, admired the generosity and warm-heartedness of the Irish people; and I must say, that if this is to be taken as a specimen of their barbarism, I would not exchange it for all the refinement and polish of the most civilized nations of the globe.

The next point to which I desire to call the attention of the House is the character of the localities to which these young creatures are consigned. The state and nature of the places in which they work form a most material consideration in this subject, for they must necessarily affect the safety and salubrity of the employment. If the ventilation and drainage of these places be good, then much protection is given to the health of the employed; if otherwise, the most fearful diseases may be engendered; and the early prostration inflicted of a working-man's capacity to obtain his livelihood. Now, it appears that the character of the places of employment differs according to the depth of the seams of coal, which vary from 10 inches in some districts, to 10 or 20 yards in others. In South Staffordshire, for instance, the places of working are described as, comparatively speaking, comfortable to those who are habituated to them. Dr. Mitchell says—"In the coal-mines of this district the state of the place of work, to persons who have been accustomed to it,. is very comfortable. The coal-beds are sufficiently thick to allow abundance of room. The mines are warm and dry. There is a supply of fresh air from ventilation, though less than there might easily be." In Leicestershire and Warwickshire they are described as being the same—but in Derbyshire the state of things in this respect is described as being very different:—"Black-damp very much abounds—the ventilation in general is exceedingly imperfect. . . . . . Hence fatal explosions frequently take place: the workpeople are distressed by the quantity of carbonic acid gas which almost everywhere abounds, and of which they make great complaint, and that the pits are so hot as to add greatly to the fatigue of the labour."

"While efficient ventilation," the report adds, "is neglected, less attention is paid to drainage. . . . . Some pits are dry and comfortable. . . . . Many are so wet that the people have to work all day over their shoes in water, at the same time that the water is constantly dripping from the roof: in other pits, instead of dripping, it constantly rains, as they term it, so that in a short time after they commence the labour of the day their clothes are drenched; and in this state, their feet also in water, they work all day. The children especially (and in general the younger the age the more painfully this unfavourable state of the place of work is felt) complain bitterly of this." It must be borne in mind that it is in this district that the regular hours of a full day's labour are 14, and occasionally 16; and the children have to walk a mile or two at night without changing their clothes. In the West Riding of Yorkshire it appears that there are very few collieries with thin seams where the main roadways exceed a yard in height, and in some they do not exceed 26 or 28 inches: nay, in some the height is as little even as 22 inches; so that in such places the youngest child cannot work without the most constrained posture. The ventilation, besides, in general is very bad, and the drainage worse. In Oldham the mountain-seams are wrought in a very rude manner. There is very insufficient drainage. The ways are so low that only little boys can work in them, which they do naked, and often in mud and water, dragging sledge-tubs by the girdle and chain. In North Lancashire, "the drainage is often extremely bad: a pit of not above 20 inches seam," says a witness, "had a foot of water in it, so that he could hardly keep his head out of water." In Cumberland, it appears, the mines are tolerably dry and well ventilated, and in South Durham the same, with some exceptions. In North Durham there are some thin seams, and in Northumberland many not exceeding 2 feet, or 2 feet 2 inches. Great complaints are made by children of pains and wounds from the lowness of the roof; but the ventilation is excellent—as good, perhaps, as it can be in the present state of that science." Yet, I regret to add, the "drainage, not being so essential to the safety of the coal-mine as ventilation, has been much less attended to in this district." In East Scotland, where the side-roads do not exceed from 22 to 28 inches in height, the working-places are sometimes 100 and 200 yards distant from the main-road, so that females have to crawl backwards and forwards with their small carts in seams in many cases not exceeding 22 to 28 inches in height. The whole of these places, it appears, are in a most deplorable state as to ventilation, and the drainage is quite as bad as the ventilation. The evidence, as given by the young people and the old colliers themselves, of their sufferings, is absolutely piteous. In North Wales, in many of the mines, the roads are low and narrow, the air foul, the places of work dusty, dark, and damp, and the ventilation most imperfect. In South Wales, in many pits, the ventilation is grossly neglected, and the report complains of the quantity of carbonic acid gas, which produces the most injurious effects, though not actually bad enough to prevent the people from working. So long as a candle will burn, the labour is continued. With respect to the mines in Glamorganshire and Pembrokeshire, the sub-commissioner states the ventilation to be most imperfect, and productive of diseases which have a manifest tendency to shorten life, as well as to abridge the number of years of useful labour on the part of the work-people.

Sir, the next subject to which I shall request your attention is the nature of the employment in these localities. Now, it appears that the practice prevails to a lamentable extent of making young persons and children of a tender age draw loads by means of the girdle and chain. This practice prevails generally in Shropshire, in Derbyshire, in the West Riding of Yorkshire, in Lancashire, in Cheshire, in the east of Scotland, in North and South Wales, and in South Gloucestershire. The child, it appears, has a girdle bound round its waist, to which is attached a chain, which passes under the legs, and is attached to the cart. The child is obliged to pass on all fours, and the chain passes under what, therefore, in that posture, might be called the hind legs; and thus they have to pass through avenues not so good as a common sewer, quite as wet, and oftentimes more contracted. This kind of labour they have to continue during several hours, in a temperature described as perfectly intolerable. By the testimony of the people themselves, it appears that the labour is exceedingly severe; that the girdle blisters their sides and causes great pain. "Sir," says an old miner, "I can only say what the mothers say, it is barbarity

—absolute barbarity." Robert North says, " I went into the pit at
7 years of age. When I drew by the girdle and chain, the skin
was broken and the blood ran down. . . . . If we said anything, they would beat us. I have seen many draw at 6. They
must do it or be beat. They cannot straighten their backs during
the day. I have sometimes pulled till my hips have hurt me so
that I have not known what to do with myself." In the West
Riding, it appears, girls are almost universally employed as trap-
pers and hurriers, in common with boys. The girls are of all
ages, from 7 to 21. They commonly work quite naked down to
the waist, and are dressed—as far as they are dressed at all—in a
loose pair of trousers. These are seldom whole on either sex. In
many of the collieries the adult colliers, whom these girls serve,
work perfectly naked. Near Huddersfield the sub-commissioner
examined a female child. He says, " I could not have believed
that I should have found human nature so degraded. Mr. Hol-
royd, and Mr. Brook, a surgeon, confessed, that although living
within a few miles, they could not have believed that such a system
of unchristian cruelty could have existed." Speaking of one of
the girls, he says, " She stood shivering before me from cold. The
rug that hung about her waist was as black as coal, and saturated
with water, the drippings of the roof." "In a pit near New Mills,"
says the sub-commissioner, " the chain passing high up between
the legs of two girls, had worn large holes in their trousers. Any
sight more disgustingly indecent or revolting can scarcely be imagined than these girls at work. No brothel can beat it."—Sir, it
would be impossible to enlarge upon all these points; the evidence is most abundant, and the selection very difficult. I will,
however, observe that nothing can be more graphic, nothing more
touching, than the evidence of many of these poor girls themselves. Insulted, oppressed, and even corrupted, they exhibit, not
unfrequently, a simplicity and a kindness that render tenfold more
heart-rending the folly and cruelty of that system that has forced
away these young persons, destined, in God's providence, to holier
and happier duties, to occupations so unsuited, so harsh, and so
degrading.

Now, Sir, it appears that they drag these heavy weights some
12,000 yards, some 14,000, and some 16,000 yards daily. " In the
east of Scotland," says the commissioner, " the persons employed
in coal-bearing are almost always girls and women. They carry
coal on their backs on unrailed roads, with burdens varying from
¾ cwt. to 3 cwt.,—a cruel slaving," says the sub-commissioner, " revolting to humanity. I found a little girl," says he, " only 6 years
old, carrying half a cwt., and making regularly 14 long journeys

a-day. With a burden varying from 1 cwt. to 1½ cwt., the height
ascended and the distance along the roads, added together, exceeded in each journey the height of St. Paul's Cathedral." Thus
we find a child of 6 years old, with a burthen of at least half a cwt.,
making 14 times a-day a journey equal in distance to the height
of St. Paul's Cathedral. The commissioner goes on : "And it not
unfrequently happens that the tugs break, and the load falls upon
those females who are following," who are, of course, struck off the
ladders into the depths below. However incredible it may be, yet
I have taken," he adds, "the evidence of fathers who have ruptured themselves by straining to lift coal on their children's backs."
But, Sir, if this is bad for the children and young persons, the case
is far worse for pregnant women. For them it is horrible. I will
quote the evidence of one woman who deposes to her own sufferings; and let me here observe that the evidence of the workpeople
themselves is worth more than all the rest ; for they know what
they suffer, and what the consequences are. I can say for them
that I have ever found their statements most accurate, and that I
have never met with attempts to mislead in the evidence given by
working men of their own condition. To return, however, to the
situation of the women in a state of pregnancy. "I have a belt
round my waist," says Betty Harris, "and a chain passing between my legs, and I go on my hands and feet. The road is very
steep, and we have to hold by a rope, and where there is no rope,
by anything we can catch hold of. It is very hard work for a
woman. . . . The pit is very wet. I have seen water up to
my thighs. . . . My clothes are wet through almost all day
long. . . . I have drawn till I have had the skin off me. The
belt and chain is worse when we are in the family way." "A
woman has gone home," says another, "taken to her bed, been
delivered of a child, and gone to work again under the week." "I
have had," says a witness, "three or four children born the same
day that I have been at work, and have gone back to my work
9 or 10 days after : four out of eight were still-born." There is
further evidence to the same effect : "The oppression of coal-
bearing," says Ellspee Thompson, "is such as to injure women in
after life, and few exist whose legs are not injured, or haunches,
before they are 30 years of age." "Jane Watson had two dead
children : thinks it was so from the oppressive work. A vast
number of women have dead children, and false births, which is
worse : they are not able to work after the latter. I have always
been obliged to work below till forced to go home to bear the
bairn, and so have all the other women. We return as soon as
able—never longer than 10 or 12 days ; many less, if they are

much needed. It is only horse-work, and ruins the women: it crushes their haunches, bends their ankles, and makes them old women at 40." Another poor girl says, "We are worse off than horses: they draw on iron rails, and we on flat floors." Another witness, a most excellent old Scotchwoman, Isabel Hogg, says, "From the great sore labour, false births are frequent, and very dangerous. . . . Collier people suffer much more than others. You must just tell the Queen Victoria that we are quiet, loyal subjects: women-people here don't mind work; but they object to horse-work; and that she would have the blessings of all the Scotch coal-women if she would get them out of the pits, and send them to other labour." Well, Sir, and I say so too. And she would have the blessing not only of all the Scotch women, but of every woman who has the least feeling of the sex within her, and of every man too who has ever known what it is to have a wife, a sister, or a mother.

But now I will call the attention of the House to the hours of work and the physical effects on the workpeople. "When workpeople are in full employment," says the report, "the regular hours of work for children and young persons are rarely less than 11; more often they are 12; in some districts they are 13. In Derbyshire, children, &c. work 16 hours out of the 24, reckoning from the time they leave their home in the morning until they return to it in the evening." As regards the east of Scotland, there is "overwhelming evidence that the labour is often continued, on alternate days, at least 15, 16, 17, and 18 hours out of the 24." Anne Hamilton, 17 years old, says— "I have repeatedly wrought the 24 hours, and after 2 hours of rest and my peas (soup), have returned to the pit and worked another 12 hours." "Now, in the great majority of these mines night-work is a part of the ordinary system of labour—one which the whole body of the evidence shows to act most injuriously both on the physical and moral condition of the workpeople, and more especially on that of the children and young persons." "Though the labour," says the report, "cannot be said to be continuous, because intervals of a few minutes necessarily occur . . . it is, nevertheless, generally uninterrupted by any regular time set apart for rest and refreshment, what food is taken in the pit being eaten as best it may while the labour continues." But in the coal-mines of Ireland a fixed time is allowed, at least for dinner. Here, too, I am glad to be able to repeat that a different system prevails in the sister island. Now, with regard to the physical effects of the labour on the workpeople, it appears that in some parts of the country a curious effect is produced by the results of this species of labour, not being discernible, in many cases, until a certain period of life.   On this head the report says— " With the exception of the east of Scotland (of which the account is deplorable), the physical condition of persons employed (so long as they can pursue their labour) derives a favourable character from the advantages of high wages, yet the testimony," it continues, " is equally full that the nature and circumstances entail ultimately grievous diseases."   This is confirmed by the evidence of the children themselves as to the effect upon their own health ; and the Sunday-school teachers depose to the extreme fatigue which the few who do attend the school exhibit when they go on the Sunday.   Mr. William Sharpe, F.R.S., a surgeon at Bradford, " has for 20 years professionally attended the Low Moor Iron Works : there are cases of deformity, and also bad cases of scrofula apparent, induced by boys being sent too early into the pits, by their working beyond their strength, by the constant stooping, and by occasionally working in water."   The chief employment of children and young persons in North Durham and Northumberland, that of " putting," is very severe—great numbers of the younger children are often completely exhausted by the labour, while those more advanced in years say that it deprives them of appetite and produces a constant feeling of sickness.   " The youngest of the putters are greatly to be commiserated; many of them declared," says the sub-commissioner, " that the severity of their labour was such that they would willingly suffer a diminution of wages to procure a limit to the hours of work."   But notwithstanding all this, the coal-fields of the north stand out in almost every respect in a very favourable contrast with the other districts.   But the east of Scotland beats them all :—From the tender age and sex of the great proportion of the workpeople, the long hours of work, the wretched condition of the pits, the meagre and unsubstantial food, the degree of fatigue produced by colliery-work, the labour in this district is extreme.   The evidence of the children is intolerably distressing.   Agnes Kew, 15 years old, says—" It is sore crushing work : many lasses cry as they bring up their burdens."   Again, another says—" It is sare fatiguing work : it maims the women."   In another place, Mr. T. Batten, surgeon of Coleford, says—" Has known cases of nervous relaxation in young boys.   Had one case of epilepsy in a boy about 13, brought on by too much exertion : another boy died of hemorrhagia purpurea, from the same cause.   The boy was not more than 7 years of age."   There is one phenomenon very remarkable in the physical condition of the miners, which is seen in their extensive muscular development : at first it was supposed that an employment which produced such a result could not be essentially prejudicial; but those well acquainted with the subject pronounce this development to be unnatural, and therefore injurious.

Now, Sir, the physical effects of this system of labour may be classed under these heads:—Stunted growth, crippled gait, irritation of head, back, and feet, a variety of diseases, premature old age, and death. "Several," says Dr. Scott Allison, "become crooked. Diseases of the spine are very common and very serious. Several of the girls and women so employed are distorted in the spine and pelvis, and suffer considerable difficulty at the period of parturition." Diseases of the heart are very frequent, say all the medical witnesses; "many are ruptured, even lads, from over-exertion; some are ruptured on both sides." But the most destructive and frequent disease is asthma. "Some are affected at 7 or 8 years of age. Most colliers at the age of 30 become asthmatic." Dr. Scott Allison adds—"Between the twentieth and thirtieth year many colliers decline in bodily vigour, and become more and more spare. . . . At first, and, indeed, for several years, the patient, for the most part, does not suffer in his general health; but the disease is rarely, if ever, cured. . . . It ultimately deprives him of life by a slow and lingering process." "The want of proper ventilation," says an old miner, "is the chief cause: the men die off like rotten sheep." There is another most curious disease, of which the House now hears perhaps for the first time. It is the melanosis, or black spittle. From the state of the atmosphere in which the people worked, there is oftentimes not sufficient oxygen to decarbonize the blood; and Dr. Thompson, of Edinburgh, says—"Workmen in coal-mines occasionally die of an affection of the lungs, accompanied with the expectoration of a large quantity of matter of a deep black colour." Dr. Makellar calls it "the most serious and fatal disease which he has had to treat among colliers—a carbonaceous infiltration into the substance of the lungs." Dr. Scott Allison says—"The symptoms are emaciation of the whole body, constant shortness and quickness of breath, occasional stitches in the sides, quick pulse, usually upwards of 100 in the minute, hacking cough day and night, attended by a copious expectoration, for the most part perfectly black. The disease is never cured. It invariably ends in the death of the sufferer." Who, then, can be surprised that the consequences are premature old age and death? Not only, however, is the death of the collier premature, but so is the exhaustion of his strength: he is early deprived of the power of earning a livelihood. Mr. Massey, clerk to the Wellington Union, says—"That when about 40 years of age, the greater part of the colliers may be considered as disabled, and regular old men." The evidence, in this respect, is universal. In the east of Scotland the system is thus spoken of by the sub-commissioner :— "Its baneful effect on the health cannot well be exaggerated. I have been informed by competent authorities, that 6 months' labour in the mines is sufficient to effect a very visible change in the physical condition of the children." The Rev. Richard Buckly, rector of Begelly, says—"The foul air of the mines seriously affects the lungs of the children and young persons employed therein, and shortens the term of life;" and here is a summary of the condition of the collier by the commissioners :— "By the same causes the seeds of painful and mortal diseases are very often sown in childhood and youth : these slowly but steadily developing themselves, assume a formidable character between the ages of 30 and 40; and each generation of this class of the population is commonly extinct soon after 50." No doubt exceptions might be quoted to these results, but I am only speaking of the great mass of persons employed in the collieries.

Here, let me observe to the House, the moral effects of the state of things which the collieries present are equally prominent and equally alarming. It begets a slave-driving system. It might, indeed, be assumed without proof; but I shall state a few cases in order to exhibit those effects to the House and the country, and to show how necessary it is, immediately, if possible, to address ourselves to the evil. A clergyman, the Rev. W. Parlane, of Tranent, says—"Children of amiable temper and conduct, at 7 years of age, often return next season from the collieries greatly corrupted, and, as an old teacher says, with most hellish dispositions." See, too, here how the system superinduces habits and feelings of ferocity that are perfectly alarming. Hannah Neale says—"My boy, 10 years old, was at work : about half a year since his toe was cut off by the bind falling; notwithstanding this, the loader made him work until the end of the day, although in the greatest pain." Isaac Tipstone says—"I was bullied by a man to do what was beyond my strength. I would not, because I could not. The man threw me down, and kicked out two of my ribs." Jonathan Watts says—"A butty has beaten a boy with a stick till he fell. He then stamped on him till the boy could scarcely stand. The boy never told, and said he would not, for he should only be served worse. Boys are pulled up and down by the ears. I have seen them beaten till the blood has flowed out of their sides. They are often punished until they can scarcely stand." John Bostock, speaking of Derbyshire, says—"The corporals used to take the burning candle-wicks after the tallow was off, light them, and burn his arms. I have known my uncle take a boy by the ears and knock his head against the wall, because his eyesight was bad, and he could not see to do his work as well as others." From the south part of the West Riding, and about Bradford and Leeds, the accounts are more favourable; but about Halifax girls are beaten as severely as boys. They strike them in the face and knock them down. "I have seen this many times," says a witness. Harriet Craven, aged 11, says—"A man flung a piece of coal as big as my head at me, and it struck me in my back." "I met," says the sub-commissioner, "the girl crying bitterly. The several marks on her person and that of her sister were sufficient proofs of ill-treatment." "I remember meeting," he adds, "one of the boys crying very bitterly, and bleeding from a wound in his cheek. I found his master, who told me, in a tone of savage defiance, that the child was one of the slow ones, who would only move when he saw blood, and that by throwing a piece of coal at him he had accomplished his purpose, and that he often adopted the like means." William Holt says—"I have seen boys get an eye knocked out by a stone flung at them by the master." No doubt there are many exceptions to this state of things; but I am sorry to say that colliers are generally spoken of and known in many places as remarkably uneducated and ferocious. Their habits besides beget an utter recklessness of human life: in no part of the habitable globe, perhaps, is there such utter indifference displayed towards the life and limbs of human beings as in these collieries. The chief constable of Oldham says—"There are so many killed, that it becomes quite customary to expect such things, and people say, 'Oh, it is only a collier!' There would," he said, "be more feeling exhibited if a policeman were to kill a dog in the streets. Even the colliers amongst themselves say so; so that when they learn which it is that is killed, that is all they think about it." But now mark the effect of the system on women: it causes a total ignorance of all domestic duties; they know nothing that they ought to know; they are rendered unfit for the duties of women by overwork, and become utterly demoralized. In the male the moral effects of the system are very sad, but in the female they are infinitely worse, not alone upon themselves, but upon their families, upon society, and, I may add, upon the country itself. It is bad enough if you corrupt the man, but if you corrupt the woman you poison the waters of life at the very fountain. Sir, it appears that they are wholly disqualified from even learning how to discharge the duties of wife and mother. Matthew Lindley, a collier, says—"I wish the Government would expel all females from mines; they are very immoral;

they are worse than the men, and use far more indecent language."
George Armitage says—" Nothing can be worse." At a meeting
of 350 working-colliers, in Barnsley, it was voted, with only five
dissentients, that "the employment of girls in pits is highly injurious to their morals; that it is improper work for females; and
that it is a scandalous practice." Indeed, it universally appears
that "wherever girls are employed, the immoralities are scandalous." The Rev. Richard Roberts says—" The practice of working females in mines is highly objectionable, physically, intellectually, morally, and spiritually." "It is awfully demoralizing,"
says Mr. Thornely, a justice of the peace for the county of York:
"the youth of both sexes work often in a naked state." The sub-
commissioner for the east of Scotland says—" The employment of
females in this district is universally conceived to be so degrading,
that all other classes of operatives refuse intermarriage with the
daughters of colliers who work in the pits." Joseph Fraser, a
collier, says—" The employment unfits them for the duties of a
mother: the men drink hard, the poor bairns are neglected; in
fine, the women follow the men, and drink hard also." "Under
no conceivable circumstances," says the sub-commissioner, "is
any one sort of employment in collieries proper for females: the
practice is flagrantly disgraceful to a Christian, as well as to a
civilized country." "I have scarcely an exception to the general
reprobation of this revolting abomination." "I am decidedly of
opinion," says Mr. Thornely, "that women brought up in this way
lay aside all modesty, and scarcely know what it is but by name.
I sincerely trust that before I die I shall have the satisfaction of
seeing it prevented, and entirely done away with." I know, Mr.
Speaker, that the commissioners have not, by any means, told
the worst of the story. They could not, in fact, commit to print
for general circulation all the facts and circumstances that had
come to their knowledge in connexion with this system; but surely
it does not require any very vigorous imagination on the part of
those who have read or heard these statements, to draw from them
conclusions which will show a state of things which is not only
disgraceful, but most perilous to the welfare of the country.

Surely it is evident that to remove, or even to mitigate, these
sad evils, will require the vigorous and immediate interposition
of the legislature. That interposition is demanded by public
reason, by public virtue, by the public honour, by the public
character, and, I rejoice to add, by the public sympathy: for
never, I believe, since the first disclosure of the horrors of the
African slave-trade, has there existed so universal a feeling on
any one subject in this country, as that which now pervades

the length and breadth of the land in abhorrence and disgust of this monstrous oppression. It is demanded, moreover, I am happy to say, by many well-intentioned and honest proprietors —men who are anxious to see those ameliorations introduced which, owing to long-established prejudices, they have themselves been unable to effect. From letters and private communications which I have received on the subject, I know that they will hail with the greatest joy such a bill as I shall presently ask leave to introduce. In that bill I propose, in the first place, and at once, to cut off the principal evils. Much, no doubt, may be left for future legislation; but there are some of the evils of so hideous a nature that they will not admit of delay—they must be instantly removed—evils that are both disgusting and intolerable —disgusting they would be in a heathen country, and perfectly intolerable they are in one that professes to call itself Christian. The first provision, then, which I shall propose will be the total exclusion of all females from the mines and collieries of this country. I think that every principle of religion—I think that every law of nature calls for such a step; and I know of no argument that can be raised against it, unless one of a most unworthy and of a completely selfish character. I believe, indeed, there are but very few proprietors who have any real interest in keeping women so employed; but there are some interested parties who wish to retain females in the pits, and I am anxious to state to the House and the country what the motives are for inducing or compelling those wretched females to undergo the shameful toil and degradation to which they are subjected. I will take the evidence of the working people themselves, one of whom says— " Girls and women never get coal; they always remain drawers, and are considered to be equal to half a man." Another collier says—" They prefer women to boys, as they are easier to manage, and they never get to be coal-getters, which is another good thing." Another witness says—" The temptation to employ women arises from their wages being lower than that of males." The underlooker at Mr. Woodley's states—" One reason why women are used so frequently in the coal-pits is, that a girl of 20 will work for 2s. a day, or less, and a man of that age would want 3s. 6d. It makes little difference to the coal-master; he pays the same whoever does the work. Some would say he got his coal cheaper, but I am not of that opinion; the only difference is, that the collier can spend 1s. to 1s. 6d. more at the alehouse." Another remarks,—" When a lad gets to be half, he is all for getting coal; but a lass never expects to be a coal-getter, and that keeps her steady to her work." I ask the House to estimate the benefits of removal, by merely observing the effect of the evil. There is no economy in the practice, for Ellspee Thompson says—"I can say, to my own cost, that the bairns are much neglected when both parents work below; and if neighbours keep the children, they require as much as women sometimes earn, and yet neglect them." Mr. M. T. Sadler, a surgeon at Barnsley, says—"I strongly disapprove of females being in pits: the female character is totally destroyed by it; their habits and feelings are altogether different; they can neither discharge the duty of wives nor mothers. I see the greatest difference in the homes of those colliers whose wives do not go into the pits." Mr. Wood, the sub-commissioner, says— "The result of my inquiries is in every case to show that the employment of female children and young persons in such labour shuts them out entirely from all useful and necessary knowledge; the wives are so little capable of rendering a house comfortable, that the husband is constantly driven to the alehouse, whence arise all the evils of drunkenness to themselves and to their families. From this source a fearful deterioration of the moral and physical condition of our working population is rapidly taking place." Now, I rejoice to say that in this matter we are not left to mere speculation, for we have the evidence of Mr. James Wright, manager for the Duke of Buccleuch, and, I have his Grace's authority for adding, a most intelligent and honest man. He says—"Four years ago I superintended Mr. Ramsay's mines; females and young children were excluded; and a vast change was observable in the comfort and condition of the colliers who availed themselves of the new regulations." He goes on: "Some families left at the period, being desirous to avail themselves of the labour of their female children, many of whom have returned, and the colliers are much more regular than heretofore." This evidence is confirmed by Thomas Hynd, coalviewer in Mr. Dundas's pits, who says—"When Mr. Maxton first issued the order, many men and families left, but many have returned, for they find, now the roads are improved, and the output not limited, they can earn as much money, and get homes. Many of the females have gone to service, and prefer it." Again, Mr. James Wright says—and here I am very anxious for the attention of the House, because I would entreat them to observe how the mischief is first engendered, and then perpetuated, by the toleration of these practices: women are allowed to work below, and because they are so, the evils here stated continue without abatement; a man would complain and resist, but a woman is submissive—"I feel confident," he says, "that the exclusion of females will advantage the colliers in a physical point of view, inasmuch as the males will not work on bad roads (females are wrought only where no man can be induced to draw or work: they are mere beasts of burden). This will force the alteration of the economy of the mines." Pray, Sir, observe what follows: "Owners will be compelled to alter their system: they will ventilate better, and make better roads, and so change the system as to enable men, who now work only two days a week, to discover their own interest in regularly employing themselves." Mr. Maxton, of Arniston, and Mr. Hunter, the mining overman, asserts— "That in consequence of a new ventilation, and an improved mode of railing roads, a man and two boys take nearly as much money as when the whole family were below, and many of the daughters of miners are now at respectable service." Mr. Maxton, of Arniston, again contends that "Women ought to be entirely disused underground; and no boys ought to be permitted to go below under 12 years of age. These have been the rules in this colliery for some time past, and already the good effects are being felt: the houses of the workmen are clean and comfortable, the children are well looked after by their mothers, the young women are going out to service, and the whole workpeople have a better moral aspect. Colliers, prior to our regulation, emigrated in the proportion of one-fourth; but now not in that of one-tenth." This is very important testimony, for the colliers, I understand, are people of very migratory habits; and now listen to this as a crowning point:—Mr. James Wright concludes: "Since young children and females have been excluded from his Grace's mines, we never had occasion to increase the price of coal." All this is confirmed by the experience of Mr. Hulton, of Hulton, who has for 25 years been in occupation of coal-pits. That gentleman has been kind enough to write to me, and has exhibited a most striking contrast in the state of the population of his mines with that of the surrounding districts.

The next point for legislation is the exclusion of all boys under 13 years of age; and this I confess may be looked upon as my weak point, for here I am likely to find the greatest opposition. I shall, however, briefly state to the House the reasons why I think it necessary to limit the admission of children into the pits to those who have arrived at the age of 13. In the first place, the Factory Act prohibits full labour under 13 years of age: in the next place, in the cotton and wool districts frequent complaints have been made of a deficiency of young persons, who, it is alleged, are called off to the print-works and coal-mines, where labour is not regulated by law. It is therefore contended that an undue advantage is thus given to these departments of industry, to the prejudice of those of wool and cotton. Now, I am extremely anxious to bring them all to this one level; and if my proposition be adopted, a due supply of children under 13 years of age will be obtained from the coal-pits, and the proprietors of wool and cotton mills, as they themselves have alleged, will be enabled to have two complete sets of workers, the demand for children under 13 years of age being thus supplied to work in two relays of 6 hours in the day each (though I should myself prefer 5), according to the provisions of the Bill introduced, but not carried, in the last session. Indeed, almost all the evidence goes to show that 14 years of age would be the proper limit required for full labour. My own feelings, I must say, lead me to that opinion; but as 13 is the age stated in the Factory Act, I am not disposed to deviate from it. If a child once goes down into a pit, he must remain in it. All who go down must work full time, and, if required, throughout the night.

As for subterranean inspection, it is altogether impossible; and, indeed, if it were possible, it would not be safe. I do not know what the case may be 25 years hence, but certainly, at the present time, I for one should be very loth to go down the shafts for the purpose of doing some act that was likely to be distasteful to the colliers below. Nor are we without evidence as to the hazard of such proceedings. Dr. Mitchell says—" Cases have occurred where diabolical characters have deranged the gear during the night; . . . and in consequence, the first party descending has been dashed to pieces." In these mines, too, the House must recollect, the miners have a morality and a policy of their own. " It is well known," says Dr. Mitchell, " that persons who have done actions not deemed very heinous by the miners, have taken shelter in the mines;" and he adds, " there are few constables who would willingly go down after them." But I urge most strongly that children are, in many cases, left altogether in these pits to the butties and overlookers, and that it is in their power to treat them as they please. There is abundant evidence, too, to show that the children never dare complain of the ill-usage they receive. Punishments may be prohibited by the masters, as in many cases they are; but, as one of the commissioners very truly remarks, these people work alone, in secluded places, at great distances from each other, and they are consequently enabled to inflict any punishment they please almost without notice. Nor is there, I contend, any necessity for employing children in such offices. One witness says—" Coal-work is at best of an o'er sair kind, and few lads can acquire the knowledge of 'heaving,' or have good strength to 'put,' till 14 years of age. Colliers frequently exhaust themselves, and if regular they would not need the assistance of such quantities of infant labour." Indeed, the very custom of taking those children into the mines had its origin in vice. The habits of irregularity and intoxication common among miners are the cause of it; and unhappily, from the system which prevails, those habits are transmitted from father to son. We have it in evidence that many of the miners work 8 or 9 days only in a fortnight, earn some money, and then spend the rest of their time, until those earnings are exhausted, in drinking, cock-fighting, and gambling. They then have to work again to make up for lost time; and thus it happens that they take down their wives and children into the pits with them, and make that cruel demand on female and infantile labour, which would be wholly unnecessary were they steady to their work and decently frugal in their habits. But take away the power of permitting young children to work in the pits; put an end at once to this abuse—this monstrous and shameful abuse—and, depend upon it, they will soon attain their legitimate ends in an honest way.

The next point is one of real importance: it is the necessity of making a provision that no person shall be employed in charge of an engine or an engine-house who is under the age of 21 years. The whole subject of accidents in coal-pits has been under the investigation of this House, and has been reported on, yet nothing has been done; but I am sure that we must speedily direct our attention to this subject, if we wish to save many heads of families for the service of their country, and many families of children from destitution and the poorhouse. Now, the frequency of their occurrence is fully proved and their cause is also elaborately detailed in the evidence. To give only one statement: Dr. Mitchell says—" The accidents which occur in the mining districts of South Staffordshire are numerous, and, to judge from the conversation which one constantly hears, we might consider the whole population as engaged in a campaign." But my proposition will be limited to a single point. In many districts it is common to draw up the miners and let them down again into the pits in baskets worked by engines. The engines are put up in small buildings near the mouth of the shaft; and those engines are frequently left in the charge of children, 12, 11, and even 9 years of age. The testimony is uniform and universal as to this shameful neglect in the districts where it prevails. One witness says—" It is common in Derbyshire, as elsewhere, to employ very young children as engineers to let down and draw up the workpeople. I have met with children only 10 years old having the lives of colliers left to their mercy, and have

seen others so inattentive to their duty as to let the corve be
drawn over the pulley, and half a ton of coals be thrown down
the shaft." These children draw up or let down six at a time.
The accidents resulting from the practice are innumerable. One
of the witnesses, a miner, says—"The worst thing that has ever
been brought about against the colliers is in the masters employing little bits of lads as engineers. Until a man has come to
maturity of age, and to know the value of a man's life, he is not
to be trusted with the management of an engine." That is a very
just and sensible remark, from an experienced working-man, and
one to which I hope the House will pay attention. But just hear
what is said by Mr. Wilde, the chief constable of Oldham—and I
call more particular notice to his statements, because it is Mr.
Wilde's duty to collect evidence for the coroner's inquests. "It
is," he says, "a general system here to employ mere children to
attend these engines and to stop them at the proper moment;
and if they be not stopped, the two, or three, or four, or five persons wound up together are thrown over the beam down into the
pit again. There have been people wound over at Oldham Edge,
at Wernertho, at Chamber Lane, at Robin Hill, at Oldbottom,
and on Union Ground here, within the last six or seven years;"
and he adds, "I do not know a case in which children were not
the engineers. Three or four boys were killed in this way at the
Chamber Lane Colliery by the momentary neglect of a little boy,
who, I think, was only 9 years of age; and who had turned away
from the engine when it was winding up, on his attention being
attracted by a mouse on the hearth." But the witnesses who have
given evidence on this point also hesitate not to state the motive
which induces the employment of those children. They say, and
with great truth, "If the masters can get such a duty discharged
by a boy, to whom they give 5*s*. or 7*s*. a week, it is so much gained
to them upon the wages of a man, whom they ought to employ."
I think the House will concur with me, therefore, in believing that
the Legislature may well interfere to check the great cause of
these lamentable results, by putting an interdict upon the practice of employing young children in such responsible occupations.

And now, Mr. Speaker, the fourth and last point on which I
appeal to this House, is one on which I trust every member of the
House will have as strong a feeling of indignation as that which
animates myself. I speak now of the practice of assigning boys
as apprentices to the butty colliers; and I do not hesitate to say
that anything more enormous was never brought under the notice
of the legislative assembly of a free country. The districts in
which this system of apprenticeship is most common are South

Staffordshire, Yorkshire, Lancashire, and the west of Scotland.
"In South Staffordshire," says the sub-commissioner, "the
number of children or young persons as apprentices is exceedingly numerous: these apprentices are paupers or orphans, and
are wholly in the power of the butties. Such is the demand for
this class of children, that there are scarcely any boys in the
union workhouses. These boys are sent on trial between 8 and 9 ;
and at 9 are bound for 12 years, that is, to the age of 21 years
complete." Now, Sir, was there ever such a thing ? "There are
probably," says Mr. William Grove, "300 apprentices belonging
to the collieries in this town of Bilston. One man has now five
in his house." Just see what an abominable system this is. Ask
yourselves whether any state of slavery is worse. Take what I
am now going to read to you as a sample :—"Many of the colliers," says the sub-commissioner, "take two or three apprentices
at a time, supporting themselves and families out of their labour."
Mark this : he is idle himself, and lives on the toil of these
wretched creatures. "As soon as either of them is old enough,
he is made a getter, and is then worth from 10*s.* to 15*s.* a week.
At the age of 14 the apprentice works side by side with other lads,
who are getting 14*s.* a week (he himself getting nothing); at 17 or
18, side by side with freemen, who may go where they please, and
are earning 20*s.* or 25*s.*" "The orphan," says the sub-commissioner, "whom necessity has driven into the workhouse is made
to labour in the mines until the age of 21, solely for the benefit of
another." Not a penny may he earn for himself, not a step may
he take without the permission of another. And is this system of
apprenticeship necessary ? It is given in evidence that there is
nothing to be learned that might not be acquired in 10 days. Dr.
Mitchell says—" Notwithstanding this long apprenticeship, there
is nothing whatever in the coal-mine to learn beyond a little
dexterity, readily acquired by short practice. Even in the mines
of Cornwall, where much skill and judgment are required, there
are no apprentices." Then, Sir, see the treatment to which these
unfortunate lads are subjected, placed as they are completely in
the power of these men, in seclusion and darkness, afraid to appeal, utterly defenceless, without friends or protectors of any sort.
Just see the horrid power exercised by these men. I will read to
you some excellent testimony, that of Mr. Baylis, agent to Mr
Lonsdale. Mr. Baylis says—"The men will send a boy where
they do not go themselves, and some have their limbs broken and
others lose their lives." Mark the cowardice of the deed. "Some
parishes will not let the butties have their pauper children. Butties get apprentices, and send their own children to learn other

trades : the apprentices have not a holiday, if there be one, or any means of employing them ;—it is the apprentices who are sent to mind the steam-engine, and pump up water on Sundays." They are not even allowed the rest of the Sunday. "It is the apprentices who on that day clean the boilers." Mr. Ellison, a master manufacturer in the West Riding of Yorkshire, gives similar testimony :—" When the colliers," says he, "are in need of hurriers, they apply to the poor-law guardians for pauper children. I have been," says he, "a guardian myself, and know it to be the fact. They cannot get them elsewhere, on account of the severity of the labour and the treatment hurriers experience."

But I will now go to the detail of cases of individual oppression, and will quote, in the first instance, the evidence given by two boys, Thomas Moorhouse and Henry Gibson. Thomas Moorhouse said, " ' My master served me very bad ; he stuck a pick into me twice.' [Here (says the sub-commissioner) I made the boy strip, and found a large cicatrix, likely to have been occasioned by such an instrument, which must have passed through the glutei muscles, and have stopped only short of the hip joint : there were twenty other wounds occasioned by hurrying in low workings.]" Henry Gibson (Wigan) said, "There is a lad called Jonathan Dicks, from St. Helen's Workhouse ; he gets thrashed very ill. I saw his master beat him with a pickaxe on his legs and arms, and his master cut a great gash in his head with a blow of a pickaxe."

Here is another case, to which I am particularly anxious to call the attention of the House, because I believe it to be a case of unparalleled brutality, and because I directed the attention of the Government to the circumstances at the time they occurred. I saw this case stated in the newspapers more than a year ago, and it appeared to me that the magistrates, under whose attention it had been brought, had awarded a very small punishment for a very great misdemeanour. I immediately went to the Home Secretary, and expressed my fears that it was too late to take any steps upon the case, adding at the same time, however, that it was a matter in which, perhaps, he might think it right to show that official vigilance was alive to such conduct. My noble friend, with that courtesy and kindness which I ever experienced at his hands, instantly made inquiry, and afterwards informed me that the facts, as I had represented them, were not only substantiated, but actually correct. I now find the case detailed at length in the appendix to the report ; and I must entreat the House to allow me to state it at full length. It is the case of "Edmund Kershaw, who (says the sub-commissioner) was apprenticed by the overseers of Castleton to a collier near Rooley-Moor. Mr.

Milner (the surgeon) examined this boy, and found on his body from 24 to 26 wounds. His back and loins were beaten to a jelly; his head, which was almost cleared of hair on the scalp, had the marks of many old wounds. . . . One of the bones in one arm was broken below the elbow, and seemed to have been so for some time. The boy, on being brought before the magistrate, was unable to sit or stand, and was placed on the floor in the office. It appeared that the boy's arm had been broken by a blow with an iron rail, and the fracture had never been set, and that he had been kept at work for several weeks with his arm in that condition. It was admitted "—what an admission!—" by the master, that he had been in the habit of beating the boy with a flat piece of wood, in which a nail was driven, and projected about half an inch. The blows had been inflicted with such violence that they had penetrated the skin, and caused the wounds described by Mr. Milner." Now, was not this enough for one poor child, at least? Not at all so;—" The boy had been starved for want of food, and his body presented all the marks of emaciation. This brutal master had kept him at work as a waggoner until he was no longer of any use, and then sent him home in a cart to his mother, who was a poor widow residing in Rochdale." Well might all the charter-masters in Shropshire speak of the system with horror, and say it was as bad as the African slave-trade. For my part, I think it quite as bad, if not worse; for, at any rate, slaves have the advantage of working in the light of the open day, besides that they may possess, sometimes, the alleviations of a domestic, if not a happy condition.

But now, I ask, what is to be said of such a system as this? These wretched apprentices have committed no crime, and even if they had so, they would not deserve to meet with such a punishment. Only a few days ago I went over the new prison at Pentonville. Never have I seen such preparations as are there made for securing a proper degree of comfort to the prisoner. Such care for light, such care for ventilation, such care that every necessary requirement of the prisoner should be furnished. He is to have books, tools, instruction—to hear the human voice at least 14 times a day. Sir, I find no fault with that; but I pray you to bear in mind that all this is done for persons who have forfeited their liberty by the laws of their country; but here you have a number of poor children, whose only crime is that they are poor, and who are sent down to these horrid dens, subjected to every privation, and every variety of brutal treatment, and on whom you inflict even a worse curse than this—the curse of dark and perpetual ignorance. Ignorant such people must be; for, from the time you take them down the shaft of the pit, not one hour have they of their own to learn their duty either to their fellow-man or to their Almighty Maker. And here I tell you that this matter nearly affects yourselves. It affects you as the makers of laws— laws which you enact in order that they may meet with obedience and respect. You are anxious to enforce these laws—you are anxious to enforce, for instance, the new poor law. I say nothing now as to the wisdom, or otherwise, of that law, but surely it is wise to relax the rigour of your laws where such relaxation is just and safe. Where is the right to inflict a servitude like this? Is orphanism a crime? To maintain such a system would be not only oppression, but an insult (I say it advisedly) to the poorer classes : but they need not fear, for they will find, I can see, a defence in this House. Here is a case made out—meet that case fully and fairly. Do not only make laws to meet such cases in future, but endeavour to meet the first injustice also. Let apprenticeship be abolished on the spot; let every existing inden- ture be cancelled. "Undo the heavy burthens, and let the op- pressed go free."

I will detain the House only a short time longer; for I know that I have already trespassed too much upon your attention. You will, however, I am sure, forgive me when you remember how long I have laboured in this cause, and how deeply I have it at heart. I ask, is all this cruelty necessary? Cannot we attain our ends by any other means? You have seen not only how needless, but how wasteful and ruinous, to themselves and their families, is the employment of females in these severe and de- grading occupations : you have seen how wasteful and ruinous is the employment of children of such tender years, when we not only deprive them of all means of education, but anticipate the efforts of that strength which should be reserved for the service and de- fence of a future generation. Sir, I am sure that, under proper regulations, the occupation itself may be rendered both healthy and happy : indeed, all the evidence goes to show that a little expense and a little care would obviate a large proportion of the mischiefs that prevail. No employments that are necessary to man- kind are deadly to man but by man's own fault: when we go beyond, and enter on the path of luxury and sensual gratification, then begins the long and grim catalogue of pestilential occupations.

Having thus endeavoured to state the case, may I occupy a few minutes to show that this present effort is not a de- sultory movement, but part of a large plan, wisely or unwisely conceived, for the social and moral improvement of the working classes. There are other reports to come, which will show a greater, a deeper, and, if I may use the term, a fiercer necessity for change of some kind. I had long observed the enormous toil of a large proportion of the community, and the total disemployment of the other—physically injurious to the one, and morally injurious to both. I thought I had a right to interpose in behalf of the children and young persons, to redress the balance, and to avert the mischief by shortening the hours of labour, and by that means to call into action those who were unemployed, and to afford some relief to those who were already overworked. This has been the limit of my exertions—I have never attempted to legislate for the adults, or interpose between master and man in the matter of wages. I have laboured to bring them within the reach of moral and religious education, knowing full well that they are the seeds of future generations of citizens; and that, in the progress of opinions and of things, there can be neither safety nor hope but by our becoming, under God's blessing, a wise and an understanding people. Sir, we can estimate our loss or acquisition of territory by geographical measurement; and so we can calculate in finance by increase or deficiency of revenue; but it is not so easy to arrive at the moral statistics of a country. Many persons love to estimate the condition of a kingdom by its criminal tables; but surely these figures exhibit very scantily the moral state of a people. A people may be in a frightful condition as citizens, and yet but few of them appear before the magistrate or infringe the laws:—why take, then, such a picture as this? I use it to show that criminal statistics are only a symptom, and not the extent of the internal disorder.

The paper which I hold in my hand is a statement taken from the police returns of Manchester, for one year, up to December 31, 1841, and in it I find the following:

| | |
|---|---:|
| Taken into custody . . . . . | 13,345 |
| Discharged by the magistrates . . . | 10,208 |
| Of these there were under 20 years of age . | 3,069 |
| Including the females . . . . . | 745 |

Surely, it would be unsound for the House to conclude that of the 13,345 taken into custody, the 10,000 discharged were perfectly innocent, immaculate in all the duties of private citizens. I do not, in general, set any great value on what are now called educational statistics; yet I cannot but observe, as a matter of curiosity, in how many of these persons one avenue to moral and intellectual improvement was absolutely closed up. Of the whole number, 6,971 could neither read nor write; 5,162 could read and write imperfectly; 220 only had superior instruction, which was, we may fairly conclude, of no very high character.  Now, in the column which follows there are many sources of crime, of immorality, of utter degradation, fatal and wide-spreading, the results of which may never be seen before a commissioner of police or a judge of assize, and will therefore never be ascertained by a statistical return.  I find within the limits of the borough of Manchester the number of

| | |
|---|---:|
| Pawnbrokers to be . . . . . | 129 |
| Beer-houses . . . . . . | 769 |
| Public-houses . . . . . | 498 |
| Brothels . . . . . . | 309 |
| Brothels lately suppressed . . . . | 111 |
| Brothels where prostitutes are kept . . | 163 |
| Houses of ill-fame where prostitutes resort . . | 223 |
| Street-walkers in the borough . . . . | 763 |
| Thieves known to reside in the borough, who do nothing but steal . . . . . | 212 |
| Persons following some legal occupation, but who are known to have committed felony, and augment their gains by habitual violation of the law | 160 |
| Houses for receiving stolen goods . . . | 63 |
| Houses suppressed lately . . . . | 32 |
| Houses for the resort of thieves . . . | 103 |
| Houses lately suppressed . . . . . | 25 |
| Lodging-houses where the sexes indiscriminately sleep together . . . . . | 109 |

Again, in the year ending September, 1840, there were confined in Durham gaol 141 pitmen; no very great number in respect of the population.  Out of these, 64 were confined for breaking some small condition of their bond.  No perfect picture, however, of the state of society among the mining people can be arrived at from this return.  How little does it reveal of that which the inquiry has disclosed!  It will be much better collected from the evidence of Mrs. Goodger, the mistress of an infant-school in that district, who states, that " when she first came, oaths were exceedingly common in the mouths of girls 5 and 7 years old," and when reprimanded for their conduct, " they did not scruple to call her the most opprobrious names that could be imagined."  The witness further declares that she " thinks the bad language might be corrected by the parents, who, instead of doing this, frequently abuse her for punishing the children."

I hope, Sir, that the House will not consider that I am speaking dogmatically on these subjects—my intercourse with the working classes, both by correspondence and personal interview, has for many years been so extensive, that I think I may venture to say that I am conversant with their feelings and habits, and can state their probable movements. I do not fear any violent or general outbreaks on the part of the population : there may be a few,-but not more than will be easily repressed by the ordinary force of the country. But I do fear the progress of a cancer, a perilous, and, if we much longer delay, an incurable cancer, which has seized upon the body social, moral, and political; and then in some day, when there shall be required on the part of our people an unusual energy, an unprecedented effort of virtue and patriotism, the strength of the empire will be found prostrate, for the fatal disorder will have reached its vitals.

There are, I well know, many other things to be done; but this, I must maintain, is an indispensable preliminary ; for it is a mockery to talk of education to people who are engaged, as it were, in unceasing toil from their cradle to their grave. I have endeavoured for many years to attain this end by limiting the hours of labour, and so bringing the children and young persons within the reach of a moral and religious education. I have hitherto been disappointed, and I deeply regret it, because we are daily throwing away a noble material!—for, depend upon it, the British people are the noblest and the most easily governed of any on the face of the earth. Their fortitude and obedience under the severest privations sufficiently prove it. Sure I am, that the minister of this country, whoever he be, if he will but win their confidence by appealing to their hearts, may bear upon his little finger the whole weight of the reins of the British empire. And, Sir, the sufferings of these people, so destructive to themselves, are altogether needless to the prosperity of the empire. Could it even be proved that they were necessary, this House, I know, would pause before it undertook to affirm the continuance of them. What could induce you to tolerate further the existence of such abominations? Just hear, Sir, and it is the last, the statement of William Hunter, a mining overs-man in the Arniston Colliery:— "I have been 20 years," says he, "in the works of Mr. Robert Dundas. Women and lasses were wrought below, when Mr. Alexander Moxton, our manager, issued an order to exclude them. Women always did the heavy part of the work, and neither they nor the children were treated like human beings, nor are they where they are employed. Females submit to work in places where no man, or even lad, could be got to labour in ; they work in bad roads, up to their knees in water, in a posture nearly double; they are below till the last hour of pregnancy ; they have swollen haunches and ankles, and are prematurely brought to the grave, or, what is worse, a lingering existence." Well might that good man Mr. Bald exclaim—" The state of these females after pulling like horses through these holes, is more easily conceived than explained : their perspiration, their exhaustion, and tears very frequently, it is painful in the extreme even to witness."

Is it not enough to announce these things to an assembly of Christian men and British gentlemen? For twenty millions of money you purchased the liberation of the negro; and it was a blessed deed. You may, this night, by a cheap and harmless vote, invigorate the hearts of thousands of your countrypeople, enable them to walk erect in newness of life, to enter on the enjoyment of their inherited freedom, and avail themselves (if they will accept them) of the opportunities of virtue, of morality, and religion. These, Sir, are the ends that I venture to propose : this is the barbarism that I seek to restore.* The House will, I am sure, forgive me for having detained them so long; and still more will they forgive me for venturing to conclude, by imploring them, in the words of Holy Writ, "To break óff our sins by righteousness, and our iniquities by showing mercy to the poor, if it may be a lengthening of our tranquillity."

* A member, in a preceding discussion, had said that " this kind of legislation would bring back the barbarism of the Middle Ages."

---

NOTE.—In answer to a question from Mr. Milner Gibson, M.P. for Manchester, Lord Ashley explained that " he had selected Manchester, not because he thought it pre-eminent in vice, but because a most accurate and important document had been drawn up relative to it—one which completely illustrated the position he wished to establish."

## *Reply to Lancashire Short-time Committee.*

MANCHESTER, SEPTEMBER 26, 1842.

GENTLEMEN,

The address which I have just had the honour of receiving demands from me a more ample reply than an ordinary acknowledgment. I will not attempt to qualify the force of your sentiments and expressions by showing how little I have deserved such commendation, for you are the best judges of the value of my efforts. I will joyfully accept your praise, and hope that it may be an incentive to myself and others to enter the broad and difficult, but not thankless field of the social and moral improvement of the working classes.

But though I am honoured and satisfied by your approval, I will not disguise from you my firm conviction that the measures which I have hitherto either carried or suggested, are but preliminaries in the great undertaking of domestic regeneration. You have spoken with kindness of the zeal I have manifested and the labour I have undergone on behalf of your constituents: yet all that has been done is small in comparison with what remains to be done; and the only reward, if any be due, that I look for at your hands, is your constant and hearty co-operation, at present and hereafter, on projects alike beneficial to yourselves, to your children, and to mankind.

The vast proportion of the evils which affect and endanger this country is not ascribable to physical or commercial causes,—these may have their influence, but in the main the mischief is to be traced to a moral origin. Over a large surface of the industrial community man has been regarded as an animal, and that, an animal not of the highest order; his loftiest faculties, when not prostrate, are perverted, and his lowest exclusively devoted to the manufacture of wealth. Women and children follow in the train of ceaseless toil and degrading occupation, and thus we have before us a mighty multitude of feeble bodies and untaught minds, the perilous materials of present and future pauperism, of violence and infidelity.

It is much to be regretted that a great part of our fellow-subjects, who might entertain or express an interest in the remedy of such evils, are altogether ignorant of their existence. Yet I am not without hope that a healthy and vigorous public opinion has been permanently awakened to the discovery and correction of all these abuses. We have seen in the Colliery Bill the first fruits of that revival. The researches of astute and able commissioners have disclosed a world of unknown abominations. Political differences were suppressed, and parties of all complexions aspire to, and may claim, an equal share in vindicating the rights of humanity and the character of the nation. Nor may we forget our deep obligations to the public press, which both in the capital and in the provinces exhibited a spectacle neither seen nor imagined in any country but this, the spectacle of the journals of extreme opinions and discordant principles combining to sustain a public man because they believed that, with no private purposes of his own, he was engaged in an honest endeavour for the public good.

I mention these things that they may impart to you, as they did to me, consolation and encouragement; they may animate you to perseverance in your just and necessary demands for a reasonable time-bill, for a measure which, by the more equal distribution of labour, shall save you from the alternation of absolute idleness and intolerable toil, and call into employment many whose energies are dormant while yours are overwrought. I entreat you to believe that, while my conviction of its necessity is greatly deepened, the resolution I had formed to persevere in the face of all kinds of opposition has undergone no abatement.

Nor must we omit to press upon the attention of the public the gradual displacement of male by the substitution of female labour, in a large proportion of the industrial occupations of the country; an evil we have long observed with fear and sorrow. This evil, as you well know, is not confined to the mills and factories of the United Kingdom, but is spreading rapidly and extensively over other departments, desolating, like a torrent, the peace, the economy, and the virtue of the mighty mass of the manufacturing districts. Domestic life and domestic discipline must soon be at an end; society will consist of individuals no longer grouped into families; so early is the separation of husband and wife, of parents and children. Thousands of young females of tender years are absorbed, day by day, in the factories and workshops; every hour is given to their toil, and that toil the most unsuited to their age and sex. In the precious season of youth there is no consideration for the harvest of adult life: they become, not a few of them, wives and mothers, but in utter ignorance of every domestic accomplishment; often unwilling, more frequently unable, to discharge any conjugal and maternal duty. I draw a veil over the enormous licentiousness which alike disgraces and endangers these pursuits. But the late unhappy disturbances have exhibited to you and to the world the pernicious results of violating the order of Providence by the abstraction of the females from their peculiar calling. Their presence, nay more, their participation in the riots, has read us an awful lesson; for when the women of a country become brutalized, that country is left without a hope. I speak these things openly and without fear, because you know that I love and respect you, and that I have ever said, as I conscientiously believe, that the working classes of these realms are the noblest materials in existence, for industry, patriotism, and virtue.

Yet, reform in these matters, great and beneficial in themselves, would be really valuable only as they preceded and conferred the opportunities of moral and religious education. This must be our principal, our only indispensable object. But in order that the children be rightly instructed, they must have leisure both to learn and practise the lessons of the school. We must keep before our eyes the undeniable but ill-considered fact, that every child in these districts is an immortal being; and that another generation, neglected like the present, and left in ignorance and sin, will probably witness the final extinction of the British empire.

You have concluded your address by a sincere and fervent prayer that it would please Almighty God to bless me and mine with prosperity and peace—may the prayer return to your own bosoms. Only let us proceed towards the attainment of our common object in dutiful submission to the law, and with due reference to the interests of all parties; and I shall still be animated by the hope, which has never deserted me, of seeing the restoration of content among all classes—the revival of good-will between master and man—a blessing on every house, and a home for every labourer.

*Education of the Working Classes.*

## HOUSE OF COMMONS,

### FEBRUARY 28, 1843.

Speech on moving " That an humble address be presented to her Majesty, praying that her Majesty will be graciously pleased to take into her instant and serious consideration the best means of diffusing the benefits and blessings of a moral and religious education amongst the working classes of her people."

SIR,

The question that I have undertaken to submit to the deliberation of this House is one so prodigiously vast, and so unspeakably important, that there may well be demanded an apology, if not an explanation, from any individual member who presumes to handle so weighty and so difficult a matter. And, indeed, had any real difference of opinion existed, I should probably have refrained from the task; but late events have, I fear, proved that the moral condition of our people is unhealthy and even perilous—all are pretty nearly agreed that something further must be attempted for their welfare; and I now venture, therefore, to offer for the discussion both matter and opportunity.

Surely, Sir, it will not be necessary as a preliminary to this motion to inquire on whom should rest the responsibility of our present condition—our duty is to examine the moral state of the country; to say whether it be safe, honourable, happy, and becoming the dignity of a Christian kingdom; and, if it be not so, to address ourselves to the cure of evils which, unlike most inveterate and deeply-rooted abuses, though they cannot be suffered to exist without danger, may be removed without the slightest grievance, real or imaginary, to any community, or even any individual.

The present time, too, is so far favourable to the propounding of this question, as that it finds us in a state of mind equally distant, I believe, from the two extremes of opinion; the one, that education is the direct, immediate, and lasting panacea for all our disorders; the other, that it will either do nothing at all, or even exasperate the mischief. That it will do everything is absurd; that it will do nothing is more so—every statesman, that is, every true statesman, of every age and nation, has considered a moral, steady, obedient, and united people, indispensable to external greatness or internal peace. Wise men have marked out the road whereby these desirable ends may be attained; I will not multiply authorities; I will quote two only, the one secular, the other sacred. "I think I may say," observes the famous John Locke, "that, of all the men we meet with, nine parts in ten are what they are, good or evil, useful or not, by their education. It is that which makes the great difference in mankind." "Train up a child," said Solomon, "in the way he should go; and when he is old he will not depart from it."

Now, has any man ever shown by what other means we may arrive at this most necessary consummation? If it be required in small states, and even in despotic monarchies, much more is it required in populous kingdoms and free governments;—and such is our position—our lot is cast in a time when our numbers, already vast, are hourly increasing at an almost geometric ratio —our institutions receive, every day, a more liberal complexion, while the democratic principle, by the mere force of circumstances, is fostered and developed—the public safety demands, each year, a larger measure of enlightenment and self-control; of enlightenment that all may understand their real interests; of self-control that individual passion may be repressed to the advancement of public welfare. I know not where to search for these things but in the lessons and practice of the Gospel: true Christianity is essentially favourable to freedom of institutions in Church and State, because it imports a judgment of your own and another's rights, a sense of public and private duty, an enlarged philanthropy and self-restraint, unknown to those democracies of former times, which are called, and only called, the polished nations of antiquity.

Sir, I do not deny, very far from it, the vast and meritorious efforts of the National Society; nor will I speak disparagingly of the efforts of some of the dissenting bodies; but in spite of all that has been done, a tremendous waste still remains uncultivated, "a great and terrible wilderness," that I shall now endeavour to lay open before you.

Sir, the population of England and Wales in the year 1801 was 8,872,980; in 1841 it had risen to 15,906,829, showing an increase in less than half a century on the whole population of 7,033,849. If I here take one-fifth (which is understated, one-fourth being the ordinary calculation,) as the number supposed to be capable

of some education, there will result a number of 3,181,365;
deducting one-third as provided for at private expense, there
will be left a number of 2,120,910; deducting also for children
in union workhouses, 50,000; and lastly deducting 10 per cent.
for accidents and casualties, 212,091; there will then be the
number of 1,858,819 to be provided for at the public expense.
Now by the tables in the excellent pamphlet of the Rev. Mr.
Burgess, of Chelsea, it appears that the total number of daily
scholars in connection with the Established Church, is 749,626.
By the same tables, the total number of daily scholars in connection with dissenting bodies is stated at 95,000; making a sum total
of daily scholars in England and Wales, 844,626; leaving, without any daily instruction, the number of 1,014,193 persons. These
tables are calculated upon the returns of 1833, with an estimate
for the increase of the Church of England scholars since those
returns, and with an allowance in the same proportion for the
increase of the dissenting scholars. But if we look forward to
the next ten years, there will be an increase of at least 2,500,000
in the population; and should nothing be done to supply our
want, we shall then have in addition to our present arrears, a
fearful multitude of untutored savages.

Next, I find as a sample of the state of adult and juvenile
delinquency, that the number of committals in the year 1841 was,
of persons of all ages, 27,760; and of persons under the age of 16
years, the proportion was 11½ per cent. I quote these tables in
conformity with established usage and ancient prejudice; but
they are, with a view to any accurate estimate of the moral
condition of the kingdom, altogether fallacious—they do not
explain to us whether the cases be those of distinct criminals or,
in many instances, those of the same individuals reproduced: if
the proportion be increased we have no clue to the discovery
whether it be real or fictitious, permanent or casual; if diminished,
we congratulate each other, but without examining how far the
diminution must be ascribed to an increased morality, or a more
effective Police—it is very well to rely on an effective Police for
short and turbulent periods; it is ruinous to rely on it for the
government of a generation. For after all, how much there must
ever be perilous to the state, and perilous to society, which,
whether it be manifested or not, is far beyond the scope of
magisterial power, and curable only by a widely different process!
I will not, therefore, attempt a comparison of one period of crime
with another; if the matters be worse, my case is established; **if**
**better,** they can be so only through the greater diffusion **of**
**external** morality. That morality, then, which is so **effective**

even on the surface of the nation, it should be our earnest and constant endeavour to root deeply in their hearts.

Having stated this much in a general way, I will now take a few of those details which form a part of the complement of this mass of wickedness and mischief—we shall thus learn the principal seats of the danger, its character and extent locally, and, in a great degree, the mode and nature of the remedy.

Sir, there have been laid upon the table within the last few days, a report by Mr. Horner and Mr. Saunders, inspectors of factories; and also the second report of the Children's Employment Commission; from these documents I shall draw very largely; and I wish to take this opportunity, as their final report has now been presented, of expressing to the commissioners my sincere and heartfelt thanks for an exercise of talent and vigour never before surpassed by any public servants.

The first town that I shall refer to is Manchester—some of those details I shall now quote I stated in the last session; but I shall venture to state them again as they bear immediately on the question before us. By the police returns of Manchester, made up to December, 1841, we find the number of persons taken into custody during that year, was 13,345. Discharged by magistrates without punishment, 10,208; of these, under 20 years of age, there were males, 3 069, and females, 745. By the same returns to July, 1842 (six months), there were taken into custody, 8341 (this would make in a whole year, were the same proportion observed, 16,682); of these, males, 5810; females, 2531. Now as to their instruction; with a knowledge of reading only, or reading and writing imperfectly, males, 1999; females, 863. Neither read nor write, males, 3098; females, 1519;—total of these last, 4617. At 15 and under 20, 2360; of these, males, 1639; females, 721. But take what may be called the "curable" portion, and there will be, at 10 years and under 15, 665; males, 547; females, 118. Discharged by the magistrates without punishment (in six months), 6307, or at the rate of 12,614 in a year. Can the House be surprised at this statement, when the means for supplying opportunities to crime and the practice of debauchery are so abundant? It appears that there are in Manchester—pawnbrokers, 129; this may be a symptom of distress; beer-houses, 769; public-houses, 498; brothels, 309; ditto, lately suppressed, 111: ditto, where prostitutes are kept, 163; ditto, where they resort, 223; street-walkers in borough, 763; thieves residing in the borough who do nothing but steal, 212; persons following some lawful occupation, but augmenting their gains by habitual violation of the law, 160; houses for receiving stolen goods, 63;

ditto, suppressed lately, 32; houses for resort of thieves, 103; ditto, lately suppressed, 25; lodging-houses where sexes indiscriminately sleep together, 109.

But there is another cause that aids the progress of crime which prevails in the town of Manchester. I will mention the fact that a vast number of children of the tenderest years, either through absence or through neglect of their parents, I do not now say which, are suffered to roam at large through the streets of the town, contracting the most idle and profligate habits. I have nere a return that I myself moved for in the year 1836, and I see that the number of children found wandering in the streets, and restored to their parents by the police in 1835, was no less than 8650, in 1840 it was reduced to 5500—having heard this table the House will not be surprised at the observations I am about to read from a gentlemen of long and practical knowledge of the place. "What chance," says he, "have these children of becoming good members of society? These unfortunates gradually acquire vagrant habits, become beggars, vagrants, criminals. It does not appear unfair to calculate that in the borough of Manchester 1500 children are added to 'les classes dangereuses' annually. Besides," he adds, "the moral evil produced by these 1500, let a calculation be made how much money per annum this criminal class costs the state."

I will next take the town of Birmingham; and it will be seen by the police returns for 1841, that the number of persons who were taken into custody was 5556, of these the males were 4537, and the females 1018. Of these there could neither read nor write, 2711; who could read only and write imperfectly, 2504; read and write well, 206; having superior instruction, 36. I feel that it is necessary to apologise to the House for troubling them with such minute details; nevertheless, details such as these are absolutely indispensable. Now from a report on the state of education in the town of Birmingham, made by the Birmingham Statistical Society—one of those useful bodies which have sprung up of late years, and which give to the public a great mass of information, that may be turned to the best purposes—I find that the total number of schools of all kinds in the town of Birmingham is 669; but then the society calls everything a school where a child receives any sort of instruction, perhaps in a place more fitted to be a sty or coal-hole. Now out of the whole mass of the entire population of Birmingham there were 27,659 scholars. A vast proportion of these schools are what are called "dame-schools;" and what these are in truth, may be known by the surveyors' report, who says of them, "moral and religious instruction forms no part of the system in dame-schools. A mistress in one of this class of schools on being asked whether she gave moral instruction to her scholars, replied, ' No, I can't afford it at 3*d.* a week.' Several did not know the meaning of the question. Very few appeared to think it was a part of their duty." This, then, being the number of the schools for educating the young, and the character of the education imparted to them, I may now be allowed to state what are the means for the practice of vice. From the police returns for 1840, it appears that the number of these places is 998, and they are thus distributed:— Houses for reception of stolen goods, 81; ditto for resort of thieves, 228; brothels where prostitutes are kept, 200; houses of ill-fame, where they resort, 110; number of houses where they lodge, 187; number of mendicants' lodging-houses, 122; houses where sexes sleep indiscriminately together, 47; add to this, public-houses, 577; beer-shops, 573. I will close this part by reading to the House an extract from a report made by a committee of medical gentlemen in Birmingham, who, in the most benevolent spirit, devoted themselves to an examination of the state of Birmingham; and who, looking to the removal of the growing evils that threaten the population, assert, that " the first and most prominent suggestion is the better education of the females in the arts of domestic economy. To the extreme ignorance of domestic management on the part of the wives of the mechanics is much of the misery and want of comfort to be traced. Numerous instances have occurred to us of the confirmed drunkard who attributes his habits of dissipation to a wretched home."

I will next take the town of Leeds; and there it will be seen that the police details would be very similar in character, though differing in number, to those of Manchester and Birmingham— the report of the state of Leeds for 1838, is to this effect:—" It appears that the early periods of life furnish the greatest portion of criminals. Children of 7, 8, and 9 years of age are not unfrequently brought before magistrates; a very large portion under 14 years. The parents are, it is to be feared, in many instances the direct causes of their crime." " The spirit of lawless insubordination (says Mr. Symons, the sub-commissioner) which prevails at Leeds among the children is very manifest; it is matter for painful apprehension." James Child, an inspector of police, states that which is well worthy of the attention of the House: He says there is " a great deal of drunkenness, especially among the young people. I have seen children very little higher than the table at these shops. There are some beer-shops where there are rooms up stairs, and the boys and girls, old people, and married of both sexes, go up two by two, as they can agree, to have connection. . . . I am sure that sexual connection begins between boys and girls at 14 and 15 years old." John Stubbs, of the police force, confirms the above testimony. "We have," he says, "a deal of girls on the town under 15, and boys who live by thieving. There are half a dozen beer-shops where none but young ones go at all. They support these houses."

I will now turn to Sheffield :—The Rev. Mr. Livesey, the minister of St. Philip's, having a population of 24,000, consisting almost exclusively of the labouring classes, gives in evidence, "Moral condition of children . . . in numerous instances most deplorable. . . . On Sunday afternoons it is impossible to pass along the highways, &c., beyond the police boundaries without encountering numerous groups of boys, from 12 years and upwards, gaming for copper coin . . . the boys are early initiated into habits of drinking. But the most revolting feature of juvenile depravity is early contamination from the association of the sexes. The outskirts of the town are absolutely polluted by this abomination; nor is the veil of darkness nor seclusion always sought by these degraded beings. Too often they are to be met in small parties, who appear to associate for the purpose of promiscuous intercourse, their ages being apparently about 14 or 15." The Rev. Mr. Farish states, "There are beer-houses attended by youths exclusively, for the men will not have them in the same houses with themselves." Hugh Parker, Esq., a justice of the peace, remarks, "A great proportion of the working classes are ignorant and profligate . . . the morals of their children exceedingly depraved and corrupt . . . given, at a very early age, to petty theft, swearing and lying; during minority to drunkenness, debauchery, idleness, profanation of the Sabbath; dog- and prize-fighting." Mr. Rayner, the superintendent of police, deposes, that "Lads from 12 to 14 years of age constantly frequent beer-houses, and have, even at that age, their girls with them, who often incite them to commit petty thefts . . . vices of every description at a very early age . . . great number of vagrant children prowling about the streets . . . these corrupt the working children. . . . The habits of the adults confirm the children in their vices." George Messon, a police officer, adds, "There are many beer-shops which are frequented by boys only . . . as early as 13 years of age. The girls are many of them loose in their conduct, and accompany the boys. . . . I remember the Chartist attack on Sheffield last winter. I am certain that a great number of young lads were among them—some as young as 15: they generally act as men."

All this was confirmed by Daniel Astwood, also a police officer; by Mr. George Crossland, registrar and vestry clerk to the board of guardians; by Mr. Ashley, master of the Lancastrian school; by Dr. Knight, and by Mr. Carr, a surgeon. Mr. Abraham, the inventor of the magnetic guard, remarks, " There is most vice and levity and mischief in the class who are between 16 and 19. You see more lads between 17 and 19 with dogs at their heels and other evidences of dissolute habits." Mr. James Hall and others of the working people say, the " morals of the children are ten-fold worse than formerly. . . . There are beer-shops fre-quented by boys from 9 to 15 years old, to play for money and liquor," Charlotte Kirkman, a poor woman of the operative class, aged 60, observes; and I much wish here to draw the attention of the House, because it is extremely desirable that they should know in what light the best and most decent of the working people regard these things, "I think morals are getting much worse, which I attribute in a great measure to the beer-shops. . . . There were no such girls in my time as there are now. When I was four or five-and-twenty, my mother would have knocked me down if I had spoken improperly to her. . . . Many have children at 15. I think bastardy almost as common now as a woman being in the family-way by her husband. . . . Now it's nothing thought about." " The evidence (says the sub-commissioner), with very few exceptions, attests a melancholy amount of immorality among the children of the working classes in Sheffield, and especially among young persons. Within a year of the time of my visit," he continues, "the town was preserved from an organised scheme to fire and plunder it, merely by the information of one man, and the consequent readiness of the troops. A large body of men and boys marched on it in the dead of the night; and a very large quantity of crowsfeet to lame horses, pikes, and combustibles were found on them, at their houses, and left on the road. Several were pledged to fire their own houses. I name this, as a further illustration of the perilous ignorance and vice prevailing among that young class between boys and full-grown men, who were known to be among the chief actors in these scenes."

Mr. Symons—and I shall the more effectively quote his opinions, because he is most strongly opposed to the political views which I venture to hold—further says, and it is right that I should state it in justice to so excellent a body of men: "If vice increases in Sheffield, the blame assuredly rests not on the clergy; few towns are blessed with so pious or active a ministry. It is not for want of exertion on their.parts if the churches and chapels are unfilled, and the schools scantily attended; and this remark applies also to part of the Wesleyan and some other religious denominations."

I shall now proceed to another district, to Wolverhampton, and there I find Mr. Horne giving the following description:— " Among all the children and young persons I examined, I found, with very few exceptions, that their minds were as stunted as their bodies; their moral feelings stagnant. . . . The children and young persons possess but little sense of moral duty towards their parents, and have little affection for them. . . . One child believed that Pontius Pilate and Goliath were apostles; another, 14 or 15 years of age, did not know how many 2 and 2 made. In my evidence taken in this town alone, as many as 5 children and young persons had never heard even the name of Jesus Christ. . . . You will find boys who have never heard of such a place as London, and of Willenhall (only three miles distant), who have never heard of the name of the Queen, or of such names as Wellington, Nelson, Bonaparte, or King George." " But," adds the commissioner, " while of scripture names I could not, in general, obtain any rational account, many of the most sacred names never having even been heard, there was a general knowledge of the lives of Dick Turpin and Jack Sheppard, not to mention the preposterous epidemic of a hybrid negro song."— This we may suppose is an elegant periphrasis for the popular song of " Jim Crow."—Mr. Horne goes on to say—" The master of the British School deposes, ' I have resided, as a teacher, for the last six years, during which I have observed that the character and habits of the numerous labouring poor are of the lowest order.' The master of the National School says ' besotted to the last degree.' "—Sir, there are many things of an extremely horrid description to be detailed concerning the physical condition of the children in these parts, but I forbear to touch them at present, being engaged only on their moral deficiency.

I now go to Willenhall, and there it is said,—" A lower condition of morals cannot, I think, be found—they sink some degrees (when that is possible) below the worst classes of children and young persons in Wolverhampton; they do not display the remotest sign of comprehension as to what is meant by the term of morals." Next, of Wednesfield, it is said the population are " much addicted to drinking; many besotted in the extreme; poor dejected men, with hardly a rag to their backs, are often seen drunk two or three days in the week and even when they have large families." The same profligacy and ignorance at Darlaston, where we have the evidence of three parties, an overseer, a col-

lector, and a relieving officer, to a very curious fact; I quote this
to shew the utter recklessness and intellectual apathy in which
these people live, caring little but for existence and the immediate
physical wants of the passing hour; they state, "that there are as
many as 100 men in Darlaston who do not know their own
names, only their nicknames." But it is said, that in Bilston
things are much better. It is remarked that the "moral condition
of children and young persons on the whole was very superior to
that in Wolverhampton;" he excepts, however, "the bank-girls,
and those who work at the screw-manufactories." Among them,
"great numbers of bastards;" the bank-girls drive coal-carts, ride
astride upon horses, drink, swear, fight, smoke, whistle, sing, and
care for nobody." Here I must observe, if things are better in
Bilston, it is owing to the dawn of education, "to the great
exertions of the Rev. Mr. Fletcher, and the Rev. Mr. Owen, in the
church; and Mr. Robert Bew (chemist), and Mr. Dimmock (iron
merchant), among the dissenters." Next, as to Sedgeley, "children and young persons," says the rector, "grow up in irreligion,
immorality, and ignorance. The number of girls at nailing considerably exceeds that of the boys; it may be termed the district
of female blacksmiths; constantly associating with depraved
adults, and young persons of the opposite sex, they naturally fall
into all their ways; and drink, smoke, swear, &c., &c., and become
as bad as men. The men and boys are usually naked, except a
pair of trowsers; the women and girls have only a thin ragged
petticoat, and an open shirt without sleeves."—Look to War-
rington; the Honourable and Reverend Horace Powys, the rector,
says, and there is no man more capable, from talent and character,
of giving an opinion,—"My conviction is—and it is founded on
the observation of some years—that the general condition of the
children employed in labour in this town is alarmingly degraded,
both religiously, morally, and intellectually." And here, too, is
the evidence of the Rev. John Molyneux, a Roman Catholic
priest, who began by stating his peculiar qualifications to give
testimony, having a congregation of 3000 persons, and chiefly
among the poorer classes. "Children in pin-works," he said,
"are very immoral—they sit close together, and encourage each
other in cursing and swearing, and loose conversation, which I
grant you they do not understand,"—a conclusion in which I
cannot agree:—"but it renders them," he adds, "prone to adopt
the acts of immorality on which they converse."—"Those girls
who from very early labour at pins go to the factories, do not
ever make good housekeepers: they have no idea of it; neither of
economy, nor cooking, nor mending their clothes."

Next, Sir, I will examine the Potteries. Mr. Scriven, the sub-commissioner, uses these expressions:—"I almost tremble, however, when I contemplate the fearful deficiency of knowledge existing throughout the district, and the consequences likely to result to this increased and increasing population. . . . It will appear," he adds, "by the evidence from Cobridge and Burslem, that more than three-fourths of the persons therein named can neither read nor write. . . . It is not from my own knowledge," he continues, "that I proclaim their utter, their absolute ignorance. I would respectfully refer you to the evidence of their own pastors and masters, and it will appear that, as one man, they acknowledge and lament their low and degraded condition." Mr. Lowndes, clerk to the board of guardians of the Burslem union, says: "It is with pain that I have witnessed the demoralizing effects of the system as it has hitherto existed. . . . It appears to me fraught with incalculable evils, both physical and moral." Mr. Grainger, a sub-commissioner, in his report respecting Nottingham, writes: "All parties, clergy, police, manufacturers, workpeople, and parents, agree that the present system is a most fertile source of immorality. . . . The natural results . . . have contributed in no slight degree to the immorality which, according to the opinion universally expressed, prevails to a most awful extent in Nottingham. Much of the existing evil is to be traced to the vicious habits of parents, many of whom are utterly indifferent to the moral and physical welfare of their offspring." "Education of the girls more neglected even than that of boys. . . . Vast majority of females utterly ignorant. . . . Impossible to overstate evils which result from this deplorable ignorance." . . . . "The medical practitioners of Birmingham forcibly point out the 'misery which ensues; improvidence, absence of all comfort, neglect of children, and alienation of all affection in families, and drunkenness on the part of the husband.'" And here I have to call the attention of the House to the testimony of a most respectable person, a simple mechanic; and I am very anxious to put forward the views of this individual, because his statements are the result of long and personal experience. I refer to the evidence of Joseph Corbett, a mechanic of Birmingham. I confess that I should like to read the whole of the report. I recommend it strongly to your attention; it will be found in the appendix to Mr. Grainger's report. I cannot, however, refrain from quoting one or two passages of it. "I have seen," he says, "the entire ruin of many families from the waste of money and bad conduct of fathers and sons seeking amusement and pastime in an alehouse. From no other single

cause alone does half so much demoralization and misery proceed."
He then adds, "from my own experience," and here he spoke with
feeling on the subject, for he referred to what he had seen in his
own home, and what he had witnessed with respect to his parents:
"My own experience tells me that the instruction of the females
in the work of a house, in teaching them to produce cheerfulness and comfort at the fireside, would prevent a great amount
of misery and crime. There would be fewer drunken husbands
and disobedient children. . . . As a working man, within
my observation, female education is disgracefully neglected. I
attach more importance to it than to anything else." I cannot
think that any one will be displeased to hear such sentiments
coming from a man in the situation of Joseph Corbett. Take
this as a proof of what the working people may be brought to, if
they cease to be so utterly neglected. This is an instance, among
many, to show what thousands of right-hearted Englishmen, if
you would but train them, you might raise up among the ranks of
the operative classes.

This, Sir, is pretty nearly the whole of the statements which I
have to make as to these districts; but there are other opinions,
by persons of great authority on this subject, and which, with the
permission of the House, I will read, although I have not permission to give the names of the writers. One gentleman, whose
opportunities of observation are unequalled, speaks of "the present existence of a highly demoralized middle-aged and rising
generation, worse and more debased than, I believe, any previous
generation for the last 300 years." A clergyman, writing
from one of the disturbed districts, says :—"The moral condition of the people is as bad as it is possible to be. Vice is
unrebuked, unabashed; moral character of no avail. . . . A
spirit of disaffection prevails almost universally—magistrates,
masters, pastors, and all superiors, are regarded as enemies and
oppressors." Another, in writing from the disturbed districts,
states :—"I took down myself the following words, as they fell
from the lips of a Chartist orator—'The prevalence of intemperance and other vicious habits was the fault of the aristocracy
and the mill-owners, who had neglected to provide the people with
sufficient means of moral improvement, and would form an item
of that great account which they would one day be called upon to
render to a people indignant at the discovery of their own debase-
ment.'" Another remarked :—"A working man's hall is opened on
Sundays, and in this 300 poor children are initiated into infidel
and seditious principles." Another said :—"A wild and satanic
spirit is infused into the hearers." An officer of great experience

to whom I put the question—"What are the consequences to be
apprehended if the present state of things be suffered to continue?"
replies: "Unless a speedy alteration be made in the manufacturing districts, a fresh and more extensive outbreak will again
occur, threatening loss to the whole nation."

I must now remark, that this condition of things prevails,
more or less, throughout the whole of England, but particularly
in the manufacturing and trading districts. The evil is not
partial, it is almost universally diffused over the surface of the
country. The time I might be allowed to occupy would be insufficient for me to travel through the whole of the details; but the
House will find, in the second report of the Children's Employment Commission, which is devoted to the statement of their
moral condition, the proof that it everywhere afflicts the country
—it is nearly universal throughout the whole of the coal and
iron-fields of Great Britain and Wales. Look to the east of
Scotland; one clergyman says:—"The condition of the lower
classes is daily becoming worse in regard to education; and it is
telling every day upon the moral and economic condition of the
adult population." Another clergyman remarks:—"The country
will be inevitably ruined unless some steps are taken by the
Legislature to secure education to the children of the working-
classes." Of North Wales we see it stated:—"Not one collier-
boy in ten can read, so as to comprehend what he reads;" while of
South Wales it is observed:—"Many are almost in a state of
barbarism. Religious and moral training is out of the question.
I should certainly be within bounds by saying that not one grown
male or female in fifty can read." In the West of Scotland I find
the same class of persons described as follows:—"A large portion
of the colliery and ironwork hands are living in an utterly depraved
state, a moral degradation, which is entailing misery and disease
on themselves, and disorder on the community." There is an
equally lamentable state of things existing in Yorkshire, Durham,
Lancashire, North Staffordshire, and Cumberland. The replies
of many of the children who were questioned by the commissioners, show a state of things utterly disgraceful to the character of a Christian country. One of the children replied to a
question put to him: "I never heard of France; I never heard of
Scotland or Ireland; I do not know what America is." James
Taylor, a boy 11 years old, said that he "has never heard of
Jesus Christ; has never heard of God, but has heard the men in
the pit say 'God damn them;' never heard of London." A girl
18 years old, said, "I never heard of Christ at all." This,
indeed, the commissioner adds, is very common among children

and young persons. She proceeded to say, "I never go to church or chapel;" again, "I don't know who God is." The sub-commissioner who visited Halifax has recorded this sentence: "You have expressed surprise," says an employer, "at Thomas Mitchell not having heard of God; I judge there are very few colliers here about that have."

Now can it be possible that such a state of things should exist without being attended with the most pernicious consequences? But I will go further, and rejoice that it is not possible—an evil unfelt is an evil unseen; nothing but an urgent and a biting necessity will rouse us to action from our fancied security.

First, Sir, observe the effects that are produced by the drunken habits of the working-classes; you cannot have a more unanswerable proof of the moral degradation of a people. I know it is frequently asserted that inebriety has yielded, in many instances, to greater habits of temperance; but suppose it to be so, the abatement is merely fractional; and no guarantee is given, in an improved morality, that those persons will not return to their former vicious courses—the abatement, however, has not taken place, at least in those districts which were lately subjected to the inquiries of the commissioners. Will the House now listen to some statements on this subject, which, lamentable as is the condition they disclose, describe but a tenth part of the evils springing out of this sad propensity? In the year 1834 a Committee was appointed, on the motion of Mr. Buckingham, to investigate the causes and effects of drunkenness. That Committee produced a report, which, by-the-by, has never received a tithe of the attention so valuable a document deserved—from that report we learn that the sum annually expended by the working people in the consumption of ardent spirits is estimated at twenty-five millions! and "I have no doubt," says a witness of great experience, "that it is, in fact, to a much larger extent." I wrote to the chaplain of a county jail, a gentleman of considerable observation and judgment, and put to him the following question, —"How much of the crime that brings prisoners to the jail can you trace to habits of intoxication?" Now mark his reply: "In order to arrive at a just conclusion, I devoted several nights to a careful examination of the entries in my journals for a series of years, and although I had been impressed previously with a very strong conviction, derived from my own personal experience in attendance on the sick poor, that the practice of drinking was the great moral pestilence of the kingdom, I was certainly not prepared for the frightful extent to which I find it chargeable with the production of crime: I am within the mark in saying that three-fourths of the crime committed is the result of **intemperance.**" In corroboration of this, I will appeal to the **very** valuable evidence given by Mr. J. Smith, the governor of **the** prison in Edinburgh. That witness states—"Having been for a number of years a missionary among the poor in Edinburgh, and having for two years had the charge of the house of refuge for the destitute, I have had, perhaps, the best opportunities of observing how far drunkenness produced ignorance, destitution, and crime; and the result of my experience is a firm conviction that but for the effects of intemperance, directly and indirectly, instead of having 500 prisoners in this prison at this time, there would not have been 50."

The next document to which I shall refer I regard as of a most important nature, and as one which deserves the most serious attention of the House. It is a memorial drawn up by a body of working men at Paisley, and addressed to their employers. It bears assuredly a remarkable testimony as to the moral effects of intemperance. I entertain a strong opinion of the great value of this paper, not only from the opinions which it expresses, but because it develops the sentiments of that class who are the agents and victims of this disastrous habit, and who speak, therefore, from practical knowledge. It states that "drunkenness is most injurious to the interests of the weavers as a body: drunkards are always on the brink of destitution. There can be no doubt that whatever depresses the moral worth of any body of workmen, likewise depresses their wages; and whatever elevates that worth, enables them to obtain and procure higher wages." This, Sir, in my opinion, is as sound political economy as ever has been spoken, written, or published. Again, I find it stated in the report of Mr. Buckingham's committee, that the estimated value of the property lost or deteriorated by drunkenness, either by shipwreck or mischiefs of a similar character, was not less than 50,000,000*l.* a-year. These are the financial losses; and it may be easy to estimate, with sufficient accuracy, the pecuniary damage that society undergoes by these pernicious practices; but it is not so easy to estimate the moral and social waste, the intellectual suffering and degradation which follow in their train. To that end I must here invite the attention of the House to evidence of another description; I will lay before them the testimony of eminent medical men, who will show what ruin of the intellect and the disposition attends the indulgence of these vicious enjoyments—we shall see how large a proportion of the cases of lunacy is ascribable to intoxication; but we shall draw, moreover, this startling conclusion, that, if thousands from this cause are deprived of their reason and incarcerated in madhouses, there must be manifold more who, though they fall short of the point of absolute insanity, are impaired in their understanding and moral perceptions.   The first medical authority to which I shall refer is a very eminent physician, well known to many members of this House, I mean Dr. Corsellis, of the Wakefield Lunatic Asylum: " I am led," he says, " to believe that intemperance is the exciting cause of insanity in about one-third of the cases of this institution ;" and he adds, " the proportion at Glasgow is about 26 per cent., and at Aberdeen 18 per cent."   Dr. Browne, of the Crichton Asylum, Dumfries, says—" The applications for the introduction of individuals who have lost reason from excessive drinking continue to be very numerous."   At Northampton, the superintendent of the asylum says—" Amongst the causes of insanity intemperance predominates."   At Montrose, Dr. Poole, the head of the asylum, says—" Twenty-four per cent. of insane cases from intemperance."   Dr. Prichard, who is well known, not only in the medical, but also in the literary world, writes to me that—" The medical writers of all countries reckon intemperance among the most influential exciting causes of insanity."   Esquirol, who has been most celebrated on the Continent for his researches into the statistics of madness, and who is well known to have extended his inquiries into all countries, was of opinion that " this cause gives rise to one-half of the cases of insanity that occur in Great Britain."   Dr. Prichard adds that " this fact, although startling, is confirmed by many instances.   It was found that, in an asylum at Liverpool, to which 495 patients had been admitted, not less than 257 had become insane from intemperance."   It is confirmed as a scientific fact by statements of American physicians almost without exception.   Dr. Rensselaer, of the United States, says that " in his opinion, one-half of the cases of insanity which came under the care of medical men in that country arose more or less from the use of strong drink."   These things, Sir, not only inflict misery and suffering on a very large class of the present community, but they entail a heavy loss on the country at large.   It cannot be denied that the state has an interest in the health and strength of her sons; but the effects of various diseases on one generation are transmitted with intensity to another !   I may also mention, to support these opinions, that the number of admissions to the Somerset Hospital, Cape Town, in the course of a year and nine months, was 1050, and of these not less than 763 were the result of intemperance.   It was also found, by *postmortem* examinations, that in the same period the number of deaths in that hospital, which was caused by intemperance, was not less than eight out of ten. Now look to the pauperism it produces; one instance shall suffice : Mr. Chadwick gave in evidence before the Committee on Drunkenness, in 1834,—"The contractor for the management of the poor in Lambeth, and other parishes, stated to me that he once investigated the cause of pauperism in the cases of paupers then under his charge. The inquiry," he says, "was conducted for some months, as I investigated every new case, and I found in nine cases out of ten the main cause was the ungovernable inclination for fermented liquors."

Next, Sir, vice is expensive to the public : Mr. Collins, in his valuable statistics of Glasgow, observes,—"The people will cost us much, whether we will or not; if we will not suffer ourselves to be taxed for their religious instruction, we must suffer to be taxed for the punishment and repression of crime." I will now just give a short estimate of the amount of the expense to which the country is subjected directly for the suppression of crime. I find that the expense of jails in 1841 was 137,449*l.* ; during the same period the expense of houses of correction was 129,163*l.* ; making together a total of 256,612*l.* The expense of criminal prosecutions in 1841 was 170,521*l.* ; the charge for the conveyance of prisoners was 23,242*l.* ; the charge for the conveyance of transports to the hulks, &c., 8,195*l.* ; and the expense for vagrants, 7,167*l.* These items make together the sum of 209,125*l.* The expense of the rural police, and it should be remembered that this is only for a few counties, is 139,228*l.* Thus the charges under the three heads which I have mentioned, amount, in a single year, to 604,965*l.* But here, Sir, is a document well deserving, I think, of the attention of the House,—a curious illustration of the facts we are asserting; I have not been able to verify it myself, but I will take it as stated. In the county of Lancaster, in 1832, the number of criminal cases tried at the assizes was 126, and the average charge for each of them 40*l.* The number of cases tried at the sessions was 2,587, and the average charge for each of these was 7*l.* 19*s.* The aggregate amount of charge was 25,656*l.* Now in addition to this average charge, let us take the estimate cost for the transportation across the seas of each person convicted at 25*l.* This would be a gross sum for the cost of each prosecution of 65*l;*—if the calculation, then, of Mr. Burgess 'be correct, that 11*s.* in the year will supply the education of one child for that term, we must confess that for the expense of a single convict, we might, during the space of twelve months, give moral and religious education to 117 children. Nevertheless, Sir, it is a melancholy fact, that while the country disburses the sums I have mentioned, and more too, for the punishment of crime, the State devotes but 30,000*l.* a year to the infusion of virtue; and yet, I ask you, could you institute a happier and healthier economy in your finances, than to reduce your criminal, so to speak, and increase your moral expenditure? Difficulties may lie in your way; mortifications may follow your attempts, but you cannot fail of raising some to the dignity of virtuous men, and many to the rank of tranquil and governable citizens.

I have not here included an estimate of the loss inflicted on society by plunder, violence, and neglect; nor can I arrive at it; it must, however, be necessarily very large. Let us use, as an approximation, a statement made by a late member of this House (Mr. Slaney) that, in one year, in the town of Liverpool alone, the loss by plunder was calculated at the enormous sum of 700,000*l.*

Thus far, Sir, I have endeavoured to lay before you an outline of our present condition, and to collect into one point of view a few of the more prominent mischiefs. A partial remedy for these evils will be found in the moral and religious culture of the infant mind; but this is not all: we must look further, and do more, if we desire to place the working-classes in such a condition that the lessons they have learned as children they may have freedom to practise as adults.

Now, if it be true, as most undoubtedly it is, that the State has a deep interest in the moral and physical prosperity of all her children, she must not terminate her care with the years of infancy, but extend her control and providence over many other circumstances that affect the working man's life. Without entering here into the nature and variety of those practical details, which might be advantageously taught in addition to the first and indispensable elements, we shall readily perceive that many things are requisite, even to the adult, to secure to him, so far as is possible, the well-being of his moral and physical condition. I speak not now of laws and regulations to abridge, but to enlarge his freedom; not to limit his rights, but to multiply his opportunities of enjoying them; laws and regulations which shall give him what all confess to be his due; which shall relieve him from the danger of temptations he would willingly avoid, and under which he cannot but fall; and which shall place him, in many aspects of health, happiness, and possibilities of virtue, in that position of independence and security from which, under the present state of things, he is too often excluded.

Sir, there are many evils of this description which might be urged; but I shall name three only, as indications of what I mean, and as having a most injurious and most lasting effect on the moral and physical condition of an immense portion of our people. I will briefly state them; and there will be then no difficulty in shewing their connection with the present motion; and how deep and how immediate is their influence on the morals of infants and adults, of children and parents; and how utterly hopeless are all systems of education, so long as you suffer them extensively to prevail.

The first I shall take is the truck system. Now hear what Mr. Horne, the sub-commissioner, says on this subject :—" The truck system encourages improvidence, by preventing the chance of a habit of saving, for nobody can save food. It prevents a family from obtaining a sufficient supply of clothes, and more comfortable furniture, in proportion to the .possession of which it is always found that the working man becomes more steady, industrious, and careful. It therefore amounts to a prevention of good conduct." In another place, he says: "The poor working man never sees the colour of a coin, all his wages are consumed in food, and of the very worst quality; and to prevent the chance of his having a single penny in his possession, the reckonings were postponed from week to week, until sometimes two or three months had elapsed." Now, as to the corrupting effects of this system, Mr. Horne, in his report, emphatically says :—" One final remark should, however, be made on the particular evil of the system, which principally relates to the moral condition of the children and young persons, nothing can be worse than the example set by the truck system—an example which is constantly before the eyes of the children, and in which they grow up, familiarised with the grossest frauds, the subtlest tricks, and the most dishonest evasions, habitually practised by their masters, parents, and other adults, in the very face of law and justice, and with perfect impunity." Such is the result of this part of the inquiry made by Mr. Horne. That gentleman uses the emphatic language that the truck system not only familiarises the mind, and the mind too of the child, with the grossest frauds, but that it tends to prevent the practice of any of the moral virtues. See, too, the effect as stated in the evidence produced before Parliament. It is notorious that the system has led to the most serious effects in several parts of the country. The whole man suffers; his experience; his thrifty habits; his resolutions of forethought; he is widely and justly discontented, becomes a bad subject, and ripe for mischief. In 1834 the existence of the truck system drove the mining districts of South Wales into open rebellion; it produced the disturbances that took place in Staffordshire in 1842; and no one can calculate the flood of the moral and physical mischiefs that devastated those counties as the result of their outbreak.

I will take, in the second place, the payment of wages in public-houses, beer-shops, and localities of that description. You have recognised the principle of interdicting such a practice in the Colliery Bill of last year; let me shew how necessary it is that a law of that kind should become universal:—" Payment of wages in cash," says Mr. Horne, " are made in a public-house (for the convenience, they pretend, of change), where it is required that every man shall spend a shilling as a rule, which is to be spent in drink. Boys have also to spend proportionately to their wages (generally sixpence), and either they thus learn to drink by taking their share, or, if they cannot, some adult drinks it for them till they can. The keeper of this house generally delays the settling of accounts, so as to give more time for drinking previously." Now, Sir, I have frequently heard discredit thrown on the exertions that have been made to promote the improvement in the moral condition of the working classes, in consequence of the criminal conduct of some who had received a moral and religious education. No doubt it is true that persons may be found in jails who have received their education in Sunday and other schools; but there is many a man who will trace his ruin to the practice I mention; whole families have been pauperized; and, by a perverted logic, moral teaching itself is declared to be useless, because the system we allow has made moral practice next to impossible.

The third, is the state of the dwellings of the poor—I will at once put before the House a picture drawn by an able hand;— Captain Miller, the valuable superintendent of the police at Glasgow, writes thus: "In the very centre of the city there is an accumulated mass of squalid wretchedness, which is probably unequalled in any other town in the British dominions. There is concentrated every thing that is wretched, dissolute, loathsome, and pestilential. These places are filled by a population of many thousands of miserable creatures. The houses in which they live are unfit even for sties; and every apartment is filled with a promiscuous crowd of men, women, and children: all in the most revolting state of filth and squalor. In many of the houses there is scarcely any ventilation; dunghills lie in the vicinity of the dwellings; and from the extremely defective sewerages, filth of every kind constantly accumulates. In these horrid dens the most abandoned characters of the city are collected; from whence they nightly issue to disseminate diseases, and to pour upon the town every species of crime and abomination." Will any man after this tell me that it is to any purpose to take children for the purposes of education during 2 hours a day, and then turn them back for 22 to such scenes of vice, and filth, and misery ? I am quite certain this statement is not exaggerated, I have been on the spot and seen it myself ; and not only there, but I have found a similar state of things existing at Leeds, at Manchester, and in London. It is impossible for language to describe the horrid and disgraceful scenes that are exposed to the sight in these places, and I am sure no one can recollect, without the most painful feelings, the thousands and hundreds of thousands, who ought to be the subjects of any system of education, that are hopelessly congregated in these dens of filth, of suffering, and infamy.

Turn, then, to the invaluable report of Mr. Chadwick on the sanitary state of the population, which has just been presented to the House. He shews clearly how indispensable it is to establish some better regulations with regard to the residences of the people, if you wish to make them a moral and religious race, and that all your attempts at their reformation will be useless, if steps are not taken to promote their decency and comfort. He says, amongst the conclusions at which he arrives towards the end of his report :—" That the formation of all habits of cleanliness is obstructed by defective supplies of water; that the annual loss of life from filth and bad ventilation is greater than the loss from death or wounds in any wars in which the country has been engaged in modern times; that of the 43,000 cases of widowhood, and 112,000 cases of destitute orphanage, relieved from the poor's-rate in England alone, it appears that the greatest proportion of deaths of the heads of families occurred from the above specified and other removable causes; that their ages were under 45 years—that is to say, 13 years below the natural probabilities of life, as shewn by the experience of the whole population of Sweden ; that the younger population, bred up under noxious physical agencies, is inferior in physical organization and general health to a population preserved from the presence of such agencies ; that the population, so exposed, is less susceptible of moral influences, and the effects of education are more transient, than with a healthy population; that these adverse circumstances tend to produce an adult population short-lived, improvident, reckless, and intemperate, and with habitual avidity for sensual gratification ; that these habits lead to the abandonment of all the conveniences and the decencies of life, and especially lead to the over-crowding of their homes, which is destructive to the morality as well as to the health of large classes of both sexes; that defective town-cleansing fosters habits of the most abject degradation, tending to the demoralization of large numbers of human beings, who subsist by means of what they find amid the various filth accumulated in neglected streets and by-places." Now, Sir, can any one gainsay the assertion that this state of things is cruel, disgusting, perilous ?—indifference, despair, neglect of every kind— of the household, the children, the moral and the physical part— must follow in the train of such evils; the contemplation of them distresses the standers-by, it exasperates the sufferer and his whole class, it breeds discontent and every bad passion; and then, when disaffection stalks abroad, we are alarmed, and cry out that we are fallen upon evil times, and so we are ; but it is not because poverty is always seditious, but because wealth is too frequently oppressive.

This, Sir, completes the picture I desired to lay before the House : it has been imperfectly, and I fear tediously drawn. There is, however, less risk in taxing the patience than in taxing the faith of indulgent hearers. I have not presumed to propose a scheme, because I have ever thought that such a mighty undertaking demands the collective deliberation and wisdom of the executive, backed by the authority and influence of the Crown. But what does this picture exhibit. Mark, Sir, first, the utter inefficiency of our penal code—of our capital and secondary punishments. The country is wearied with pamphlets and speeches on jail-discipline, model-prisons, and corrective processes; meanwhile crime advances at a rapid pace; many are discharged because they cannot be punished, and many become worse by the very punishment they undergo—punishment is disarmed of a large part of its terrors, because it no longer can appeal to any sense of shame;—and all this, because we will obstinately persist in setting our own wilfulness against the experience of mankind and the wisdom of Revelation, and believe that we can regenerate the hardened man while we utterly neglect his pliant childhood. You are right to punish those awful miscreants who make a trade of blasphemy, and pollute the very atmosphere by their foul exhibitions; but you will never subdue their disciples and admirers, except by the implements of another armoury. You must draw from the great depotory of truth all that can create and refine a sound public opinion —all that can institute and diffuse among the people the feelings and practices of morality. I hope I am not dictatorial in repeating here, that criminal tables and criminal statistics furnish no estimate of a nation's disorder. Culprits, such as they exhibit, are but the representatives of the mischief, spawned by the filth and corruption of the times. Were the crimes of these offenders the sum total of the crimes of England, although we should lament for the individuals, we might disregard the consequences; but the danger is wider, deeper, fiercer; and no one who has heard these statements and believes them, can hope that 20 years more will pass without some mighty convulsion, and displacement of the whole system of society.

Next, Sir, observe that our very multitude oppresses us; and oppresses us, too, with all the fearful weight of a blessing converted into a curse. The King's strength ought to be in the multitude of his people; and so it is; not, however, such a people as we must shortly have; but in a people happy, healthy, and virtuous : " Sacra Deûm, sanctique patres." Is that our condition of present comfort or prospective safety? You have seen in how many instances the intellect is impaired, and even destroyed, by the opinions and practices of our moral world; honest industry will decline, energy will be blunted, and whatever shall remain of zeal be perverted to the worst and most perilous uses. An evil state of morals engenders and diffuses a ferocious spirit; the mind of man is as much affected by moral epidemics as his body by disorders; thence arise murders, blasphemies, seditions, everything that can tear prosperity from nations, and peace from individuals. See, Sir, the ferocity of disposition that your records disclose : look at the savage treatment of children and apprentices; and imagine the awful results, if such a spirit were let loose upon society. Is the character of your females nothing?—and yet hear the language of an eye-witness, and one long and deeply conversant with their character : " They are becoming similar to the female followers of an army, wearing the garb of women, but actuated by the worst passions of men; in every riot or outbreak in the manufacturing districts the women are the leaders and exciters of the young men to violence. The language they indulge in is of the most horrid description—in short, while they are demoralised themselves, they demoralise all that come within their reach." People, Mr. Speaker, will oftentimes administer consolation by urging that a mob of Englishmen will never be disgraced by the atrocities of the Continent. Now, Sir, apart from the fact that one hundredth part of " the reign of terror " is sufficient to annihilate all virtue and all peace in society, we have never, except in 1780, and a few years ago at Bristol and Nottingham, seen a mob of our countrymen in triumphant possession. Conflagration then and plunder devastated the scene; nor were they forgotten in the riots of last year, when, during the short-lived anarchy of an hour, they fired I know not how many houses within the district of the Potteries.

Consider, too, the rapid progress of time. In 10 years from

this hour—no long period in the history of a nation—all who are 9 years of age will have reached the age. of 19 years; a period in which, with the few years that follow, there is the least sense of responsibility, the power of the liveliest action, and the greatest disregard of human suffering and human life. The early ages are of incalculable value; an idle. reprobate of 14 is almost irreclaimable; every year of delay abstracts from us thousands of useful fellow-citizens; nay, rather, it adds them to the ranks of viciousness, of misery, and of disorder. So long as this plague-spot is festering among our people, all our labours will be in vain; our recent triumphs will avail us nothing—to no purpose, while we are rotten at heart, shall we toil to improve our finances, to expand our commerce, and explore the hidden sources of our difficulty and alarm. We feel that all is wrong, we grope at noonday as though it were night; disregarding the lessons of history and the Word of God, that there is neither hope nor strength, nor comfort, nor peace, but in a virtuous, a " wise and an understanding people."

But if we will retrace our steps, and do the first works—if we will apply ourselves earnestly, in faith and fear, to this necessary service, there lie before us many paths of peace, many prospects of encouragement. Turn where you will; examine the agents of every honest calling, and you will find that the educated man is the safest and the best in every profession. I might quote the testimony of distinguished officers, both military and naval, and they will tell you that no discipline is so vigorous as morality. I have here the earnest declaration of various manufacturers, that trustworthiness and skill will ever follow on religious training. You have heard the opinions of the judges at the late special assizes, more particularly the charge of that eminent lawyer and good man, Chief Justice Tindal. I have read correspondence of the clergy in the disturbed districts, and they boldly assert, that very few belonging to their congregations, and none belonging to their schools, were found among the insurgents against the public peace; because such persons well know that, however grievous their wrongs, they owe obedience to the laws, not on a calculation of forces, but for conscience' sake.

Nor let us put out of mind this great and stirring consideration, that the moral condition of England seems destined by Providence to lead the moral condition of the world. Year after year we are sending forth thousands and hundreds of thousands of our citizens to people the vast solitudes and islands of another hemisphere; the Anglo-Saxon race will shortly overspread half the habitable globe. What a mighty and what a rapid addition to the happiness of mankind, if these thousands should carry with them, and plant in those distant regions, our freedom, our laws, our morality, and our religion!

This, Sir, is the ground of my appeal to this House; the plan that I venture to propose, and the argument by which I sustain it. It is, I know, but a portion of what the country requires; and even here we shall have, no doubt, disappointments to undergo, and failures to deplore; it will, nevertheless, bear for us abundant fruit. We owe to the poor of our land a weighty debt. We call them improvident and immoral, and many of them are so: but that improvidence and that immorality are the results, in a great measure, of our neglect, and, in not a little, of our example. We owe them, too, the debt of kinder language, and more frequent intercourse.—This is no fanciful obligation; our people are more alive than any other to honest zeal for their cause, and sympathy with their necessities, which, fall though it often-times may on unimpressible hearts, never fails to find some that it comforts, and many that it softens. Only let us declare, this night, that we will enter on a novel and a better course—that we will seek their temporal, through their eternal welfare—and the half of our work will then have been achieved. There are many hearts to be won, many minds to be instructed, and many souls to be saved: *" Oh Patria! oh Divum domus !"*—the blessing of God will rest upon our endeavours; and the oldest among us may perhaps live to enjoy, for himself and for his children, the opening day of the immortal, because the moral, glories of the British empire.

---

The following TABLE, showing the state of parts of London, which it was intended to quote, was accidentally omitted.

*The London City Mission Report of two districts just examined,* 1842.

In a small district immediately contiguous to Holborn Hill, found,

| | |
|---|---:|
| families | 103 |
| Consisting of, persons | 391 |
| From 6 years and upwards, could not read | 280 |
| Of these, above 20 years of age | 119 |
| In five courts and alleys in the Cow-cross district:— | |
| Heads of families | 158 |
| Cannot read | 102 |
| Young persons, between 7 and 22 | 106 |
| Cannot read | 77 |

" Can we be surprised," says the Report, " at the number of public criminals? Neighbourhoods such as these chiefly supply our jails with inmates. So late as October last there were in the House of Correction alone 973 prisoners, exclusive of children, and out of these 717 had no education at all."

# Condition of the Labouring Population.

STURMINSTER, NOVEMBER, 1843.

AT the annual dinner of the Sturminster Agricultural Society, in Dorsetshire, Lord Ashley occupied the chair, and replied to the toast of his health proposed by Lord Grosvenor, now Marquis of Westminster.

GENTLEMEN,

The language of my noble friend in proposing my health, and the manner in which you received his proposition, so far exceed anything that I could have expected, that I am at a loss to conceive what I can have done to obtain such high and undeserved approbation—but such as you award me I accept, assuring you that while it urges me to continued and still greater exertions, I shall desire no larger recompense on earth than the esteem and co-operation of my fellow-citizens.

It is customary on these occasions to make a few observations from the Chair, relative to the business of the evening, and I am desirous of conforming to the custom, not only because it is the custom, but because there seems to be, and is, at the present time, a more serious demand for our single and combined efforts, a more pinching necessity to mitigate, nay, by God's blessing, altogether to remove, many sad and perilous evils that threaten to impoverish and degrade the labouring population. On these topics, gentlemen, I can speak to you with great freedom, because I feel assured that no one here present is chargeable with any share in the mischiefs we so much deplore; nay, more than this, that every one of you will cheerfully lend his aid to remove every source of complaint, whensoever it shall be proved. The first step towards a remedy is in a knowledge and an abhorrence of the existing wrong; the second, in that sense of duty which commands us, both great and small, rich and poor, with hearty faith and Christian diligence, amidst all the alternations of failure and success, of disappointment and hope, to use all appropriate means, to exhaust every legitimate power, and never to desist until we shall have either accomplished our end, or ascertained it to be impossible.

Gentlemen, I shall not be considered as departing from the business of the day, or as thrusting in irrelevant matter, if I dwell more on the condition of the workman than on the progress and prospects of live and dead stock. The paper I hold in my hand sets forth, no doubt, many subjects of agricultural importance; but we are not, and ought not to be, excluded from discussing others of primary value—for our first duty and our dearest interests lie in the physical and moral welfare of our people. To begin elsewhere is to begin at the wrong end, and to postpone to mere display or personal advantage the fulfilment of those obligations which alone can sanctify the possession of property, and render its tenure a joy to all classes, alike honourable, beneficial, and secure. Gentlemen, if we be agreed in this, as I am sure we are, I shall have no difficulty in obtaining your approval of an abstinence from all controverted topics while at this table—every topic has its time and place; let those which the Parliament has undertaken be reserved for Parliament, for the hustings, or places specially appointed—our business is of a higher cast, local, it is true, but, because local, within our reach, if we will but go to our work with the smallest amount of zeal and self-denial.

Now the county of Dorset is in every man's mouth—every paper, metropolitan and provincial, teems with charges against us; we are within an ace of becoming a byword for poverty and oppression. As Englishmen, as human beings, and as Christians, we ought to examine these accusations, refute whatever is untrue, and remedy what cannot be denied. I do not think that your task will be very difficult; for these charges, though somewhat founded in truth, have been pushed, by other parties than those who first made them, with woful exaggeration; that which is only partial, is assumed to be universal; all that is good is suppressed, all that is bad most zealously produced; and the owners and occupiers of land in this county are represented as guilty of much that they have never done, and of much that they cannot control. Nevertheless, the statements are weighty, and the period important; they are made by no nameless or spiteful reporter, but by an officer of the Government, and by a landed proprietor of your own county. The language of Mr. Austin and Mr. Sheridan must not be overlooked; it is not necessary here to repeat their statements; many of you must have heard, and all of you must have read them; I wish, too, to avoid touching on any points which may excite individual feeling; but I must confess that, as your compatriot and representative, I had rather incur your utmost displeasure, and even the hazard of forfeiting your friendship, than refrain from declaring fully, freely, and immediately, that these things ought not to be. In so doing I cannot be charged with any unworthy motive; and I regret that such imputations have been thrown upon Mr. Sheridan, who, I am convinced, by all that I have seen of him, acts by a higher and nobler impulse. Gentlemen, are we prepared to look these charges in the face, discuss their justice, repel what is false, but correct what cannot be gainsayed? Do we admit the assertion that the wages of labour in these parts are scandalously low, painfully inadequate to the maintenance of the husbandman and his family, and in no proportion to the profits of the soil? If we are able to deny this statement, we shall also be able to disprove it—let us do so without delay; but if the reverse, not an hour is to be lost in rolling away the reproach. I do not pretend to give advice as to the precise mode of doing these things, I am not sufficiently practical, or conversant with the hiring and payment of labour; but this I know, that if a larger self-denial, an abatement of luxuries, a curtailing even of what are called comforts, be necessary to this end, let us begin at once with the higher and wealthier classes—it must be done; there is neither honour, nor safety, nor joy (setting aside all higher considerations) to dwell in a house, however fair the outside, which rests on such rotten and crumbling foundations. Do we deny that the dwellings of the poor are oftentimes ruinous, filthy, contracted, ill drained, ill ventilated, and so situated as to be productive of many forms of disease and immorality? If we do, let us take the same course, and refute our accusers; but if not, let us hasten to wipe out the stain; the remedy is within our reach; it needs no deliberation; and, I must say, allows of no delay—shall we suffer these hot-beds of misery and sin to afflict and devour their victims? for even where the life of the labourer is spared, his health is broken down, and he becomes incapable of toil to support either himself or his family. There is a mighty stir now made in behalf of education, and I heartily thank God for it; but let me ask you to what purpose it is to take a little child, a young female for instance, and teach her for six hours a day the rules of decency and every virtue, and then send her back to such abodes of filth and profligacy, as to make her unlearn by the practice of an hour the lessons of a year, to witness and oftentimes to share, though at first against her will, the abominations that have been recorded. Gentlemen, if you desire to have a moral and well-conducted people, you must do your best to place, and to keep, them under such circumstances that they may have the means and opportunity to bring into action the lessons they have been taught, the principles they have acquired. People go to their boards of guardians, and hear the long catalogue of bastardy cases, they cry out "sluts and profligates," assuming that, when in early life these persons have been treated as swine they are afterwards to walk with the dignity of Christians.

And now, gentlemen, notwithstanding the openness with which I have spoken to you I hope, nay, I believe, I shall obtain your forgiveness—it would have been easy to take a safer course, hold a more flattering language, and, by suppressing the reality, indulge the imagination; but I should not then have done either my duty to you, or had respect to the consistency of my own principles. You ought to know and reflect on these things; and I ought not to be lynx-eyed to the misconduct of manufacturers, and blind to the faults of landowners. We have the means of a vast superiority in virtue and comfort over the thickly-crowded districts; let us do our best to profit by the advantage, and attain the desirable issue that our great and only rivalry should lie in a competition of moral and physical benefits to all our people. Set yourselves to mitigate the severity of the poor-law; its greatest supporters admit that it is severe; but that severity may be mitigated or increased by the mode of its administration; begin a more frequent and friendly intercourse with the labouring man—we have lost much in departing from the primitive simplicity of our forefathers; respect his feelings; respect his rights; pay him in solid money; I say it again emphatically, pay him in solid money; pay him in due time; and, above all, avoid that monstrous abomination which disgraces some other counties, but from which, I believe, we are altogether free, of closing your fields in the time of harvest; give to the gleaner his ancient, his Scriptural right; throw open your gates, throw them wide open, to the poor, the fatherless, and the widow. Gentlemen, these men appeal to you with every claim of justice, service, and affection—they and their fathers have tilled your fields; they have replenished, and still replenish your armies in order to extend your dominion, and defend your shores—often have I heard the great Duke of Wellington declare that all his ability and courage would have effected nothing, had he not been called to command so noble a material as the British labourer. Such service they have rendered once; they may be summoned to do so again; and surely then we shall find our account in a vigorous and loyal peasantry. But let us draw our resolutions from a higher source, recollecting that all wealth, talent, rank, and power, are given by God for his own service, not for our luxury; for the benefit of others, not for the pride of ourselves; and that we must render an account of privileges misused, of means perverted, of opportunities thrown away. Employ them aright, and they sanctify the possession of property, bless its use, and grace its enjoyment—accomplishing still higher and better ends by leading the poor, who experience their value, to thoughts of piety and peace; and, in their heart and prayer, to bless Almighty God that such men (and such we all must strive to become), are invested with station and leisure, and property and power.

## Ten Hours Factory Bill.

---

## HOUSE OF COMMONS,

### Friday, March 15, 1844.

---

Speech in moving that the word ' Night,' in the second clause of the Ten Hours
Factory Bill, shall be taken to mean from six o'clock in the evening to six
o'clock on the following morning.

Mr. Speaker,

Nearly eleven years have now elapsed since I first made
the proposition to the House which I shall renew this night.
Never, at any time, have I felt greater apprehension or even
anxiety; not through any fear of personal defeat, for disappointment is "the badge of all our tribe;" but because I know well the
hostility that I have aroused, and the certain issues of indiscre-
tion on my part affecting the welfare of those who have so long
confided their hopes and interests to my charge.

And here let me anticipate the constant, but unjust accusation
that I am animated by a peculiar hostility against factory-masters,
and have always selected them as exclusive objects of attack. I
must assert that the charge, though specious, is altogether untrue.
I began, I admit, this public movement by an effort to improve
the condition of the factories; but this I did, not because I ascribed
to that department of industry a monopoly of all that was pernicious and cruel, but because it was then before the public eye,
comprised the wealthiest and most responsible proprietors, and
presented the greatest facilities for legislation. As soon as I had
the power, I showed my impartiality by moving the House for the
Children's Employment Commission, for an inquiry into the moral
and physical condition of children engaged in the various departments of industry. The curious in human suffering may decide
on the respective merits of the several reports; but factory-labour
has no longer an unquestionable pre-eminence of ill-fame, and we
are called upon to give relief, not because it is the *worst* system,
but because it is oppressive, and yet capable of alleviation.

Sir, I confess that ten years of experience have taught me that avarice and cruelty are not the peculiar and inherent qualities of any one class or occupation;—they will ever be found where the means of profit are combined with great and virtually irresponsible power—they will be found wherever interest and selfishness have a purpose to serve, and a favourable opportunity. We are all alike, I fully believe, in the town and in the country—in manufactures and in agriculture—though we have not, all of us, the same temptations, or the same means of rendering our propensities a source of profit. And oftentimes what we will not do ourselves we connive at in others, if it add in any way to our convenience or pleasure. Look at the frightful records of the London dressmakers—for whom do they wear out their lives in heartbreaking toil? Why, to supply the demands and meet the sudden and capricious tastes of people of condition! *Here* is neither farmer nor manufacturer at fault; the scene is changed, and the responsibility too: we must ascribe it entirely to the gentler sex, and, among them, not a little to our own intimacies and connections.

And here it is just to state, that if I can recite many examples of unprincipled and griping tyranny, I can quote many also of generous and parental care, and of willing and profuse expenditure for the benefit of the people. If there are prominent instances of bad, there are also prominent instances of good men. I will suppose, for the sake of argument, that *all* are the victims, rather than the causes of the system; but whatever the cause, the condition inflicts a great amount of physical and moral suffering. I know I am arousing a fierce spirit of reply—be it so—" Strike me, but hear me."

I shall, for the present, altogether leave to others that part of the question which belongs to trade and commerce. I am neither unwilling, nor perhaps unable, to handle it; but I desire to keep myself within the bounds that I have always hitherto observed in the discussion of this matter, and touch only the consideration of the moral and physical effects produced by the system on the great body of the workpeople.

I am spared, too, the necessity of arguing the propriety or impropriety of interfering to regulate the hours of labour for persons under certain ages; the principle has long been conceded and acted on by parliament. Our controversy can relate only to the degree in which it shall be carried out. I have never omitted an opportunity of asserting the claim I ventured to put forward nearly eleven years ago; and I return, therefore, this evening to my original proposition.

Sir, I assume, as one ground of the argument, that, apart from

considerations of humanity, which, nevertheless, should be
paramount, the State has an interest and a right to watch over
and provide for the moral and physical well-being of her people.
The principle is beyond question; it is recognised and enforced
under every form of civilized government. Let us see what is
done by the powers of Europe.

Now, what has been determined by Russia in this matter? In
a despatch addressed some time ago by, I think, Count Nesselrode
to the then Secretary of State for Foreign Affairs of this country
—the noble lord, the member for Tiverton (Lord Palmerston)—
this subject is alluded to, and it is stated that, "the Emperor
admits the necessity of supervision—considering," says the memorandum by the Minister of Finance, "that the number of children
occupied in spinning mills is likely to increase every year, the
Imperial government deemed it indispensable to take such pre-
paratory measures as will lead to legislative enactments hereafter."
Then follow many regulations respecting the moral and physical
treatment of the children.

In Austria "the period of labour is cruelly long, often fifteen,
not unfrequently seventeen hours a day. The question of shortening the labour of children is under discussion." In Switzerland
the regulations are very strict: "in the Canton of Argovia no
children are allowed to work, under fourteen years, more than
twelve hours and a half; and education is compulsory on the millowners." In the Canton of Zurich "the hours of labour are
limited to twelve; and children under ten years of age are not
allowed to be employed. The clergy are the inspectors, and the
system of inspection is very rigorous." In France a bill has been
framed almost on the same principles as our own, with the same
restrictions. The system is, however, but imperfectly carried out
on account of defective machinery; but the principle is recognised;
and there are 1,200 unpaid inspectors. In Prussia, by the law of
1839, no child who has not completed his or her sixteenth year is
to be employed more than ten hours a day; none under nine years
of age to be employed at all.

Now, if foreign powers consider it a matter both of duty and
policy thus to interpose on behalf of their people, we, surely,
should much more be animated by feelings such as theirs, when
we take into our account the vast and progressively increasing
numbers who are employed in these departments of industry.
See how it stands. In 1818, the total number of all ages and
both sexes employed in all the cotton factories was 57,323. In
1835, the number employed in the five departments — cotton,
woollen, worsted, flax, and silk—was 354,684. In 1839, the

number in the same five departments was 419,590; the total number of both sexes under eighteen years of age, in the same year, was 192,887.

Simultaneously, however, with the increase of numbers has been the increase of toil. The labour performed by those engaged in the processes of manufacture is three times as great as in the beginning of such operations. Machinery has executed, no doubt, the work that would demand the sinews of millions of men; but it has also prodigiously multiplied the labour of those who are governed by its fearful movements. I hope the House will allow me to go through several details connected with this portion of the subject; they are technical, it is true, but, nevertheless, of sufficient importance to be brought under your attention.

In 1815, the labour of following a pair of mules spinning cotton-yarn of Nos. 40—reckoning twelve hours to the working-day—involved a necessity for walking eight miles. That is to say, the piecer who was employed in going from one thread to another in a day of twelve hours performed a journey of eight miles. In 1832, the distance travelled in following a pair of mules spinning cotton-yarn of the same numbers, was twenty miles, and frequently more. But the amount of labour performed by those following the mules is not confined merely to the distance walked. There is far more to be done. In 1835, the spinner put up daily on each of these mules 820 stretches; making a total of 1,640 stretches in the course of the day. In 1832, the spinner put upon each mule 2,200 stretches, making a total of 4,400. In 1844, according to a return furnished by a practised operative spinner, the person working puts up in the same period 2,400 stretches on each mule, making a total of 4,800 stretches in the course of the day; and in some cases the amount of labour required is even still greater.

The House will now, probably, like to know how I have arrived at these conclusions. The calculations on which they are founded have been made by one of the most experienced mathematicians in England: At my request he went down to Manchester, and himself made the measurements and calculation upon the spot. The measurements, I should state, were made in five different mills, spinning, respectively, yarns of the following numbers :—14, 15, 30, 38, and 40. In the mill spinning No. 14 yarns the least distance possible to be travelled over was seventeen miles per day; the greatest possible twenty-seven miles. In that spinning No. 15 yarns the least distance was nineteen—the greatest twenty-nine miles. In that spinning 30 the least distance was twenty-four—the greatest thirty-seven miles. In that spinning 38 the least distance was fifteen—the greatest twenty-three miles; but this was a machine of an old construction. In that spinning 40 the least distance was seventeen—the greatest twenty-five miles. Now, the mules which are to be followed advance and recede—as they advance the yarn is elongated; and, by bearing this in mind, honourable gentlemen may see how the calculations were made. The yarn is stretched in elongated threads, and the calculations were made thus :—In the first case, the least, the assumption is, that only one thread would be broken in each movement of the mule. In the second case, that which shows the greatest amount of labour, the calculation is made upon the assumption of four threads being broken. Now it is almost impossible that only one thread shall be broken; and, on the other hand, it is very improbable that four threads should be in the same condition. We may, therefore, discard these extreme suppositions, and take the average of supposing two threads to be broken. On this assumption, then, the following will be the distances travelled :—In a mill spinning No. 14 yarns, twenty-two miles; No. 15 yarns, twenty-four miles; No. 30 yarns, thirty miles; No. 38 yarns, nineteen miles (old machine); and No. 40 yarns, twenty-one miles. While these calculations were in progress the machinery was not driven at its full speed; it might have been impelled at one-third, at least, of greater velocity.

But this is not all : there is another portion of the labour which is very oppressive, particularly to young persons—and to show its character I will read a note made by the measurer upon the spot :—" I may also suggest that in estimating the fatigues of a days' work, due consideration should be given to the necessity of turning the body round to a reverse direction not less than from four to five thousand times in a day, besides the strain of continually having to lean over the machine and return to an erect position." The House will be aware of the great strain requisite, after leaning over the machinery, in bringing the body back to an upright position—it often happens, indeed, that the body is bent forward in the form of a right angle. Now, in the fine mills, spinning, for instance, No. 100 yarns, the distance travelled will be far less. It will only be 14 miles; but then the House must bear in mind that though the distance is less, the labour is equal, and in some respects greater. The exertion of leaning over the machinery is in these cases much increased, by reason of the more frequent breakages, and consequent toil in repairing them. Some of the measurements to which I have alluded were made in the mill of a gentleman named M'Connell, to whom I must express my obligation for the kindness with which he offered every facility to the gentleman who went down to the manufacturing districts for the purpose. Mr. M'Connell stood by the measurer, and made calculations simultaneously with him. At the close of the work they compared notes; and it was found that Mr. M'Connell's measurements gave a less distance than those of the mathematician. But when they came to inquire into the reason of this difference, it was found that Mr. M'Connell had left out of his calculation all the diagonal movements. He had calculated only the straight movements, without reckoning the immense number of paces which the piecer has to make on either side. Now, these calculations are substantiated by those of several practical men. The honourable member for Oldham, Mr. Fielden, has himself measured in his own mill the distances travelled by the piecers; and the results of his observations he published in a pamphlet in 1836. The distance laid down by the honourable member is twenty miles. But I have still another authority. I submitted the case to the operative spinners of Manchester; and I have a document here, signed by twenty-two of these men, in which they state that twenty miles is the very least distance travelled, and they believe it to be still greater. I have another document, sent to me in 1842, by another set of operative spinners, confirming what I have said, and stating that the labour is progressively increasing—increasing not only because the distance to be travelled is greater, but because the quantity of goods produced is multiplied, while the hands are, in proportion, fewer than before; and, moreover, because an inferior species of cotton is now often spun, which it is more difficult to work. Well, now, I know that the measurements which I have stated to the House have been disputed by a mill-owner of great respectability—by Mr. Gregg, a very well-known gentleman, with large capital, who carries on one of the most extensive concerns of this kind in Europe. This gentleman published his contradiction to the statement which I have made, in which he estimated the distance at eight miles; and I submitted it to the same mathematician who made the original calculation. The moment he looked at it he said, "It is altogether inaccurate; Mr. Gregg cannot know anything of the matter;" and after speaking of the details, he thus sums up the question:—" Referring the matter to scientific considerations, Mr. Gregg's table must either be the result of some strange and most grievous blunderings, or of a gross perversion of observed facts, which, though extremely rude and ill-chosen for the object professedly in view, could not, by any possibility, carry a fair and judicious inquiry so very far away from the truth as to give only about one-third of the real distance." Now this is the toil imposed upon a very large portion of the population of the manufacturing districts—this is the labour imposed in the spinning-room. In the carding-room there has also been a great increase of labour—one person there does the work formerly divided between two. In the weaving-room, where a vast number of persons are employed, and principally females, an operative, writing to me, states that the labour has increased, within the last few years, fully ten per cent., owing to the increased speed of the machinery in spinning. In 1838, the number of hanks spun per week was 18,000; in 1843, it amounted to 21,000. In 1819, the number of picks in power-loom weaving per minute was 60—in 1842 it was 140, showing a vast increase of labour, because more nicety and attention are required to the work in hand.

Now, Sir, it is no difficult transition from such a statement of daily toil, passed as it is in crowded rooms, heated atmospheres, noxious gases, and injurious agencies of various kinds, to the following statement of physical mischiefs to the workers employed. Since 1816, eighty surgeons and physicians, and three medical commissioners in 1833 (one of whom, Doctor Bisset Hawkins declared that he had the authority of a large majority of the medical men of Lancashire), have asserted the prodigious evil of the system. The government commissioners themselves furnish a summary of particulars:—" The excessive fatigue, privation of sleep, pain in various parts of the body, and swelling of the feet, experienced by the young workers, coupled with the constant standing, the peculiar attitudes of the body, and the peculiar motion of the limbs required in the labour of the factory, together with the elevated temperature, and the impure atmosphere in which the labour is often carried on, do sometimes ultimately terminate. in the production of serious, permanent, and incurable diseases." Dr. Loudon states—" I think it has been already proved that children have been worked a most unreasonable and cruel length of time daily, and that even adults have been expected to do a certain quantity of labour, which scarcely any human being is able to endure. As a physician, I would prefer the limitation of ten hours for all persons who earn their bread by their industry." Dr. Hawkins says—" I am compelled to declare my deliberate opinion, that no child should be employed in factory labour below the age of ten, that no individual under the age of eighteen should be employed in it longer than ten hours daily." When I was myself in the manufacturing districts, in the year 1841, I went over many of the hospitals, and consulted many of the medical men in that part of the country. The result is contained in a note which I drew up at the time, and which is

as follows:—" Scrofulous cases apparently universal; the wards
were filled with scrofulous knees, hips, ankles, &c. The medical
gentleman informed me that they were nearly invariably factory
cases. He attributed the presence of scrofula to factory employment under all its circumstances of great heat, low diet, bad
ventilation, protracted toil, &c." Now the same evils are found
to exist in other parts of the world where the same system is
followed. A very admirable work was published a few years ago
by a French physician, Dr. Villermé, employed by the Académie
des Sciences to examine and report upon the condition of
artisans. He states, when speaking of factories in France, that,
"In the operations of the cotton business, cough, pulmonary
inflammation, and the terrible phthisis, attack and carry off
many of the workpeople; but numerous as are the victims of
these disorders, their premature death seems to me less deplorable
than the development of scrofula in the mass of our workpeople
in manufactories." Mark that: he considers death a less evil
than the terrible prevalence of scrofulous disorder. Another
effect produced by the system is an injurious affection of the eyesight. Any person conversant with the cotton business knows
how early in life the eye is apt to become so enfeebled as scarcely
to be of any effective service. There is one more fact to which
I wish to call the attention of the House. Those honourable
gentlemen who have been in the habit of perusing the melancholy
details of mill accidents should know that a large proportion of
those accidents—particularly those which may be denominated
the minor class, such as loss of fingers and the like, occur in the
last hours of the evening, when the people become so tired that
they absolutely get reckless of the danger. I state this on the
authority of several practical spinners.

Hence arise many serious evils to the working classes—none
greater than the early prostration of their strength, their premature superannuation, and utter incapacity to sustain their families
by the labour of their hands. I will prove my assertions by the
following table, from which you will observe that at the very
period of life at which, in many other departments of industry,
men are regarded as in the prime of their strength, those employed
in the cotton manufacture are superannuated and set aside, as
incapable of earning their livelihood by factory labour. The ages
above forty are seldom found in this employment. Now, during
the great turn-out in 1831, from forty-two mills in Mosely, Ashton,
and in other parts of Lancashire, out of 1,665 persons who joined
in that turn-out, there were between forty-five and fifty years of
age, only fifty-one. In 1832, it appeared by certain returns from

mills in Harpur and Lanark, that out of 1,600 persons, there were above the age of forty-five, only ten individuals. In 1839, the returns from certain mills in Stockport and Manchester showed that the number of hands employed in these mills was 22,094. Now of all that immense multitude, how many does the House suppose were above forty-five years of age? Why, only 143 persons; and of these, sixteen were retained by special favour, and one was doing boy's work. I have in my hand, also, a list of 131 spinners, made out in 1841, only seven of whom were above forty-five years of age, and almost all of these people had been refused employment. Why? Because it was declared that they were too aged for labour! I have other authority, too, to prove the state of matters in this respect. I hold in my hand a letter from a person who went down to Bolton to make returns for me, in which he states—" I have just seen fifty reduced spinners; two are more than fifty years of age, the rest will not average forty years of age. One man, T. E., worked for sixteen years at Mr. O.'s mill; he is forty-three years of age; he has frequently applied for work, but is invariably answered, he is too old." The same evil exists in France and other countries where the manufacturing system prevails. Dr. Villermé says—" There are few cities in which one meets with old people employed in manufactories; it is found to be more economical to pay younger workmen, though at a higher rate." In the year 1833, a letter was addressed to me by Mr. Ashworth, a very considerable mill-owner in Lancashire, which contains the following curious passage :—" You will next very naturally inquire about the old men, who are said to die, or become unfit for work, when they attain forty years of age, or soon after." Mark the phrase, " old man," at forty years of age! " As all spinners (he continues), whether young or old, are paid the same price per pound for spinning, the production of an old man is at greater expense by reason of the diminished quantity; this, and not ill-health, may sometimes occasion his discharge." . . . . " Old men of every description adhere to habits contracted in early life; hence they are troublesome to manage, and often disagree with the overlookers—this may sometimes lead to their discharge; but it appears not unfrequently that they become disinclined to work when the earnings of their families are sufficient to maintain them." Indeed! why, there cannot, I think, be a more alarming feature in the case than the last-mentioned fact—that men, of perhaps forty, should be maintained in idleness by the labour of their families. But I have the additional testimony of a government commissioner, Mr. M'Intosh, who, in his report in 1833, says—" Although prepared by seeing childhood occupied in such a manner, it is very difficult to believe the ages of men advanced in years, as given by themselves, so complete is their premature old age." Now, Sir, I am the more inclined to rest my case with confidence on these commissioners, because they were sent expressly to collect evidence against that taken by the committee of 1832; and it is upon their reports, in considerable measure, that I will ground my appeal to this House.

Now, let this condition of things be contrasted with the condition of agricultural life; and let us see how much longer is the duration of the working powers in that class of labour. In June, 1841, on an estate in Worcestershire, out of forty-two agricultural labourers, there were, over forty-five years of age, twenty. Out of twenty-five on one in Lincolnshire, eleven exceeded forty years of age. At a place in Wales, out of thirty-three labourers, twelve exceeded the age of forty, and seven were above sixty. At another estate in Lincolnshire, out of sixty-two labourers, thirty-two exceeded forty years of age. At one in Scotland, out of sixty labourers, twenty-seven were over forty years of age. Again, in England, out of thirty-nine labourers, twenty-nine exceeded forty years of age. On an estate in the Isle of Wight, out of eighteen labourers, there were found ten exceeding forty years of age. On another, out of seventeen, seven were above forty years of age. On another farm, out of fifteen labourers six were over forty years of age; and, on an aggregate of farms in the neighbourhood, there were thirty labourers, every one of them exceeding forty years of age! So that the total shows, that of 341 labourers, 180 were above forty years of age. Contrast the condition of these people with that of a multitude of 22,000, of whom only 143 were above the age of forty-five. There is yet another instance. On an estate in Dorset, in 1844, out of 427 labourers 118 are above forty-five years of age. And these men may go on much longer; for I can appeal to honourable gentlemen on both sides of the House, whether they have not known agricultural labourers at the ages of fifty, sixty, and seventy years, still capable of working and of earning wages.

You will, naturally enough, inquire what becomes of many of these worn-out and superannuated spinners and factory hands. A few may retire to other businesses; those who have, by nature, a more vigorous mental and physical constitution may, in some instances, survive; but a large proportion sink into a state of pauperism and decrepitude.

I hold in my hand a statement which will give the House some idea of the condition into which a vast mass of these people fall when it becomes impossible for them to earn their subsistence by factory labour. It will be borne in mind that the present system has prevailed so long, and is of such a nature as completely to have destroyed every idea of thrift and economy. The education both of males and females is such that domestic economy is almost wholly unknown to them; and it very rarely happens that they have the foresight to accumulate savings during the period at which they can work to subsist upon in the days of their old age. It will be also remembered that their strength is so wholly exhausted that they are unable to enter into any different active occupation when discharged from the mill; and that, therefore, they sink down into employments of the nature of which I will give a specimen to the House. In June, 1841, from a return which was presented to me, it appeared that in 11 auction rooms in Manchester, out of 11 common jobbers, as they are called, 9 were discharged factory hands. Of 37 hawkers of nuts and oranges, 32 were factory hands; of 9 sellers of sand, 8 were factory hands; of 28 hawkers of boiled sheep's feet, 22 belonged to the same class; of 14 hawkers of brushes, 11 were factory hands; of 25 sellers of coals, 16 were factory hands—thus out of 113 persons pursuing these miserable occupations, 89 were discharged factory hands. I may add that, upon a further examination being made, it was found that of 341 discharged factory hands, 217 were maintained entirely by the earnings of their children. In Bolton, many discharged spinners were employed in sweeping the streets; and of 60 sellers of salt and gatherers of rags, 50 were factory hands. In 1842 an inquiry was made in Manchester, and it was found that of 245 cast-off spinners, there were maintained by the earnings of their children 108. The rest were following such occupations as I have already alluded to, or engaged in begging, picking up dung, and other miserable avocations. With reference to these men, I asked the question, how many may expect to be taken up on a revival of trade? The answer was, scarcely one; that the masters required young hands and unexhausted strength, and that they would rather take men of twenty-five than of thirty-five years of age; and Dr. Bisset Hawkins, one of the commissioners in 1833, gives similar testimony, that—"The degree in which parents are supported by their youthful offspring at Manchester is a peculiar feature of the place, and an unpleasing one; the ordinary state of things in this respect is nearly reversed."

Sir, neither the existence nor the consequences of these destructive causes have escaped the attention of continental writers and legislators. Their testimonies and their laws strongly confirm the opinions and statements of those who, in this country, have so long urged upon the public consideration the perilous necessity of withstanding the further progress of such pernicious agencies. By the system we permit, the laws of nature are absolutely outraged, but not with impunity. The slow but certain penalty is exacted in the physical degradation of the human race, including, as it does, the ruin of the body, and the still more fatal corruption of the moral part.

In the year 1840 a commission was issued in France. A report was made to the French Chamber of Peers by M. Dupin, the Baron Charles Dupin; and to that eminent person I am indebted for the copy of the report from which are taken the extracts to which I am about to refer. I hope the House will attend to the facts adduced by this gentleman.

" We were desirous," says the reporter, " of ascertaining the amount of difference, in force and physical power, between the parties which have respectively attained the age of manhood in the parts of France most devoted to agriculture, and those where manufacturing industry is more generally diffused. The councils of revision in the recruiting department exhibited the following facts :—For 10,000 young men capable of military service, there were rejected as infirm, or otherwise unfit in body, 4,029 in the departments most agricultural: for 10,000 in the departments most manufacturing, there were rejected 9,930." The reporter then proceeds to speak in detail :—" There were found," he says, " for 10,000 capable of military service, in Marne, 10,309 incapable; in the Lower Seine, 11,990 incapable; in L'Eure, 14,450 incapable." Now, what is the comment of the reporter on this? I will take the liberty of reading it to the House, because of the solemn warning it conveys to all governments and nations. "These deformities," he proceeds, " cannot allow the legislature to remain indifferent; they attest the deep and painful mischiefs—they reveal the intolerable nature of individual suffering; they enfeeble the country in respect to its capacity for military operations, and impoverish it in regard to the works of peace. We should blush for agriculture if, in her operations, she brought, at the age adapted to labour, so small a proportion of oxen or horses in a fit state for toil with so large a number of infirm and misshapen." Now, this is a return which I have once before quoted; but I quote it again because it is so singularly adapted to our present position. We have no means of applying to our population the same test as that in France, because we have not the same courts for examination into the ability of people to carry arms; but if such tribunals existed I fear that they would set forth results far more distressing. If, for the comparatively short time that manufactures have been established in France, such terrible results are exhibited, what must be the case in England, where they have prevailed for considerably more than half a century? Just see what Dr. Villermé says. Dr. Villermé, having enlarged on the pernicious effects of factory labour, adds—" In examining men from twenty to twenty-one years of age, I found them physically unfit for the military service in proportion as they came from the working classes of the factory (*classe ouvrière de la fabrique*) at Amiens. One hundred fit men required 193 conscripts from the middling class; 100 fit men required 343 conscripts from the working class."

Is this all? By no means—we have, if possible, yet stronger testimony from Prussia. The sovereign of that country thought fit to enforce a law of protection for all under sixteen years of age, against more than ten hours' labour in the course of the day. What was the reason assigned?—here is the document!—From the *Official Gazette of Laws, 9th March,* 1839.

" His Majesty was pleased to direct the attention of his ministers to a report from Lieutenant George Von Horn, that the manufacturing districts would not fully supply their contingents for the recruiting of the army, that the physical development of persons of tender years was checked, and that there was reason to believe that in the manufacturing districts the future generations would grow up weaker and more crippled than the existing one was stated to be—employed from eleven to fourteen hours daily in excessive labour, frightfully disproportioned to the powers of persons from eight to eighteen years of age." Then followed an inquiry very similar to our own, which fully confirmed every statement; and the document proceeds—" The preceding facts show that urgent necessity for legislative interference felt by the King to put a stop to such premature, unnatural, and injurious employment of the young operatives in factories."

I need not detain the House by an endeavour to show that similar or worse mischiefs must have arisen in our own country—I speak of those districts only where the manufacturing system has long and extensively prevailed; I know that the agricultural parts and hilly regions of Yorkshire and Lancashire still send forth a noble race of human beings. But let me here impress upon the House the necessity of deeply considering these important statements. The tendency of the various improvements in machinery is to supersede the employment of adult males, and substitute in its place the labour of children and females. What will be the effect on future generations, if their tender frames be subjected, without limitation or control, to such destructive agencies?

Consider this: in 1835, the numbers stood thus—the females in the five departments of industry, 196,383; in 1839, females, 242,296; of these, the females under 18, 112,192. The proportions in each department stood—females in cotton, 56¼ per cent.; ditto worsted, 69½ ditto; ditto silk, 70½ ditto; ditto flax, 70½ ditto. Thus, while the total amount of both sexes and all ages in the cotton manufacture, in 1818, were equal only to 57,323, the females alone in that branch, in 1839, were 146,331. Now, the following is an extract of a letter from a great mill-owner in 1842:—"The village of ——, two miles distant, sends down daily to the mills in this town at least a thousand females, single and married, who have to keep strictly the present long hours of labour. Seven years ago, these persons were employed at their own homes; but now, instead of the men working at the power-looms, none but girls or women are allowed to have it." But, Sir, look at the physical effect of this system on the women. See its influence on the delicate constitutions and tender forms of the female sex. Let it be recollected that the age at which the "prolonged labour," as it is called, commences, is at the age of thirteen. That age, according to the testimony of medical men, is the tenderest period of female life. Observe the appalling progress of female labour; and remember that the necessity for particular protection to females against overwork is attested by the most eminent surgeons and physicians—Dr. Blundell, Sir Anthony Carlisle, Sir William Blizard, Dr. Elliotson, Sir George Tuthill, Sir Benjamin Brodie, John Henry Green, Esq., of St. Thomas's, Charles Aston Key, Esq., George James Guthrie, Esq., Mr. Travers, Sir Charles Bell, Dr. Hodgkin, John Morgan, Esq., of Guy's Hospital, Samuel Smith, Esq., surgeon, of Leeds, Dr. Young, of Bolton, John Malyn, Esq., Peter Mark Roget, Esq., some time physician to the Manchester Infirmary. Here are some specimens of their evidence:—"Is it not especially necessary to give protection from excessive labour to females when approaching the age of puberty?—Quite important; if they are afterwards to become mothers, quite essential;" this is an universal opinion. Many anatomical reasons are assigned by surgeons of the manufacturing towns, that "the peculiar structure of the female form is not so well adapted to long-continued labour, and especially labour which is endured standing." Mr. Smith, of Leeds, declares—"This (the operation of the factory labour) occasionally produces the most lamentable effects in females, when they are expecting to become mothers." On the anatomical difficulty of parturition, he states—"It is often the painful duty of the accoucheur to destroy the life of the child. I have seen many instances of the kind, all of which, with one single exception, have been those of females who have worked long hours in factories." "There is a foundation in nature," says Dr. Blundell, "for the customary division which assigns the more active labour to the male, and the sedentary to the female"—"among savages, the woman is often the drudge." George James Guthrie, Esq.: "Have you not been a medical officer in the armies of this country for a considerable length of time?—Yes. Would you sanction, for a continuance, soldiers being actually under arms for twelve hours a day for a succession of days?—Such a thing is never done nor thought of; a soldier is never kept under arms more than five or six hours, unless before the enemy. Is the female sex well fitted to sustain long exertion in a standing posture?—It is not. Is it not more than ordinarily necessary to protect females against excessive labour when approaching the age of puberty?—Certainly it is." "The ten hours," he adds, "you propose to give to the children in factories is the work you would not give to soldiers, even when soldiers are employed in public works; they would not then be worked more than twelve hours, granting them time for their meals; and for the work they would have additional pay."

Now, Sir, mark the fearful superseding of adult workers; "the tendency of improvements in machinery," say all the inspectors, "is more and more to substitute infant for adult labour." Dr. Villermé, in his *Tableau d'état physique et moral des ouvriers*, urges the same results, that "children and women are employed instead of men." In one mill (1831) adults, 70; spindles to each, 104; piecers, 305. In the same mill (1841) adults, 26; spindles to each, 223; piecers, 123; being one-sixth, instead of one-fifth, as before, of the hands employed. In Bolton (1835) thirty-nine mills set up 589,784 spindles; the same mills set up (1841) 740,000 spindles; piecers to these spindles (1835), 2,443; ditto in 1841, 2,426; spinners to them in 1835, 797; ditto in 1841, 727. Observe, too, the process of double-decking and self-actors. In 1831, twenty-three mills employed 1,267 spinners (Manchester); in 1839, the same twenty-three mills employed 677 spinners; thus throwing out 590 spinners, without any abatement of productive power. In 1829, in Manchester, spinners, 2,650: 1841, in Manchester, spinners, 1,037; thrown out entirely, 1,613. In 1835, 2,171 spinners worked 1,229,204 spindles; in 1841, 1,037 spinners worked 1,431,619 spindles. Observe, too, that the labour is greatly increased upon children in all mills alike. In 1829, in the mill of

Mr. ———; spinners, 70; spindles worked, 43,680; piecers, 230.
In 1841, in same mill, spinners, 26; spindles, 43,796; piecers, 134.
In 1829, in a mill, spinners, 53; spindles, 23,800; piecers, 125.
In 1842, spinners, none; spindles, same number; piecers, 84. In
1829, in thirty-five mills, spinners, 1,088; spindles, 496,942. In
1841, in same mills, spinners, 448; spindles, 556,375; self-actors,
473, wrought by children and young persons only. A working
spinner makes this statement, and it is a fair sample of the
whole—"My wheels are trebled; the piecers reduced to eight;
thus two do the work of three. Self-acting greatly augments
labour by the increased velocity of the machine, and the greater
number of spindles apportioned to each piecer."

Here, Sir, pause to consider the multitudes of females on whom
this system must exercise its influence, and their great increase
since 1835. "Mr. Orrell's mill," says the inspector, and I will
quote this as an example, "at Heaton Norris, is by far the largest
in Stockport. We are employing (says Robert M'Lure, the
manager) altogether in that mill, and in connection with it (as
carters, gas-men, and others), 1,264 hands at this time, of whom
846 are females. The whole number of looms is 1,300, all standing
on one flat, attended by 651 females, and twenty-one males." But
there is a reason for this substitution; I will show, by an extract
from a letter dated in March, 1842, the motives that actuate some
minds. "Mr. E., a manufacturer (says the writer), informed me
that he employs females exclusively at his power-looms; it is so
universally; gives a decided preference to married females,
especially those who have families at home dependent on them
for support; they are attentive, docile, more so than unmarried
females, and are compelled to use their utmost exertions to procure the necessaries of life."

Thus, Sir, are the virtues, the peculiar virtues, of the female
character to be perverted to her injury—thus all that is most
dutiful and tender in her nature is to be made the means of her
bondage and suffering! But consider again, I entreat you, what
a multitude of females it is on whom this system has its operation. Just survey the enormous increase since 1835. This is the
further testimony of the Sub-inspector Baker, in his report of 1843.
There are employed in his district more than in 1838, 6,040
persons; of these, 785 males, 5,225 females. "The small amount
of wages," says the Inspector Saunders, "paid to women acts as
a strong inducement to the mill-occupiers to employ them instead
of men, and in power-loom shops this has been the case to a great
extent." Now hear how these poor creatures are worked. Mr.
Baker reports, as to "having seen several females who, he was

ure, could only just have completed their eighteenth year, who had been obliged to work from 6 A.M. to 10 P.M., with only one hour and a half for meals." In other cases, he shows, females are obliged to work all night, in a temperature of 70 to 80 deg. Hence Mr. Saunders (1843) deduces the necessity of a law protecting all females, up to the age of twenty-one; adding, medical men invariably declare the urgent necessity of protecting from excessive labour all females up to that period of life. "I found," says Mr. Horner, October, 1843, "many young women, just eighteen years of age, at work from half-past five in the morning until eight o'clock at night, with no cessation except a quarter of an hour for breakfast, and three quarters of an hour for dinner. They may fairly be said to labour for fifteen hours and a half out of twenty-four." "There are," says Mr. Saunders, "among them, females who have been employed for some weeks, with an interval only of a few days, from six o'clock in the morning until twelve o'clock at night, less than two hours for meals, thus giving them for five nights in the week six hours out of its twenty-four to go to and from their homes, and to obtain rest in bed." "A vast majority," says Mr. Saunders, in January, 1844, "of the persons employed at night, and for long hours during the day, are females; their labour is cheaper, and they are more easily induced to undergo severe bodily fatigue than men."

Where, Sir, under this condition, are the possibilities of domestic life? how can its obligations be fulfilled? Regard the woman as wife or mother—how can she accomplish any portion of her calling? And if she cannot do that which Providence has assigned her, what must be the effect on the whole surface of society? But to revert to the physical effects. Mr. Saunders says in the same report, "The surgeon distinctly condemns such employment; though the effect may not be immediately apparent, it must have a tendency to undermine the constitution, produces premature decay, and shortens the duration of human life. No female," he adds, "ought to work more than ten hours; and that twelve hours produces severe injury to those in a state of pregnancy;" he often witnesses the effect of so much standing when parturition comes on; adding, "work in the night is the most injurious; it is unnatural, and not adapted to the constitution of women." Another surgeon, of great experience in Lancashire, writes to me that, "after thirteen is the age when young women begin to be most susceptible of injury from factory work," and much more at this period of their lives "than at the earlier ages." He proceeds to details: "the effects of long-continued labour in factories become more apparent after childbirth. The infants are at birth below the average size, have a stinted, shrivelled appearance. I would take a score of factory births, and the same of healthy parents, and distinguish between them." "Children are much confided by factory mothers to care of others—opium administered to the infants in various forms—the quantity of this pernicious drug thus consumed would almost stagger belief—many infants are so habituated to it, that they can scarcely exist when deprived of the stimulus—immense numbers fall victims to hydrocephalus —mothers' milk becomes deteriorated—infants fed upon substitutes in her absence—hence internal disorders, of which the usual remedy is gin." "Miscarriages very frequent, and all the physical and surgical mischiefs of mistreated pregnancy—varicose veins produced by the continued evil practice—aggravated greatly in pregnant women." "Again, troublesome ulcers of the legs, arising from varicose veins, which in some cases burst and bring on a dangerous and sometimes fatal hæmorrhage." "The practice of procuring abortion is very frequent, even among married women." "I have, moreover, the personal testimony of several females to the truth of these statements—they speak of the intolerable pain in their breasts by such long absences from children, and the suffering of returning to work within ten days of confinement."

Look again to the effects on domestic economy; out of thirteen married females taken at one mill, only one knew how to make her husband a shirt, and only four knew how to mend one. I have the evidence of several females, who declare their own ignorance of every domestic accomplishment. The unmarried declare, "not a single qualification of any sort for household servants." The married, "untidy, slovenly, dirty; cannot work, sew, take care of children, or the house.; cannot manage expenses; perpetual waste and extravagance." But hear the history of their daily life from their own lips.

"M. H., aged twenty years, leaves a young child in care of another a little older for hours together; leaves home soon after five, and returns at eight; during the day the milk runs from her breasts until her clothes have been as wet as a sop." M. S. (single) leaves home at five, returns at nine; her mother states she knows nothing but mill and bed; can neither read, write, knit, nor sew. H. W. has three children; leaves home at five on Monday, does not return till Saturday at seven; has then so much to do for her children that she cannot go to bed before three o'clock on Sunday morning. Oftentimes completely drenched by the rain, and has to work all day in that condition. "My breasts have given me the most shocking pain, and I have been dripping wet with milk." I will conclude this part with an extract from a letter dated February, 1840, by Dr. Johns, Superintendent Registrar of the Manchester district—an important document, when we consider that it was written to controvert some of my statements respecting the mortality of those districts. " Very young children," says Dr. Johns, " are by the existing system not sufficiently taken care of by their mothers; as regards themselves during gestation, and their offspring after childbirth—the women during pregnancy continue as long as possible at their work; and sooner than they ought they again attend the factories, leaving their infants to the care of ill-paid and unsuitable persons, to take the oversight of the children in their absence; nor ought we to omit that soothing drugs—the well-known nostrum, Godfrey's cordial— are often had recourse to, with a view to lull the troubles of the little unfortunates, and hence, perhaps, may be attributable to the improper use of narcotics the frequent deaths from convulsions. It is most desirable that mothers should not be, if possible, abstracted from their attention to their helpless infants, certainly not during the period of lactation and teething."

So much, Sir, for their physical and, if I may so speak, their financial condition: the picture of their moral state will not be more consolatory. And, first, their excessive intemperance:—

Mr. Roberton, a distinguished surgeon at Manchester, says, in a published essay—" I regard it as a misfortune for an operative to be obliged to labour for so long hours at an exhausting occupation, and often in an impure atmosphere. I consider this circumstance as one of the chief causes of the astounding inebriety of our population." I read in a private letter from Manchester, 1843 — " Intemperance is making progress; on Sundays there is more drinking than there has been for many years; the people who sell ale, &c., state to me that they never sold more on Sunday, nor as much as they now do." Mr. Braidley, when boroughreeve of Manchester, stated that in one gin-shop, during eight successive Saturday evenings, from seven till ten o'clock, he observed, on an average rate, 412 persons enter by the hour, of which the females were 60 per cent. Many females state that the labour induces " an intolerable thirst; they can drink, but not eat." I do not doubt that several of the statements I have read will create surprise in the minds of many honourable members; but if they were to converse with operatives who are acquainted with the practical effects of the system they would cease to wonder at the facts I have detailed. I might detain the House by enumerating the evils which result from the long working of males and females together in the same room. I could show the many and painful effects to which females are exposed, and the manner in which they lament and shrink from the inconveniences of their situation. I have letters from Stockport and Manchester, from various individuals, dwelling on the mischievous consequences which arise from the practice of modest women working so many hours together with men, and not being able to avail themselves of those opportunities which would suggest themselves to every one's mind without particular mention. Many mills, I readily admit, are admirably regulated, but they are yet in a minority—were all of such a description as several that I have seen, they might not, perhaps, require any enactments. But to return. Mr. Rayner, the medical officer of Stockport, says—"It has been the practice in mills gradually to dispense with the labour of males, but particularly grown-up men, so that the burden of maintaining the family has rested almost exclusively on the wife and children, while the men have had to stay at home, and look after household affairs, or ramble about the streets unemployed." But listen to another fact, and one deserving of serious attention; that the females not only perform the labour, but occupy the places of men; they are forming various clubs and associations, and gradually acquiring all those privileges which are held to be the proper portion of the male sex. These female clubs are thus described:—"Fifty or sixty females, married and single, form themselves into clubs, ostensibly for protection; but, in fact, they meet together to drink, sing, and smoke; they use, it is stated, the lowest, most brutal, and most disgusting language imaginable." Here is a dialogue which occurred in one of these clubs, from an ear-witness:—"A man came into one of these club-rooms, with a child in his arms. 'Come lass,' said he, addressing one of the women, 'come home, for I cannot keep this bairn quiet, and the other I have left crying at home.' 'I won't go home, idle devil,' she replied; 'I have thee to keep, and the bairns too, and if I can't get a pint of ale quietly, it is tiresome. This is only the second pint that Bess and me have had between us; thou may sup if thou likes, and sit thee down, but I won't go home yet.'"

Whence is it that this singular and unnatural change is taking place? Because that on women are imposed the duty and burthen of supporting their husbands and families—a perversion as it were of nature, which has the inevitable effect of introducing into families disorder, insubordination, and conflict. What is the ground on which the woman says she will pay no attention to her domestic duties, nor give the obedience which is owing to her husband? because on her devolves the labour which ought to fall to his share, and she throws out the taunt, "If I have the labour,

I will also have the amusement." The same mischief is taking place between children and their parents : the insubordination of children is now one of the most frightful evils of the manufacturing districts. " Children and young persons take the same advantage of parents that women do of their husbands, frequently using oaths and harsh language, and, if corrected, will turn round and say, '—— you, we have you to keep.' One poor woman stated that her husband had chided two of their daughters for going to a public-house; he made it worse, for they would not come home again, stating, 'they had their father to keep, and they would not be dictated to by him.'" This conduct in the children is likewise grounded on the assertion that the parents have no right to interfere and control them, since, without their labour, the parents could not exist; and this is the bearing of children, many of whom are under thirteen or fourteen years of age! Observe carefully, too, the ferocity of character which is exhibited by a great mass of the female population of the manufacturing towns. Recollect the outbreak of 1842, and the share borne in that by the girls and women; and the still more frightful contingencies which may be in store for the future. "I met," says an informant of mine, " with a mother of factory workers, who told me that all the churches and chapels were useless places, and so was all the talk about education, since the young and old were unable to attend, either in consequence of the former being imprisoned in the mills so many hours, and being in want of rest the little time they were at home; and the latter being compelled to live out of the small earnings of their children, and cannot get clothing, so they never think of going to churches or chapels. She added, ' when you get up to London, tell them we'll turn out the next time (meaning the women), and let the soldiers fire upon us if they dare; and depend upon it there will be a break out, and a right one, if that House of Commons don't alter things, for they can alter if they will, by taking mothers and daughters out of the factories, and sending the men and big lads in.'" But further, what says Sir Charles Shaw, for some years the superintendent of the police of Manchester—what is his opinion of the condition of the females of that town, and the effects produced, by the system under which they live, on their conduct and character ? " Women," says he, " by being employed in a factory, lose the station ordained them by Providence, and become similar to the female followers of an army, wearing the garb of women, but actuated by the worst passions of men. The women are the leaders and exciters of the young men to violence in every riot and outbreak in the manufacturing districts, and the language they indulge in is of a horrid description. While they are themselves demoralized, they contaminate all that comes within their reach."

This will conclude the statement that I have to make to the House. And now, Sir, who will assert that these things should be permitted to exist? Who will hesitate to apply the axe to the root of the tree, or, at least, endeavour to lop off some of its deadliest branches? What arguments from general principles would they adduce against my proposition? What drawn from peculiar circumstances? They cannot urge that particular causes in England give rise to particular results: the same cause prevails in various countries; and wherever it is found it produces the same effects. I have already stated its operation in France, in Russia, in Switzerland, in Austria, and in Prussia; I may add also in America; for I perceive by the papers of the first of February, that a bill has been proposed in the legislature of Pennsylvania to place all persons under the age of sixteen within the protection of the " ten hours " limit. I never thought that we should have learned justice from the city of Philadelphia. In October last I visited an immense establishment in Austria, which gives employment to several hundred hands; I went over the whole, and conversed with the managers, who detailed to me the same evils and the same fruits as those I have narrated to the House—prolonged labour of sixteen and seventeen hours, intense fatigue, enfeebled frames, frequent consumptive disorders, and early deaths—yet the locality had every advantage; well-built and airy houses, in a fine open country, and a rural district; nevertheless, so injurious are the effects, that the manager added, stating at the same time the testimony of many others, who resided in districts where mills are more abundant, that, in ten years from the time at which he spoke, " there would hardly be a man in the whole of those neighbourhoods fit to carry a musket." Let me remind, too, the House of the mighty change which has taken place among the opponents to this question. When I first brought it forward in 1833, I could scarcely number a dozen masters on my side—I now count them by hundreds. We have had from the West Riding of Yorkshire a petition signed by three hundred mill-owners, praying for a limitation of labour to ten hours in the day. Some of the best names in Lancashire openly support me. I have letters from others who secretly wish me well, but hesitate to proclaim their adherence; and even among the members of the Anti-Corn-Law League I may boast of many firm and efficient friends.

Sir, under all the aspects in which it can be viewed, this system of things must be abrogated or restrained—it affects the internal tranquillity of those vast provinces, and all relations between employer and employed—it forms a perpetual grievance, and ever comes uppermost among their complaints in all times of difficulty and discontent. It disturbs the order of nature and the rights of the labouring men, by ejecting the males from the workshop and filling their places by females, who are thus withdrawn from all their domestic duties, and exposed to insufferable toil at half the wages that would be assigned to males for the support of their families.

It affects, nay, more, it absolutely annihilates all the arrangements and provisions of domestic economy—thrift and management are altogether impossible; had they twice the amount of their present wages they would be but slightly benefited—everything runs to waste; the house and children are deserted; the wife can do nothing for her husband and family; she can neither cook, wash, repair clothes, or take charge of the infants; all must be paid for out of her scanty earnings, and, after all, most imperfectly done. Dirt, discomfort, ignorance, recklessness, are the portion of such households; the wife has no time for learning in her youth, and none for practice in her riper age; the females are most unequal to the duties of the men in the factories; and all things go to rack and ruin because the men can discharge at home no one of the especial duties that Providence has assigned to the females. Why need I detain the House by a specification of these injurious results? They will find them stated at painful length in the Second Report of the Children's Employment Commission.

Consider it, too, under its physical aspect. Will the House turn a deaf ear to the complaints of suffering that resound from all quarters? Will it be indifferent to the physical consequences on the rising generation? You have the authority of the government commissioner, Dr. Hawkins, a gentleman well skilled in medical statistics—" I have never been," he tells you, " in any town in Great Britain or in Europe, in which degeneracy of form and colour from the national standard has been so obvious " as in Manchester. I have, moreover, the authority of one of my most ardent antagonists, himself a mighty mill-owner, that, if the present system of labour be persevered in, the " county of Lancaster will speedily become a province of pigmies." The toil of the females has hitherto been considered the characteristic of savage life; but we, in the height of our refinement, impose on the wives and daughters of England a burden from which, at least during pregnancy, they would be exempted even in slaveholding states, and among the Indians of America.

But every consideration sinks to nothing compared with that which springs from the contemplation of the moral mischiefs this system engenders and sustains. You are poisoning the very sources of order and happiness and virtue; you are tearing up, root and branch, all the relations of families to each other; you are annulling, as it were, the institution of domestic life decreed by Providence himself, the wisest and kindest of earthly ordinances, the mainstay of social peace and virtue, and therein of national security. There is a time to be born, and a time to die—this we readily concede; but is there not also a time to live, to live to every conjugal and parental duty?—this we seem as stiffly to deny; and yet in the very same breath we talk of the value of education and the necessity of moral and religious training. Sir, it is all in vain; there is no national, no private system that can supersede the influence of the parental precept and parental example—they are ordained to exercise an unlimited power over the years of childhood; and, amidst all their imperfections, are accompanied with a blessing. Whose experience is so confined that it does not extend to a knowledge and an appreciation of the maternal influence over every grade and department of society? It matters not whether it be prince or peasant, all that is best, all that is lasting in the character of a man, he has learnt at his mother's knees. Search the records, examine the opening years of those who have been distinguished for ability and virtue, and you will ascribe, with but few exceptions, the early culture of their minds, and above all, the first discipline of the heart, to the intelligence and affection of the mother, or at least of some pious woman, who, with the self-denial and tenderness of her sex, has entered as a substitute on the sacred office. No, Sir, these sources of mischief must be dried up—every public consideration demands such an issue—the health of the females, the care of their families, their conjugal and parental duties, the comfort of their homes, the decency of their lives, the rights of their husbands, the peace of society, and the laws of God; and, until a vote shall have been given this night—which God avert—I never will believe that there can be found in this House one individual man who will deliberately and conscientiously inflict on the women of England such a burthen of insufferable toil.

Sir, it is very sad, though perhaps inevitable, that such weighty charges and suspicions should lie on the objects of those who call for, and who propose this remedial measure. I am most unwilling to speak of myself; my personal character is, doubtless, of no consequence to the world at large; but it may be of consequence to those whose interests I represent, because distrust begets delays, and zeal grows cold when held back in its career by the apprehension that those whom it would support are actuated by unworthy motives. Disclaimers, I know, are poor things when uttered by parties whom you listen to with suspicion or dislike; but consider it calmly; are you reasonable to impute to me a settled desire, a single purpose, to exalt the landed and humiliate the commercial aristocracy? Most solemnly do I deny the accusation; if you think me wicked enough, do you think me fool enough for such a hateful policy? Can any man in his senses now hesitate to believe that the permanent prosperity of the manufacturing body in all its several aspects, physical, moral, and commercial, is essential, not only to the welfare, but absolutely to the existence of the British empire? No, we fear not the increase of your political power nor envy your stupendous riches; "Peace be within your walls, and plenteousness within your palaces!" We ask but a slight relaxation of toil, a time to live, and a time to die; a time for those comforts that sweeten life, and a time for those duties that adorn it; and, therefore, with a fervent prayer to Almighty God that it may please him to turn the hearts of all who hear me to thoughts of justice and of mercy, I now finally commit the issue to the judgment and humanity of Parliament.

*Ten Hours Factory Bill.*

## HOUSE OF COMMONS,

### MAY 10, 1844.

On moving "That the Clause (And be it Enacted, That from and after the 1st day of October in the present year, no young person shall be employed in any Factory more than eleven hours in any one day, or more than sixty-four hours in any one week; and that from and after the 1st day of October, 1847, no young person shall be employed in any Factory more than ten hours in any one day, or more than fifty-eight hours in any one week; and that any person who shall be convicted of employing a young person for any longer time than is in and by this Clause permitted, shall for every such offence be adjudged to pay a penalty of not less than £  , and not more than £  ,) be now read a second time."

IT may seem to be almost superfluous, after three distinct declarations of this House (and in a single session), to appeal again, by rhetoric or argument, to your feelings or understanding. We determined only seven weeks ago, three times, actually, that the period of labour should be less than twelve hours; and twice, virtually, that it should not exceed ten. The world at large believed that a middle term would be offered; but her Majesty's Ministers have refused concession—they have invited, nay, more, have compelled us to revive the debate, and now summon the House of Commons to revoke its decision. We, then, who stand in the old paths, and protest against this novel and somewhat questionable course, shall not be regarded as guilty of wearying your attention, and wasting your time, if we urge every possible consideration, and press forward every hitherto-omitted argument, as some counterpoise to the enormous weight of ministerial influence and official authority.

Sir, I cannot but be aware that enough has been said on the physical and social condition of the people—one way or the other, the minds of all are fully made up; and it is, indeed, unnecessary to say more, as all, even the hottest of my opponents, admit that a reduction of the hours of labour, could it be effected without injury to the workmen and manufacturers, would be highly desirable. The only objection, then, in the minds of many honourable and thinking men, is the danger to the people themselves; and I find myself in the condition of being summoned to refute the charge that I, who propose the scheme, am far more inhuman than those who resist it. Now I, for one, will reject the use of such epithets as these; nor will I retort any accusations that, here or elsewhere, have cast on me the imputation of malignity or cant. I regret but one thing in the course of these debates; I deeply regret that I should have been accused of calumniating the whole body of masters. I totally disclaim it. I should be ashamed of myself if I held such language towards a class of men that can boast of as worthy and munificent individuals as ever supported or adorned the institutions of this country; nor am I, because I address myself to a particular evil, to be considered as the enemy of the Factory System. Remove some few imperfections, and it may become a blessing, if not absolutely, at any rate relatively, to the present state of our labouring people.

Sir, when I first introduced this subject, I did not attempt to handle the commercial argument—I did not think it necessary for my view of the question, nor do I now; but I owe it to those whose interests I represent to show that I have not left any part without due consideration; that I have not rushed, like an enthusiast, into this career, neither knowing nor caring what consequences might ensue from the attainment of my ends. I said then that I entertained a full confidence that what was morally wrong could not be politically right; I had, and I have, an equal confidence that what is morally right cannot be politically wrong; and everything that I can acquire by thinking, reading, and, above all, by communication with those who are able to instruct me from their practical experience, confirms my conclusion.

And now, Sir, I shall entreat, with much respect and earnestness, the indulgence of the House to a subject always, perhaps, dry, and now both dry and somewhat exhausted.

Now, after all that has been written and said on the subject, I can discover no more than four arguments urged by our opponents against this measure—all of which are comprised in the Manchester Petition lately presented to this House.

1st. That the passing of a ten hours' bill would cause a diminution of produce.

2nd. That there would take place a reduction, in the same proportion, of the value of the fixed capital employed in the trade.

3rd. That a diminution of wages would ensue, to the great injury of the workmen.

4th. A rise of price, and consequent peril of foreign competition.

Even supposing that these assertions be separately, they cannot be collectively, true; it is very fair to place before us a variety of possible contingencies, but it must not be urged that we are threatened by a combination of them. Any one event may occur; but such an occurrence prevents, in one case at least, the full accomplishment of the other.

Let us look at the first argument, that "the passing of a ten hours' bill would cause a diminution of produce." It has hitherto been urged by all our antagonists that a reduction of one-sixth of the time would involve a corresponding reduction of one-sixth of the produce. I am happy to say that the opponents of the Bill have somewhat receded from their ground, and state, in their petition, an abatement of one-seventh; this is so far a gain on our side of the argument. But is the case so? What authority do they urge for the assertion? do they quote any facts? None on the face of the petition. But I think I shall be able to urge some very sufficient reasons to disprove altogether these general assertions, and establish some more favourable to myself.

The first statement to which I shall refer is contained in a letter from a gentleman who carries on a very large concern, employing, I believe, no less than 1,200 hands; it is dated March, 1844. "It is a mistaken notion," writes this gentleman, "to suppose that the produce of yarn or cloth from machinery would be curtailed in an arithmetical proportion to the proposed reduction of working hours from twelve to ten, because in very many instances the workman can produce much or little during the day, as he feels disposed, or as his strength enables him; and in my own trade, in which we employ at least 1,200 hands, I have proved beyond a doubt that, whenever we have reduced the hours for working from twelve to ten per day, which is equal to one-sixth, the quantity of work produced has not fallen below one-tenth or even one-twelfth." Another very important testimony is to be found in a valuable essay, published in 1831, entitled, "An Inquiry into the State of the Manufacturing Population," and written, I believe, by the owner of the largest establishment in Europe, Mr. Gregg. "That a reduction of the hours of labour would cause a corresponding reduction in the quantity produced," says the writer, "we entirely deny; it is probable that, if factories were to work ten hours instead of twelve, the loss in the quantity produced would not be one-sixth, but only about one-twelfth, and in mule-spinning scarcely so much. We know that in some cases, when the mills only worked four days in the week, they have often produced five days' quantity, and the men earned five days' wages. That this would be the case to a considerable extent every one must be aware, as all men will be able to work much harder for ten hours than they can for twelve." Another gentleman, who is the proprietor of a large establishment, writes to me thus:—"I am persuaded by experience, and from actual experiment, that the mill-occupier would lose very little by such a regulation (a ten hours' bill); the workers would be so improved in their physical condition, that they would do very nearly as much work in ten and a half as in twelve hours." Now, I have been anxious to obtain upon this point the opinion also of the operative cotton-spinners themselves, and I submitted two questions to them, to which I have received answers from twenty of the principal towns in Lancashire. My first question was—"Is the reduction in the produce in the direct proportion of the reduction in time—that is, would a reduction of one-sixth in the hours of work lead to the reduction of one-sixth in the amount of produce?" The answer I have received from twenty principal manufacturing towns was— "Certainly not." My next question was—"At how much do you estimate the reduction of produce?" The answer took the view the most advantageous to my opponents, and was—"Not more than one-eighth."

So far, then, as argument can go, and practical opinion, the case is established; there is no set-off to this statement—at least I have heard none; our adversaries have nowhere adduced actual facts to show that the abatement of produce is, in any degree, proportionate to the abatement of time.

Now the second argument may very probably follow on the foundation of the first, that " a reduction would take place, in the same proportion, of the value of the fixed capital employed in the trade;" this is not unlikely; but what does it amount to? Great authorities have calculated the diminution of produce by one-twelfth, or about 8 per cent. Let us admit this sum, as indicating the amount of the diminution of value on the fixed capital. Is this pure loss? are there no compensating circumstances? Look at this estimate, furnished to me by one of the largest proprietors in the cotton trade of England. Here it is:—

" Calculations of expenditure saved by diminution of hours of labour.—Horse power at work in the concern, 200; Original fixed capital, 100,000*l.*, or 500*l.* per horse power, which is the usual estimate. Diminution of produce by reason of two hours less labour, I will say 10 per cent., putting the argument advantageously for my opponents, for the reduction of produce will not exceed 1-12th. The calculation will then stand thus :—On 12 hours time, or 69 hours per week, the quantity of production is now measured by 69 hours; and this table will show the yearly cost of fixed capital :—

| | |
|---|---:|
| Interest on fixed capital at 5 per cent. per annum | 5 |
| Depreciation by wear and tear | 6 |
| Coal, oil, tallow, repairs, &c. | 12 |
| Gas (nearly) | 1 |
| | 24 |

That is, 24 per cent. of the fixed capital for carrying on the concern, for a production of 69—say 69,000 bundles of manufactured goods—then 24 divided by 69=24-69, which is nearly $\frac{3}{8}$ per cent. per annum of the fixed capital for each thousand bundles.

" On 10 hours time, or 59 hours per week, the production being calculated at 10 per cent. less, may be measured by 62 hours production :—

| | |
|---|---:|
| Interest on fixed capital at 5 per cent. per annum | 5 |
| Depreciation by wear and tear | 5 |
| Coal, oil, tallow, repairs, &c. | 10 |
| Gas (half) | $\frac{1}{2}$ |
| Total | $20\frac{1}{2}$ |

That is, $20\frac{1}{2}$ per cent. of the fixed capital for carrying on the concern for the production of 62,000 bundles—then $20\frac{1}{2}$ divided by $62=20\frac{1}{2}$-62, which is a trifle less per 1,000 bundles than when working 12 hours, so far as the fixed capital is concerned. Now from the above table it appears that the cost of goods (allowing the wages to be reduced in proportion to the work done) will be less than at present."

But the cardinal argument of my honourable opponents is hung on the supposed reduction of the operatives' wages, and on the calculated mischiefs that would ensue to the workpeople from so large an abatement of their weekly earnings. Sir, I have already observed, and I must observe again, that these statements, founded as they principally are on the researches of Mr. Horner, must be taken with many grains of allowance. Mr. Horner, with perfect candour, admits the plea, when he tells us that he draws all his inferences from the statements made by the masters, and that he has never been able to obtain, on the other side, the statements of the workpeople. This is an important consideration; the men themselves take a different view; and while they admit an abatement of earnings, urge that it will be in a lower proportion. Sir, very hard things are said about the folly and the nonsense, with other expressions equally pointed, of expecting twelve hours' wages for ten hours' work. Sir, I am not aware that anybody expected any such thing. It should be borne in mind that the earnings of these workpeople are regulated by the piece, and not by time; that a man receives every week a certain sum, not for the labour, but for the produce of sixty-nine hours; and the abatement of his wages will be estimated, not by the limitation of the time, but by the reduced amount of yarn or cloth that he carries to the counting-house. A reduction of one-sixth of the time may involve, as I have endeavoured to show, a reduction of one-twelfth of their earnings. Should the demand continue—and there is nothing in this bill to affect either the demand or the rate of spinning per pound—the wages will fall only in proportion to the abatement of produce, one-tenth or one-twelfth, for the prices of labour will be governed, like those of all commodities, by the demand and supply.

To this extent the operatives anticipate fully a reduction of their earnings. I endeavoured to show, some short time back, the calculations of household economy, by which they were prepared to meet even an abatement of one-sixth; this, however, is beyond the mark. The countervailing advantages of a reduced time are so great, as compared with a reduction of wages, that they readily accept the loss, and find their interest in the improvement of health of body and mind; in social and domestic comfort; in the practice of household economy; and specially in the prolongation, by three or four years of their working life, of their physical capacities to obtain a livelihood.

The fourth and last argument with which I have to deal is founded on an apprehended rise of price, and consequent advantages to the foreign competitor. Now, on this head I must produce two calculations exhibiting very minutely the degree to which such a result may take place. I will state it as founded on two establishments. The amount of sunk capital in each is 20,000*l.*, each having 40-horse power at work; one spinning No. 36, the principal count of yarn used; the other manufacturing shirting cloth from the same.

SPINNING ESTABLISHMENT, *Working* 69 *Hours per Week, and Spinning* 16,000 *lbs. of No.* 36.

|  | £. | s. | d. |
|---|---|---|---|
| Weekly wages paid . . . . | 87 | 10 | 0 |
| Wear and tear, coal, oil, gas expenses, carriage, &c. . . . . | 49 | 0 | 0 |
| Interest on capital sunk, at 5 per cent. | 19 | 5 | 0 |
| Depreciation on capital, at 5 per cent. | 19 | 5 | 0 |
| Profits at 10 per cent. per annum, on the capital . . . . . | 38 | 10 | 0 |
|  | £213 | 10 | 0 |

WEAVING ESTABLISHMENT, *Working* 69 *Hours per Week, and Weaving* 3,350 *Pieces of Shirting.*

|  | £. | s. | d. |
|---|---|---|---|
| Weekly wages paid . . . . . | 233 | 6 | 8 |
| Wear and tear, oil, coal, gas expenses, carriage, &c. . . . . | 78 | 3 | 4 |
| Interest on capital sunk, at 5 per cent. | 19 | 5 | 0 |
| Depreciation on capital at 5 per cent. | 19 | 5 | 0 |
| Profits, at 10 per cent. per annum, on the capital . . . . . | 38 | 10 | 0 |
|  | £338 | 10 | 0 |

Again, the time being reduced to 60 hours, or one-seventh less, as before observed, the production will not be reduced more than one-eighth, that is to say :—

SPINNING ESTABLISHMENT, *Working* 60 *Hours per Week, will Produce* 14,000 *lbs. of No.* 36 *Yarn.*

|  | £. | s. | d. |
|---|---|---|---|
| Weekly wages paid . . . . . | 76 | 10 | 0 |
| Wear and tear, coal, oil, gas, &c., expenses, carriage, &c., being 1-7th less . . . . . . | 42 | 0 | 0 |
| Interest on capital sunk, at 5 per cent., as before . . . . . | 19 | 5 | 0 |
| Depreciation on capital, at 5 per cent., less 1-7th . . . . | 16 | 10 | 0 |
| Profits, at 10 per cent. per annum, on capital, as before . . . | 38 | 10 | 0 |
|  | £192 | 15 | 0 |

This is the total cost for spinning 14,000 lbs., allowing profits and interest to remain the same, which is $3\frac{3}{10}d.$ per lb., or 1-10th part of a penny more when working 60 hours instead of 69.

WEAVING ESTABLISHMENT, *Working* 60 *Hours per Week, will Produce* 2,950 *Pieces of Shirting.*

|  | £. | s. | d. |
|---|---|---|---|
| Weekly wages paid . . . . . | 205 | 0 | 0 |
| Wear and tear, coal, oil, gas expenses, carriage, &c., 1-7th less . . . | 67 | 0 | 0 |
| Interest on capital sunk, at 5 per cent., as before . . . . . . | 19 | 5 | 0 |
| Depreciation on capital, at 5 per cent., less 1-7th . . . . . . | 16 | 10 | 0 |
| Profits, at 10 per cent. per annum, on capital, as before . . . . | 38 | 10 | 0 |
|  | £346 | 5 | 0 |

Which is the total cost for manufacturing 2,950 pieces of shirting, being 2s. 4d. per piece, or $\frac{3}{8}$ths of a penny more when working 60 hours instead of 69, allowing profits and interest to remain the same.

This, then, on a minute and accurate calculation, is the fair estimate of the advantage, if advantage it can be called, which is offered to the foreigner as a set off to the great advantages to be bestowed on our own people !

But, Sir, I should like to try the question by the test of experience, and examine what has really been the effect upon production and upon the earnings of the workmen in all those cases where the hours of labour have been reduced. Forebodings were uttered of the most melancholy description—were they, any of them, fulfilled? This great question was agitated from 1815 to 1819. Several witnesses of experience and character maintained before Committees of the Lords and Commons in 1816, 1818, and 1819, the same propositions as those laid down in the Manchester Petition of the present year; that is to say, " the diminution of produce, the rise of price, the reduction of wages." Now observe; the hours of labour, before the restriction of 1820, ranged between thirteen and sixteen in the day. The Secretary to the Associated Mill Owners, in 1819, gave in the following table, which falls short of the exact truth; but this is its result—

The total number of cotton mills was 325. Of these 5 worked

66 hours a week; 19 ditto, 68 to 68½; 38 ditto, 69, the present
duration—in all, 62. But the 263 which remained worked in a
range from 70 to 93 hours a week. The population employed in
the 62 mills was 7,486. But the population in the 263 mills was
nearly 50,000. Here observe what a large proportion of the
workers were occupied on the long periods of labour. Well, what
was the result? In 1819 the Act passed, to take effect from
January 1, 1820, which reduced the hours in all the cotton
factories to twelve actual working hours. It had been most
boldly asserted that there would be a diminution of produce;
but how was this confirmed? I will just compare the prophecy
and the issue. In three years, from 1817 to 1819 inclusive, the
cotton wool imported was 451,934,946 lbs. Now, 1820 was the
first year under restriction of labour to 12 from 14 and 15 hours a
day; in three years, from 1821 to 1823 inclusive, the cotton wool
imported was 466,776,751 lbs. The estimated weekly consumption
in those years, before restriction, was, in 1817, 2,051,400 lbs.;
1818, 2,132,000 lbs.; and 1819, 2,116,809 lbs. In the three years
after restriction the weekly consumption was, in 1821, 2,476,800
lbs.; 1822, 2,750,100 lbs.; and 1823, 3,025,000 lbs. You must
observe, too, there was no falling off in aggregate production; for
instance, the average quantity of cotton yarn retained for home
consumption, and exported in each year, before restriction, from
1818 to 1820, both inclusive, was 134,420,757 lbs.; whilst in the
three years, from 1821 to 1823, after restriction, the quantity was
140,142,224 lbs. The official value of cotton goods exported from
Great Britain in two years, 1818 and 1819, before restriction, was
37,988,893*l.* In the three years after restriction, from 1821 and
1822, the official value was 46,202,208*l.* The official value of yarns
for the two years exported, before restriction, in 1818 and 1819,
was 2,882,529*l.* In the two years after restriction, 1821 and 1822,
the value was 4,250,450*l.* Look to the aggregate of goods for five
years before and five years after restriction; from 1815 to 1819,
both inclusive, the aggregate official value of goods exported was
95,787,626*l.* From 1821 to 1825, the aggregate official value was
124,090,698*l.* The statement of yarns, did I enter upon it, would
be still more striking.

But now, with respect to the second apprehension, which lay in
"the consequent advance of prices, and in the advantage to the
foreigner;" that argument has proved no more true as to the past
than I believe it will as to the future. The declared value of the
cotton goods exported in 1818 and 1819, together, was 29,032,412*l.*
before restriction. But the declared value of cotton goods exported
in 1821 and 1822, together, was after restriction only 28,321,210*l.,*

being an increase of twenty-one and a half per cent. in the quantity, and a decrease of two and a half per cent. in the price. The same statement holds good in respect of the yarns exported. The declared value of yarns exported in 1818 and 1819 was 4,902,088*l.* The declared value in 1821 and 1822 was 4,915,207*l.*, being an increase of forty-seven and a half per cent. in the quantity, as nearly as possible, at the same cost. The same might be seen on an aggregate of five years. The declared value of goods exported before restriction from 1815 to 1819, both included, was 75,445,940*l.* The declared value from 1821 to 1825, after restriction, was 72,249,105*l.* But let us consider still further the advantage given, as is said, to the foreigner, with respect to two countries from which the competition is the greatest. The import of cotton wool into France for consumption in 1820 was 20,203,000 kilogrammes, or, at 100 kilogrammes to 220½ lbs., 44,547,615 lbs. The same in 1840 was 52,942,000 kilogrammes, or about 116,737,110 lbs., being an increase of 162 per cent. The export of cotton twist and woven cottons from France in 1820 was 1,441,000 kilogrammes. The same in 1840, 4,440,000 kilogrammes, being an increase of 208½ per cent. The consumption of cotton in America in 1826 (I cannot obtain an earlier year) was 103,483 bales, or 38,392,193 lbs. The same in 1840 was 297,288 bales, or 110,293,848 lbs., being an increase of 187 per cent. The total value of manufactures exported from America in 1826 was 1,138,125 dollars, as stated in *Hunt's Merchant's Magazine,* published at New York. The total value in 1840 was 3,549,607 dollars, being an increase of 212 per cent.

The statements respecting the French trade I believe to be strictly accurate—they are taken from Mr. MacGregor's tables. But now turn to the British trade. The imports of cotton wool into Great Britain for consumption in 1820 was 152,829,633 lbs. The import of cotton wool in 1820 was 592,488,010 lbs., being an increase of 288 per cent. The total of manufactured cottons (twist and goods) exported from Great Britain in 1820, as by official value, was 22,531,079*l.* The total value exported in 1840 was 73,124,730*l.*, being an increase per cent. of 225. Thus, while foreign countries increased 162 per cent. in the first case (France), and 187 per cent. in the second (America), on the amounts respectively of 44,547,615 lbs., and 110,293,848 lbs., the British trade increased 288 per cent. on the amount of nearly 153 millions. In support of my argument I quote Mr. M'Culloch. "It is ludicrous indeed," says that able writer, "to suppose that a half-peopled country like America, possessed of boundless tracts of unoccupied land of the highest degree of fertility, should be able successfully to contend in manufacturing industry with an old, settled, fully-peopled, and very rich country, like Great Britain." Mr. M'Culloch speaks like a man of sense.

Now, the third point of alarm which I wish to test by the experience of the past, is the question urged so strongly then, and with double vehemence now, the reduction of wages. Now, here is the actual statement of the case, which will show how weak was the ground on which the assertion was based. I will take the facts, without pretending to assign the causes. In 1818 and 1819, the two years preceding the limitation of the hours of labour, these were the wages of the operatives :—The fine spinners made 1*l.* 12*s.* per week, the coarse spinners from 20*s.* to 28*s.* per week, the women spinners 17*s.* per week, the reelers 10*s.*, the stretchers 14*s.*, the pickers 9*s.* I find from the same table—a table in Tooke's "High and Low Prices"—that in 1820, the first year of the limitation, the wages continued the same. I have not been able to get any tables to show the state of their earnings in the two following years; but the subject is a very important one, and we can arrive at it by an easy process. The records of the operative spinners in Lancashire show for many years the prices paid for spinning per lb. In 1818 and 1819, in the Manchester and Bolton district, those prices were for 40*s.* 3½*d.* per lb.; 60*s.* 5½*d.* per lb.; 80*s.* 8¼*d.* per lb.; 100*s.* 9*d.* per lb.; 150*s.* 1*s.* 10*d.* per lb.; and 200*s.* 5*s.* 4*d.* per lb. I find that, in 1821 and 1822, the years following the limitation of labour, the same prices were obtained for spinning as in 1818 and 1819. I have already shown to the House that the weekly consumption of cotton-wool, in the three years following the restriction, was greater than in the three years preceding the restriction. Therefore, as there was a greater quantity of cotton wool to be worked up, and the prices of working it up were not reduced, we have good ground for asserting that wages continued at least at the same level. So much for the predictions of wages to be reduced.

Did the loss then fall on the profit of the manufacturer? Suppose, for the sake of argument, that it was so; surely an adequate return must have been left, for I find that the

| | | |
|---|---|---|
| Cotton wool imported in 1818 amounted to | | 177,282,158 lbs. |
| But in 1842 to . . . . . . | | 475,060,700 lbs. |
| The total number of cotton establishments in 1819 . | | 344 |
| The same by latest returns (1839) . . . . | | 1815 |

And mills are, at this moment, in course of construction in every quarter. But let people say what they will, the whole subject is contained in an extract from a letter written to me in March, 1844, by a very large proprietor :—

"When," says he, "we see around us men of all trades and professions going into the cotton trade, some with little capital, others with less knowledge or experience of the business—when we see gentlemen, brokers, merchants, doctors, lawyers, drapers, tailors, &c., leaving their respective professions and trades, and see them building mills in almost every town in Lancashire—when we see capital thus finding its way into the spinning and manufacturing business, surely the profits cannot be so small that a little reduction of the hours of labour to suffering thousands is impracticable."

Now, Sir, I have long been regarded as a monomaniac on these subjects, as a man of peculiar opinions, one having a fixed idea, but without support, or even countenance, in my wild opinions—yet is it not the fact that the reduction of the hours of labour is a question maintained and desired by many great manufacturers in the cotton trade? I may quote in this House the members for Oldham, Salford, Ashton, and Blackburn—I will just indicate a few without its walls, firm friends of the measure; Mr. Kay, of Bury; Mr. William Walker, of Bury, perhaps the largest consumer of cotton in that district; Mr. Hamer, of the same place, a partner in the firm of the late Sir Robert Peel; Mr. Cooper, of Preston; Mr. Tysoe, of Salford; and Mr. Kenworthy, of Blackburn. I set great store by the opinions of this gentleman last named, because he has passed through all the gradations of the business, and has by his own talent and integrity raised himself from the condition of an operative to the station of a master. I may add, too, the name of Mr. Hargreaves, of Accrington—no inconsiderable person in Lancashire—who feels so strongly on this subject, that he attended a public meeting in support of the question, and moved a resolution himself.

Now, consider here the famous argument of Mr. Senior—an argument urged almost more frequently than any other—to prove the folly and mischief of my demand. Every one, no doubt, will readily acknowledge the talents and learning of this gentleman, but practical experiments are worth ten thousand of his calculations. Mr. Senior declares that the profit of the manufacturer arises from the labour of the last two hours! Now observe—this assertion might be met in various ways by reasoning, but a fact is far better. I find a letter addressed, in April, 1844, to the editor of the *Bolton Free Press*, and signed, a Bolton Cotton Spinner, but known to be by Mr. Thomason, a highly respectable mill-owner,—he speaks from personal experience; and what does he say? These are his words:—" There is also another consideration for employers, namely, that in a day's work of twelve hours, the last hour, by reason of the exhaustion and listlessness of the workers, more especially young children of thirteen or sixteen, is the least productive in quantity, and the least satisfactory in quality." And he adds—now mark this,—" The probability is, that the twelfth hour produces more spoiled work than any other two hours of the day." Here is the opinion of a practical cotton-spinner; and it is confirmed by every statement that I have received on the subject; not a few experienced persons having declared that they could tell, by the feel and the appearance of the cloth, whether it had been made at the earlier or later periods of the day. But, further, I submitted the question to the operative spinners of Lancashire; and this is the answer I received from twenty principal towns :—" What is the character of the work of the two last hours; is it equal in quality to that of the first ?" The answer which they have given me is,— " Certainly not, especially in the winter months."

Sir, is it necessary further to detain the House by proofs that the arguments of Mr. Senior rest by no means on the firmest grounds ? The commercial argument, in truth, is really feeble; it has always been urged, and has never been verified, and yet experience should go for something in these great considerations, —it was broached in 1816; repeated and enforced in evidence before committees, in speeches and pamphlets, in 1817, 1818, and 1819, and utterly refuted by the whole subsequent history of the cotton trade from that day to the present—you had no diminution of produce, no fall in wages, no rise in price, no closing of markets, no irresistible rivalry from foreign competition, although you reduced your hours of working from 16, 14, 13, to 12 hours in the day. What change has there occurred so mighty as to prevent a similar result in 1845 ? Is British energy so exhausted, or skill so decayed, our resources so dried up, that two hours taken from 12 will produce nothing but misery, when 2, 3, or 4, taken from 16, 14, or 13, produced nothing but good ? You argue, moreover, as though there existed no difference of opinion among master cotton-spinners—as though every commercial authority lay on your side, and were not found in equal weight and character upon ours.

But while your financial argument has failed, not so that arising from moral considerations. The antagonists, even, of the restriction pronounce it desirable, could it be safely effected; and your own inspectors have told you that without such a limitation of the hours of toil, there can be no hopes for the social or moral improvement of the working classes. Here, then, springs up a curious and important problem for solution by this House—no, not by this House, for they have already resolved it—but for her Majesty's Government, who deny our conclusions, and oppose themselves to the thrice-recorded wishes of the British empire. Which is the preferable condition for a people—high wages, with privation of social and domestic enjoyment, without the means of knowledge or the opportunities of virtue, acquiring wages, which they waste through ignorance of household economy, and placed in a state of moral and physical deterioration? or lower earnings, with increased advantages for mental improvement and bodily health; for the understanding and performance of those duties, which now they either know not, or neglect; for obtaining the humble but necessary accomplishments of domestic life, and cultivating its best affections? Clouds of witnesses attest these things; clergy, ministers of every persuasion, doctors, master-manufacturers, and operatives, have given, and are ready to give again, the most conclusive evidence; but her Majesty's Ministers refuse to listen, and will neither adopt the remedy we propose, nor assist us with one of their own.

Sir, this House is now placed in a novel position; it is summoned to rescind its resolution, not because new facts or new conditions have appeared, but because the Minister has declared his hostility. Nothing has been stated that was not stated before —no fresh knowledge communicated, no unseen dangers discovered. The House is summoned to cancel its vote, not upon conviction, but to save a government. The Minister surely has no right to expose his supporters to this alternative—either to abandon their opinions or dislodge their political friends. A determination such as this should have been signified beforehand, and not reserved until a time when it will be obeyed certainly with great pain, and perhaps not without disgrace. Sir, I do think that members should pause to consider the precedent they are about to establish. Very alarming words fell from my honourable friend, the member for Somersetshire—manly and conscientious, as is everything that he says or does—that while he retained his opinions, he should change his conduct, because he found himself at variance with the Minister. And so it is come to this, that great questions are to be tried, not by their merits, but by their aspect, as affecting the will or the fancies of a government, opposing, be it remembered, not a set of principles to introduce a new system of rule or policy, but asserting a mere opinion against the extension of an existing law, hastily taken up, and somewhat arbitrarily maintained. Sir, the whole question of representative governments is at stake—votes have been rescinded before, but never such as this; you are almost declaring, to those who are your ordinary friends, that they shall never exercise a vote but at the will of the Minister. This is a despotism under the forms of the constitution; and all to no purpose; for your resistance will be eventually and speedily overcome, but your precedent will remain, more fatal to true liberty and independence than all the Reform Bills.

Sir, it is possible, nay, more, it is probable (for their efforts have been great), that her Majesty's Ministers will carry the day; but for how long? If they would render their victory a lasting one, they must extinguish all the sentiments that gave rise to mine. Their error is stupendous—"Scilicet illo igne, vocem populi, et libertatem senatûs, et conscientiam humani generis aboleri arbitrabantur." Could you, simultaneously with your extinction of myself, extinguish for a while the sense of suffering, or at least all sympathy with it, you might indeed hope for an inglorious repose, and by the indulgence of your own ease, heap up, for your posterity, turmoil, anxiety, and woe. But things will not end here. The question extends with numbers, strengthens with their strength, and rises with their intelligence. The feeling of the country is roused; and, so long as there shall be voices to complain and hearts to sympathise, you will have neither honour abroad, nor peace at home, neither comfort for the present, nor security for the future. But I dare to hope for far better things—for restored affections, for renewed understanding between master and man, for combined and general efforts, for large and mutual concessions of all classes of the wealthy for the benefit of the common welfare, and specially of the labouring people. Sir, it may not be given to me to pass over this Jordan; other and better men have preceded me, and I entered into their labours; other and better men will follow me, and enter into mine; but this consolation I shall ever continue to enjoy—that, amidst much injustice, and somewhat of calumny, we have at last lighted such a candle in England as, by God's blessing, shall never be put out.

*Treatment of Lunatics.*

---

# HOUSE OF COMMONS,

## TUESDAY, JULY 23, 1844.

---

Speech on moving for an Address to the Crown, praying Her Majesty to take into her consideration the Report of the Metropolitan Commissioners in Lunacy to the Lord Chancellor, presented to the House by command of Her Majesty.*

LORD ASHLEY said it would be necessary for him shortly to explain the reasons which actuated him. First, the nature of the subject and the protraction of inquiry had inevitably delayed the production of the Report to this period of the Session. Secondly, the statute under which the Commissioners acted would expire in the next Session, and it would be necessary to call upon the House to consider in what form and to what extent power should be confided to any administrative body for the government of lunatics throughout the kingdom. It was desirable, therefore, that the country should not be taken by surprise, but that these weighty matters should be maturely considered during the approaching recess. He had been unwilling to bring forward this subject at all, but his colleagues in the Commission had thought that the novelty of the subject, the great expenses incurred, and the vast numbers who were subject to this jurisdiction, would justify him in calling the attention of the House to it. Though the Report embraced a variety of matters, those with which he had to deal were limited to the civil and external government of lunacy; it was the duty of the House to prescribe the conditions under which a man should be deprived of his liberty, and also those under which he might be released; it was their duty to take care that for those who required restraint there should be provided kind and competent keepers, and that, while the patient received no injury, the public should be protected.

Insane patients were lodged either in single houses, in public or county asylums, or in private asylums where paupers were

* From Hansard.

received. With respect to the first class there were no Returns; the Commissioners were precluded by the statute from any interference in such circumstances; and he must take the opportunity of saying that he thought this a most unfortunate enactment, not that he wished to claim for the Board the invidious and burthensome power of examining and censuring the neglect of private families, but because he believed that a power of this kind ought to be confided to some hands that would hunt out and expose the many horrible abuses that at present prevailed. No doubt there were many worthy exceptions, but the House had no notion of the abominations that prevailed in those asylums. It was the concession of absolute secret and irresponsible power to the relatives of lunatics and the keepers of the asylums, and exposing them to temptations which he believed human nature was too weak to resist. There were many patients in these single houses for whom were paid not less than 500*l.* per annum. This was a temptation to keep such a patient in perpetual confinement, because with the returning health of the sufferer the allowance would be discontinued. So strong was his opinion of the bad effect of this, that if Providence should afflict any near relative of his with insanity, he would consign him to an asylum in which there were other patients, and which was subjected to official visitation. The only control they had over the single houses was this—that if a patient resided in one more than a twelvemonth, the owner of the house was compelled to communicate under seal the name of that patient to the Clerk of the Commission. But for the most part no notice whatever was taken of this law, and it was frequently evaded by removing the patient, after a residence of eleven months, to some other lodging. He knew the delicacy of the subject, but it was one with which the Legislature ought to interfere.

The second class of houses was the county asylums. The total number of lunatics and idiots chargeable to unions and parishes on the 1st of January, 1844, was 16,821; in England, 15,601; in Wales, 1,220. In county asylums there was provision for no more than 4,155 persons, leaving more than 12,000, of whom there were in asylums under local acts eighty-nine, in Bethlehem and St. Luke's 121, in other public asylums 343, while others were disposed of otherwise, leaving in workhouses and elsewhere 9,339. Although a few of the existing county asylums were well adapted to their purpose, and a very large proportion of them were extremely well conducted, yet some were quite unfit for the reception of insane persons. Some were placed in ineligible sites, and others were deficient in the necessary means of providing out-door employment for their paupers. Some also were ill-contrived and defective in their internal construction and accommodation. Some afforded every advantage of science and medical treatment; others were wholly deficient in these points. All of them, however, had the advantage of constant supervision, and of not giving any profit to the superintendents, so that it was not necessary that the keeper should stint and spare his patients in the articles necessary for the curative process, with the view of realising a profit. Some of the country asylums were stated in the Report to be admirably managed. It might be invidious to specify, but he would mention those of Wakefield, Hanwell, Lincoln, Lancaster, and Gloucester. Why, then, were not these institutions multiplied? At this moment there were twenty-one counties in England and Wales without any asylum whatever, public or private. The expense was one cause; in some cases the cost of construction had been exceedingly great; the asylum most cheaply constructed was that of Wakefield, of which the average cost per head was 111*l.*; while the highest priced was that of Gloucester, which had cost, on the first accommodation, 357*l.* per head. In many cases the cost of construction had exceeded 200*l.* per head. The cost of the Bedford asylum, for 180 patients, was 20,500*l.*; that of the Gloucester, for 261 patients, 51,366*l.*; that of the Kent, for 300 patients, was 64,056*l.*; that of Hanwell, for 1,000 patients, was 160,000*l.*, exclusive of 36,000*l.* paid since July, 1835, for furniture and fittings. On the other hand, the best constructed union houses in the country had not cost more than 40*l.* a head. No doubt a lunatic asylum was more expensive, but not in that enormous degree. The reason of this difference he did not know, except that many of them had been constructed with a great display of architecture. The Commission had no wish to advise the erection of unsightly buildings, but they thought that no unnecessary cost should be incurred in the erection of asylums. Some asylums were far too large, and on this subject the Report said:

"The asylum for Kent will contain 300, for Surrey 360, for West Riding 420, for Lancaster 600, and for Middlesex 1,000. From the best opinions that we have been able to collect, and from the result of our own observations and experience, we think it is highly desirable that no asylum for curable lunatics should contain more than 250 patients, and that 200 is perhaps as large a number as can be managed, with the most benefit to themselves and the public, in one establishment."

The principle had been recognized in the district asylums of Ireland, and they had the great authority of Dr. Conolly for saying that 100 persons were the highest number that could be managed, with convenience, in one of these asylums. It would be better to have two of a moderate size than one very large, to which patients would be brought from a great distance. The asylums of Lancaster and Middlesex were so excessively overgrown that it was impossible to do full justice to the patients kept in them. And yet he feared that further enlargements were in contemplation.

The third class was that of private asylums, which received persons who paid their own expenses, and also paupers. The total number of private patients in asylums of various descriptions, on the 1st of January, 1844, was 4,072; of these there were in metropolitan licensed houses, 973; in provincial, 1,426. The paupers in private or licensed houses were—metropolitan, 854; provincial, 1,920. With respect to these a very serious question arose, how far any house should be licensed to take patients or paupers for payment. He knew there were some very good houses of that description, but the principle was very dangerous. Whatever might be the opinion of the House as to places of reception for wealthy and independent patients, he considered there could be very little doubt as to cases in which paupers were sent to such houses to be maintained, at the low rate of seven or eight shillings, out of which the proprietor was to feed, and clothe, and house the patient, and carry on the remedial process, paying all these expenses, and still getting a profit. In the metropolitan districts, at one time, the competition was so great that they were preparing to take persons at seven and even six shillings a head; but the Commissioners had done everything they could to discountenance this, and to a certain extent they had succeeded, though they were still taken at eight and nine shillings. But in the country this evil was still altogether unchecked, as the extracts from the Report which he should now read to the House would show.

" Many asylums had formerly been private houses; the mansion was sometimes engrossed by the proprietor and a few private patients, while the paupers were consigned to buildings formerly used as offices and outhouses."

The following were the remarks of the Commissioners on some of these houses :—

" West Auckland—Thirteen males, sixteen females; the violent and the quiet, the dirty and the clean, shut up together; only one small yard, and when the one sex was in it, the other shut up; in the day room of the males five restrained by leg-locks, and two wearing, in addition, iron handcuffs and fetters from the wrist to the ankle, all tranquil, but they would otherwise escape; chains fastened to floor in many places, and to many of the bedsteads; the males throughout the house slept two in a bed. Wreckenton, near Gateshead—Chains attached to the floor in several places, and it was the practice to chain patients by the leg upon their first admission, in order, as it was said, to see what they would do; bedding filthy, cell offensive, also sleeping room; improved by visitation, but still unfit. Licensed house at Derby—Damp, unhealthy; bedding in a disgusting condition from running sores. At Lainston, in Hants—Even on third visit seven female paupers in chains; these seven and three others chained to their beds at night; the usual accompaniments of dirty, wet, and ill-clothed. Kingdown-house, at Box—the same details. House of Industry, Kingsland, near Shrewsbury—Containing from eighty to ninety insane persons. They were nearly all fastened to their beds by chains to the wrists. Union House, Redruth, in Cornwall— Forty-one insane persons, several violent and requiring restraint. Ditto at Bath—Twenty-one insane persons. At Leicester— Thirty insane persons; namely, eleven males and nineteen females, of whom three males and nine females were dangerous. Of the males, W. K. was a noisy maniac, very cunning, and occasionally striking the other men in the ward. P. R. was subject to maniacal attacks, during which he was placed in a strait waistcoat: he was raving mad about two months before our visit, and was consequently fastened to his bed at night, to prevent him from injuring or annoying the other inmates. A. H. was violent and passionate, and tried to cut others with knives, and all these persons were dangerous. Amongst the other cases J. L., an epileptic; J. D., a case of melancholia; J. G., formerly in the asylum, and still insane, noisy, and abusive: the rest of the males of the class appeared to be either harmless idiots, or in a state of mental imbecility. The three most dangerous of the females were C. B., admitted June 12th, 1839, a destructive and dangerous idiot; M. H., admitted the 23rd of February, 1839, an abusive and dangerous lunatic: she was brought to the workhouse in a state of violent excitement by two policemen. M. A. R., admitted the 24th of February, 1841, a quarrelsome and dangerous idiot, once knocked out the teeth of a child. To these may be added the following, as properly coming within the description of dangerous lunatics:—M. B., a sullen, ill-tempered person, who refused to be employed, and had threatened, when at home, to kill her mother. A. W., in the workhouse three years, an abusive lunatic, who had occasionally struck most of the women in the ward, particularly a paralytic patient, who could not defend herself.

J. S., an irritable mad woman, who threw knives at those whom she happened to have a dispute with. E. H., a violent, irascible person, subject to maniacal excitement, and dangerous when irritated. She had been twenty-six weeks in the county asylum, having become unmanageable at home after the death of her mother sixteen years ago, and was said to strike the inmates maliciously. A. H., a harmless lunatic, with delusions, was most improperly sent to the workhouse instead of the asylum four years ago. Besides the above, there were in the house six quiet female lunatics, all confirmed cases, and five idiots. Workhouse at Birmingham—Seventy-one insane persons, amongst them was an unusual proportion of epileptics, namely, eleven males and sixteen females. Several of these were idiots, others were subject, after their paroxysms of epilepsy, to fits of raving madness or epileptic fever, during which they were stated to be excessively violent. Besides these, there were several patients who were occasionally under great excitement and furiously maniacal, two of the females had strong suicidal propensities, and one of them had attempted suicide. There is no class of persons more dangerous than are those epileptics who are subject to attacks of epileptic furor or delirium."

Of Plympton, in Devonshire, the Commissioners said,—

" In one of the cells in the upper court for the women, the dimensions of which were eight feet by four, and in which there was no table, and only two wooden seats fastened to the wall, we found three females confined, there was no glazing to the window, and the floor of this place was perfectly wet with urine. The two dark cells which adjoin the cell used for a day room are the sleeping places for these three unfortunate beings; two of them sleep in two cribs in one cell. The floor in the cell with the two cribs was actually reeking wet with urine, and covered with straw and filth, and one crib had a piece of old carpet by way of bedding besides the straw, but the other appeared to have had nothing but straw, without any other bedding. In the other cell, the patient who had slept in it had broken her crib to pieces, and a part of it was remaining in the cell, but the straw was heaped up in one corner, and as far as we could rely upon what was said, she had slept upon the straw upon the ground at least one night. The straw itself was most filthy, the floor was perfectly wet with urine, and part of the straw had been stuck to the wall in patches with excrement. It must be added that these two cells, and one other adjoining to it, have no window and no place for light or air, except a grate over the door, which opens into a passage. The persons of these three unfortunate women were extremely dirty, and the condition in which we found them and their cells was truly sickening and shocking. Adjoining to the two sleeping cells of these women, and opening into the same passage, was a third cell, which was occupied as a sleeping place by a male criminal of very dangerous habits and an idiotic boy. This cell was dirty and offensive, and the floor of it wet with urine, but it was not in so filthy a state as the other two. The criminal was fastened at night to his bed with a chain. We strongly objected to these men being confined in a cell closely adjoining to the females. The whole of these cells were as damp and dark as an underground cellar, and were in such a foul and disgusting state that it was scarcely possible to endure the offensive smell. We sent for a candle and lantern to enable us to examine them."

That asylum had since been improved, but it was in consequence of repeated visitations. To correct these evils (proceeded the noble Lord) there was no remedy but the multiplication of county asylums; and if advice and example failed, they ought to appeal to the assistance of the law, to compel the construction of an adequate number of asylums over the whole country. If constructed, however, on the same principles as had been adopted in many of those now existing, they would be little better than useless, and mere hospitals for incurables. Great benefit, it was to be observed, as well as great saving of expense, resulted from the application of curative means at an early stage of insanity. The keepers of all the great asylums stated that numbers of persons, especially pauper lunatics, were sent there at so late a period of the disease as totally to preclude hope of recovery. It was the duty of the State to provide receptacles for the incurable patients, apart from those devoted to the remedial treatment: it would be necessary also to enact that the patients should be sent without delay to the several asylums. On this subject he would read a few observations of the Commissioners. With reference to Hanwell they said:

" The county asylum is nearly filled with incurable lunatics, and almost all the recent cases are practically excluded from it. When we visited it in March last, there were 984 patients, of whom only thirty were reported curable, and there were 429 patients belonging to the county out of the asylum, who, if they wait for the rota before they are admitted, will probably have become incurable, and will be lunatic annuitants upon the county or their parishes. Lancaster asylum contains 600 patients, of whom 546 are considered incurable; and there are more than 500 pauper lunatics in the county for whom it has no accommodation. Surrey Asylum, opened in 1841; on 1st January, 1844, number in asylum, 382, of whom 362 are reported incurable; there are belonging to the county of Surrey 591 pauper lunatics. This was a most costly system. The superintending physician of Hanwell Asylum published a table in 1842, to show how long each patient had been confined there. There were 936 in the asylum; 696 had been there more than two years, and were pronounced incurable. The average duration of confinement of these 696 was upwards of six years and nine months. The yearly cost was about 22*l.* 4*s.* for each patient; each patient, therefore, will have cost 140*l.*" " It should not be forgotten," the Report said, "that many pauper lunatics have families, who would no longer be thrown on parishes for support, if their mental maladies could be removed, or even materially ameliorated."

But the benefits of early attention were most evident from the following statements. It was impossible that they could press too much upon the attention of all parish officers the immense benefit which arose from early attention to all cases of lunacy, and an early attack, medicinally, upon the disease, before it became confirmed. In general, all the best practitioners at county asylums complained of the late stage of the disease at which patients were sent in, and hon. Members would see that the Commissioners were obliged to make frequent complaints upon that subject, and the state of filth and rags in which the poor creatures were transmitted from their parishes. Into the asylum at Forston, in Dorsetshire, during the course of last year, out of thirty-seven pauper lunatics, six had been sent in within three months of their being attacked with the disorder, and the result was most cheering, for out of the six, five were dismissed cured within four months after their arrival, and the sixth, although a female of seventy-five years of age, was in a state of convalescence, and he had no doubt she was also now restored to her family. Into St. Luke's it was well known that no patient was admitted after he had been labouring under the attack for more than twelve months. He was astonished to find, from the Returns made from that hospital, that, in 1842, the cures averaged 70 per cent., and that last year they reached 65 per cent. His curiosity was so excited upon the subject that he wrote a letter to Dr. Sutherland, the visiting physician, to ask him whether those cases were merely temporary, or whether they were real and substantial cures. In answer the Doctor said:

" All the cures mentioned in the Report, page 81, are permanent. Our rule is, that if any patient who has been discharged from the hospital as cured relapses within three months, he is readmitted, not as a fresh but as a relapsed case; the period he has been at home is deducted, and he is kept in the hospital to the end of the twelve months, or till he is again cured; but all such relapsed cases are deducted from the list of cures; however, we very seldom have instances of relapses—three or four during the year is the average."

Was not that a most satisfactory statement? Contrast that with reports from other parts of the country. The Commissioners report that—

"In the asylums of Lincoln, Leicester, Nottingham, and North-ampton, the superintendents and visiting physicians have ex-pressed their unanimous opinion that pauper lunatics are sent there at so late a period of their disease as to impede or prevent their ultimate recovery. Opinions to the same effect from almost every county lunatic asylum." Chester may be taken as a sample. "Paupers are brought in a very bad state, in filth and rags, and, from too long delays, in a state where there is little or no chance of recovery."

He believed that one reason why parochial authorities were so backward in sending in patients was their ignorance of the great benefit arising from early care and medical attendance, partly, too, the want of a sufficient accommodation, but the great ob-jection was the increased expense. They liked much more to keep such unfortunates in the workhouse at an expense not exceeding 2*s.* per week, rather than sending them to the county asylum, where the minimum charge was 7*s.* per week. He verily believed that even in the matter of expense, a first outlay, which might be considerable in the beginning, would prove eminently profitable in the end. His full conviction was, that the number of cures which would be effected, and looking at it merely as a question of expense, would fully repay the expenditure in ten years. Now, it was true that they could show but few instances of restoration to reason; how was it possible? They could show a mighty improvement in the condition of the sufferers, the alleviation of their state, their occupations and amusements (all, with some bright exceptions, of recent date), and that the services of religion had infused a momentary tranquillity; but they could show little else; and unless the Legislature should interfere, and bring these unfortunates by force within the reach of sympathy and care, for every one restored to his senses we should see a hundred in whom the light of reason would be extinguished for ever.

Next, there were two points of deep interest to which the House would do well to advert for a moment—the questions of restraint, and the admission and liberation of patients. Upon restraint it was unnecessary to dwell very long, as it was a matter of internal arrangement, and beyond their immediate legislation; but he wished to direct the attention of the House to the chapter in the Reports which handled that subject, that it might share the general satisfaction, and give praise to those good and able men, Mr. Tuke, Dr. Hitch, Dr. Corsellis, Dr. Conolly, Dr. Vitrè, Dr. Charlesworth, and many more, who had brought all their high moral and intellectual qualities to bear on this topic, and had laboured to make the rational and humane treatment to be the rule and principle of the government of lunacy. Respecting the admission of pauper patients it would be necessary to make very stringent regulations: for their admission into private asylums a certificate was required, signed by a medical man; county asylums also, though not compelled by law, had made similar regulations for their own guidance; but for the transfer of them to any lunatic ward in a workhouse no authority was required but that of the master. This power was open to the greatest abuses. The Report suggested that, until a sufficient number of asylums had been created, certain portions of stated workhouses should be licensed, and subjected to all the conditions and superintendence of the appointed visitor.

The admission into licensed houses offered a better guarantee of security; and the Commissioners were satisfied that it was, on the whole, well guarded, as they had not found a single instance of which they could say that the first confinement was unquestionably, and beyond all doubt, improper; but they have found some instances in which the confinement was unnecessarily prolonged. The question of liberation was very delicate; they had two parties to consider, the patient himself, and the public, which must not be exposed to the evil of persons who may become violent and dangerous being allowed to wander at large. What was to be done? There was one point to which he wished to direct attention with reference to this portion of the subject, and that was, the fact that no more frequent cause of insanity existed than was found in intoxication; the number of persons who were confined in lunatic asylums, and whose insanity originated in drunkenness, was very great, and would surprise any person who was not aware of the effects of this habit. In a majority of cases, a few days' curative treatment produced a cure; but then the patient relapsing into former habits became again insane, and underwent a series of repeated cures and repeated relapses; in many instances such persons, if set at liberty, endangered not only their own lives but those of others; this was one of the most difficult points to adjudicate. He (the noble

Lord) had frequently urged upon the House, and especially in his Motion upon Education, the frightful consequences of inebriety— a habit fostered among the people as much by the system of things we permitted, and the temptations to which we suffered them to be exposed, as by their own tendencies.

He would now call the attention of the House to the state of Wales with respect to pauper lunatics. In 1843, by the Poor Law Returns, the number of Welsh pauper lunatics was 1,177. Of these thirty-six were in English county asylums, forty-one in licensed houses in England, ninety in union workhouses, and 1,010 living with their friends. Many of these were in a wretched condition. The Commissioners stated—

"It has been represented to us that many of the Welsh lunatics who have been in the English asylums have been very violent, and have been sent to them in a wretched and most neglected condition."

He (Lord Ashley) had been charged for having included South Wales in a reproach that belonged only to the north; but what was the fact? In a letter from South Wales, one of the Commissioners, now on a visitation, stated—

"We have met with one case which we think most atrocious. A. B. was sent to the Hereford Asylum from near Brecon, on Nov. 28, 1843. She died on January 30; she was in such a shocking state that the proprietor wished not to admit her; she had been kept chained in the house of a married daughter. From being long chained in a crouching posture, her knees were forced up to her chin, and she sat wholly upon her heels and her hips, and considerable excoriation had taken place where her knees pressed upon her stomach. She could move about, and was generally maniacal. When she died, it required very considerable dissection to get her pressed into her coffin! This might be taken as a sample of Welsh lunatics."

But it had been urged as a reason for not building lunatic asylums in Wales, that the pauper lunatics could be easily provided for in the English lunatic asylums, and in consequence it had not been attempted to institute a curative system in that country. This appeared to him, and would, no doubt, appear to every one to be a great cruelty. "The greatest of all cruelties," said Dr. Lloyd Williams, in speaking of this subject, "was to send the wretched pauper to a people whose language he could not understand;" and the general result was that the lunatic—whose state of mind, in general, was characterised by suspicion of all who approached him, not being able to understand the language of those around him, or to communicate with them—became excited and inflamed, and passed from the incipient or curable stage of insanity to confirmed lunacy. It was true that the foundation of an asylum had been lately laid at Denbigh; but the present activity of all parties must be ascribed in great measure to the inquiry which had been instituted by the Commission which had travelled throughout the country, and which had shown that it was the determination of Parliament not to permit these crying evils any longer to go unchecked and unredressed.

He now came to the criminal lunatics, the number of whom in April, 1843, was 257, distributed in the following manner :—In gaols, 33; in Bethlehem Hospital, 85; and in various asylums, 139. With respect to those criminals who were confined in the various private asylums, he would put it to the House whether it was not an improper and unnecessary aggravation of their miseries towards the other lunatics to subject them to confinement in the same place and under the same regulations as criminal lunatics—he spoke not of crimes of a lighter dye, but of those of whom some had committed the most atrocious crimes, such as murder and detestable offences. He assured the House it was felt by such lunatics to be a serious hardship that they should have to associate with these persons : the regulations, also, which were enforced in those places where criminals were confined were more severe than elsewhere, and their severity was felt by all the lunatics alike. They were likewise debarred from much indulgence which, under other circumstances, their melancholy situation would have procured for them.

The noble Lord then proceeded to say that the whole course of experience, and the judgment of all the most enlightened and humane men who had reflected on the subject, went to establish the necessity of instituting and maintaining the most vigilant system of frequent visitation. It was in itself a most salutary mode of executing a duty so essential to the comfort of the unhappy objects whose welfare was concerned, while it afforded the opportunity of bringing to bear upon those institutions the influence of public opinion and public notoriety, and of exposing their administration to praise or blame. Now it was believed, that, within the metropolitan districts of late years, vigilance had generally been exercised; but he could not say the same in the provincial districts; an exception could be made in favour of the county asylums, where the visiting justices had shown the greatest attention, and in some few, though very few, of the borough and rural asylums. In general this duty had been shamefully neglected. It would be needless for him to detain the House by enumerating facts that spoke for themselves; for if the parties to whom the duty of visitation had been entrusted had discharged their office with but common vigilance, the Commissioners would never have been able to have collected such materials for the Report that had been laid on the table. But he should like to state to the House the beneficial effects of continual visitation. He would mention a case, which he felt warranted in doing from a sense of justice to the proprietor of a very great establishment in this town, whose asylum was the original cause of the Commission of Inquiry being appointed in 1818, but whose asylum now presented, as far as it was possible for an institution of that nature to present, a most agreeable and a most consolatory picture of what might be done by vigilant inspection. He spoke of Dr. Warburton's asylum at Bethnal Green. He remembered that the state of that asylum was so bad, that in 1826 a Commission of Inquiry was instituted, when scenes of the most cruel and disgusting nature were revealed, which made one shudder at the very recital of them. He remembered well the sounds that assailed his ear, and the sights that shocked his eye, when visiting that abode of the most wretched. But what was that asylum now? Altogether changed. There was, however, an original and inherent sin in all private asylums, because they must be made to yield a profit to the keeper. But Dr. Warburton had expended large sums to make improvements in his establishment. He had extended his grounds for affording opportunities of exercise, and had adopted every means for the amelioration and care of his patients. As a proof of the very great change in the system adopted at that asylum, he (Lord Ashley) would simply mention that, whereas, in 1828, there was commonly from 150 to 200 of the patients restrained by leg-locks, chains, and other fetters—certainly during the night —in 1844 there were out of 582 patients only five whose violence rendered this species of restriction necessary; and even the confinement or coercion resorted to was of the most moderate description, and, in the opinion of the visiting officers, most necessary. He would point to that case as to a sample of the salutary influence which was exercised by watching the proceedings carried on in these places of confinement, which but for such constant vigilance would again become dens of iniquity and oppression.

Sir, these subjects may be dull, and want the light and shade of more exciting topics; but the expense which is incurred, the numbers that suffer, and the nature of their sufferings will, perhaps, justify the present demand upon your time and patience. The House possesses the means of applying a real and a speedy remedy. These unhappy persons are outcasts from all the social and domestic affections of private life—nay, more, from all its cares and duties—and have no refuge but in the laws. You can prevent, by the agency you shall appoint, as you have in many instances prevented, the recurrence of frightful cruelties; you can soothe the days of the incurable, and restore many sufferers to health and usefulness.. For we must not run away with the notion that even the hopelessly mad are dead to all capacity of intellectual or moral exertion—quite the reverse; their feelings, too, are painfully alive—I have seen them writhe under supposed contempt, while a word of kindness and respect would kindle their whole countenance into an expression of joy. Their condition appeals to our highest sympathies,

"Majestic, though in ruin;"

for though there may be, in the order of a merciful Providence, some compensating dispensation which abates within, the horrors manifested without, we must judge alone by what we see; and I trust, therefore, that I shall stand excused, though I have consumed so much of your valuable time, when you call to mind that the motion is made on behalf of the most helpless, if not the most afflicted, portion of the human race.

## *Legislation for the Labouring Classes.*

ON the evening of the 26th of October, Lord Ashley met the Lancashire Central Short Time Committee, and a few of their friends, at the Brunswick Hotel, where considerable difficulty was experienced by the committee in preventing the room from being crowded.

Lord Ashley said: Gentlemen, I now rise, with feelings of unusual gratification, to thank you for the address which has just been presented to me. I may say that I am more than satisfied with those expressions of thanks and renewed confidence contained in the document which I now hold in my hands. It is quite as much as I can expect for any past services I may have rendered in this good cause; but I have much more to require for the future than a mere approval of my own conduct. I have to require at your hands, that you will persevere in demanding this measure of justice for your children, in the same spirit of respectful but determined entreaty which has hitherto characterized the whole of your operations. Gentlemen, I must, in this stage of our proceeding this evening, express, in your presence, the obligations both you and I are under to my friend—for as such I am proud to call him—I mean your delegate to London during the last session of Parliament, and whom you have chosen, on this occasion, to put this address into my hands. I have had many opportunities of judging of his zeal and efficiency, and I assure you that very much of our success in the last session of Parliament is attributable to his services, and those of his worthy colleague; nor should I be doing my duty, when, if in Manchester, did I omit to mention, with the greatest respect, the names of some excellent friends to this cause, and to whose efforts in former years the present position of the question is in no small degree attributable. I do not think that, in the town of Manchester, the name of your best and earliest friend, Nathaniel

Gould, can ever be forgotten.  After him came that great and good man, who is now gone to his rest, I mean the late Michael Thomas Sadler—a man designed by God to promote this cause at a time when good, courageous, and powerful minds were alone adequate to the task, and without whose preliminary labours, I hesitate not to say that my efforts would have been altogether unavailing.  Gentlemen, that man must never be forgotten.  But there are others whose services must not be passed over.  I trust I shall never omit to mention the name of John Wood, of Bradford; for if ever there was Christianity in the heart of man, it is to be found in that excellent person.  He has ever stood your friend, sparing neither toil nor money; and I can tell you that at this moment his zeal is as warm, and his spirits as unbroken, as on the very first day he undertook to mix himself up with this mighty question.  Surely, among your allies in Lancashire, your minds will recur to the names of Mr. Brotherton and Mr. Fielden.  Their services to your cause in Parliament are beyond commendation.  They have ever, since the first day I was engaged in this matter, been to me, in all its stages, the most staunch and untiring friends.  There are two other friends to be named with deep gratitude—Mr. Oastler and Mr. Bull.  Mr. Oastler I have lately seen, and I know that his feelings are unchanged on this subject; and I am told that Mr. Bull is as warm-hearted and as vigorous as he ever was in your cause.  I have thought it right, being in Manchester, and at a meeting of the workpeople, to make honourable mention of those men who, when the question was surrounded with greater hazards than it is at present, did not fear to come forward and declare in the face of contempt, and prejudice, and power, that, by the aid of God's blessing, they would strive against every difficulty, and persevere until they had brought the struggle to a successful termination.

Let us now consider the position of the measure at the present time.  Just bear in mind this important fact, that from the very first hour it was mooted in Parliament to the present day it has continually advanced, by slow degrees, it is true, yet by safe and certain improvements.  It has struck root downwards, and be assured it will soon bear fruit upwards.  If this be so (and who can doubt it?) then I say there is great cause to rejoice in the progress which has been made; and if you are of the same mind as when I first began the measure, and as resolved as you were then, that it is indispensable to your physical and moral welfare, you would be wrong to distrust the Providence which watches over you.  There is every reason to hope that the day is not far distant when our labours will be brought to a happy issue; and that the women and children of this great empire will, God helping them, eventually enjoy these social and domestic blessings which, for so many years, we have been seeking to obtain. Gentlemen, I should like to point out to you, in a few words, what are the advantages that we have gained since we first began to stir in this question. I have had occasion, in my tour through these districts, to address my friends; and I have asked them to tax their memories, and contrast the present state of the mills with what it was sixteen years ago. Why, gentlemen, if you consider your position now as compared with that period, you could scarcely believe you were living under the same system. In the act which we obtained last session of Parliament, there were provisions which ought to repay both you and me for all the exertions we have made since we first began our labours. The first is an enactment for children of tender years—judge by yourselves—you know what a blessing it would have been to you had your labour in youth been limited to six hours a day; what an inexpressible advantage had two or three hours each day been assigned for wholesome instruction!—what a benefit if in early life you should have had two or three hours left for healthy recreation and enjoyment! You know well what a blessing all this would have been to you, and therefore you have great cause to lift up your hearts to God, and thank him for the mercy now extended to your children. There is another clause in this bill to which I shall briefly allude; you must know, from sad experience, how numerous and cruel are the accidents, deaths, and mutilations that occur in these districts from the unguarded state of machinery;—it is no trifling point to have gained by the present law that, so far as human provision can go, your lives and limbs will be protected against these sad mischiefs. The legislature has said that your persons shall not be exposed to unnecessary danger; that any neglect on the part of the proprietors which shall have caused injury to any human being shall be prosecuted at the public expense. This is a novel, but it is almost a divine principle of protection to those who cannot protect themselves. I will not here further allude to it, as I wish to avoid saying anything needlessly, which, by recurring to the past, may lead to exasperation; I have simply mentioned the circumstance now, to show you what strides we have already made in the right direction. But there is another provision contained in the present bill, founded on justice and nature; one which, I feel convinced, will work out very great and beneficial results. I speak of the clause which provides that no woman, of whatever age, shall be worked in any mill or factory more than twelve hours a day. I wish that the limitation had been reduced much lower; but this is a good point gained; and it is a consolation to know that respect has been paid to the claims and weakness of the sex, to such a degree as that no woman may, in any circumstances, be forced to toil more than twelve hours in the day. This provision alone is, I have declared already, and I declare again, worth all the labour, and anxiety, and sacrifice, we have endured since we commenced the advocacy of this question to the present time.

Now, my object in coming here is, first, to explain any little obscurity that there might appear to be as to the mode I adopted in dealing with the subject in the last session of Parliament; and next, that I may both give and receive counsel in the present state of the question. How far explanation is necessary as to the course I adopted is for you to determine; and I shall be ready and most willing to explain any matter which may appear obscure, and answer any questions which any operative may think proper to put to me; but at present I hardly think it advisable at this hour of the night, after the toil you have endured during the day, to detain you with lengthy details of matters that even then may be difficult to be understood by those who are not conversant with the forms of the House of Commons. It will perhaps be sufficient to say, that it was necessary for me to adopt the course I pursued in order to preserve the bill which is now become law, and to obtain which had required great care and watchfulness. It was in constant jeopardy, and a false step on our part would have caused the loss of it, perhaps, for ever. Here was our difficulty; we had to combine two objects,—the preservation of the bill, and the affirmation of our own great principle of the ten hours. It is my firm conviction that I have succeeded; the bill is now the law of the land; and the principle of ten hours is as fresh and vigorous as at any period, and scarcely even retarded by the prodigious exertions of official power.

Gentlemen, it has been said that I am the enemy of the factory masters and of the factory system: allow me to say a few words on this point. To call me the enemy of the factory masters is to call me both insane and unchristian; there is neither justice, nor principle, nor common sense in being the enemy of any one class of gentlemen, and particularly of a class of gentlemen which presents as many instances of intelligence and virtue as any other in this community. I have never been the enemy of factory masters; I should be ashamed to entertain any hostility against that class amongst whom I know so many that are ornaments to our country; men who have exhibited a degree of generosity and benevolence that I have seldom found equalled amongst other classes of the community. In so large a body of men there must be, as in other classes of society, some far better than others; some, no doubt, very greatly inferior. If all factory masters were like some that I could name, there would be no necessity for the legislature to interfere; but in this, as in every other case, laws of the statute book are made to restrain the vicious, who will not be restrained by the laws of humanity and justice. But if ever I had been the enemy of the manufacturers (which I deny), I have, since the commencement of my present tour in these districts, experienced sufficient of their courtesy to force, were it necessary, a change of opinion. I must say, that to whatever place I have gone, I have been received by all the masters whom I have waited on, and by those even who differ from me in my views upon this question, with kindness, and offers even of hospitality. They have given me all and every information I could desire, and with the utmost willingness. For me to admit, then, that I am the enemy of the whole class, would be to allow that I am justly chargeable not only with the greatest folly, but the greatest wickedness. Now, it would be almost equally foolish and wicked in me were I to call myself the enemy of the factory system. I am the enemy of its abuses, but not of the system itself. Why, it would be the very extreme of absurdity for any one to call himself the enemy of a system by which hundreds of thousands of human beings have obtained, and must, moreover, continue to obtain, an honest livelihood. Did I attempt to endanger its existence, I should consider myself the greatest enemy of the working people, who derive from it all their maintenance. No, gentlemen, I am only the enemy of its abuses; and those abuses we seek to remedy. Let us but shorten the term of daily labour, giving, thereby, to those employed the means of enjoying their inalienable right of time for self-improvement and domestic life, and I believe that, in the present state of the country, the factory system might thus be made the channel of comforts and even blessings to this large community. When I have contemplated a multitude of twelve or fourteen hundred people, congregated under a single roof, governed by the revolutions of a single engine, all within reach of daily intercourse, of watchful care, of every happy influence, I have often reflected what prodigious means of doing good had been placed by Providence in the hands of such employers. I do say, when I have contemplated one of these enormous buildings, alive with human beings, and under the authority of a single proprietor, I confess I have often said to myself—" I wish to God I were a factory owner." I do, indeed, believe that by such an instrumentality as this ancient sympathies might be revived, and ancient habits restored between master and man—a state of society so beautifully expressed in the book of Ruth, when " Boaz said unto the reapers, The Lord be with you. And they answered him and said, The Lord bless thee."

Now, just consider what and how valuable are the objects we seek. It is to purify the social system; to restore the woman to her domestic duties and the care of her family; to provide that the younger part may have time to learn what is necessary to fit them for their future stations in life; and that, as wives and mothers, they may have leisure to practise those duties which they shall have learned as children. It is to establish a better understanding between master and man; to allay heart-burnings and effect an interchange of conciliation. We seek to give men time for religious and intellectual improvement, for something beyond mere animal life. If such be the objects we have in view, we must surely consider the ways by which they are to be attained. You must ever bear in mind that you are immortal beings, in pursuit of certain ends now, yet of still higher ends hereafter. Though you have a right to demand this boon from the legislature, you are, at the same time, bound to demand it with forbearance. Ask whatever is fitting from your employers; but you will not forget that those things must also be asked for from higher sources—from Him who alone can give, turn the hearts of your opponents, and afterwards enable you, when you shall have received them, to use all for your own advantage and His glory. I may honestly assert that, were I not fully convinced that such were your intentions, and that such would be the result of our exertions, I, for one, would have nothing more to do with the conduct of this question. There are here and elsewhere various gentlemen who have long been your friends in this cause. Why do you suppose that we have been ready to undergo all this toil, and anxiety, and almost peril in your behalf ? Why do you suppose that I have been ready to break my political friendships, and sever many ancient connexions ? It is because we believed that these duties have been imposed upon us by our common Master. God has given me leisure and freedom from the necessity of daily toil; and I willingly therefore devote them to the service of those people who have neither the one, nor the other of these responsible gifts. But I will seize the occasion of impressing upon your minds that, if such be the character of these principles, you must look with reverence to the source from which they are derived. I cannot too often repeat it; it is my most fervent desire to impress upon you the solemn obligation, that, when you shall have obtained the measure you so earnestly pursue, you should turn it to the high purpose for which it has been sought by myself, and, I believe, by all your friends in Parliament and in the country. While you are respectfully soliciting from man that concession to which you are so justly entitled, I myself will never relax in my efforts, or compromise one jot of your righteous demands; I will persevere with an unbroken and determined spirit, until our labours shall have reached a happy consummation. But remember that your first request must be made to God, and your second to man; you will then go forward with resolution and strength, sure of ultimate success, and exhibiting, in the manner both of the pursuit, and of the enjoyment of such a happy issue, the high and patriotic example of a wise and an understanding people.

*Children in Calico Print-Works.*

# HOUSE OF COMMONS,

## February 18, 1845.

Speech on moving " That leave be given to bring in a Bill to regulate the Labour of Children in the Calico Print-Works of Great Britain and Ireland."

Lord Ashley rose to bring forward the motion of which he had given notice, and addressed the House to this effect :—Sir, the subject which I feel bound to submit to the consideration of the House is so much akin to others which I have had the honour to bring forward, that I fear I cannot promise anything in the way of novelty in the evidence I have to adduce, or in the arguments I shall derive from it; but, nevertheless, I do hope that the House will extend to me its patient indulgence while I lay before it the case of a large class of our fellow-subjects, whose claims have never yet been represented in this assembly. I am about to speak in behalf of a large body who have been much oppressed, and I may say, have been altogether forgotten; but whose interests not only are of great value to themselves, but, if taken in connection with those of their contemporary labourers, are calculated to have a powerful influence on the destinies of the empire.

It will be recollected that in the year 1840 I had the honour to move in this House for a commission to inquire into the employment of children in the various departments of labour. That commission made a very voluminous report; and in a summary of that report, from which I shall read a few extracts, they stated what was the condition of many thousands, I may almost say hundreds of thousands, of children. I do not here mean those employed in the factories, but those employed in the various trades and branches of labour in these realms, and who are compelled to commence labour at very tender years. There are instances of their beginning to work at the early age of 3 and 4 years; more between 5 and 6; and, in many instances, regular employment begins from 7 to 8, and in most instances, between 8 and 9. With respect to the employment of girls, the report states, that " A large proportion of the children and young persons employed in this branch of trade are girls, the proportion in Lancashire being upwards of one-third of the whole number under thirteen." It further appears from the report that the young girls work as long each day as the adults, which sometimes extends to 16, 17, and even 18 hours consecutively. Schools are wholly out of the reach of these poor children, in consequence of the early age at which they are set to work; and the result is, that the greatest demoralization prevails in those districts. This is the summary presented by the commissioners, and adduced from a close survey of large numbers employed in various trades in the realm.

Of all these cruel and pernicious employments—pernicious, I mean, in the extent to which they are carried on—only one has been brought under the consideration of the House. I had the honour of proposing to the House the removal of females from employment in collieries; but of all the trades and manufactures that have been inquired into, that is the only one with respect to which any measure of relief has been afforded, or any motion made. In all other respects nothing has been done,—or, rather, everything has been left undone; not one hour has been struck off from their term of labour,—not one hour added to their instruction. They have not had even the advantage of public opinion being awakened in their favour,—public opinion, which has such powerful influence when brought to bear on other cases, has been of no advantage to those on whose behalf I have ventured to come forward. I own I do not wonder at this reluctance when I consider the enormous labour it would require to wade through those ponderous folios of the evidence collected by the commissioners, to arrive at all the information they contain, and to drag to light those records of suffering, ignorance, and shame.

But it may perhaps be said that I myself am chargeable with this neglect; for it was my duty, being more cognizant of the evil, to endeavour to find a remedy. Undoubtedly it was more my duty than that of any other; but my excuse is, that I have lacked the opportunity, and it will not be denied that I have not had any great encouragement. I am, however, now prepared to take up the subject, and I do trust that in consideration of the urgency of the case, and also of the moderation of what I am about to propose, the House may be induced to give me a part, if not the whole, of what I ask on behalf of these young persons.

Now, I hope it will be borne in mind, throughout the whole of the discussion on this question, that I limit my demand entirely to children under the age of 13, which are children according to the definition of the Factory Act—a vast number of these children are females, and therefore entitled to the special protection of this House. Sir, I do not consider that in the exclusion of those of more advanced age from the operation of the measure which I shall propose either justice or humanity will be satisfied; but the demand which I now make is more in accordance with what I hope to obtain than with what I think to be just.

Calico printing, to which I beg now to call the attention of the House, is thus described in the commissioners' report:—" Calico printing, with its subsidiary processes of bleaching and dyeing, is carried on to the greatest extent in the cotton districts of Lancashire, Cheshire, Derbyshire, and the west of Scotland. There are also a few print-works near London, and several near Dublin." With respect to the age of the children employed, the report said:—" In Lancashire, Cheshire, and Derbyshire, instances occur in which children begin work in this employment as early as between 4 and 5, and several between 5 and 6 inclusive; many between 6 and 7, still more between 7 and 8, and a great majority between 8 and 9. Out of 565 children, taken indiscriminately from returns obtained from each section of this district, it appears that one child began work between 4 and 5; three between 5 and 6; 68 between 6 and 7; 133 between 7 and 8; 156 between 8 and 9; 127 between 9 and 10; 49 between 10 and 11; 26 between 11 and 12; and 2 between 12 and 13. In the east of Scotland children commence work at the same early ages." The Rev. John Dempster, Minister of Denny, states that infants may be seen at work as early as 5 years of age, having got at school little more than a knowledge of the alphabet, and that they go to a continuous employment at all ages, from 7 upwards. The Rev. J. A. Bonar states, " our common schools now often look like infant schools, from the paucity of older children." But the print-fields in Kent afford, in regard to infant labour, a remarkable exception to all others in the United Kingdom. In the works of Mr. Swaisland there were found only two girls and five boys, and in Mr. Applegath's, only six boys under 13 years of age.

There are instances in Ireland of children beginning work at 6; but, says the sub-commissioner, " out of 833 persons visited, only 109 were under 13 years of age." In Ireland the system presents, as I have shown, a remarkable contrast to the state of things in England, showing, as it does, a remarkable care for children of tender years. Now a word as to the numbers employed. From returns made from print-works in Lancashire, Cheshire, and Derbyshire, the children under 13 years amount to 5,646. "But," says the report, "it must be borne in mind that these returns give only the number of children employed at the time the return was made; and it has often happened that at that time half the tables in the works have been standing idle." But we can arrive at it by calculation; there are block tables in these establishments, each requiring one child, amounting to 8,156; long tables, each requiring two, 168; total, therefore, if the tables are in full work, 8,492. It is estimated that in the print-fields in the whole of Scotland there are teerers amounting to 5,000. "But this estimate," says the commissioner, "by no means includes the total number; . . . there are several other departments in which, though they commence somewhat later than as teerers, many children are employed. The works also at West Ham, in Essex, are on the largest scale, and those at Carshalton, in Surrey, are considerable." Total number, therefore, as stated in the report, 13,492. But this is confessedly much under the truth; and when we add the number employed in bleach-fields and calendering departments, sometimes detached from printing-works, we cannot put the whole numbers at less than 25,000,—and I have reason to believe, from inquiry that I have made, that this amount is under the reality.

I now beg leave to call the attention of the House to what must have an important effect on the moral and physical condition of those employed—I mean the state of the places in which this work is carried on. On this point the commissioners state:—"There is perhaps no description of manufacture in which the convenience and comfort of the places in which the various operations are carried on differ so materially in different establishments, and even in different departments of the same establishments as in calico-printing. . . . With the view of lessening, as far as practicable, the noxiousness of these operations, some proprietors spare neither trouble nor expense to secure proper ventilation, temperature, and drainage; but in great numbers of cases those conditions of the place of work are deplorably neglected." Here are samples. The hooking and lashing-out rooms, and the singeing-rooms, are very disagreeable places, the air of which is filled with dust, and in the latter with small burnt particles, which irritate the eyes and nostrils exceedingly. "On going into this room with a friend," says the sub-commissioner, "we were both instantly affected, our eyes began to smart, and we felt a ticklish sensation in the throat and nostrils, much the same as that produced by taking snuff. We noticed, too, that all the children who were employed in this room were more or less affected with inflammation and copious discharge of the eyes." I specify these things, not as arguments against the employment of children in these works, which may probably be unavoidable, but as good and cogent reasons against the sad prolongation of labour in such localities. Again, " the temperature of the work-shops usually varies from 65 to 80 degrees. . . . The stoves are often overheated, and I have," he adds, " occasionally seen them red-hot. The temperature to which the stenters are exposed is very high, from 85 to 100 degrees. I have found them, between 11 and 12 years old, working 14 hours. The temperature at which," says the commissioner, " I usually found these stoves, when the girls were filling them, was 110 degrees, or fever heat, and the steam rising from the wet goods as they are hung up is still more suffocating and oppressive than dry heat would be." I will now read some of the evidence on this point :—" Robert Crawford, block-maker, states, that in the kiln, where the block runs through on rollers to dry the colours, no one can work above three, or at most five minutes. Mary Moody and Mary Maxwell, stove-girls, state that the girls often faint from exhaustion caused by the heat. John Rodger, machine-printer, states that the girls who attend on the dash-wheel have to stand with the feet and petticoats always wet, and that this in severe weather causes great hardship. Mr. David Young, surgeon, of Bridgetown, says, that from his experience as a medical man, he knows that at certain periodical seasons the dash-wheel produces very injurious effects on women. But a far different account is given of Mr. Swaisland's works in Kent; there the whole of the premises, particularly the room where the teerers work, are clean, spacious, lofty, and well ventilated, heated in winter by warm-water pipes, and thoroughly drained. The same is said of the works of Mr. Applegath, and at West Ham, in Essex;" showing, therefore, that health and cleanliness may be consulted by care and atten-tion, and without any formidable diminution of profits.

Now, Sir, to give a complete picture of the case I have to present to the House, I must likewise show them what is the nature of the employment in which these children are engaged. It is quite true that the labour is not in itself heavy; it is the continuity of it during so many hours that produces a debilitating effect on both body and mind. Sir, I quote from the Report of the Commissioners :—" The work of the teerers does not require much muscular exertion, while it admits of some variety, as they occasionally bring the colour from the colour-shop, and it is also their duty to wash the blocks and cleanse the sieves; but, on the other hand, their exertion of attention must be almost unremitting; they must keep their arms in a continual rotatory motion, and during the whole time they are at work they must be upon their feet."

And now consider what are the hours of work. "The regular hours of work in the different departments of the print-field are rarely less than 12, including the time allowed for meals, but it is by no means uncommon in all the districts for children from 5 to 6 years old to be kept at work for 14, and even 16, hours consecutively." "In those of Lancashire, Cheshire, and Derbyshire, the nominal (the nominal, be it observed, not the actual) hours of work are 12, including meal hours; but there can scarcely be said to be any regular hours, for all the block-printers are in the habit of working overtime, and as they are paid by the piece, and are independent of machinery, they are at liberty to work what hours they please." Now, what is the testimony on this subject of the persons employed in these works? These matters, I fear, must be stated, though I am perfectly aware that, in bringing forward evidence of this kind, I am trespassing on the patience of the House. But I would rather lay before you a true picture of facts, than indulge in any general rhetorical display that might, after all, leave you ignorant of the exact truth. Thomas Sidbread, block-printer, says—"I began to work between 8 and 9 o'clock on Wednesday night, but the boy had been sweeping the shop from Wednesday morning. You will scarcely believe it, but it is true, I never left the shop till 6 o'clock on the Saturday morning, and I had never stopped working all that time; I was knocked up, and the boy was almost insensible." "There were men there, and children too, who came on a Monday morning and stayed till Saturday night." Henry Richardson states—"At 4 o'clock I began to work, and worked all that day, all the next night, and until 10 o'clock the following day. I had only one teerer during that time, and I dare say he would be about 12 years old. . . . I have known children made ill by working too long hours; the boy that worked for me at the Adelphi was sometimes unable to come to his work from being sick with over working." In the west of Scotland "the regular hours for work are from 6 to 6, with two intervals for meals, sometimes of one hour each, leaving about ten working hours." "I have been hitherto," says the sub-commissioner, "describing the regular hours; but these, I am sorry to say, are but too frequently prolonged by over hours. . . . Two or three hours of over work a day is, however, not uncommon, making on the

whole 14 or 15 hours, including meals." The sub-commissioner
adds—"Instances were found of girls working at the steam cans
for 38 hours in succession." In some establishments, however,
these long hours are not allowed. Mr. T. Greig, of the firm of
Watson, Jackson, and Greig, stated to the sub-commissioner that
in three years the utmost number of hours actually worked
by any one was 13 per day, and the utmost for the children was
10 a day, the average not being above nine-and-a-half. Does not
that prove most undoubtedly that the protracted hours I have referred to are not necessary? Does it not show that the profits of
the employer need not be derived from the exhaustion of the
child? It is undoubtedly true that this labour is not continued
throughout the whole year. The trade has its flushes and its
pauses; such is the technical expression to denote periods of
great demand and cessation from labour. But this excess on
either side is highly injurious—extreme toil or absolute idleness;
the one cannot be considered as a healthy compensation for the
other. It must, moreover, be borne in mind that the print-works
are always most busy during the winter, in preparation for the
spring trade—at that time of year when toil and exposure are the
least endurable.

But of all the features of this employment, that which I am
now about to describe is the most abominable—I speak of the
practice of night work. The commissioner says—"The occasional
practice of night work in print-grounds in all the districts is
universal, while in many it is so general and constant that it may
be regarded as a part of the regular system of carrying on this
branch of the trade. In Lancashire, Cheshire, and Derbyshire,
night work is stated to be so common that those establishments
in which it does not exist are exceptions to the general practice.
In working in the night, relays of printers and children are
almost invariably used; the contrary is rarely the case except
where there is a difficulty in procuring children." "Relays are
sometimes from 6 to 6, or 12 o'clock in the day to 12 o'clock at
night (called twelving), or from 4 in the morning till 12, and from
12 to 9 at night." Now just hear what are the depositions of the
young persons themselves as to the period they work, as well as
to the effects produced on them. The first I shall mention is
Margaret Isherwood, eight years old. She says—"Before she
was six years and a half old she worked all night three or four
nights a week." Henry Hughes, nearly 9, teerer, says—"I have
worked all night many a time. I have worked all day and all
night too, without stopping, except for meals." Julia Cunliffe,
aged 10, says—"I came on Friday morning at 7 o'clock, worked all

day and all night until Saturday morning at 6 o'clock. . . . I took snuff to keep myself awake." Ellen Radcliffe, aged 10, says—"I was once a teerer, but I could not stand the work. I once worked three nights teering blue colour, but it made me sick and giddy in my head." Margaret Morris, going 10, says—"Many times I worked all day and all night too. Sometimes I have gone at 8 o'clock in the morning, worked all day and all night until 8 o'clock the next morning." "Robert Kellat, block-printer, has seen a child named Hellin, seven years old, work from 6 o'clock in the morning until 11 o'clock at night for a week together on an average; he teered for his father, who worked him quite beyond his strength." "I have known a man," says William Archer, a foreman, "work three days and three nights, without ever going home, and he had the same teerer all the time." In the west of Scotland night work appears to be very common occasionally in almost all establishments. In the east of Scotland the evidence shows that night work is not uncommon; but in Ireland, which again appears to the greatest advantage, it is said—"In general there is no night work in the print-fields of Ireland. . . . There are exceptions to this, though rare."

With respect to treatment, the commissioners state, that the "tendency of the improvements progressively made in the processes of calico-printing has been to diminish the labour of the children, and to lessen their danger of injuring their work; at the same time there has been a growing disapprobation on the part of the workpeople of any oppressive treatment of the children. . . . Severe punishment, which was formerly common, is now scarcely known." This, Sir, is matter for rejoicing, and, so far as it goes, we thankfully accept it. But here comes the fearful and important consideration for the Parliament and the country—the physical suffering is bad enough, but the moral degradation is worse. The commissioners state, and this is their general report, that "the evidence collected in the Lancashire district tends to show that the children employed in this occupation are excluded from the opportunities of education; that this necessarily contributes to the growth of an ignorant and vicious population; that the facility of obtaining early employment for children in print-fields empties the day schools; that parents without hesitation sacrifice the future welfare of their children through life for the immediate advantage or gratification obtained by the pittance derived from the child's earnings." This is not my language; it is the language of the report. But this is not all. The evil is a growing one. The state of things is becoming worse. Mr. Emery, master of the school at Disley, says—"When I first came into this district, which is now many years since, my scholars stayed much longer with me; and I then had a chance of making something of them. On looking at the number of scholars, it appeared that they had diminished one half since 1832, notwithstanding the remarkable increase of population in this district within the last ten years." Mr. Emery attributes the falling off of the school "to the facility of getting employment at high wages for very young children, and to the indifference of the parents about the education of their children. . . . The block-printers," he adds, " can make from 20s. to 30s. a week, and of course they might afford, at 2d. a week each, to send their children to school." The testimony to this effect is almost general. " Of the means of instruction," says the commissioner for Scotland, " that are provided, the children of the manufacturing population generally, and those employed in the print-fields in particular, cannot avail themselves, on account of the early age at which children are removed from school, and the long hours during which their labour is continued." Again: "Of many of the children in the print-grounds of Lancashire, and especially of those who have been the least educated, it is stated that they appear to have no sense of moral obligation; they are generally not trustworthy, and are given to pilfering, lying, and fighting. . . . Of the same class in Scotland, it is stated that the ease with which parents are enabled to rid themselves of the burden of their children's support weakens all parental and domestic ties, saps the foundation of morality, and stops all progress in the mental and moral culture of the children." Well, then, with these facts before them, with this concurrent testimony from all parts, is it surprising that the Central Board should have reported, in language to which I must implore the serious attention of the House—"That the girls are prevented, by their early removal from home and the day-schools to be employed in labour, from learning needlework, and from acquiring those habits of cleanliness, neatness, and order, without which they cannot when they grow up to womanhood economise their husbands' earnings, or give to their homes any degree of comfort—and this general want of the qualifications of a housewife in the women of this class is stated by clergymen, teachers, medical men, employers, and other witnesses, to be one great and universally prevailing cause of distress and crime among the working classes ?"

I shall not weary the House with any further evidence as to the moral and physical condition of children engaged in the print-works. But I will ask if that be a state of things which should be allowed to continue ? Any effort we may make may, in the outset, be imperfect, on account of the difficulties that stand in the way of all legislation on such a subject; but at any rate we may strike at the main evil, and correct the law as far as we can. In spite of all obstacles, I will not shrink from proposing a remedy. In the first instance, I shall propose the total abolition of night work for all females of whatsoever ages, and all of both sexes under thirteen, to commence in October next. I am quite sure that in this I am not proposing anything that can be in the least injurious to the interests either of the workmen or their masters. If the House will allow me, I will state on what evidence I found that opinion. Morally and physically, nothing can be more injurious than this night work. W. Archer, a foreman, was asked—"Did night work affect your health?" and the answer was —"Yes; it is the worst part of our trade. I always felt very unwell in the morning—almost the same as if I had been drunk over night." "What is your opinion of night work?" "It is my opinion that night work is the greatest injury, both to the children and printers; night work ought to be stopped." John Williams, operative, says—"The working by gas injures the eyes. . . . More affected at morning after working by night, than in the night after working by daylight." Daniel Hawthorn, gas-engineer, says—"Children always look pale and sickly when they have been working night and day." A deputation of calico printers say—"Night work is doubly distressing on this account, where a great quantity of gas is burning in a room badly ventilated; the air is hurtful to breathe, and bad for the constitution. Children of delicate constitutions are obliged, in a long succession of night work, to desist from coming to the shop, otherwise they die off." "When children first come to work, from being robust they will become pallid and weak." "Almost all classes of witnesses in all the districts concur in stating that the effect of night work is most injurious, physically and morally, on the workpeople in general, and on the children in particular." The Rev. J. Harbottle, Baptist minister, says—"I consider the unseasonable hours during which young persons are oftentimes employed, as unfitting them for any improvement in mind, as well as exceedingly injurious to health." "One general effect is, that when any meeting takes place of an evening for moral and religious purposes, the workpeople seem quite overcome with the effect of having been at work so many hours, young persons especially."

Sir, I may venture to assert that night work is neither necessary nor advantageous to the trade. The Report says—"No countervailing advantage is ultimately obtained from it even by

the employers." Again : " In working in the night it is generally
considered that more work is spoiled than in the day, and an
abatement is made for bad work." Mr. Robert Hargreaves, of
Accrington, one of the highest authorities in the kingdom, says—
" I do not like the principle of night work; there is danger of
fire, and a necessity for a double set of superintendents. The
work done is much worse." The sub-commissioner for the west
of Scotland reports, that . " The great majority of printers would
not object to a prohibition of night work for children and young
persons." Mr. Gilbert Innes, manager of Cogan print-works, " is
very strongly of opinion that over hours are injurious both to
workmen and employers." He " considers that a law reducing
and regulating hours of work in print-fields would put all on a
footing, and so would soon produce no inconvenience." Mr. Kennedy, the sub-commissioner for Lancashire, Cheshire, and Derbyshire, reported—and this is a most valuable statement, to which
I should desire to call the especial attention of the House—" I
have been favoured," says he, " by an influential house with an
inspection of those books which show rates of production in their
roller printing-machines, during a period of four months, when
they worked fifteen hours a day. . . . The proportion of spoiled
work from the beginning of the first to the end of the fourth
month actually doubled itself, whilst the average production of
the machines decreased from 100 to 90 per cent. In fact, the
amount of spoiled work increased. to such an alarming degree,
that the parties referred to felt themselves completely obliged to
shorten the hours of labour to avoid loss, and as soon as the
alteration was made, the amount of spoiled work sank to its
former level. I am informed," he adds, " the general experience
of this branch of trade is, that under whatever circumstances
night work is tried, the produce is distinguished by a larger
share than ordinary of spoiled work." Now, just consider the
whole force of this statement ; observe the false economy, the
actual waste, of excessive toil, and disregard of the times and
seasons that nature has appointed—a large decrease in the quantity produced ; a still larger deterioration in the quality of the
article—the causes of all this mischief, night work and over toil,
are removed, and then the good and the marred produce return
to their former proportions. I have also permission to read the
following extracts from the letters of two most respectable and
intelligent persons. Mr. John Graham, superintendent of the
works at Mayfield, says—" So far as we are concerned at Mayfield,
it would be advisable to give up night work for women, young
persons, and children, night work being understood as those hours

between 10 P.M. and 6 A.M." Mr. David Cooper, of Primrose Works, Clithero, observes—"I allude only to Messrs. Thomson's works. There may be other printers who may be unable to adopt such regulations." He says that Mr. Thompson for many years carried on night work, but had for years been induced to give it up, partly from feelings of humanity, and partly from motives of economy, because he found it injurious to his workpeople, and because the amount of spoiled work was so considerable. It is clear, therefore, that a law may be proposed with benefit to all, to save these unfortunate children from the effects of such a system.

I would next propose a reduction of the hours of labour in behalf of those under a certain age—under the age of thirteen, for instance. I am bound to state that those two gentlemen whom I last quoted—Mr. David Cooper and Mr. John Graham—do not recommend a reduction of the hours of labour—they confine their recommendation to the abolition of night work; but I hold, Sir, that the evil of excessive labour on the part of these young persons is so manifest and extensive, that it must not be left without a check. I propose, therefore, that in October, 1846, allowing thereby nearly two years before the operation of the enactment, none under thirteen years of age shall be allowed to work more than eight hours a day for six days in the week, or more than twelve hours a day for three alternate days in the week. I shall propose also, in conformity with the provisions of the Factory Bill, that two hours a day of schooling should be required with respect to those children who work eight hours a day for six days in the week; and three hours of schooling on alternate days with respect to those who work twelve hours a day for three days in the week. Should more labour be required, it may be obtained by relays, to which the trade is accustomed.

I do not know whether it is necessary for me to notice the various arguments which I may anticipate as likely to be urged against my proposed provision with respect to the education of the children. In the first instance, I may be told that parents may be safely trusted to attend to the physical and moral welfare of their children. Now, in answer to this I may refer to the results of the investigations of the commissioners, which prove the utter carelessness of the parents of those children in reference to their education, even when they have ample means of providing for that education. Mr. Kennedy says—"One of the chief points for observation is the carelessness of the parents as to the future welfare of their offspring, as shown by depriving them of the advantages of education. This they invariably do without reference

to their ample means of supporting them." Commissioners were
sent to examine all the various mining and manufacturing districts ; and one of them, Mr. Fellowes (Derbyshire), states the
sole wish of parents examined by him to be to make all they could
of their children at as early an age as possible, without regarding
their future welfare.     Mr. Austin (Lancashire) says, parents
will not avail themselves of the many facilities offered in that
district for the education of their children ; they will not send
them to school.   In Scotland, all classes of witnesses state that
the difficulty is to get the parents to send their children to school ;
and as respects Wales, it is stated that the parents estimate even
one penny a week as more than education is worth.   But perhaps
I may be told that poverty is the cause of this reluctance on the
part of the parents ; but attend to the statement made by that
intelligent individual, Mr. Symons.   He, on the contrary, says
that the evidence of all witnesses shows that when trade improves
fewer children will remain in school, and that sensual gratifica-
tions are far oftener the obstruction to education than poverty.
Mr. Fletcher says, that the earnings of the population in the
neighbourhood of Oldham in prosperous times are amply sufficient
to enable parents to pay for their children's education ; but they
will take nothing but Sunday-school instruction, because it does
not interfere with work and costs nothing.   Mr. Grainger says,
many of the parents are utterly indifferent to the moral and
physical welfare of their offspring ; and it would be a serious
error to mistake this indifference for desperation arising from
distress and misery.   He adds, that in the best of times, when in
Birmingham, for example, many mechanics were earning from
2*l.* to 5*l.* or 6*l.* a week, instead of making provision for the future
and promoting the welfare of their families, these large wages
were but too often wasted in vice and extravagance.   Now, Sir,
in this deplorable state much of the population is being brought
up.   It must, I think, be evident to every one, that unless parents
themselves receive the benefit of education, they will be indifferent
to the education of their progeny ; and yet we are bringing up a
race of parents in an entirely demoralized condition, and who
will be ignorant of the great advantages which must ever accompany religious improvement ; the present generation of these
children is utterly neglected, physically and morally ; and we
find, in consequence, that such a complication of evils has
been suffered to accumulate, that even the powers of this House
will scarcely be able to extricate the population from the evils
that surround them.

Sir (continued the noble Lord), I have very great fears that, not only in the delivery of individual speeches, but in the frequent reproduction of subjects of the same class, I shall become exceedingly tedious to the House. It may, therefore, be some compensation to know that I suffer nearly as much as I inflict. The labour of research, the extent of correspondence, the trespass on the time of this House, cheered by little or no prospect of success —may be urged as an adequate proof that these endeavours have not been wantonly undertaken; but where the interests are so serious, much may and ought to be hazarded; and it is better to fail in the attempt than never to have aspired to such a measure.

Sir, I am at a loss to conceive on what grounds an opposition will be made to my proposal; it cannot be said that I have selected one interest only as the object of attack—this is the third in the series that I have ventured to reform. I have, too, I hope, been careful, for such at least was my intention, in my language respecting the conduct and character of individual print masters; I have endeavoured to expose the pernicious system of their labour, but without imputing to them either the authorship or the encouragement of the mischiefs that afflict the present generation—the evil has, as it were, come down to them by inheritance.

Now, in every debate on similar subjects it has been invariably conceded that protection should be extended to young children; their inexperience, their helplessness, the deep interest that the State was supposed to have in their moral and physical welfare extorted this admission. There may have been some, though very few, who thought differently, and believed that they might safely be left to the affectionate solicitude of parents and guardians; these objections were overruled, and the legislature has, in various enactments, asserted the principle for which I now contend; I ask no other—this bill, I must again observe, will affect young children only, those only of the age which the government, in the Factory Bill of 1833, protected by a limitation of eight hours of daily labour and regular attendance at school; a measure of unequal and imperfect success, but productive, nevertheless, of much moral and physical benefit to thousands of the workers.

Sir, in the various discussions on these kindred subjects, there has been a perpetual endeavour to drive us, who seek the aid of the law, from the point under debate, and taunt us with a narrow and one-sided humanity; I was told that there were far greater evils than those I had assailed, that I had left untouched much worse things. It was in vain to reply that no one could grapple with the whole at once. My opponents, on the first introduction of the Ten Hours' Bill, sent me to the collieries; when I invaded the collieries, I was referred to the print-works; from the print-works I know not to what I shall be sent, for can anything be worse? Yet, if I judge by what I have heard and read out of doors, I conclude that it will be to the Corn-laws; but let me appeal to the most zealous advocate for their abolition, and ask him what their repeal could do more for the benefit of the manufacturing classes than perpetuate the present state of commercial prosperity? We have cheap provisions and abundant employment, but what, nevertheless, is the actual condition of these children? The repeal of the Corn-laws would leave these infants as it found them, neither worse nor better, precisely in the condition in which they are in those countries where no Corn-laws prevail, in France or Belgium. Whatever it might do for others, it would do nothing for these; but I solemnly declare that, if I believed the removal of the impost would place these many thousands in a position of comfort, and keep them in it, I would, in spite of every difficulty, and in the face of every apprehension, vote at once for the entire abolition.

Sir, it has been said to me more than once, " Where will you stop?" I reply, without hesitation, " Nowhere, so long as any portion of this mighty evil remains to be removed." I confess that my desire and ambition are to bring all the labouring children of this empire within the reach and the opportunities of education, within the sphere (if they will profit by the offer) of happy and useful citizens. I am ready, so far as my services are of any value, to devote what little I have of energy, and all the remainder of my life to the accomplishment of this end; the labour would be great and the anxieties very heavy; but I fear neither the one nor the other; I fear nothing but defeat. I should cheerfully undertake it all had I but the hope of your countenance and support.

And who will deny that it is a matter well worthy of the time and deliberations of this august assembly? Look to the increasing numbers of your people, look to the increasing facilities for mischief. I speak not of this class or that, manufacturing or agricultural, the principle is the same in both, though the danger may be less in the one than in the other—the march of intellect, as it is called, bearing with it good and evil, while it multiplies the agents of mischief, leaves millions of the poorer sort only as fuel for the fire; crime is increasing in amount and deepening in character and intensity; the valuable tables of criminal offenders prepared at the Home Office attest the accuracy of this assertion

—in 1843, "thirteen persons were hung for murder." Of these, says the preface, three were females for the murder of their husbands, two were males for the murder of their wives, one for the murder of his child, one of his father. And in a summary deduced from these tables, written by Mr. Jelinger Symons, and published in a most able article of the " Law Magazine " for last December, it is stated—" Murders, and attempts to murder and maim, have increased 38 per cent. on the average of the last four years, rapes 57 per cent., other horrid offences 53 per cent. Arsons, which exhibit malice in its worst shape, have increased by 28 per cent., and if those of the present year were taken into account the increase would be far greater." The public journals confirm to the full this horrid statement; scarcely a week elapses but that the newspapers detail some crime that, in novelty and atrociousness, exceeds the imagination of mankind. I will not dwell on many cases; of two only I will ask, whether the records of sin in England present any instances of similar wickedness:— one mother, a year ago, who poisoned her four children in succession for the sake of their burial-money; another, within these few days, who held her own daughter alive over the fire until the wretched infant was roasted to death ?

To what, Mr. Speaker, will all this grow, if no remedy be applied or even attempted ? If we will not, as a nation, undertake the mighty task, let us not, by a continuance of the present system, render it impossible to private enterprise. Within the last few years the means of education, though still inadequate, have been greatly diffused, schools are multiplied, and zealous and qualified persons, within and without the Established Church, are ready to devote their energies to this service; but the entire absorption of the children by almost unceasing toil in so many departments of industry defeats their efforts and breaks all their hopes. Does this state of things afford us any security ? Far from it. Time was when men believed, or rather maintained, that utter ignorance and excessive labour were the best guarantees for the tranquillity of the people—a sad delusion; for the most hardly worked, and the most brutally ignorant, can ever find time and intellect for mischief. Hundreds throng to the beershops and pothouses to listen to seductive compositions in prose and verse, in which vice and violence are dignified into heroism; compositions written with fancy and power and embellished with all the excellence of modern art. What a monstrous perversion of the noblest faculties, of talents bestowed to refine and elevate mankind ! But their guilt is our guilt, we incur it by conniving at it—certainly, by not repressing it.

> " Oh, gracious God ! how far have we
> Profaned thy heavenly gift of Poesy ;
> Made prostitute and profligate the Muse,
> Debased to each obscene and impious use,
> Whose harmony was first ordained above,
> For tongues of angels, and for hymns of love !!"

Sir, I much fear that I shall appear dogmatic if I again presume to impress upon this House the hollowness and danger of our actual position. We may obtain a surplus and reduce taxes, increase our fleets and extend our commerce—excellent things in their way, but all unavailing, if they rest not on the moral and physical prosperity of the great mass of our people. We may flourish for a while, and we may exchange congratulations; but an hour of difficulty will soon disclose that we have done nothing whatever to assure our external dignity or internal peace.

But while there is life there is hope; we have little to fear but from indifference or delay; and facilities for mischief, now so rife, are, in the order of a merciful Providence, alike facilities for good. The march of intellect, the restless activity, the railroads and steamboats, the stimulated energies of mind and body, the very congregating of our people into masses and large towns, may be converted into influences of mighty benefit. Let the State but accomplish her frequent boast, let her show herself a faithful and a pious parent; such efforts, be assured, will not be lost in the sight of God, and, in security and joy, her children will be "like olive plants round about her table."

# Regulation of Lunatic Asylums.

## HOUSE OF COMMONS,

### FRIDAY, JUNE 6, 1845.*

Speech on bringing forward two Bills, for the Regulation of Lunatic Asylums, and
for the Better Care and Treatment of Lunatics in England and Wales.

LORD ASHLEY said: My motion requires some preliminary
explanation. By the two bills I intend to effect the repeal of
many existing acts respecting the treatment of lunatics, and
substitute such other enactments in their place as time and
circumstances have rendered necessary. Before entering ·into
the general principle of my motion, I wish to observe that my
proposition will apply only to England and Wales. I wish that
circumstances enabled me to extend the bills to Ireland and
Scotland; for I believe that not in any country in Europe, nor in
any part of America, is there any place in which pauper lunatics
are in such a suffering and degraded state as those in Her
Majesty's kingdom of Scotland. I assume, in the first place, that
the House, or at least a considerable portion of those hon. Members
who may honour me with their attention, have read the Report of
the Commissioners in Lunacy made in the last session of Parliament; and I will also assume that it is unnecessary for me to
repeat the statement which I made in the course of last year on
the subject which I now seek to bring under your notice. You
will allow it, perhaps, to form a part of my present speech.

It is necessary I should begin by reminding you that the laws
affecting lunatics may be divided into four classes, and that that
law, as it now stands, is embodied in nine several statutes. These
nine several statutes may be divided, as I have said, into four
classes; first, those which are relative to county asylums; second,
those relating to licensed asylums, public asylums, and the
visitation of those respectively; third, relative to persons found

* From "Hansard."

lunatic by inquisition, the appointment of visitors, and of a "commission in lunacy," to perform duties formerly discharged by masters in Chancery; fourth, relative to criminal lunatics. Now, I do not intend to touch more than the first two of these classes. I mean to amend the single act contained under class 1, as well as to amend and combine the three which are contained under class 2. The three bills contained under class 2 are as follows :—2nd and 3rd of William IV., c. 107; 3rd and 4th of William IV., c. 64; and 5th and 6th of Victoria, c. 87. These various statutes I propose to consolidate into one, entitled " A Bill for the regulation of the Care and Treatment of Lunatics in England and Wales;" and I must solicit, for a topic in itself uninviting and dry, your forbearance and indulgent attention.

But before I proceed further with this part of the subject, I may be permitted for a moment to recur to the state of the law as it existed under the 14th of George III., the only law for the regulation of private asylums previously to 1828. In those days there was no power of punishing any offence—there was not even the power of revoking or refusing any license. There was also extreme laxity in the signature of certificates, one only being deemed sufficient; and that might be, nay, it often was, signed by a person not duly qualified, or by the proprietor of the mad-house in his medical capacity; and to the care of this person the alleged lunatic was consigned. Houses licensed under this act were not required to be visited more than once a year. There was no power to discharge any patient who might prove to be of sound mind. Licenses could be granted only on one day in the year. Pauper lunatics were sent without medical certificates; there was no return of pauper patients made to the board; and no plans were required of houses previously to the granting of licenses. There were no returns of the cases of lunatics kept singly in houses for gain; there were no visits of medical persons to the patients required. A measure was then introduced by Mr. Gordon, in 1828, to remedy these defects; and no enactment on your statute book has been attended with more satisfactory results. I stated them at some length in my speech of last year. Evasions, no doubt, will be found wherever temptation and opportunity are combined; we can only pretend to mitigate, not to abolish the evil.

Now, the first of the bills which I intend to submit to the consideration of the House will establish a permanent commission, and thereby secure the entire services of competent persons. It will give the power of far more detailed and frequent visitation, and fix the limits of expense, now regularly increasing. It will place "hospitals" or subscription asylums under proper regulations, by requiring them to have the same orders and certificates as are necessary in licensed houses, and by subjecting them to the same visitations as county asylums. My bill will also provide an additional security against the improper detention of pauper patients, by requiring that the person signing the order for their confinement shall personally examine them beforehand, and that the medical officer who certifies as to their insanity shall see them within seven days previous to their confinement. I may add that neither of these safeguards exists at present. I propose, also, that my measure should compel every person receiving a patient to state his condition, mental as well as bodily, when first admitted, and the cause of his death when he dies. It will also direct that every injury and act of violence happening to a patient shall be recorded, and will require a case-book to be kept, thereby affording additional securities against mismanagement, and showing how far the patients have the benefit of medical treatment. It will also authorize the visitors to enforce a proper supply of food (in licensed houses) to pauper patients, who are at present fed at the discretion of the proprietor. Further, it will enable the visitor to order the admission of a patient's friends; at present, they are admitted or excluded at the caprice of the person who signs the order for the patient's confinement. It likewise will enable the visitors to sanction the temporary removal of a patient in ill health to the sea-side, or elsewhere. It, moreover, will enforce an immediate private return of all single patients received for profit, and authorize the members of a small private committee, named by the Lord Chancellor, to visit them if necessary. This is the provision of the law in France: in that country licenses are prescribed for every house, and certificates and visitors for every lunatic. The abuses and cruelties perpetrated in these retreats for single patients would surpass the belief of the House. I have said before, and I say again, that, should it please God to afflict me with such a visitation, I would greatly prefer the treatment of paupers in an establishment like that of the Surrey Asylum, to the treatment of the rich in almost any one of those receptacles. These returns are universally evaded at present, the law rendering it unnecessary to make any return, unless the patient has been confined for twelve months. The bill will give the Chancellor power to protect the property of lunatics against whom a commission has not issued by a summary and inexpensive process, and it subjects all workhouses in which any lunatic is kept to regular visitation.

The second bill which I intend to lay before the House is called for by the report of the commissioners, and the facts which I produced in my statement of last year; and, presuming that the House will accept this for granted, I think it may not be necessary for me to go over the evidence that was then laid before the House; nevertheless, I do feel it necessary to call the attention of the House to the principal defects which are pointed out by our report as to pauper lunatics and county asylums. First, that there are 40 counties in England, and only 16 county asylums; and 12 counties in Wales, and only one disgraceful borough asylum. Of the 24 counties in England having no asylums, one has 500, two upwards of 400, three upwards of 300, seven upwards of 200, and 11 nearly one hundred lunatics each; and Wales has 1,000 lunatics. The second is, that of the 16 counties which have asylums, one has 800, one has 600, one has 500, one more than 300, three more than 200, and the rest more than 100 lunatics, for whom there is no accommodation in the asylums which have been erected, and no other receptacle. The third defect is, that all the existing asylums are full of incurables, or persons said to be incurable. The fourth defect is, that no system has been adopted in the county asylums to give preference to urgent cases, or those capable of cure. The fifth fault in the present state of the law is the detention of lunatics in workhouses, where there is no sufficient medical or moral treatment. At the Union workhouse of Redruth, there were 40, and of Leicester 30 lunatics; and at Birmingham not in the Union 70 lunatics. The sixth is, there is no real visitation or true account of those lunatics who are not in asylums; for example, the lunatics of North and South Wales, and those in England not in asylums, being 9,339 with their friends or in workhouses.

I think I may now proceed to illustrate the necessity for these alterations by reference to one or two cases. I find, from the report before me, that in the Leicester Union workhouse—

"There were thirty insane persons, of whom three males and nine females were dangerous lunatics, in the strict sense of the word, and most unfit inmates of the place, and where, as we were informed, they had been long detained in spite of the remonstrances of the visiting surgeon and some of the magistrates. In the parish workhouse at Birmingham there were seventy-one insane persons, subject to insanity in various forms, several of them being epileptics, liable after their paroxysms of epilepsy to fits of raving madness, during which they were usually excessively violent and furiously maniacal."

Take the case of a private house at Derby visited in 1842:

" The straw in the paupers' beds was found filthy, and some of the bedding was in a disgusting condition from running sores, and was of the worst materials and insufficient; two cells in which three sick epileptic paupers slept were damp, unhealthy, and unfit for habitation; the beds of some of the private patients were in an equally bad state; nearly all the provisions of the law for the regulation of licensed asylums were violated. . . . The magistrates of the borough, who are its visiting justices, had not visited the house for the space of a year minus eight days. . . . In 1843 it was again in a very bad state; the paupers were still occupying what had been the coachhouse and stables; the rooms were low, comfortless, and ill-ventilated, and one of the apartments most offensive. It has been visited within the last six weeks of the present year; the commissioners report that the condition of the private patients was improved, but that of the paupers was so bad that another communication must be made by the board to the magistrates of the borough."

Now, here is an excellent sample—though there are exceptions, I admit—of the mode and measure of provincial visitation by the provincial magistracy. I am speaking in reference to the visitation of private asylums only; the supervision and care of the county asylums are, on the whole, extremely satisfactory; but look at this, the justices in the preceding year visited the asylum but once; they received a shock, no doubt, by the spectacle they witnessed, and they took a good course to avoid a repetition of it; for, says the report, " during the last year no visiting justices were appointed." It is very true that many private asylums are of a superior character; but the tendency of such establishments is to this state of things. Every one must perceive that the pittance of seven shillings or eight shillings a week given to the proprietor of an asylum for the maintenance and cure of a pauper lunatic is altogether insufficient; the proprietor actually and justifiably looks to realize a profit; and, however great his humanity, which I have seen in frequent instances, will not generally go beyond that point which will leave him an adequate return for himself.

I will now, by a very striking example, illustrate the deplorable condition in which some of the pauper lunatics in Wales have been placed. I will mention the case of Mary Jones, who was consigned, be it observed, to the care of her mother. The report made upon her case I will now read, with the permission of the House:

"We went to the cottage between eight and nine o'clock in the evening, accompanied, at our request, by Dr. Lloyd Williams, who interpreted to us the answers given to questions put through him. In a dark and offensive room over a blacksmith's forge, upon opening a bolted door, we discovered the miserable object of our search. The only window was closed up by boards, between which little air could find admission, and only a feeble glimmering of light. In the middle of this loathsome chamber was Mary Jones, the lunatic, on a foul pallet of chaff or straw, and here she had been confined for a period of fifteen years and upwards. She was seated in a bent and crouching posture on her bed of nauseous and disgusting filth. Near to her person, and just within her reach, was a cup into which she was accustomed to pass her excretions, which she emptied from time to time into a chamber utensil. This last vessel contained a quantity of feculent matter, the accumulation of several days. By her side were the remnants of some food of which she had partaken. Within a few feet of the pallet, which was on the floor, stood a large earthen jar, nearly full of fetid urine, the produce of the three other persons in the cottage. It had, as stated by the mother, been placed there in order that it might, from the warmth of the room, undergo a more speedy decomposition for the purpose of being used in dying wool. The stagnant and suffocating atmosphere, and the nauseous effluvia which infected it, were most intolerable."

Listen to the effects of this treatment:

"This long and close confinement had produced in Mary Jones's person the most frightful distortions. The chest bone protruded forwards five or six inches beyond its natural place, and there was an excoriation of the parts below. The legs were bent backwards, and the knee-joints were fixed and immoveable. The ankles and feet were also greatly twisted and deformed. She was emaciated in the last degree; her pulse was feeble and quick; and her countenance, still pleasing, was piercingly anxious, and marked by an expression of despair. Her garments were loathsome, and from her person was emitted a most offensive odour. . . . For about ten years past she had been confined to the dismal chamber in which we found her, the window of which had been boarded during nearly the whole of that time."

Now, observe the whole enormity of this case: this poor woman was removed to the hospital. What says Dr. Williams?

"We have the clearest evidence that if this poor creature had been properly treated in the first instance, she would have been completely cured."

He adds:

" August 14, 1844,—After I wrote to you yesterday I gave her (*i. e.*, Mary James), some money to buy calico, and I was gratified to find that she took a needle and thread and commenced sewing very tidily."

On the authority of Dr. Williams, of Denbigh, I am enabled to say that she must have been at one time fully capable of cure, and that she still had sufficient intellect to enjoy existence, when she was placed in favourable circumstances.

It is time that I should now come to that part of my statement which has reference to the alterations that I intend to propose. The second bill which I shall ask leave to introduce will be an extension of the act of the 9th of George IV., c. 40. We have taken this act for our basis, and have been scrupulous in departing as little as possible from its provisions : the act is far from perfect, but I must speak with deference of a law that has laid the foundation of such asylums as Surrey, Hanwell, and others. The principal amendments are these :—1st. Instead of permitting, I propose to require every county and borough which has no asylum to provide one, either for itself or in union with some other county or borough. 2nd. That every county which has an asylum, but insufficient accommodation, is to provide further accommodation. This is according to the law in France ; every department in that country is compelled to furnish adequate receptacles for its insane poor. 3rd. In erecting new asylums, and providing further accommodation where it is required, regard should be had to the proportion of curable and chronic lunatics ; I purposely avoid the use of the term "incurable." Separate buildings I propose should be provided for the chronic at a less cost, and parts of the workhouses, with the consent of the Poor Law Commissioners, may be adapted, in which case they are to be separated from the other part of the building, and to be deemed county asylums. 4th. Counties having asylums may unite with other counties not having one. 5th. To extend the act to boroughs having courts of separate quarter sessions, and to every place not contributing to county rates. 6th. To assist magistrates in erecting asylums, and ascertaining the proportionate numbers of curable and chronic lunatics, and providing separate buildings for them, and for diminishing the expense of building asylums, the plans are to be submitted to the Commissioners in Lunacy, and the estimates to the Secretary of

State; it is provided also that asylums for boroughs may be erected without the boundaries of the borough. 7th. The time for the repayment of money borrowed for building asylums I propose to extend from fourteen to thirty years. 8th. General rules for the government of asylums should be submitted to the Secretary of State. 9th. Copies of the accounts of asylums are to be sent to the Secretary of State. We also propose that all recent cases of lunacy are to be sent immediately to an asylum : this is an indispensable provision, for it is clear that if such cases are met with instant attention, the number of cures will be, as I shall presently state, in the proportion of from 70 to 90 per cent. ; whereas if they are suffered by neglect to become chronic or inveterate cases, the amount curable is scarcely anything per cent., or at the very outside, and under the most favourable results, only from 6 to 8 per cent. We next provide for the reception of all lunatics who are not chargeable, whether wandering or otherwise : they are to be apprehended, and those whose friends cannot pay for them are to be admitted into the asylum as paupers. Our next provision is, that a quarterly inspection of all lunatics who are not in asylums is to take place by a medical man, who shall return lists of them, describing their condition, to the Commissioners in Lunacy. Amongst other provisions appertaining to this part of the bill is one by which every pauper lunatic shall, in the first place, be deemed to belong to the parish from which he is sent until he shall be proved to belong to another; and, with reference to this proviso, a clause will be introduced in order to protect counties from this casual charge becoming permanent, in cases where adjudications shall be made respecting lunatic paupers; and, lastly, power is to be given to remove chronic lunatics to the asylums provided for such cases. These are the main enactments; the others may be reserved for a future stage of the bill.

But now as to the actual state of the pauper lunatics in the existing county asylums. I will take the great asylum of Hanwell, in Middlesex. In that asylum there were, in the month of March, 1844, 984 patients, of whom thirty only were reported to be curable. There were waiting for admission 429 pauper lunatics, all of whom were, in consequence of the delay in applying a curative treatment, fast becoming incurable. Within the first three months of 1844 there were no less than forty lunatic patients, to whom admission was refused into the Hanwell asylum, making in the whole year 160 patients. Of these, supposing that 6 per cent. were curable, there would remain permanently thrown upon the county of Middlesex for support no less than 150 lunatics in each year. The second instance to which I shall refer is that of the lunatic asylum of the county of Lancaster, which contained in the year 1844 about 600 lunatics. Of these nearly all had been previously detained in the workhouses of their different parishes so long as to greatly diminish all probability of their cure. In the whole county there were then waiting for admission into the asylum about 500 lunatics, for whom no room whatever could be made. I next turn to the Surrey Lunatic Asylum, where I find, on the 1st of January, 1844, no less than 382 patients, of whom 362 were reported as incurable, whilst there were in private asylums and elsewhere in the county 209 lunatics waiting for admission. I take these very magnificent establishments, because they afford striking examples of the want of provision for the treatment of recent cases, and they likewise offer the most convincing proofs of the increase of incurable lunatics throughout the counties in consequence of the neglect of early treatment. Let us now look to the treatment pursued in other asylums, and contrast the effects of recent attention with those where the cases have experienced neglect of longer or shorter date. I refer in this respect to the report of the Dorset County Lunatic Asylum, made at the Epiphany Sessions for the year 1845, which states that there had been discharged during that year twenty-three lunatics as cured, of whom seventeen had been admitted in the same year. And what did the superintendent say with respect to this fact? He reports thus :

" This is a larger number of recoveries than has taken place in any year since the opening of the institution, and may be attributed to a greater number than formerly being admitted in the incipient stage of the disorder."

Of sixteen persons who had been admitted during the first three months of their attack no less than thirteen were cured, making 81 per cent. In cases even of relapse, the proportion of cures was not less than 58 per cent., and in the cases themselves the disorder had existed for more than three but less than twelve months. In St. Luke's Hospital the cures during 1843 amounted to 63¾ per cent., and in 1842 to 70¼ per cent., the cases in many instances having been of several months' standing. I find, too, in a paper recently read before the Medical Society, communicated by Dr. Forbes Winslow, a gentleman who has paid much attention to this class of disorders, and who is justly entitled to be heard, an opinion that a large proportion of the many thousand incurable

lunatics in England and Wales had been reduced to this melancholy state by the neglect to which they had been subjected in the
incipient state of the malady. In fact, that nine out of ten cases
recovered if subjected to treatment within the first three months
of the attack. There is similar testimony in other countries; from
the reports of the State Lunatic Asylum of New York for the
year 1844, sent to me by Dr. Brigham, I find it stated that—

"Few things relating to the management and treatment of the
insane are so well established as the necessity of their early treatment. . . . By examining the records of well-conducted asylums
it appears that more than eight out of ten of the recent cases
recover, while not more than one in six of the old cases are cured."

And I find the same facts reported by the physicians of the
Hartford Lunatic Asylum, in the United States. Many impediments, however, are thrown in the way of the speedy application
of the curative treatment in cases of pauper lunacy,—first, no
magistrate, in any county having a public asylum, has it in his
power to authorize the transmission of pauper lunatics to a
private asylum for treatment in case the county asylum should
be too full to receive them. The law has been so determined by
a late decision in the Court of Queen's Bench, which renders it
additionally necessary for the government to apply themselves to
a removal of existing difficulties; the parish authorities, moreover,
are indolent, indifferent, or they seek to avoid the expense; but,
after all, the main impediment lies in the want of adequate accommodation. And whence is this defect? It may be traced to the
past and present fear of the enormous cost to be incurred in the
construction of asylums.

Here, then, I approach the financial part of our project; and,
although I admit that this is a most dry and uninviting topic, I
still am under the necessity of entering upon some details respecting this branch of the subject, as it is of the most essential
importance; and hon. Members will allow that without some
explanation on this head I shall have but little hope for any bill.
The main impediments in the way of constructing county
asylums has been, I have already said, and at present is, the fear
of the enormous expense supposed to be necessarily attendant
upon such undertakings. Now, the county asylum at Hanwell
has cost in all the sum of 196,000*l.* On the original cost the rate
per head for 1,000 patients was 160*l.*, and on 800 patients 245*l.*
The Surrey Asylum cost 85,000*l.*, or 237*l.* per head for each
patient. But this is far too large an estimate to be taken as an

allowance of the cost per head; it is the opinion of the commissioners that 80*l.* per head would be an ample allowance for the construction of lunatic asylums, and to provide that the enlightened curative system in the treatment of patients recommended by the best authorities be adopted and acted upon. Of this we shall be able to furnish ample proofs in the committee on the bill. The great error, as it has appeared to us, in the construction of lunatic asylums, is that they are all built upon the presumption that every one of the patients is of the same character, requiring the same minute care and the same precautions. This view of the question greatly enhances the expenses; but we look at the matter in a totally different way. We make a distinction between the different classes of lunatics; we provide a distinction between chronic cases and recent cases. For chronic cases of lunacy we provide good diet, warmth, clothing, air, and exercise; and, in addition, occupation, which we recommend to be of the healthiest description—I mean occupation in the open air, such as gardening, or on farms. But the chronic patients do not require the same careful supervision which the recent cases would constantly call for, nor do they require the same medical attention as the patients who are under curative treatment demand; and therefore the care and attention shown to them is not by any means so costly as that of the patients who are undergoing the whole of the curative process, and towards whom every minute precaution and care must be constantly observed.

Let us take therefore the proportions of these respective classes of patients, and adapt them to the estimates for building new asylums. Suppose we take 12,500 pauper lunatics to be the number requiring accommodation. From this number deduct 10 per cent. for the harmless lunatics, who may safely be left at home under the care of their relations, but also under medical supervision. Of the remainder, 40 per cent. are considered to be curable, and 60 per cent. are chronic or inveterate cases. Apply this to a county asylum having 300 lunatics; deduct 10 per cent., there will be 270 left; of these 40 per cent., or 108, are curable, and to be admitted into the "recent-case" hospital: the remainder, 60 per cent., or 162, are patients for the chronic department of the asylum. The gross expense of such an asylum would be as follows:—taking the recent cases at 80*l.* per head, they would amount to 8,640*l.*; and taking the chronic cases at 50*l.* per head, they would be 8,100*l.*: making in the whole 16,740*l.* for these two classes; but, as all cases of epilepsy and of violent patients must be under especial care in the recent-case hospital, I will add one-sixth of the whole expense, or 3,290*l.*, to the sum already mentioned as the cost of this extra care, by which the sum total for 300 patients in an asylum will be 20,030*l.* We propose to extend the term of repayment, out of the county rates, of the cost of these asylums from fourteen to thirty years; thus the annual burden on the county rates in the case I have referred to would only be 666*l.* Now, compare the burden which our plan would impose with that under the present system; the average expense of construction of eleven county asylums has been 170*l.* per head, Thus, under the old plan, an asylum for 300 lunatics cost 51,000*l.*; under the new plan, as I have just shown, it will cost 20,030*l.* Take then the gross expense of providing for 12,500 lunatics, at 170*l.* per head, it would be 2,125,000*l.* throughout England and Wales; whilst under our plan it would be 813,750*l.*, being a difference of 1,311,250*l.*, leaving for the thirty-six counties in England and Wales unprovided with asylums an average of 22,604*l.* (and in many counties much less), repayable in thirty years. Now, if we look to the number of chronic cases, and to the mode of their treatment, we cannot wonder at the enormous expense which lies on the counties. There are pauper lunatics in asylums, say 7,000; in workhouses and elsewhere, 10,000; curable in asylums, 20 per cent., or 1,400; in workhouses, 20 per cent., 2,000; making together 3,400. Incurable in asylums, 5,600; in workhouses, 8,000; making together 13,600. Now, the average duration of the lives of lunatics has been calculated by Dr. Conolly at ten years, which is a very low average. Observe this; the following would be the average annual cost, at 20*l.* per head :—60 per cent. of 5,600 (or 3,660) lunatics in asylums, at 20*l.* per head, would have cost, for one year, if cured, 67,200*l.*; if allowed to become incurable, and they live the average of ten years, 672,000*l.* : in same way, 60 per cent. of 8,000 (or 4,500) lunatics, would have cost 96,000*l.*; if incurable, 960,000*l.* Now, with respect to the duration of life in an insane person, I am strongly persuaded that the average of ten years is far too low a basis to calculate upon. Dr. Hitch, of Gloucester, says that insanity by no means shortens life, and he gives tables to show this. He asserts that out of 105 deaths, there were sixteen above fifty years of age, seventeen above sixty, and seventeen above seventy, being nearly 50 per cent. of the whole mortality. I may here call attention to another feature in the economy of the plan which we propose, namely, that exhibited in the case of the Hanwell Asylum, which is, in fact, the case of every asylum. By the present system, the cures only average 6 per cent. instead of 60. The number of applications refused every year is 160. There are thus 150 incurable lunatics thrown upon the county annually, instead of sixty-four, being an annual difference of ninety-six. Now, had these been sent and cured within the first six months, they would have cost at the annual rate of 16*l.* 11*s.* 6¾*d.* each, or 1,591*l.* 10*s.* But supposing them to become incurable, and live the usual period, the cost would be 31,830*l.* This system prevailing throughout the whole kingdom, the present plan would reduce the additions to the chronic lists from ninety-four to thirty annually; and the calculations which I have laid before the House show that in Middlesex alone there would be an annual saving of 30,000*l.* This is a saving which, in the course of ten years, will more than cover the whole additional outlay for the construction of a new asylum.

But this is not all the good that will result from our plan. By recovering the patient, not only will the expense of his maintenance for life in a lunatic asylum be avoided, but he will be restored to his occupation—and his family, instead of being thrown upon the parish for support, will again look to him for their means of existence. The system which we propose to substitute for the present one will effect a cure in seventy cases out of every hundred. But other and very great advantages will arise by reducing the size of these asylums. They are by far too large for an efficient administration of the curative process. There must be, to insure success, a minute attention to diet, exercise, and classification— the patients must be seen daily, sometimes hourly, and occasionally, in certain circumstances, during the night. No one man can undertake the charge of more than 300 patients : the experience of all practical men is concurrent on this point : no one presses it more vigorously than Dr. Conolly. Hear the testimony of Dr. Julius, an eminent physician at Berlin :

" Every public or private institution," he writes, " has certain limits in which it must be restricted." He insists particularly " on schools, hospitals, and, more than all, penitentiaries and lunatic asylums, as places where the individualising treatment of every case will contribute much, and more than anything, to its success."

He proceeds to lament the extension of Hanwell, and adds, that

" This institution, excellent as it is, warns mankind not to en- large asylums beyond the limits which are traced by the moral and physical powers of the individual that has to guide and manage it."

Our present business, however, is to affirm that indigent lunatics ought to be maintained at the public charge. I entertain, myself, a very decided opinion that none of any class should be received for profit; but all, I hope, will agree that paupers, at any rate, should not be the subjects of financial speculation. How is it possible that the proprietor of the house should, out of 8s. a week, give the patient everything that is required—full diet, ample space of house and grounds, all the expensiveness of the non-restraint system, and realize in the remainder an adequate return for himself and his family? The thing is next to impossible, and ought not to be attempted.

And now, Sir, it seems to me unnecessary to weary the House any further by preliminary matter; for whatever remains and requires explanation, may be made the subject of discussion, should the House be pleased to permit the introduction of these Bills, and the subsequent consideration of them in committee. Still more is it unnecessary to urge upon this House, an assembly of educated, humane, and Christian men, the duty of coming forward to the aid and protection of this utterly helpless class, who, under the marked visitation of a wise though inscrutable Providence, demand an unusual measure of our sympathy. Sir, it is remarkable and very humiliating, the long and tedious process by which we have arrived at the sound practice in the treatment of the insane, which now appears to be the suggestion of common sense and ordinary humanity. The whole history of the world, until the era of the Reformation, does not afford an instance of a single receptacle assigned to the protection and care of these unhappy sufferers, whose malady was looked upon as hardly within the reach or hope of medical aid. If dangerous, they were incarcerated in the common prisons; if of a certain rank in society, they were shut up in their houses under the care of appointed guardians. Chains, and whips, and darkness, and solitude, were the approved and only remedies. The practice has descended to our own day; and Dr. Conolly assures us that he has formerly witnessed—

" Humane English physicians daily contemplating helpless insane patients bound hand and foot, and neck, and waist, in illness, in pain, and in the agonies of death, without one single touch of compunction, or the slightest approach to a feeling of acting either cruelly or unwisely. They thought it impossible to manage insane people in any other way."

The honour of these discoveries, and the first practice of them belongs unquestionably to the French nation; it is to the genius and humanity of their professors that we owe such mighty

advances in the science of mental disorders.   Some improvements
were attempted in the early part of the last century; but it was
reserved for Pinel, in the centre of Paris, in the very moment of
the reign of terror, to achieve a work which, for genius, courage,
and philanthropy, must ever rank him amongst the very principal
of mankind.   The narrative is so graphic and interesting, that I
must entreat permission to detain the House by the recital of a
few passages :—

"Pinel undertook what appeared to be the rash enterprise
of liberating the dangerous lunatics of the Bicêtre.   He made
application to the commune for permission.   Couthon offered
to accompany him to the great bedlam of France.   They were
received by a confused noise; the yells and angry vociferations
of 300 maniacs mixing their sounds with the echo of clanking
chains and fetters, through the dark and dreary vaults of the
prison.   Couthon turned away with horror, but permitted the
physician to incur the risk of his undertaking.   He resolved to
try his experiments by liberating fifty madmen, and began by
unchaining twelve.   The first was an English officer, who had
been bound in his dungeon forty years, and whose history everybody had forgotten.   His keepers approached him with dread; he
had killed one of their comrades by a blow with his manacles.
Pinel entered his cell unattended, and told him that he should be
at liberty to walk at large, on the condition of his promising to
put on the camisole or strait-waiscoat.   The maniac disbelieved
him, but obeyed his directions mechanically.   The chains of the
miserable prisoner were removed; the door of his cell was left
open.   Many times he was seen to raise himself and fall backwards
—his limbs gave way; they had been fettered during forty years.
At length he was able to stand, and to stalk to the door of his
dark cell, and gaze, with exclamations of wonder and delight, on
the beautiful sky."

I ask, Sir, was there ever such an instance of needless suffering !

"He spent the day in walking to and fro, was no more confined,
and during the remaining two years which he spent at Bicêtre
assisted in the management of the house.   The next madman
liberated was a soldier of the French Guard, who had been in
chains ten years, and was the object of general terror.   His
disorder had been kept up by cruelty and bad treatment.   When
liberated, he assisted Pinel in breaking the chains of his fellow-
prisoners.   He became immediately kind and attentive, and was
ever after the devoted friend of his deliverer. . . . The result was

beyond all hope. Tranquillity and harmony succeeded to tumult and disorder; even the most furious maniacs became tractable."

This was indeed a man to be honoured by every nation under heaven! Would to God that such were the character, the motive, and end, of all our rivalry with that great people. Well would it be for mankind, if, by our mutual harmony, we kept the world at peace, while we prosecuted and enforced their noble discoveries. I could furnish to the House many recent instances of similar triumphs in our own country; but I will not now detain them by the narrative. The system passed from France into this country, but was of slow growth. We are mainly indebted for it to the Society of Friends, and that remarkable family of the Tukes who founded the Retreat at York, soon after the victories of Pinel in France. Samuel, the son of William Tuke, is still alive, a man of singular capacity and benevolence; and surely he must be gratified to perceive that his example has obtained not only the approval, but the imitation of the best and wisest men of this country, and I may add, of America; for I have here very copious documents, sent to us by Dr. Brigham, the eminent physician of the State Asylum of New York, which show the zealous and liberal efforts of the local governments in these great and necessary undertakings.

But, Sir, to secure not only the progress, but even the continuance of this improved condition, we have need of a most active and constant supervision; if this be denied, or even abated, the whole system will relapse. There is the strongest tendency, and it is not unnatural, amongst the subordinate officers of every asylum to resort to coercion; it gratifies all the infirmities of pride, of temper, and indolence. The disclosures of the former state of the public hospital at Bedlam, of the private one at York, and more recently, of a large portion of the country, in our report of last year, sufficiently attest how indispensable are the provisions we have suggested for visitation and publicity. Such arrangements will supersede the necessity of much minute legislation: on no one point is Mr. Tuke more hearty in his concurrence, with a view to prevent the return of those disgraceful practices which have both afflicted and dishonoured mankind. Clearly then, Sir, it is our duty, and our interest too, while we have health and intellect—" *Mens sana in corpore sano,*" leisure and opportunity—it is our duty and our interest, I say, to deliberate upon these things before the evil days come, and the years of which we shall say that we have no pleasure in them.

Here we are sitting in deliberation to-day—to-morrow we may be the subjects of it. Causes, as slight apparently as they are sudden, varying through every degree of intensity—a fall, a fever, a reverse of fortune, a domestic calamity—will do the awful work, and then, "Farewell, king!" The most exalted intellects, the noblest affections, are transformed into fatuity and corruption, and leave nothing but the sad though salutary lesson, how frail is the tenure by which we hold all that is precious and dignified in human nature. But, Sir, it is the temper of our times—and most heartily ought we to thank God for it—and especially of our own country, to view all such things as incentives to earnest and vigorous action. I invite you, therefore, in this spirit, to accept or to amend the proposition I have submitted to your consideration; and be assured that it is not in the order of Providence that such labour should be altogether without fruits; for one of two results you cannot fail of attaining: either you will behold the blessings of happiness and health revisiting the homes of the emancipated sufferers, or you will enjoy the satisfaction of having laboured with disinterestedness and zeal for those who cannot make you the least compensation.

## Social Condition of the Labouring Classes.

LORD ASHLEY addressed the meeting as follows:

" Mr. Sutcliffe, and Gentlemen,—Although most of those who are present are fully aware of the circumstances to which I am indebted for the honour of an introduction to you, I think it will be advisable that I should shortly review them as a preliminary to the few observations which I shall touch upon in my address. When, in obedience to a sense of duty, as no longer deeming it right to oppose the repeal of the Corn Laws, I resigned my seat for the county of Dorset, I was almost willing to retire altogether from public life, and all its distracting vocations; for, however tempting to the young and inexperienced—however full of promise of usefulness and of honour to those who have never tried it —the House of Commons does not present to its more practised Members such an amount of unalloyed enjoyment as to render it of all sublunary things the most to be desired. The immense consumption of time, the constant demand on the moral and physical energies, the enormous effort which is required to do the smallest good, and the misunderstanding and abuse which constantly attend that attempt—these circumstances, when seen and felt, greatly diminish the attraction of parliamentary honours. Add to these the state of public parties, the uncertainty of the opinions of your own ordinary political friends, and the total impossibility of reposing entire confidence in any public man— consider all these things. and you have but little left to inspire any inordinate desire of senatorial privileges.

But these sentiments, although they would not justify a man in surrendering a trust that was confided to his hands, would, I think, release him from the obligation of seeking a renewal of it at the cost of much toil, vexation, and expense. So far as my past and public life was concerned, matters still were incomplete. The Factory Bill, on behalf of which I had so long laboured, was struggling for legislative existence, and many other questions of social interest of the highest importance remained unadjusted. It was then that your offer was presented to my notice. An offer so honourable demanded my most serious and respectful consideration. In these days a man may not choose inactivity; and, therefore, as you well know, the issue was that I did not venture to decline the flattering proposition. It seemed to me, in a great degree, a providential summons, and I obeyed it. And now I stand here as no man's enemy; nor am I chargeable with having wantonly disturbed the peace of your city. Had I thrust myself, unsolicited, on your notice, I might, perhaps, have been justly exposed to such an imputation; but you have a right—and I in accepting your offer recognize that right—nay, more, you have a solemn duty, in the discharge of your responsible trust, to select that person who, according to your judgment, will best represent your principles in the councils of the nation, and give them beneficial effect by a steady and judicious course of action in the legislature. I say, then, I am not chargeable with having disturbed the peace of your city, because, as I said before, you have the right to select the representatives who shall best declare the principles which you profess.—And what are those principles? I think I may infer them from the facts of the requisition which I had the honour to receive, so numerously and so respectably signed. I gather that your principles are those which have governed nearly the whole of my parliamentary life, because I cannot conceive any qualification that should recommend me to the notice of the electors of Bath but that which is founded on an examination and approval of my parliamentary course. Now, gentlemen, I decide at once that you will avow, and will maintain, the great principles of our constitution in Church and State—those great principles which, ever since the revolution of 1688, have been recognized and cherished by the people of these realms—the Crown, the Bishops, the Houses of Lords and Commons, and every institution ecclesiastical and civil. I say the great principles of the Constitution, because the mere bigoted adherence to details, probably only external, is manifestly impossible in the present day. The growing demands, and, indeed, the exigences of the realm, require an occasional adaptation to the necessities of the times; and I rejoice, and we may be thankful, that our system of polity is capable of a safe and most beneficial expansion. You may lengthen your cords, and strengthen your stakes, and in the very elongation of the support.

ing power make the edifice you would sustain more erect and symmetrical.

But it is not by reference to speculative statements—it is by reference to practical statements, that we in this country ascertain our unity of sentiment; because it is better that we understand each other in seeing in what we have acted, rather than what, before trial, we had professed together; and I will, therefore, touch on some of the principal topics of the day, in hope—nay, in the full belief—that you and I shall find abundant matter for harmony and co-operation. Now, I will not dwell long upon questions of foreign policy, because they are not the stirring topics of the present time. We are often charged in this country with an indifference to foreign politics; and no doubt they do occupy a secondary place in our consideration. And I see no harm in that; on the contrary, I rejoice in it. I rejoice that the attention of the public is drawn to subjects within its reach, under its own observation, and affecting its real interests. But we may, by referring to this subject, thank God that there is, in this country, an increased and increasing desire to avoid, not only for ourselves, but for all others, the horrors, and also the glories, of war. That minister who, whilst not tarnishing the honour of the nation, will make the greatest efforts, and even sacrifices, for the maintenance of peace, will stand the highest in the esteem and in the affection of the people. No; it is to social questions that the attention of the public is mainly directed; it is to the cleansing away of that enormous mass of filth and suffering, physical and moral, which for years has been suffered to accumulate around our internal polity, poisoning the very sources of public and private life, and endangering the national security, most certainly the national honour, in the almost indefinite mass of domestic corruption. Now, I have some experience of these things, both of the evils that prevail and of the remedy which may be applied to them. When, some years ago, these subjects were first mooted, I remember that throughout the manufacturing districts there were thousands and tens of thousands who were brought in no respect within the pale of education, or within the sound of the gospel. Observe the different effect which has been produced; at this moment there may be within those manufacturing districts no less, I believe, than upwards of forty thousand children, between the ages of eight and thirteen, who are receiving an excellent education. But I will touch more on that by-and-by : I wish now to return to those social questions to which I was before referring; because I maintain that these are the questions which not only do and ought to engage your principal attention, but that they are those which involve most seriously the permanent interests of this realm. Now observe, can there be greater wisdom in the government of a country than to devote itself to the internal condition of all its interests ? What nation can be so secure as that which is built like a city at unity with itself ? What nation can be so free from internal tumult and from external assault ? " Out of the heart," says the wise man, " proceed the issues of life." The heart of a country is its people. Let that people, in their habits, their thoughts, and their manners, rise in the scale of civilization and Christianity, and then you will drink water abundantly out of your own cisterns, and you will not only enjoy them yourselves, but will diffuse them in streams of richness and plenty for the delight and refreshment of other lands.

But, gentlemen, one obstacle, prodigious and almost insuperable, meets us at every turn, darkening with its shadow every burst of sunshine, and stopping, by its mass, every avenue to social improvement. Faith, we know, can remove mountains, and faith, we believe, will remove the evils of Ireland ; but it must be no ordinary faith, perseveringly exhibited in no ordinary efforts. I never can speak of that country without shame and remorse. Centuries of misgovernment and neglect have brought that island into the condition it now is in, from which all the wisdom, the zeal, and the hearty desire of every government for the last quarter of a century has not been able to extricate it. The evils of that country spring from her social system, and spring from her religion, both alike traceable to this country, and both demanding the succour and the sympathy of the English people. Her Majesty's present Ministers have determined boldly and most wisely in their endeavours to improve the social condition of that country. I do not deny the hazardousness of the experiment ; I cannot but regret the embarrassment likely to arise to the landed proprietors of that portion of the realm ; but poor-laws for Ireland were emphatically demanded ; they were just, necessary, and inevitable. It may be called amputation, but you know amputation is often necessary to preserve life ; and all that we can require is confined to the expression of the simple wish that certain persons who call so emphatically for this terrible operation should administer it under the soothing and beguiling influence of the ether of courteous sympathy and civil language. Turning to the other suggestions which are made for the improvement of Ireland, I do not think there are many here who will not take very large exceptions to the plan of encouraging the Roman Catholic religion, fostering its colleges, and endowing its priest-**hood; for** these things involve great concession of principle, without any compensating or proportionate benefit. Those who take the highest ground of opposition declare that they are sinful; those who assume a lower ground maintain that they are useless in one aspect, and perilous in another. That they are useless as means of conciliating you have the experience of the last twenty years, and more especially in the recent legislation upon the College of Maynooth. The fact is, that all our statesmen lie under a grievous mistake; they endeavour to control the people through the priests, whereas they should endeavour to control the priests through the people. Depend upon this—the difficulty does not lie with the Irish nation; the difficulty lies with the sacerdotal and monkish orders, who, reversing the piety of Aaron, stand between the living and the dead—the living word of God and the dead congregation. Only allow profound security of life and limb, with free discussion and an open Bible, and you will cease to be perplexed in your determination how Ireland is to be governed—Ireland,

> "Great, glorious, and free;
> Bright flower of the earth, and first gem of the sea."

Then that quotation, so often used in the agitation of that unhappy country, and used for purposes other than those for which I use it now, will have its fulfilment, and Ireland will occupy her true position, not as a gangrene in the side of England, but, as she ought to be, and as, by God's blessing on our efforts, she will eventually become—her true and powerful arm of strength. Now, gentlemen, to continue upon these subjects, there are matters of much interest in the present day. I do not anticipate that you and I shall be much at variance in consequence of the part which I thought it my duty to take in respect of the repeal of the corn-laws. It is, in fact, a consequence in some measure of the part which I then took, that I have now the honour to stand before you. I will not enter into any discussion of that measure, either of the causes which gave rise to it, or of the results which may follow. The time is yet too early for us to decide either upon the good or the evil which may spring therefrom. But this thing must be manifest to every one, be he friend or foe to that measure, that if those corn-laws had been in existence when the present scarcity occurred, there would not have been found in the kingdom one party able to oppose their suspension; and being suspended, I do not believe there would have been found a single party to renew their operation. But when we are taunted with being bound, as they say, to go a little further into legislation, injurious to all classes of the trading community, I reply at once that I deny not only the character of the obligation, but the obligation itself. We are bound to nothing that we were not bound to before. We were bound then, as we are bound now, to do all that we believe in our conscience to be for the welfare of the realm, the peace of the world, and the advantage of mankind. And this brings me to another point of no small interest in the present day, upon which I will detain you for a few minutes, because it certainly is wrapt up with the vital interests of this nation. Most assuredly, the condition of the large mass of the people of these realms, both in secular and in religious knowledge, is not such as can give to those who inquire into these matters either satisfaction or hope. No doubt in late years great advances have been made; but the population has widely outstripped the provision made for it, and thousands may be found in our highways and hedges, in our streets and alleys, in our courts and lanes, who are living in a state of practical heathenism—a heathenism as complete as if they were found in California or Timbuctoo. Now, heathenism, wherever it prevails, produces a deep moral and physical degradation, and those people are not exempt from the operation of that universal law. You may see that, in their countenances, and their persons, many of them bear the impress of a disordered life. Now I will return to the point which I indicated some time ago. I have seen some of the evils, and I have seen some of the remedies. I have seen the effects produced on large masses of the children engaged in factory operations; I know what they were when the work of legislation was begun in 1830, and I know exactly what they are now; and I will give you the testimony of their own people, written to me when I desired operatives of intelligence to give me their opinions as to the effect produced, first, by the limitation of hours, and then by the education of the children; and the answer given to me was this: "So greatly are they improved that you would not know them to be the same race of human beings." I go further (and I am indicating these things because at the time that I point out the mischief I wish to show you there is a remedy at hand)—I go further, and talk of the condition of those who are engaged beneath the surface in the mines of the earth. Go over those districts where that system once prevailed; take with you the blue books which record what their condition was, and with your own eyes see what their condition is now; and you will tell me, as has been told me by several in those districts—ay, and by masters themselves who were opposed to the legislation I had the honour to introduce—you will, I have no doubt, say at the conclusion of your voyage of inspection, that by the restoration of women to their true position in society we have revived that which ought to be the glory and strength of every country—I mean the domestic system; we have restored to those districts the domestic system and the benign influence of females, and we have there planted seeds of strength which will grow up, I doubt not, when the present generation is dead and gone, into a tree, the leaves of which shall be for the refreshing of the nation. You may go to the print-works, and see thousands and thousands of children extricated from the most cruel and debasing toil, and not only put under a limitation of the hours of labour, but provision made that they should be taught their duty to God and to man. The same effects that followed in the first instance have followed in this; and be assured, they will follow in every instance where you go forward with faith in your hearts, and the word of God in your hands, for the purpose of making Him known to human beings who may differ from you in this world in the degrees of life, but who are equal to the best of us in the light of immortality.

This, however, is only a fraction of what remains to be done; this is but a fraction of all that must be overhauled and examined before the good old ship Britannia will be able to float erect, and defy all the enemies of her honour and her peace. In examining the records of the reports made by the Children's Employment Commission, which I moved for in 1840, I see enumerated a number of cruel and distressing trades exhausting the energies of the tender plant, sending many to a premature grave, and consigning all the rest to a degrading existence in after life. Examine those records, and see what remains. I will not detain you by an examination of this; I will pass on to one other class who are now beginning to occupy some of the public attention, found in great numbers in our large towns—found, I believe, in a smaller degree in the city of Bath, but principally in London, Liverpool, and Manchester—that class known by the singular denomination of ragged scholars. Which of you will take the trouble to perambulate those great concentrations of human life? If you will penetrate these alleys and courts, and dive into the recesses of suffering, darkness, and ignorance, you will see a state of things which I will defy either Dickens to describe, or Hogarth to paint. You will see a state of things which will offend every physical sense, that will shock every moral feeling; and if you do not close that walk with a determination that you will devote every energy you can spare towards the evangelization of that wretched class, you are not the men I take you for, and I do not desire to be your representative. But it is because I hold you to be men of a different mould, and that you are animated by these great and divine principles, that I shall esteem it a special honour to be the representative of Bath. It is not necessary that I should enlarge here on the duty of training a child in the way he should go; that is, I know, with you, a foregone conclusion. Neither is it necessary to say that the State has already seen it most just that it should no longer confide altogether to the voluntary principle so important a matter as the education of the people. I do not say that a national scheme of education is within our reach—it is, in fact, beyond our reach; but, nevertheless, let us do all that in us lies; let us strengthen the things that remain; let us seize every opportunity; let none slip of doing partial, if we cannot effect entire, good; trusting that, in the good providence of God, the day will come when we shall openly confess as we now feel, and reduce it to action, that, after all, we have one Lord, one faith, one baptism. I do not mean to say that education is a panacea for all the evils, or for the very largest proportion of them, that affect this country; and certainly not such an education as we find in the greater number of our schools, consisting in dexterous displays of mental arithmetic, geographical information, and all those exhibitions which pander to the vanity of the master, and deteriorate the character of the boy by feeding that quality of the mind in him which we ought rather to check. No; that education which we should all desire for the children of this realm is most admirably described in the language of our catechism, "To learn and labour truly to get my own living, and to do my duty in the station to which it has pleased God to call me." Reflect, and you will see that education is a much wider thing than the mere lessons and lectures of the schoolroom: it ought to be connected with the discipline of the parent and the whole domestic system. And if it be so decided, that the education of the children of these realms must be connected with the discipline of the parents, the domestic system, and social example, just consider the impediments presented in many of our rural districts—but in many more of the districts of our great and overgrown cities—to the grown poor of these realms. Let me first direct your attention to that to which I have no doubt you have already given some thought; just consider, first, the state of the dwellings of a large proportion of the poor; just see how, in many of these dwellings, you may find two, and three, and four families in a single room; you may see, as I have seen, as many as thirteen or fourteen persons sleeping in the same narrow apartment. Consider the position in which they are; consider the total want of all the necessaries and the decencies of life; consider how pernicious the atmosphere in which they live, the total want of drainage, and the mephitic vapours perpetually exhaling; consider the total defect of water for purposes of health and cleanliness. I am directing your attention to these things, because you will see in a moment the conclusions I wish you to draw from them. They are producing a result on the physical and moral condition of our people that can be estimated only by a personal inspection. My firm belief is, that the physical condition of our people arises, in no small measure, from our long neglect, from suffering these things to grow up without any restriction—above all, from exaggerating that principle which some persons are so exceedingly anxious to promote, the principle of non-interference. The fact is, we have come to the present state of mischief because we did not interfere in time; if we had interfered in time we should have but few of these evils to contend with now. Again, many of the difficulties which beset this country, I would say to the extent of one-half of its pauperism, are caused by the condition in which, in our towns, and, I regret to say, in many of our rural districts, we suffer large masses of the population to dwell. The physical condition which is superinduced by the mephitic air, by the want of ventilation, by the defect of water, by all the circumstances I have mentioned, bring on such a general depression of the whole health, as drives hundreds and thousands to the beerhouse and the gin-palace; I have seen myself many persons in the prime of health, and able to maintain their families on their earnings—I have seen those persons being compelled, in order to be near their work, to live in those miserable and unhealthy localities, brought down from strength to weakness, and from weakness to the grave, leaving on the world a widow and children to be maintained by the parish or by private bounty. And we find a great fact testified by the records of the fever hospitals, that some of these localities are never free from fever (I believe that you, in Bath, can scarcely understand this; you have no such places as are to be found in Liverpool, and Manchester, and London), and when it gets on the ascendant its victims are—who? They are not the young, and the weak, and the feeble; but the records of the fever hospitals will testify that these dreadful fevers invariably settle on the heads of families in the prime of life, and their ravages are principally among persons between the ages of twenty-two and thirty-five, those who generally leave, when carried to their graves, the largest number of helpless and destitute orphans.

Now, these things cannot be allowed to remain as they are.

If you search the records of the Health of Towns Commission you will be able to see at a single glance more than I could tell you if I detained you here a considerable time; but they are records which must be searched if you wish to understand what is the great and crying social evil of the day in which we live. These things cannot be left as they are—yet one advantage we have gained, we have learnt that these mischiefs arise from known and preventible causes. Private duty will do a great deal towards the removal of them, but legislation will do a great deal more, by directing and stimulating our lagging efforts. But these things must not remain as they are, if we have the slightest regard for the welfare of our country. Although I will not go quite so far as to say that to preach the gospel to these people is altogether useless, inasmuch as we know that the word of God will not return to Him empty, this I do know, that, in the present state of things, we are encouraging a fatal and deadly agency, unceasingly, actively, and powerfully retarding every hope of the physical and moral improvement of the people. Now, I will not weary you by a specific enumeration of all the evils we dread, and the remedies we propose. It may be summed up in this—that our statesmen must not be content, as hitherto, to await the development of the mischief, saying that sufficient for the day is the evil thereof; but they must search out and nip the system in the bud, and take for their text in all that they do, zeal for the honour of God, and all imaginable good for the children of men. It is that system of waiting until the mischief is developed which has brought us into our present difficulty, for then it is developed in all its gigantic proportions, and it fills those who contemplate it with alarm and despair. But let the mischief be searched out and strangled in its birth. And now there is no longer any excuse for idleness, because we know the whole extent of the mischief; and I am sure that the constituencies of this realm will support those who shall declare that they will direct their attention and direct all their energies to the removal of these great evils. Whether we have such ministers at the present day —whether we have men actuated by such a spirit and wisdom— remains to be seen. I confess that I am disposed to rely somewhat on Lord John Russell, and one or two of his colleagues. I confess that I have seen in his policy, and have read in the expression of his sentiments, that which elicits from me the expression of a desire to repose in him a certain amount of confidence.

Now, gentlemen, I have dwelt at some length on these matters, because I think it right that there should exist as little room as possible for misunderstanding between a representative and his constituents. I have rather indicated principles than stated precise measures, and I hold myself free to decide the time and the mode of asserting them. But I cannot conclude without a passing observation upon the aspect of affairs at the present day. There is much that is dark—much of various kinds—moral, religious, and political —to excite our apprehension; much from without, and not a little from within. Disunion prevails everywhere. We cannot resist the common enemy, nor can we combine to defeat him. The present scarcity has grievously and perilously affected our country, and the failure of a single root has brought sorrow upon our peasantry, and stained the path of all our glory. But we hope that an abundant harvest will, by the blessing of God, restore us what we have lost, and bring with the enjoyment of it a larger measure of sobriety and thankfulness. Yet amidst all these calamities we may discern indications of a better state of things; we may see the dawn of a better spirit, which acts in every relation of public and private life. Aggressive war is denounced, and commerce is fostered—not only as a means of making wealth, but as a happy and legitimate method for the civilization of nations, and the revival of brotherly intercourse among all the families of the earth. We have begun to attach a loftier value to man as such, be he noble or be he plebeian, be he black or be he white, collectively and individually, both as a mortal and as an immortal being. These are, indeed, times of progress; nothing is stationary, and the invention of to-day is antiquated to-morrow. The astounding powers of locomotive intercourse, railways, and electrical telegraphs (the rapid growth of the last few years), the running of many to and fro, and the multiplication of knowledge, are manifestly tending towards some great and unseen issue. Evil, no doubt, will be mixed with the good; and, like all other faculties given to man, many will pervert them to the vilest purposes. But it is for us who recognise whence they came, and for what end they were proposed, to labour and to pray, with all our hearts, that they may speedily accomplish the true and blessed object of their mission, which is, "Glory to God in the highest, on earth peace, good-will towards man."

## Ten Hours Factory Bill.

---

# HOUSE OF COMMONS,

## THURSDAY, JANUARY 29, 1846.

---

Speech on moving for leave to bring in a Bill for limiting the hours of labour of young persons in factories to ten hours.

LORD ASHLEY said: Sir, it has so often been my duty to solicit the indulgence of the House, that I may seem to be acting merely in conformity with ceremonial when I prefer my earnest entreaty for its patient attention on this occasion; but at no time have I felt it more necessary to make this request. I am about to revive the discussion of a proposition oftentimes propounded in this House, and as often rejected; one upon which I can offer no novel arguments, and which moreover was submitted to the House at a period not very distant, and was then determined and decided. I think, however, that I can assign good reasons for the course I am about to take. In the first place, I must assert very respectfully, though very positively, that the decision was not a decision of the House; it was the decision of the Minister. This House has twice affirmed my proposition; and we all know in what way the reversal of that judgment was obtained. Next I observe, that a very large majority of those gentlemen who from their position and knowledge must be best acquainted with the feelings of the manufacturing and commercial districts, indeed no less than thirty-three of forty-two of the representatives of those districts, supported my proposition, and voted for the Ten Hours Bill through all its divisions; and I confidently expect a similar exhibition of local opinion on the present occasion. Moreover, I must assert the continued and undiminished desire of the workpeople for this measure—a desire that, instead of abating, seems, as far as I can see, to gather strength and resolution under every defeat. Nearly two years have elapsed since I last submitted this question to the House; and during the interval events have occurred of such a character as will illustrate in the most forcible manner the truth and the safety of the principles I have endeavoured to maintain; I have also obtained from foreign countries most important information, justifying, as I think, the strongest assertions and strongest arguments, I have ever been able to adduce in this House. It will be my endeavour to abstain from wearying hon. Members by the production of evidence which has oftentimes been brought before it in various reports and debates. I believe it will be some disadvantage to my argument, if I abstain from refreshing the memory of gentlemen present, with a detail of all that evidence which shows the great pressure upon the physical condition of the workers; but I will forego the advantage, because the question now is narrowed to this single proposition—can this be done without injury to the manufacturer, and without a serious diminution of the wages of labour? For I have met with no one, wherever I have been, who will deny the great moral and physical benefits to be derived if this limitation were assigned to the hours of work.

The first matter to which I shall call the attention of the House is a series of experiments instituted in the manufacturing districts by various parties in respect of the reduction of the hours of labour. Mr. Gardner, a gentleman who has very large mills in Manchester and Preston, instituted those experiments; and he was good enough, in the course of last year, after his experiments had run through twelve months, to send up his son and his principal agent to London, to give me an account of his operations. I put to them several questions, the answers to which were committed to writing; and they are so exceedingly important that I must solicit the indulgence of the House while I read them; they completely prove that the hours of labour may be reduced, not only without loss, but with actual benefit both to the master and operative. The first question I put to them was with respect to the comparative produce of labour where the limitation was eleven hours instead of twelve. The reply was this—

"The produce of eleven hours at Mr. Gardner's mills was not reduced at all."

He added an observation—

"I could not understand how it was that our men could turn off as much work (and some a little more) in eleven hours as ever they did in twelve. I said to one of them, 'John, will you tell me how it is that you can do more work in eleven hours than you did in twelve?' 'Why,' said he, 'we can lay to in eleven hours a day better than we could when we worked twelve, because we get more rest at night, and we are in better spirits all the day through, and, besides, the afternoons are not so long.' He could spin, he said, ten years longer, if Mr. Gardner would keep on eleven hours."

I could give you more such cases. The second question I put to them was, Was the quality of the produce for eleven hours better or worse than that from twelve? To this I received the following answer:

"The work is decidedly better since the change to eleven hours; when we worked twelve hours I had very often to find fault with the spinners for not making their cops hard enough. Most of our spinners are generally spinning pin cops, which have to be wove wet, and if they are not made very hard they will fly off in the weaving, and they are nothing but waste. I can say that since the change the work is decidedly better. At the present speed at which the machinery is generally run it is very hard work for the spinners to keep up and make such work as will give satisfaction, particularly where they spin coarse numbers and work twelve hours in the day."

The next question I put was—

"Were the wages reduced or raised, or kept at the same level in eleven hours as compared to twelve hours?"

The answer was to the effect that the wages were the same. And the gentleman then gives a statement showing the average rate of wages paid for a certain number of weeks, when they worked twelve hours, and eleven hours; and by this it appears that in fact there was a slight increase of wages under the eleven-hour system as compared with the twelve. The next question I put was—

"What were the effects of the change of system upon the health of the workers?"

To this it was answered, that—

"The hands undoubtedly have better health since the change to eleven hours, and I could give you several cases of both weavers and spinners; I will give but one. Joseph Parker, a very sober, industrious man, and a very good spinner, having been in the employ of Mr. Gardner for seventeen years, was so often off his work in the winter time, when we worked until half-past seven, that he was obliged to conclude that he could not stand spinning any longer. . . . Since the change to eleven hours he has done more work than ever he did before, and has only been off work once through sickness, which will be very soon two years."

The next point to which I turned my inquiries was, whether the means of improvement (if any) which the diminution of daily labour gave to both sexes for the comfort and duties of domestic life had been turned by the parties concerned to any advantage in their social and moral condition? To this I received the following reply :—

"Whenever mills worked twelve hours the numbers that attended night school were twenty-seven; and a few months after the change they increased to ninety-six. The female part of our hands turn their leisure time more to the needle, and those that are married to their domestic concerns. I believe there is a better taste for reading among the workpeople. Mr. Gardner intimated that, as he was a subscriber to the Bible Society, he wished his hands to have Bibles and Testaments at the society's prices; and the first week I sold myself 136 books, and every week's end I sell a few."

On asking as to the feeling produced between employers and employed under the operation of this system, I received the following information :—

"I can confidently say, that there is not a gentleman in all Lancashire that stands so high in the estimation, not only of his own workpeople, but of all the operatives. I will conclude by saying, first, that at the present speed at which machinery is generally run it is impossible for the hands to keep up, when they work 12 hours a day. Secondly, when the speed and time they work, and the atmosphere they breathe, is taken into consideration, no one will wonder at the death-like appearance of the factory-workers; and if the hours of labour were reduced, it would be like giving them so much more life."

But Mr. Gardner himself published a letter describing the results of his experiments. He says—

"I am quite satisfied that both as much yarn and power-loom cloth may be produced at quite as low a cost in 11 as in 12 hours a day. . . . All the arguments I have heard in favour of long time appear based on an arithmetical question; if 11 produce so much, what will 12, 13, or even 15 hours produce? This is correct so far as the steam-engine is concerned; whatever it will produce in 11 hours, it will produce double the quantity in 22; but try this on the animal—horse—and you will soon find he cannot compete with the engine, as he requires time both to rest and feed."—" It is, I believe, a fact not to be questioned that there is more bad work made the last one or two hours, than the whole of the first nine or ten hours."

I saw this gentleman in October last, and he still maintains all the opinions he has expressed heretofore, as to the result of the limitation-of-time system. But there are various other places where this system is in operation, and with similar advantageous consequences. The Messrs. Horrocks and Jackson, of Preston, have made similar experiments, and with equal success. These gentlemen have been working on the eleven-hour system since May last. Mr. Knowles, of Bolton, a very considerable spinner, commenced the reduction in April last.

" I saw Mr. Knowles," says the writer of a letter, " three weeks since, and he said so satisfied was he with the change, that he never intended to work his mill any longer than 11 hours per day. He had been connected with the working of factories more than 40 years, and he always thought that the hours in factories were far too long. I asked him respecting the work turned off in 11 hours compared with 12 hours. He said, when he made the change, he never expressed any wish that his hands would turn off as much work in 11 hours as in 12; but some of the spinners did as much work in 11 hours as ever they did in 12; others did a little less, but not in proportion to the diminution of time. The difference was so little, that he had no hesitation in saying, that he did not lose one penny in the year by the change."

The following is an extract of a letter from a large power-loom weaver in Scotland, which he communicated to me, knowing the part I have always taken with regard to this question; he writes to me thus:

" Six months ago we came to the resolution of employing our workpeople only 65 hours a week instead of 69. It has been entirely successful; we have had no reason to regret the change, neither have our workpeople. We make no alteration in the wages, and there never was more earned in our works than at present by those employed at work paid by the piece. We have it in contemplation now to reduce our time to 60 hours. The more I have considered the matter, the more convinced have I become, that for all parties a Ten Hours Bill would be advantageous."

A communication received from a worsted mill, near Bradford, informs me—

" The proprietor has lately been trying the ten hours principle with his weavers, and with profit and advantage."

From a woollen mill near Leeds I have received the following :—

" The limitation of the hours of labour has been of the most incalculable benefit to the people in that neighbourhood, not only in relieving physical suffering, but in distributing wages over a longer period during the year."

From the West Riding of Yorkshire, a worsted manufacturer writes as follows :

" I have been trying the ten hours principle ; I get nearly as much work as ——— gets, who works a longer time for the same wages. ——— used to work 16 hours a day ; he declares that he gets more work and better work than ever he did in 16."

These were the experiments made in various parts of England, and in every single instance you have found that the amount of produce has not fallen off, neither have the wages of the operatives been diminished ; and the general facts show a great moral and social improvement in the condition of the people. I was anxious also to ascertain what was the result of this system in Prussia, where, in 1839, the king passed a decree limiting the hours of labour, to children under 16 years of age in factories, to 10 hours, and where the system has been in full operation ever since. In reply to various questions of mine, I received the following answers from Elberfeld :

" There has been no diminution of work in consequence of the limitation of the time for children at 16 and under to 10 hours a day."—" The salutary influence of the law on the physical as well as moral condition of the labouring classes is evident."— " There is no diminution of the wages perceptible in consequence of the limitation of the hours of labour."—" At first there was undoubtedly a very strong feeling against the law in a considerable body of the millowners ; but this has literally disappeared."

With respect to the observance of the law, on making inquiry of the Director of the Home Department, he says—

" Not a single remonstrance has been addressed by any one of the millowners to the government or the provincial states, much less has any resistance taken place."

He further says—

" There were some malcontents. They were afraid of foreign competition ; but they seem soon to have been satisfied that this fear was imaginary, the produce of the work not having dimi: nished."

The example we have set with respect to the regulation of

labour in factories has been followed by various foreign countries. It has been followed by France; and the French government has passed a law as nearly as possible a transcript of our own. Our example has forced the government of Prussia into an enactment which provides for the moral and physical improvement of the operatives of that country; and you may depend upon it that if we persevere in the course on which we have entered, we shall compel foreign countries to adopt a similar policy.

Let me just point out to the House what are the general results of our factory regulations on the moral, physical, and financial condition of our operatives. I request the particular attention of the House to this subject, for I believe that the results in question offer a complete contradiction to all the opinions put forward in the year 1833, against the measure which I introduced at that period. Let the House see what were the predictions then made, as compared with the actual results of our legislation. I recollect that in the year 1833, when I first brought forward a bill for a limitation of the hours of labour, there were four predictions, which were constantly ringing in our ears, which were repeated at every meeting, and were transcribed into every journal adverse to the measure. The first of these predictions was, that the great cotton trade would be destroyed by any limitation of the hours of labour; the second was, that the wages of the protected parties would be diminished; the third was, that the wages of children would be reduced to a mere fraction; and the fourth was, that the children would be dismissed, and that great suffering would universally ensue. Now, let the House permit me to state the actual results, as compared with those predictions. It has been said, in the first place, that our great cotton trade would be destroyed by any diminution of the hours of labour. In answer to that prediction, I need only refer to the state of our cotton trade in the years 1835 and 1836, and during the last three years; and it is not, I believe, necessary that I should dwell any further upon that part of the question. But it was predicted, in the second place, that the wages of the protected parties would be diminished. Now, there were two classes who were at that time protected by our legislation. There were, first, persons under the age of thirteen, who were called "children;" and there were, secondly, persons between the ages of thirteen and eighteen, who were called "young persons." The law enacted that young persons between the ages of thirteen and eighteen should not be exposed to a longer duration of work than twelve hours in the day. Now, before the year 1833, the average wages of those young persons were 5s. 4d. per week, while their average wages since that period have been 6s. 11d. per week; thus showing an increase of 30 per cent. in the averages drawn from the four great towns of Manchester, Bolton, Preston, and Oldham. Let us next pass to the third prediction, that the wages of children would be reduced to a mere fraction. The average wages of children under thirteen years of age, for twelve or more than twelve hours' labour a day, were, before 1833, 3s. 1d. per week; and, since 1833, their average wages for six hours' labour a day have been 2s. 2d. per week. But although there has been in that case an apparent abatement of wages, the families have not, in many instances, suffered in consequence; because, by that admirable provision restricting the labour of children to six hours a day, a greater demand has been created for the labour of those children, and many families which could formerly obtain employment for one child only now find employment for two children; so that the aggregate wages are at present frequently greater than the wages received under the old system. Let us look at the fourth prediction, which was that the children would be dismissed, and that much physical suffering would ensue. It is very difficult to obtain statistical returns with respect to children under thirteeen years of age employed before the year 1833. But this we know— that very few of them indeed were receiving any education at all; whereas, I have grounds for asserting that there are now 30,000 children, under thirteen years of age, working six hours a day, and receiving education during three hours, that education being in many instances of a very excellent description, and having been much improved during the last two or three years. I have also been informed that in the towns of Manchester, Bolton, and Preston, the increase of children at school has been, since the year 1833, as eight to one, exclusive of those who attend night schools; while the increase of those above thirteen years (who labour twelve hours a day), in places for teaching persons of that age, has been little or none. Let me add the remarks of the Committee of Operative Spinners upon that point — remarks which ought to carry with them great weight, for they had been extremely opposed to the clause which limited the labour of children to half time. They have written to me as follows:

" We also instituted an inquiry into the moral and physical condition of piecers and young persons now, as compared with the same class in 1833, and from every quarter we learn that it is much improved; and since the bill of 1833, which restricted the hours of labour to eight in the day, and that of 1844 to six in the day, with enactments for education, their physical and moral condition has been improved to such an extent, that they do not appear to

be the same race of beings.  We have recently conversed with a
large number of the operatives and those men especially who
have devoted a large portion of their time and much of their
means to the promotion of this question, and they all declare that
the benefits which have arisen to themselves and their children
are more than sufficient to repay them for their time and sacrifices, and that sooner than go back to their old system they would
part with the last shilling they have in the world in defence of the
restrictive system of factory labour."

I have felt great satisfaction in reading that statement, for it
not only justifies my past conduct, but gives me great assurance
of future success in my efforts upon this subject.  I hope I am
not assuming too much for our efforts, when I ascribe to them the
collateral advantage of the half-holiday system for warehousemen
in Manchester,-and other great towns, at one time so energeti-
cally opposed, but now as warmly approved by the employers.  I
have reason to know that the system has been attended with the
most beneficial results; and I believe that the hon. Member for
Durham will bear me out in that statement.  Among all the
alterations that have been effected since the year 1833, I am sorry
to perceive that nothing has been done for the benefit of young
persons between the ages of thirteen and eighteen.  Those young
persons are exposed under the existing law to twelve hours' actual
labour per day ; now a very large portion of them are females,
and I think I may appeal to the House to say, whether it is not
cruel to take a young female on the very day on which she has
passed the age of thirteen, at the most tender period of her life,
and to demand of her precisely the same work in duration, and
frequently the same in intensity, which is demanded from ripe
and vigorous manhood ?   Observe the results to which this
practice must lead.  I believe every one will admit that it is a
matter of vital importance to the peace and welfare of society,
and to the comfort and well-being of the working classes, that
females should be brought up with such a knowledge of domestic
arts and household concerns as may enable them efficiently to
discharge the various duties of wives and mothers.  But how can
it be possible that young women, whose labour has been so heavy
and so prolonged that they are in many cases unable to cook
their own suppers, or even to eat the suppers prepared for them—
how is it possible that they should learn the details of domestic
life, which constitute the comfort of the working man's home, and
contribute so powerfully to the morality of the rising generation,
because women must have, and ought to have, almost undivided

influence on children during the earliest and most impressible years of their existence? I am not expressing my own opinions merely upon that point, because the commissioners appointed in the year 1840 to inquire into the employment of young persons went so far as to state, that it was the universal opinion of clergymen, medical men, teachers, and others, that the condition of the women was one great and universally prevailing cause of the distress among the working classes. I will now read to the House the result of an experiment made by a friend of mine, who had set up in the neighbourhood of several large factories a night school, for the purpose of affording education to the young people employed in those factories. That gentleman writes to me as follows :—

" In October, the schoolmaster opened two evening classes, one for the young men, and the other for the young women, employed during the day in the mills of ——. Each class met twice in the week, on alternate evenings, and between the hours of eight and nine. The eagerness to receive instruction was so great, that forty young men and thirty-eight young women entered immediately. . . . Some of the pupils, after leaving the mills at eight in the evening, came the distance of nearly two miles to the classes. But so great was the fatigue they had undergone during the day, that although they evinced an earnest desire to be instructed, it was soon found that their physical powers were too much exhausted by the day's work to enable them to give proper attention to the teachers, and as many as four and five together were observed to have fallen asleep. Within the space of a few months, the classes were deserted by all but five young men. They were accustomed to excuse their want of attention to the teachers, by saying that they were up at five o'clock in the morning, and that after leaving the classes they had to take their suppers ; and, consequently, did not get to bed till eleven, and that owing to the long hours and short nights' rest, they found it impossible to keep awake during the evening lessons."

I have often heard it said, that there is a factory establishment in another country which completely proves that twelve hours labour a day are quite consistent with health, comfort, happiness, and moral and intellectual improvement; and when discussing this subject we have always been referred to the case of Lowell, in the United States. Now, I believe that this case of Lowell fully establishes everything that I have urged upon this matter. Let us begin by assuming—for it is only nominally the case—that the hours of labour are the same in both countries—that is to say, twelve hours a day. You must still observe, at the very outset, that there is one great and leading distinction. Dr. Bartlett, an eminent physician of the United States, wrote a book, entitled "A Vindication of Lowell," and in that book he states—

"By a statute of the commonwealth it is provided that no person under the age of 15 years shall be suffered to work more than nine months of any year in a manufacturing establishment, the remaining three months to be passed at school."

Dr. Bartlett further avers, that—

"The law is enforced with unflinching strictness, so that even in times of scarcity of hands no plea that he ever heard of was admitted for the wresting of the law from its important design."

There is another very great and leading distinction. What is the case in the English factory? In the English factory, children having reached the age of 13 years are admitted to the full period of 12 hours' labour, and for the whole year. What is the period at which the young people at Lowell begin to work? The average age is very much higher than in England. Out of nearly 2,000 girls employed there, the average age was 23 years. I will take two or three mills. In one mill, 657 young women are employed—what is their average age? Twenty-two years and a quarter; and the average time during which they have been at work in the mill is three years and three quarters; and, consequently, at the period of their entry they were about 19 years of age. In English factories they begin to work 12 hours a day at 13 years of age. I will take the instance of another mill, in which there are 203 young women, whose average time of employment is four years and a quarter. They also were about 19 years of age when they began work. I will just quote now from a most interesting and authentic work, published at the end of last year, called "Lowell as it was, and as it is," published by an American clergyman, the Rev. Henry Mills, who wrote the work at the solicitation of the great proprietor of Lowell, who furnished him with the necessary statistics for the purpose. Observe another great and leading distinction between our factory people and those at Lowell; observe whence they come, and how long they remain in the mills. What does the Rev. Mr. Mills say? He says—

"We have no permanent factory population. This is the wide gulf which separates English manufacturing towns from Lowell; only a very few of our operatives have their homes in this city; the most of them come from the distant interior of the country."

They are mostly, says Dr. Scoresby, the daughters of the provincial farmers. Mr. Mills goes on to say—

"To the general fact here noticed should be added, that the female operatives in Lowell do not work, on an average, more than four and a half years in the factories; they then return to their homes, and their places are taken by others. Here then (he says), we have two important elements of distinction between English and American operatives. The former are resident operatives, and are so for life, and constitute a permanent dependent factory caste—the latter come from distant homes, to which in a few years they return. The English visitor to Lowell, when he finds it so hard to understand why American operatives are so superior to those of Leeds and Manchester, will do well to remember what a different class of females we have to begin with —girls well educated in virtuous rural homes."

Now, let us look at the statistical returns respecting female operatives. On inquiry it has been found that—

"Of the 6,320 female operatives in Lowell, 527 have been teachers in common schools."

Again, it is to be observed—and this is another very leading distinction between the two countries—that with us "there are more married women," says Dr. Scoresby, "than at Lowell." Just let me point out that even at Lowell there is the same predominance of females employed in mill labour, an evil of which we have complained so often in this country, and which I have so often heard ascribed to the operation of the Corn Laws. The total population of Lowell is 30,000, of which the operatives number about 10,000, of which 2,915 are males, and 6,320 females. So, you observe, even in that country there is the same predominance of female over male labour; and it must be ascribed to some other cause than to those commercial restrictions that are said to be the cause of so much mischief with us. Well, but now observe again, that notwithstanding all these flattering statements as to the condition of Lowell, notwithstanding that there is in America complete freedom from all commercial restrictions, no limitation, nothing which can prevent the free action of the manufacturer in any way he may think proper—yet in Lowell, with all these advantages, you may hear the language of complaint; you may hear the same language which you hear in this country; you will hear stated by operatives, by word of mouth as well as by petition, the same complaints of over-toil, of premature decay, of sinking health, and an early grave. Look at these documents. I quote now from a public document, proceeding from the commonwealth of Massachusetts House of Representatives :

" Special Committee report that four petitions, signed by 2,139 persons, of which 1,151 are from Lowell, mostly females, have been presented, praying the Legislature ' to pass a law providing that ten hours shall constitute a day's work.' The petitioners declare that they are confined from thirteen to fourteen hours per day in unhealthy apartments, and are thereby hastening, through pain, disease, and privation, down to a premature grave.

If that be true, how much more true must be the language if applied to the case of our own operatives, who begin their labour at eight years of age, confined in the unhealthy towns in which labour is carried on, and continue their work till the latest period at which they are able to gain their livelihood ? What opinion does the Select Committee, to whom the petition was referred, express ?—

" We think (say the committee) there are abuses. We think many improvements may be made. We think it would be better if the hours of labour were less—if more time was allowed for meals—if more attention was paid to ventilation and pure air. '

They then proceed to comment, with very great severity, and in many instances with unfairness, on the state of the English factories and the people engaged in them. They go on to say—

" We acknowledge all this ; but we say the remedy is not with us. We look for it in the progressive improvement of art and science— in a higher appreciation of man's destiny—in a less love for money, and a more ardent love for social happiness and intellectual superiority."

These are the opinions of the committee, expressed in their special report; and it appears to me that they have passed an opinion which is applicable, in all respects, to the case before us. Sir, it would really be well for all parties, both master and operative, if this long-agitated question could be finally set at rest. If you will not concede the whole that we require, concede at first some part of it, and let the success or the failure of the experiments determine the further progress or revocation of the measure. Nothing, you may be assured, will be easier than to repeal such a law should its results prove injurious; the operatives will themselves be the first to cry out if their condition be seriously affected; should the results be beneficial, we shall trust to your willingness to accomplish our desires, and give us the remainder of our present prayer. We are ready at any rate to try that issue. But without some such arrangement as this the manufacturing population will never desist from their efforts for redress; vain is the hope to weary them out by perpetual refusals; they gather resolution under defeats; and at no period have they been more unshaken and courageous than in this present hour, in which I am urging, for the tenth time, I believe, their just and reasonable demands. You cannot wonder at their perseverance; it is natural and praiseworthy; they feel the pressure of intolerable and all-absorbing toil; they perceive the success of experiments towards the alleviation of it in their own department of industry; they perceive too the contemporaneous efforts, arising in no small degree out of their own, to obtain the half-holiday system and the early closing of shops, both of which, wherever practicable, have proved highly beneficial. Their growing intelligence shows to them the moral and physical advantages of abridged labour; and their claims, when stated in this House, always meet with respect, and sometimes with considerable support.

In stating these claims I have abstained from a repetition of evidence adduced, at various times, to exhibit the amount of moral and physical suffering endured by these young persons. This has been a disadvantage to my argument, but I was fearful of wearying the House. I have abstained also from repeating the several calculations made by experienced operatives themselves, on which we maintained that either there would be no abatement of wages, or that, if there were any, they would be enabled, under a reduced period of labour, to establish such economies as would more than compensate for a diminished income. Be this as it may, I say emphatically on their behalf, that they are fully prepared—and I did not, when I proposed the question to them, hear a dissentient voice—to submit to any contingency in return for this concession to their prayers. Sir, we have reason to thank this House, that its successive interpositions in behalf of the factory population have produced most beneficial results, and specially by its enactments which enjoin that certain hours in every day should be set apart for the education of the younger workers; but the education of a people requires something more than this one provision: you must give them time, not only for the acquisition of the necessary elements, but time to retain and practise them. You give to the children, by your present system, a certain amount of literary teaching until the age of 13; they are then, at that period, when the acquisition and experience of whatever is practical would begin, advanced to the full extent of labour, and debarred by their unceasing occupation from the attainment of knowledge, useful—we may say indispensable—to their welfare in after life. This is especially true of the females, who form so large a proportion of the manufacturing population. Their accomplishments, though few and simple, yet unspeakably important to society at large, must be learned in the daily detail of household affairs. They are unsexed in nature and habits by such constant abstraction from domestic duties—duties which they alone can perform—and the community suffers in their toilsome devotion to employments which demand the powers and habits of men. It can find no compensating circumstances in any system which hinders the peace, the comforts, or the honour of the working man's home; but these things will rise or fall with the character and condition of the females; and all the statesmen of every age, and all the maxim-mongers have never surpassed the concentrated wisdom of Madame Campan, who, in answer to a question of the Emperor Napoleon, "What shall I do for the benefit of France?" replied, without hesitation, "Give us, Sire, a generation of mothers."

Sir, I cannot conclude the appeal that I have now ventured to make to the House without a retrospect at the manner in which the question has been conducted from the beginning to its present position. I believe that it has been eminently beneficial to the operatives themselves. Of oversights and mistakes, through human infirmity, I may have committed an abundance, but in expressions and in sentiments I have nothing to recall or even to regret. I have carefully abstained, both here and among the people themselves, from all exciting language; I have studied to produce and to maintain a good understanding between the employer and the employed; I have never ceased to exhort those who confided this measure to my charge, that their thoughts, their feelings, and their actions, must be brought under the dominion of self-control. Well, Sir, I rejoice to say that the effort has been successful. I might have resorted to other means, and kept up their zeal by every inflammatory topic on a subject— be assured—not less interesting to them than the repeal of the Corn Laws; I might have collected them, not by hundreds but by thousands, and talked to them of their wrongs and their rights, of where submission ends, and where resistance begins; but I have done no such thing; and I may now say, to the high honour of those who have so long and so patiently sustained this conflict, that I have never witnessed one menacing effort, or heard from them one vindictive expression. Sir, we must not shut out of our view the wide surface of society to be affected by our decision. It is the concern of many thousands. This single class has been selected out of many to bear the forefront of the battle; but the vote of this evening will affect them all alike, for it may fairly be taken as a representative of the whole: it will be a fatal night whenever you decide adversely, for you will have closed all hopes of moral, and even of secular improvement to multitudes of the young and helpless. And will not this tend to widen the interval—already a deep and yawning gulf—that separates the rich from the poorer sort? The rise of the more affluent classes is very observable; numberless luxuries of mind and sense, hitherto attainable by none but the wealthy, are brought within the reach of much smaller people—they are elevated proportionally in the scale of society. The overtoiled operatives, both as children and as adults, are alone excluded from the common advantage; a few, it is true, of special genius, may triumph over every opposing obstacle; but the mass are abandoned to a state of things in which moral and intellectual culture, forethought and economy, and the resources of independent action, are far beyond their means, and not even in their contemplation. This, surely, is an unsound and fearful position; the contrast is seen, felt, and resented; it revives and exasperates the ancient feuds between rich and poor; and property and station become odious because they seem founded on acquirements from which multitudes are excluded by the prevailing system.

Sir, I cannot fail to perceive that to weary the House with repetitions of these things would be useless, and, therefore, disrespectful. I will persist, nevertheless, to anticipate success, though I must, perhaps, remember that the array of capitalists, backed by the weight of the Ministry, will present an obstacle almost insuperable by persons of far greater power and station than myself. By my course in the last few years, I have accumulated such an amount of public and official odium and distrust, that I cannot but feel I am addressing many whose minds are already averted from the proposition. Should I be defeated, I shall wait for fairer times, and more propitious hearts, conscientiously resolved never to abate one iota of my principles; and fully convinced that if this now mighty nation be destined to sustain its independence, and glory, and power, the counsels of thinking and unselfish men, for the social and religious improvement of all classes of the realm, must eventually and abundantly prosper.

### REPLY.

LORD ASHLEY, in reply, said he would now refer to two statements made by the hon. Member for Durham.\* The statements which had reference to the increased rate of speed of Mr. Gardner's mills, he, on the best authority, had reason for believing to be incorrect. As to the other statement, he had requested the hon. Member for Durham to wait until he had explained the circumstance to which he had referred. [The noble Lord inquired if the hon. Member was in the House, and having been informed in the negative, proceeded.] He had to complain of great discourtesy on the part of the hon. Member for Durham, who, having made a charge against him—a charge of a personal nature—had not remained in the House to hear his reply to it, though he had been requested by him (Lord Ashley) to do so. The circumstance to which the hon. Member alluded was briefly this. The year before last he was in Lancaster, on a visit to the hon. Member for Oldham; and it occurred to him that, as he was within a short distance of Rochdale, where were situated the mills of the hon. Member for Durham, he might as well go over there. He believed himself to be perfectly conversant with all the operations of mills, and therefore did not deem it necessary to add to his experience by an additional inspection of the mills at Rochdale; but he visited them simply and solely that he might see the hon. Member, or leave his name, because the hon. Member, having attacked him in the House in a way which was highly unjustifiable, he thought he would be acting, in colloquial phrase, "like a gentleman," to show him that he entertained no resentment towards him, and wished to meet him on friendly terms. He saw the hon. gentleman's brother on his arrival—conversed for half an hour with him, but said that he did not think it necessary to go over the mills. Why did he say so? In the first place, because he was afraid, had he done so, that it would have been said by the hon. Member that he wanted to spy out some defect, or discover some mismanagement in their arrangement: and secondly, because he had never said a word in disparagement of the conduct of those mills. That, and that only, he solemnly declared, to be the reason why he did not inspect them. He could not help, therefore, stating that he thought the hon. Member for Durham had travelled a little out of the record, when he stated that he was one-sided in all his statements because he had not gone over his mills; for he could assure the House that he had given them the whole history of the case.

\* John Bright, Esq.

## *Dwelling-places of the Working Classes.*

Extract from Speech delivered by LORD ASHLEY at the Hanover Square Rooms, at a meeting of the Society, founded in the year 1842, " for improving the Condition of the Working Classes."

BUT the great matter upon which we rest our claim to your further support, is the experiment that we have instituted, and with great success, for the improvement of the dwelling-places of the working classes. Now, I believe of all the physical questions that affect the condition of the working classes of the present day, there is no one point of so much importance as the condition of the dwelling-places where they and their families reside. I do not speak merely from book; I do not speak merely from the accounts that have been given to me; because I have, not only in past years, but during the present year (having, from present circumstances, rather more leisure than I formerly had), devoted a very considerable number of hours, day by day, to going over some of the worst localities in various parts of this great metropolis. And all that I have seen tends to confirm the opinion I have formed from all that I have heard, both publicly and in private, and which I have stated in public meetings and in the House of Commons. I have ever maintained the opinion, and I defy any person to gainsay it, that a large proportion of our efforts will be thrown away—whether they be directed to the improvement of the physical condition of the people, whether they be directed to their moral and spiritual improvement, to the establishment of schools for their education, to church extension, or domiciliary visitations—all these efforts will be thrown away, so long as we leave the working people in the condition in which they may be seen in various parts of this great metropolis; living in crowded rooms, sometimes two or three families in a single apartment; these rooms and places so foul and so dark, that they are exposed to every physical mischief that can beset the human frame: without light, without water, without drainage, without ventilation. I can assure you that some of those places in which large families reside, are so filthy, that I have found it impossible to go into some of them. The stench, the closeness of the air, pressed so strongly upon the senses, that I was unable to do so; and, in spite of all the resolutions I made at the entrances of some passages, I never could succeed in penetrating to the bottom of them. And I am not singular in that; for when I went on an inspection last year with an eminent physician, he told me that, habituated as he was to enter places of that description, he was frequently obliged to write his prescriptions outside the door. In these courts and rooms, thronged with a dense and most immoral population of every caste and grade of character, but almost every one of them defiled by perpetual habits of intoxication, amid riot and blasphemy of every description, noise and tumult accompanied with every indecency that I have ever seen or read of, reside multitudes of the poor; and, I ask, to what purpose is it that you take children of tender years out of these rooms : that you educate them for some hours during the day; that you give them an excellent moral and spiritual education, if you send them back at night to unlearn, in ten minutes, all that it cost you five hours to teach ? The fact is, this is the great and pressing evil of the day—of that, I mean, which affects the material condition of the people, and is principally prevalent in the metropolis and the large towns of the kingdom. The dwelling-houses of the working people in many of the rural districts are in an infamous condition, and must be looked to when there is the time and the means; but these are things which can be remedied by the proprietors, if the proprietors be excited to a sense of their duty,—and if they do not care for their duty, to a sense of their danger. In these districts, improvement can be more easily introduced. But in the metropolis, and the great towns of the kingdom, you have not the same means of working on the people and the fears of the proprietor. Many of these alleys, many of these courts, belong to small persons, on whom you can produce no effect whatever. Many holders of house property—if you were to endeavour to produce an effect, and they were as open as others to a sense of duty, and the spirit of humanity —are in such a state of poverty and destitution themselves, that they have not the means, I really believe, of improving the condition of the dwelling-houses where so many of the poor reside. This is, therefore, a matter you must look to; and I say, most emphatically, it is the duty of every person who has the least regard for the welfare of his species, to endeavour, either by his own efforts, or else by contributing to the efforts of this or of kindred societies, to roll away from this kingdom, and especially from this metropolis, that great and disgusting reproach. You may have seen that we have established a certain number of houses for artizans of a certain standing in society, persons who may be estimated as making from 15s. to 30s. a week on the average. We have also established models of houses for destitute persons, for widows, who may there enjoy every comfort, quiet intercourse, with every material advantage, at a very low rate.

We are now proceeding, and, if we succeed in obtaining the requisite funds we shall proceed, to found a building which is of far greater importance, with a view to general imitation, than almost any other institution, that I can well conceive, in this great metropolis. Our intention is, if, by God's blessing, we succeed in obtaining the funds, to erect in the heart of the parish of St. Giles's, a model lodging-house—a house where a young man coming up from the country for the first time, or others, who wish to live in a place where some, at least, of the decencies of life are observed, may find a place of retirement and of shelter at a moderate rent. No person can know, except those who have been in the habit of going over this great metropolis,—no person can know the condition, physical and moral, of the various lodging-houses in this town. This very day, I have had an interview with a person of very great experience in these matters, and who has gone over these disgusting tenements.. He tells me, there is every reason to believe that many of these dens are places where half the burglaries and half the violence perpetrated in London and the neighbourhood are concocted by the parties who frequent them. Now, just conceive the condition into which many of these young people are thrown! Many of these young men come up, having received a decent education, and many of them charged with very good principles and very excellent intentions, without any one to advise or guide them. They resort to the first lodging-house they find on their path, which affords them a bed for four-pence or three-pence halfpenny per night. The probabilities are most terribly against that party, that he may fall into the worst connections by taking up his abode in such a receptacle; and I believe that, if you trace the first cause of the fall of many of these men, who come up from the country to engage in the various artisan trades that are carried on here, you will find it is owing to the bad connections they formed within the first few days of their arrival, by having been driven to betake themselves to some of

these detestable places of abode, which are the resort, and necessarily the resort, of the worst characters in the town. And it is
to no purpose to appeal to the police. You may say to them,
" Here is an evil house to be got rid of;" and the police interfere ;
but it is only to knock it down in one place that it may be set up
in another, because these persons have no better refuge. The occupiers of these lodging-houses are persons of the worst description ;
and if you drive them from one locality, they only betake themselves to one a little removed. Unless, therefore, some parties
in the condition of this Society will come forward and institute
buildings such as I have mentioned, which will give them everything that health and decency can require, placed, too, at the same
time, under careful and moral regulations, I do not think that you
will be able, in any one degree, by resort to the law or by the aid
of the police, to abate the smallest fraction of this great and prevailing mischief.

## *Public Health Bill.*

---

# HOUSE OF COMMONS,

### MAY 8, 1848.

---

### Speech on the Adjourned Debate.*

LORD ASHLEY was anxious to impress on the House the absolute and indispensable necessity of instituting some measure which might remove some portion at least of the grievances that pressed so severely on the working population. His honourable friend near him said the other night that this was essentially a working man's question, and he had never in his life said a truer thing, for it affected the whole of the working man's life: it began at home; it affected his capacity to eat and sleep in comfort, to go abroad, and to gain a livelihood by which he might be enabled to rear his family in decency and respectability. He knew that this question was well comprehended by the working classes, and was one of the matters they had really at heart. He had not attended a single meeting of working people in which this had not been a prominent feature; he had constant correspondence with them from all parts of the country, and in every part he found them alive to this question. He need only mention that the other day, when there was a meeting of trade delegates in the metropolis, amongst the grievances urged, and the first on which they came to a resolution, which they did him the honour to communicate to him, was the sanitary condition in which they and their families were left by the neglect of legislative enactments. He, therefore, assured the House that this was a most important question, not only with respect to the moral condition of the working classes, but also in reference to the amount of political content or discontent which they would find existing amongst the masses. Nor was this a question which touched persons of a higher class at second-hand only. They knew the result of sanitary abuses by the large addition to the rates, by the increased demands on private charity, by accessions to the bills of mortality; and, more, they knew it in some cases by the results on themselves.

* From " Hansard."

Fever might break out in some noxious and remote district; but when at length it came to desolate some contiguous and wealthier region, then they began to see the consequences of this intolerable evil. He did not mean to conceal or deny that there were great difficulties in legislating on this subject, and no doubt the proposition of remedies was beset by every species of obstacle. A great number of local interests were to be encountered, a great number of local feelings to be provoked, and it no doubt required some fortitude and perseverance to devise a legislative measure which should apply a remedy to all those prodigious evils. But that could be no argument whatever for stopping this measure on the very threshold, for refusing to go into committee, and there seeing whether they could draw the teeth and pare the talons of this wild beast which had created so much terror.

He gave the Government the highest praise for the manner in which they had addressed themselves to this subject, and the boldness with which they had encountered the opposition and braved the difficulties surrounding the question. But he would fairly tell them, that he thought the measure was susceptible of very great improvement; but whether it was so or not, he implored the House to let the Government have an opportunity of dealing with the measure in committee; for it was one, as he said before, which had taken such strong hold of the minds of the people, that it was essentially necessary to prove to them, not only by general argumentation, but in detail, what was feasible in regard to the removal of the various abominations in existence. He confessed he was very much astonished when he heard it stated by certain dissentients in that House, and out of it, that the law as it now stood was adequate to the removal of those evils. If they looked at the list of Acts on the statute book, they would find no doubt, a great number levelled at abuses of this nature, which might perhaps be remedied if all those acts were enforced; but who was to enforce them? to say that the statute-book was open to all, was like the well-known saying, that the London Tavern was open to all: it was open, no doubt, provided it could be paid for. But this was a most perplexing and tedious process, which you could not call upon the working men, or any number of them, to put in operation. The old laws might be equal to the removal of abuses, but they were by no means equal to the institution of improvements; there was a law for removing masses of filth or noxious stenches, but there was none by which you could furnish to the working classes a pure, ample, and constant supply of water.

The honourable member for West Surrey (Mr. H. Drummond) had remarked that some persons had got up an agitation for the purpose of forcing this measure on the country. He (Lord Ashley) had been most deeply implicated in the movement, and was earnestly anxious to carry a legislative measure in furtherance of the object; he, therefore, took to himself all the blame the honourable member conveyed in the rebuke, and left him to prove what selfish interests he (Lord Ashley) had entertained in the matter. He asked the honourable gentleman whether it was not the case that in the opposition to this measure there was full as much of selfish and pecuniary interest as in the advocacy of the great reform to which the Bill was directed? When the honourable member treated this subject with such great jocosity, he (Lord Ashley) really thought the honourable member must have forgotten, or perhaps have never known, the very deep feeling entertained upon this question throughout the country, and could not have known that in almost every large town and populous locality boards had been formed for the purpose of making periodical reports, and exciting public interest on the subject, all beginning and ending with one and the same complaint, the utter inadequacy of the law for the removal of the great and pressing evils now endured. The city which he (Lord Ashley) represented might almost be said to be in clover as regarded this question. Two petitions, very amply and respectably signed by the inhabitants of Bath, had been presented to the House; one to the effect that, approving of many parts of the Bill, they thought that, on the whole, they could make out such a case for Bath that it ought to be exempted from the operation of the law; the other that, though many people took exceptions to parts of this Bill, yet upon the whole they thought it exceedingly good, and called for by the necessities of the country, and therefore requested their representatives not to give way to any local interests, but to suffer the general necessity to overrule them. He should, therefore, vote for going into committee, with a view to the introduction of such amendments as might be found necessary.

The honourable member for West Surrey had asked, what possible connection there could be between typhus and crime? Could there be a doubt that the same condition of things and habits of life which give rise to fever, also powerfully stimulated the action of immorality and violence? If the honourable member would consider the modes of life so prevalent amongst some unfortunate classes, and the noxious influences by which they were surrounded, he would perceive with the slightest attention that their operation on the physical state was such as made it impossible for them to practise, or even remember, many of the lessons of decency and virtue which they might have been taught in their early life. The noble Lord then quoted, in illustration, the statements of Dr. Neil Arnot respecting the condition of Glasgow, and Mr. F. Cooper respecting that of Southampton:

" In Glasgow, which I first visited, it was found that the great mass of the fever cases occurred in the low wynds and dirty narrow streets and courts, in which, because lodging was there cheapest, the poorest and most destitute naturally had their abodes. From one such locality, between Argyle Street and the river, 754 of about 5000 cases of fever which occurred in the previous year were carried to the hospitals. In a perambulation on the morning of September 24, with Mr. Chadwick, Dr. Alison, Dr. Cowan (since deceased, who had laboured so meritoriously to alleviate the misery of the poor in Glasgow), the police magistrate, and others, we examined these wynds, and to give an idea of the whole vicinity I may state as follows:—We entered a dirty low passage like a house door, which led from the street through the first house to a square court immediately behind, which court, with the exception of a narrow path round it, leading to another long passage through a second house, was occupied entirely as a dung receptacle of the most disgusting kind. Beyond this court the second passage led to a second square court, occupied in the same way by its dunghill; and from this court there was yet a third passage leading to a third court and third dungheap. There were no privies or drains there, and the dungheaps received all filth which the swarm of wretched inhabitants could give; and we learned that a considerable part of the rent of the houses was paid by the produce of the dungheaps. Thus, worse off than wild animals, many of which withdraw to a distance and conceal their ordure, the dwellers in these courts converted their shame into a kind of money by which their lodging was to be paid! The interiors of these houses and their inmates correspond with the exteriors. We saw half-dressed wretches crowding together to be warm; and in one bed, although in the middle of the day, several women were imprisoned under a blanket, because many others who had on their backs all the articles of dress that belonged to the party were then out of doors in the streets. This picture is so shocking that, without ocular proof, one would be disposed to doubt the possibility of the facts; and yet there is, perhaps, no old town in Europe that does not furnish parallel examples. London, before the great fire of 1666, had few drains, and had many such scenes, and the consequence was a pestilence occurring at intervals of about 12 years, each destroying at an average about a fourth of the inhabitants. Who can wonder that pestilential disease should originate and spread in such situations? And, as a contrast, it may be observed here, that when the kelp manufacture lately ceased on the western shores of Scotland, a vast population of the lowest class of people, who had been supported chiefly by the wages of kelp labour, remained in extreme want, with cold, hunger, and almost despair, pressing them down—yet, as their habitations were scattered and in pure air, cases of fever did not arise among them."

With respect to Southampton, Mr. Francis Cooper, surgeon, stated:

" During the period of my parochial attendance on the poor, I have more than once been compelled, in the depth of winter and at midnight, to stand in the street, and walk to and fro till my assistance has been required, not being able to breathe the air of the apartment in which the wretched sufferer lay.  And very recently, on being sent for to a poor woman, I was obliged to absent myself till the very moment of parturition, the air being so bad, so offensive, that a sort of stupor and lassitude rendered me unable to remain.  On visiting the patient the following morning, I was curious to ascertain the actual dimensions of the outlet at the back of the tenement, and found it 6 feet long by 3 feet wide, and at the end of the yard, so called, a privy was erected, only about 3 feet deep, and from which the urine and other liquid deposits were carried away by ground leakage, thus keeping up continual smells of a most noxious character, and acting as one of the most active agents of destruction to health.  The rooms, too— only one above and below—were so low and small, so ill-contrived, as to be unfit for human residence; the structural arrangements so utterly bad as to be a reproach, not only to our civilization, but to our very humanity.  There was no water laid on, no convenience for stowage, the coals being under the stairs, and the pantry (I suppose I must call it so) being placed between the back-door, opening on the yard and the sitting-room, into which every breeze from the west carried the effluvium from the spot at the back of the dwelling, and which, in warm weather, was continually breathed by the occupiers, whose powers of resistance to the deadly influence of such malaria could not possibly continue for any length of time.  The tenements, several in number, were erected at the back of others of large dimensions, and on the side of undrained privies, without drainage, without water, with no positive useful structural arrangement of any kind—mere brick and mortar run up, as the technical expression is, no party-wall (the Act of Lord Normanby is constantly evaded), no basement elevation, no internal appliance for securing comfort or preserving health, and yet 3*s.* 6*d.* per week was paid for rent, 9*l.* 2*s.* a year, or

18 per cent., for what could not have amounted to more than 50*l.* or 60*l.*, at the outside, as the original cost of erection. Who can wonder at the poverty and wretchedness of the poor ? Who can be surprised that disease makes such havoc amongst the labouring population ? Need we comment on the disastrous tendencies which such a state of things suggests ?"

The unhappy beings who were compelled to live in scenes of such putridity and filth grew gradually debilitated and powerless. They became unable to do a day's work, and, sinking into the most abject condition of pauperism, were tempted to perpetrate deeds of violence, and to commit crimes of the foulest and most disgraceful description. There was no man whose evidence on matters affecting the poor was of higher authority than Dr. Southwood Smith; and in his examination before the Commissioners for Inquiring into the State of Large Towns and Populous Districts, he gives the following evidence :

" Do you think that neglect of decency and comfort is likely to render those persons reckless of consequences, and inclined to a mode of getting their living dishonestly ?—The neglect of the decencies of life must have a debasing effect on the human mind; and hopeless want naturally produces recklessness. There is a point of wretchedness which is incompatible with the existence of any respect for the peace or property of others; and to look in such a case for obedience to the laws when there is the slightest prospect of violating them with impunity, is to expect to reap where you have not sown.

" I have myself seen a young man, 20 years of age, sleeping in the same bed with his sister, a young woman 16 or 17 years old. That incestuous intercourse takes place under these circumstances there is too much reason to believe; and that when unmarried young men and women sleep together in the same room, the women become common to the men, is stated in evidence as a positive fact; but I regard another inevitable effect of this state of things as no less pernicious; it is one of the influences which, for want of a better term, may be called unhumanizing, because it tends to weaken and destroy the feelings and affections which are distinctive of the human being, and which raise him above the level of the brute. I have sometimes checked myself in the wish that men of high station and authority would visit these abodes of their less fortunate fellow-creatures, and witness with their own eyes the scenes presented there; for I have thought that the same end might be answered in a way less disagreeable to them. They have only to visit the Zoological Gardens, and to observe the state of society in that large room which is appropriated to a particular class of animals, where every want is relieved, and every appetite and passion gratified in full view of the whole community. In the filthy and crowded streets in our large towns and cities you see human faces retrograding, sinking down to the level of these brute tribes, and you find manners appropriate to the degradation. Can any one wonder that there is among these classes of the people so little intelligence—so slight an approach to humanity—so total an absence of domestic affection, and of moral and religious feeling? The experiment has been long tried on a large scale with a dreadful success, affording the demonstration that if, from early infancy, you allow human beings to live like brutes, you can degrade them down to their level, leaving to them scarcely more intellect, and no feelings and affections proper to human minds and hearts. Have you examined frequently the houses of individuals among the poor in these neglected districts?—Yes. Have you noticed particularly the state of the air in their apartments?—I have; and it sometimes happens to me in my visits to them, as physician to the Eastern Dispensary, that I am unable to stay in the room even to write the prescription. I am obliged, after staying the necessary time at the bedroom of the patient, to go into the air, or to stand at the door, and write the prescription; for, such is the offensive and unwholesome state of the air, that I cannot breathe it even for that short time. What must it be to live in such an atmosphere, and to go through the process of disease in it?"

There was another witness also, whose testimony on such questions as those was of the very highest importance, the Rev. J. Clay, chaplain of Preston gaol; and he, too, was most decidedly of opinion that the physical condition of human beings exercised a most potent influence over their moral condition:

" It should be impressed upon every one desirous of the melioration of his kind, that filthiness of person and sordidness of mind are usually united; and if you would banish squalor and sickness from the labourers' cottage, you must remove ignorance and corruption from his head and heart. Amidst the dirt and disease of filthy back courts and alleys and yards, vices and crimes are lurking altogether unimagined by those who have never visited such abodes."

Nothing could be more distinct, continued the noble Lord, than the reverend gentleman's statement of the connection between disease and crime, and between filth and immorality. His own personal observation entirely corroborated the testimony of Dr. Southwood Smith and Mr. Clay. From the examinations he had himself made, as well as from the evidence he had been able to collect, he had arrived at the conclusion that more than one-half of the habits of intoxication which disgraced large towns and populous districts arose from the sanitary condition in which the population were permitted to live. It was impossible to visit the squalid localities in which the poor were huddled together in many of the towns of England, and to view their pallid, sinking, worn-out forms, and their livid, hueless faces, without experiencing a feeling of compassion which almost prompted one to justify the act of human beings, who, to escape from the contemplation of their unutterable anguish, and to prop a sinking constitution, had recourse to ardent spirits, or other modes of deleterious excitement. He had gone over the records of the fever hospitals of London, and was able to trace in them the connection between the sanitary and moral condition of the people. He had also discovered this terrible and startling truth, that fever, which was the offspring of bad air and defective drainage, fell, in the large proportion of cases, not on children, not on old people, but on adults in the very prime of life. It did not cut off those who, being very young, could not contribute to the general prosperity of the realm; nor those who, being very old, were a burden to it; but it hurried to the grave the heads of families, who left behind them a flock of children and a widow or widower, as the case might be, to be sustained out of the parish funds, or by the charity of private individuals. If the honourable member for West Surrey, or any one else, doubted this statement, he would implore of him, before he hazarded another opinion, to perambulate the pauper districts of the metropolis and judge for himself. He would then be able to know, by means of personal inquiries, whether the fact was so, and also whether the poor people thus miserably circumstanced were or were not sensible of their condition, and did or did not desire to be relieved from it. He (Lord Ashley) had repeatedly heard, from the lips of the inhabitants of these filthy localities, this sickening and awful complaint—the full force of which might be felt with peculiar emphasis, just at this moment when we were enjoying so genial an atmosphere—that they looked with terror at the approach of fine weather. What was a blessing to others was to them a positive curse; for they assured him that when the sun shone forth in its full splendour, the " summer stinks "—that was their phrase—became altogether intolerable. Well, can anything be more pitiable, more touching, or more deplorable than the reflection such a complaint presented to the imagination?

But the most cogent aspect in which this question could be viewed, was that which had reference to the influence of the physical condition of those poor people on their moral nature.

Let them collect the evidence of all the ministers of all religious denominations—let them collect the evidence of all the Scripture-readers, district visitors, and city missionaries throughout the kingdom—and if, out of the entire body, there could be found twenty to deny that there was an intimate connection of misery with filth, and of crime with both—if there could be found twenty to deny that the connection between the moral and physical condition of the poor was most intimate and inevitable, he (Lord Ashley) would not only oppose the present Bill, but would undertake to join any man, or any number of men, in an effort to resist any proposition that might at any future period be made to make this question the subject for a legislative enactment. His noble friend the member for Plymouth had been taunted for saying that all attempts to diffuse education amongst the poor were little better than vain and profitless, so long as they were permitted to continue in their present sanitary condition; but the noble Lord had said nothing more than had been already expressed on many occasions by others. He (Lord Ashley) concurred unreservedly in the statement, and was most distinctly of opinion that it was next to impossible that any genuine or lasting good should result from education so long as Parliament left the people in their present physical and domiciliary condition. His experience of the ragged schools confirmed him in the conviction, for he there saw the extreme difficulty, if not the absolute impossibility of training children in the way they should go, who, after school-hours, were permitted to return to the filthy purlieus from which they had issued in the morning, there to unlearn in one hour what their preceptors had spent a week in endeavouring to teach them. In a few isolated cases the power of education might prevail over all evil influences; but on the great mass of cases its beneficial effect would be wholly counteracted.

He had to thank the House for the kindness with which they have heard him, and should apologize for having trespassed at such length on their attention. In conclusion, he would express an earnest hope that the House would permit the Bill to go into committee, there to undergo such alterations and amendments as might be considered necessary. He trusted that they would concede thus much; and by so doing make one onward step to the recovery of those unhappy people, and to the recognition of their right to be placed on a level with sentient and immortal beings.

## *Emigration and Ragged Schools.*

# HOUSE OF COMMONS,

### JUNE 6, 1848.

Speech on a motion to bring under the notice of the House the state of a portion of
the juvenile population of the Metropolis, and to move, " That it is expedient
that means be annually provided for the voluntary Emigration to some one of
Her Majesty's Colonies, of a certain number of young persons of both sexes,
who have been educated in the schools ordinarily called ' Ragged Schools,' in
and about the Metropolis."

SIR,

The House will, I am sure, excuse me, not only from bringing
under their deliberation the subject of which I have given notice,
but also for entreating their most patient attention. It has been
my lot, on many occasions, to introduce questions very deeply
affecting the condition of the working classes ; but on no occasion
have I ever introduced a subject more vitally interesting to the
parties that I represented, or more intimately connected with the
honour and welfare of the whole community.

Of the existence of the evil no one can doubt who perambulates
the streets and thoroughfares of this vast city, and observes the
groups of filthy, idle, tattered children either squatting at the
entrances of the courts and alleys, or engaged in occupations
neither useful to themselves, nor creditable to the locality. If he
proceed to estimate their moral by their physical condition (and it
will be a just estimate),—if he examine the statements before the
police officers, or the records of the various tribunals—or, above
all, if, by personal inspection, he seek to understand the whole
mischief, he will come to the conclusion that these pressing and
immediate evils must be met by the application of an immediate
remedy. This state of things afflicts every sense of humanity ; it
appeals to every notion of justice ; and I must say, in reference to
the character of the age and the temper of the times in which we
live, that it is matter for grave consideration to all, who consult,

not only the reputation, but even the safety, of this great metropolis.

I am happy to say that this is no controversial question; no interest is assailed—I cannot anticipate any opposition except from those who believe that they can suggest a better plan; and, indeed, it is less from any overweening confidence that I have hit the true method, than from a desire to excite discussion, and stimulate general effort, that I have propounded this matter for our present debate.

I may, perhaps, assume that the evil is acknowledged, but I do not think that it is fully estimated. I wish much to show the nature and extent of the mischief, to prove that it cannot be dealt with in any ordinary way, nor brought under the separate influence of any existing agencies—the evil is peculiar, and must be met by peculiar means, administered by a peculiar agency.

Till very recently, the few children that came under our notice in the streets and places of public traffic, were considered to be chance vagrants, beggars, or pilferers, who, by a little exertion of magisterial authority, might be either extinguished or reformed. It has only of late been discovered that they constitute a numerous class, having habits, pursuits, feelings, manners, customs, and interests of their own; living as a class, though shifting as individuals, in the same resorts; perpetuating and multiplying their filthy numbers. For the knowledge of these details we are mainly indebted to the London City Mission; it is owing to their deep, anxious, and constant research; it is owing to the zeal with which their agents have fathomed the recesses of human misery, and penetrated into places repulsive to every sense, moral and physical; it is owing to such exertions, aided by the piety, self-denial, and devotion of Sunday-school teachers, that we have advanced thus far. Certain excellent persons, who gave their energies to Sabbath training, were the first to observe these miserable outcasts : and hoping, by the influence of the gospel, to effect some amendment, opened schools in destitute places, to which the children were invited, not coerced. Hence the clue to a vast amount of information, a part of which I shall now proceed to lay before the House!

Our first consideration must have reference to the numbers of this particular class—it is difficult to form an accurate estimate; but from all the inquiries that I have been able to make—and I can assure the House that no trouble has been spared—I should say that the naked, filthy, roaming, lawless, and deserted children in and about the metropolis, exceeded, rather than fell short of, 30,000. There are, doubtless, many more in this vast city who may be considered as distressed children, objects of charity and of the public care; but I speak now of that generation in particular, which is distinct from the ordinary poor, and beyond the observation of the daily perambulators of squares and thoroughfares.

The House will, perhaps, be curious to learn what are the habits and dispositions of this wild race; their pursuits, modes of livelihood, the character of their dwelling-places, and the natural history, as it were, of the species, so that some steps may be taken to extricate them from their sad condition, and place them in a situation where the exercise of virtue may at least be possible. Depend upon it, that while they are left in their present state, and exposed to all the detestable circumstances that surround them, the efforts of the clergyman and the missionary will be in vain; you undo with one hand the work of the other: it is a Penelope's web, woven in the morning but unravelled at night.

Now look at the result of an examination of 15 schools in which these children are occasionally congregated; I find the number on the lists to amount to 2345, ranging between 5 and 17 years of age; but the average attendance may be taken at 1600. Now of these 1600, 162 confessed that they had been in prison, not once, nor twice, many of them, several times; 116 had run away from their homes, the result, in many instances, of ill-treatment; 170 slept in lodging houses, and on this head I shall say a few words presently. I may just observe, in passing, that these receptacles are the nests of every abomination that the mind of man can conceive; 253 confessed that they lived altogether by begging; 216 had neither shoes nor stockings; 280 had no hats, caps, bonnets, or head covering; 101 had no linen; 219 never slept in beds, many had no recollection of having ever tasted that luxury; 68 were the children of convicts; 125 had stepmothers, to whom may be traced much of the misery that drives the children of the poor to the commission of crime; 306 had lost either one or both parents, a large proportion having lost both. Now, taking the average attendance at the schools as 4000, and applying to it the calculations applied to the number just stated, we shall have 400 who confess that they had been in prison; 660 who lived by begging; 178 the children of convicts; and 800 who had lost one or both parents!

So much for their domestic position. Their employments are in strict keeping; we may class them as street-sweepers, vendors of lucifer-matches, oranges, cigars, tapes, and ballads; they hold horses, run on errands, job for "dealers in marine stores;" such is the euphonous term for "receivers of stolen goods," a body of large influence in this metropolis, without whose agency juvenile crime would be much embarrassed in its operations. See, too, where many of them retire for the night, if they retire at all; to all manner of places; under dry arches of bridges and viaducts; under porticos, sheds, and carts; to out-houses, in saw-pits, on staircases, in the open air, and some in lodging-houses. Curious, indeed, is their mode of life. I recollect the case of a boy who, during the inclement season of last winter, passed the greater part of his night in the large iron roller of the Regent's Park. He climbed, every evening, over the railings, and crept to his shelter, where he lay in comparative comfort. Human sympathy, however, prevails even in the poorest condition; he invited a companion less well provided than himself, promising to "let him into a good thing;" he did so, and it proved a more friendly act than many a similar undertaking in railway shares.

Let me proceed now to the lodging-houses. I attach no small importance to the review of this part of the subject, because I know how many of these unfortunate children are doomed to live in these sinks of wretchedness and vice; and how difficult, if not impossible, it is to deal with them by any ordinary means, so long as they are forced to resort to such haunts of pollution. I will trouble you to listen to the descriptions of a lodging-house. I have seen many of them myself, and they are abominable; but the statement I shall now read is given on the authority of a city missionary, who had been appointed to inspect these dens, and report upon them. It is not an exaggerated picture of several of those places, in which hundreds and thousands of the human race are nightly congregated. The "parlour,"—you will observe the elegance of the terms,—" the parlour measures 18 feet by 10. Beds are arranged on each side of it, composed of straw, rags, and shavings. Here are 27 male and female adults and 31 children, with several dogs; in all, 58 human beings in a contracted den, from which light and air are systematically excluded. It is impossible," he says, "to convey a just idea of their state—the quantities of vermin are amazing. I have entered a room, and in a few minutes I have felt them dropping on my hat from the ceiling like peas." "They may be gathered by handfuls," observed one of the inmates. "I could fill a pail in a few minutes. I have been so tormented with the itch, that on two occasions I filled my pockets with stones, and waited till a policeman came up, and then broke a lamp that I might be sent to prison, and there be cleansed, as is required before new comers are admitted." "Ah!" said another, standing by, "you can get a comfortable snooze and scrub there;" but nowhere else it is manifest—the jail is a resource for these unfortunate people. Many boys of tender years frequent these houses; and not a few of them are for the promiscuous reception of boys and girls. I press on these matters, because I wish to show the variety of circumstances that stand in the way of their moral and physical improvement—here is a proof in the existence of such resorts ! Inquire, and you will find it to be true, not only of the metropolis, but of the smaller as well as greater towns throughout the country, that 7-10ths of the crime perpetrated in the various localities, are concocted by the society that assemble in these caverns. The Warwick magistrates say, and it is equally applicable to London, "such houses are the general receptacle of offenders. Here the common vagrants assemble in great numbers at nightfall, and, making the lodging-houses the common centre, traverse their several beats." "I have no hesitation," says a public officer, "in declaring my belief that the principal robberies have been concocted in a vagrant lodging-house, and rendered effectual through the agency of the keepers." But this is not all. When a boy leaves the lodging-house, and emerges into the open air, he is exposed to influences quite as deleterious to his moral and physical well-being. I will read a description of a court which I have witnessed myself. Now observe, it is in such places that a large mass of the community are now dwelling. In one of those courts there are three privies to 300 people ; in another two to 200 people. This is a statement made by a medical man,—" In a place where these public privies existed scenes of the most shocking character were of daily occurrence. It would scarcely be believed that those public privies often stood opposite the doors of the houses ; modesty and decency were altogether impossible." But in a private house—what a strange misnomer !—is the boy exposed to better influences than in the lodging-house ? Very often several families are found in one room. That is a fortunate family which has one room for itself. Everything is transacted in that room. Cleanliness is impossible; it is a scene of filth, misery, and vice. The House will now, I hope, permit me to pass to the description of a locality which affords a fair sample of the class of abodes; for those children are a peculiar race, to be found in almost all instances in the most filthy, destitute, unknown parts of the metropolis—places seldom trodden by persons of decent habits. "These courts and alleys are in the immediate neighbourhood of uncovered sewers, of gutters full of putrified matter, nightmen's yards, and privies, the soil of which is openly exposed, and never or seldom removed. It is impossible to convey an idea of the poisonous condition in which those places remain during winter and summer, in dry weather and wet, from the masses of putrifying matter which are allowed to accumulate." Now these statements are by no means exaggerations. I would not make such assertions if I could not do so on my own personal knowledge. I have gone over many parts of those districts, and have devoted a considerable portion of my time to the prosecution of investigations on this subject. When, in 1846, I lost my seat in Parliament, and finding myself "studiis florentem ignobilis otî," I determined to explore the unknown parts of the metropolis. In company with a medical man and a city missionary, I have ventured to go over many of those places, and I am able to say that the description I have now given is below the truth. And sure I am, that if I could persuade any honourable member to visit those disgusting localities, there would be no more need for argument or description; they would join, one and all, in a general effort to wipe away a state of things so disgraceful to the kingdom, and so injurious to the peace and welfare of the whole community.

The House will have anticipated, I think, the statement of their physical condition. The children are thus described by Dr. Aldis: "They are emaciated, pale, and thin, and in a low condition. They complain of sinking, depression of the strength, loss of spirits, loss of appetite accompanied by pains in different parts of the body, with disturbed sleep." "The depressed and low condition of health in which these people are always found induces habits of intemperance, unfortunately so common among them." "The children," says another, "are diminutive, pale, squalid, sickly, irritable; I rarely saw a child in a real healthy state."

One of the most pious, intelligent, and active clergymen of London, the Rev. Mr. Champneys of Whitechapel, has told me of the singular aptitude of those children to learn. He could only attribute it to their nervous susceptibility, produced by the circumstances in which they were placed. But he added, that while it would enable them to learn what was good, the readiness with which they learned what was bad was most alarming. The condition of those children is very peculiar. Their nervous susceptibility is stimulated so that they acquire instruction with a promptitude and activity beyond their years. Their energies are quick and lively; but they are speedily exhausted, and come to a premature grave. Many, from the condition in which they have been brought up, are greatly enfeebled; and though much may be done to restore their health and strength by giving them proper food, and allowing them to breathe a purer air, yet upon examination it is often found that these children have all some defect or other which is sufficient to exclude them from employment. A friend of mine, a Lord of the Admiralty, had arranged that if any of those children could be selected who were fit for employment, they should be taken on board a ship in Her Majesty's service. Five were sent to be examined; but in the twinkling of an eye the examiner rejected them, though they were the picked boys of the school. But after those children had been for a few months at the school, where they were fed and brought under proper care, they appeared to be changed. They became strengthened, fit for work, and showed to what condition they may arrive, when recovered from the neglect to which they had been originally abandoned. If they are only placed where they may breathe fresh air and receive a moderate supply of food, they will become as efficient for the purposes of labour as any children to be found in any part of Her Majesty's dominions, for the disease from which those children in their original condition suffered is of that kind which arises from bad air and from the want of sufficient sustenance. There is a school for such children in the neighbourhood of the House where we are now sitting; there they get sufficient food; and they are, in consequence, fit for any labour to which children can be put; and if such an opportunity again offers itself as had been offered by my noble friend the Lord of the Admiralty, I have no doubt that a number of them would be passed, because they would be found fully competent for the labour.

Of their moral condition I need say little beyond the report of one of the schools:

"The boys had been sent out daily by drunken parents to beg and steal, being often cruelly treated if unsuccessful: others were employed in vending and assisting in the manufacture of base coin. . . Another says, of 74 admitted this year between 8 and 14, known thieves, 16; beggars and hawkers, 27." But there is a most remarkable statement made on the authority of a city missionary in a district of the east of London. His house is the open resort of all who choose to come to pay him a visit, and ask his advice. From January to December he received from these children and young persons, 2343 visits, averaging 334 per month. Of these, under 10 years of age there were 2 per cent.; under 12, 9 per cent.; above 12 and under 15, 44 per cent.; above 15 and under 18, 37 per cent.; above 18 and under 22, 8 per cent. Of these 39 per cent. voluntarily acknowledged they had been in prison; 11 per cent. had been in once; 4 per cent., twice; 5 per cent., thrice; 2 per cent., four times; 1 per cent., six times; 3 per cent., seven times; 1 per cent., eight times; 2 per cent., ten times; and there were 10 per cent. uncertain as to the number of times.

This is a curious picture of juvenile society in the great metropolis! and whence has it arisen? from various causes: it has arisen, in a great measure, either from the desertion or the bad example of parents. In many instances it is good for the children that they have been deserted; in many instances, no doubt, is is good that they have no parents in existence, for not unfrequently they are misled by their bad example—still more frequently are they tempted by necessity. There are hundreds and thousands in this great city who, from their earliest years, have never obtained a meal except by begging, or by stealing, or by some avocation of a questionable kind. Children, in truth, are encouraged by their parents to that course of life. Even in those instances where parents do not bring up their children to habits of theft, they take very good care when property is brought in of a suspicious character to ask no questions, and to bestow praise for adroitness in such transactions.

But whence are the parents affected? a vast proportion of the evils which surround them arises from the sanitary condition in which they are left. The same causes which operate on the children operated on the parents before them—an irresistible depression of health, a gradual, but certain, decline of the physical energies, followed by intemperate habits, and a hopeless pauperism, have rendered them utterly reckless of decency, of comfort, of regard for the spiritual and temporal welfare of their children, reckless almost even of life itself.

With these facts under its notice, the House will not be surprised to learn the figure that these children cut before the courts of the police, and the tribunals of justice. We may see, from the reports of the Metropolitan Police, reports drawn up with much skill and accuracy, that in the year 1847 there were taken into custody 62,181 persons, of all ages, and of both sexes. Of these 20,702 were females, and 41,479 were males; whereof there were under 20 years of age, 15,698; between 10 and 15, 3682; under 10, 362. Of the whole 62,000, 22,075 could neither read nor write; and 35,227 could read only or read and write imperfectly. I do not quote this statement from any belief that mere literary attainments will have a very material influence in amending the conduct of the young; but I quote it to show the neglect in which they must have passed their early years; the want of all internal or external discipline, during the most impressible period of life, when moral instruction is most easily communicated. But mark another striking statement at the close of the tables; out of these 62,000 persons taken into custody, there were no less than 28,118 who had no trade, business, calling, or occupation whatsoever. They were merely vagabonds living by their wits, wandering from one place to another, and making the whole world a prey for their subsistence.

Now, when we bear in mind the condition of these children, is it surprising that there should be such a mass of persons without any employment ?—thousands in tattered garments, unable to read or write, known only as wandering beggars, may offer themselves as applicants for work—is it not obvious that, untrained as they are, no one will engage them, more especially when such a pressure exists that oftentimes the best workmen are compelled to sustain a severe struggle ? few, however, make any application, because they are sure to be rejected. But it is a serious fact, that so many thousands should be habituated to idleness, or that diseased activity which is the result of it; because they think that they have a necessity for living as much as any other, and they take measures accordingly. Nor may we disregard the temper of the times ;—the condition of these persons renders the state of society more perilous than in any former day. Be assured that the mischief does not admit of delay; the Legislature is called on to make an immediate effort for the mitigation, if not the total overthrow, of this portentous evil.

The statements that I have already made afford but a mode of approximating to the extent of the evil; the records of the tribunals and police courts show only the numbers of those whom the constable is quick enough to apprehend. But there is a vast amount of unseen and undetected crime; many breaches of the public order; many injuries to the peace, property, and safety of individuals; and a great prevalence of that training which forms these children to a character perilous to the well-being of society. I believe that the majority of criminals, in and about London, arises out of this class; if we were to extinguish, or greatly improve this strange tribe, we should not, I allow, extinguish crime altogether; crime is inseparable from our fallen nature; but I hold that it would be considerably abated, inasmuch as the large proportion of it is, manifestly, the work of the classes so neglected, and exposed, by their necessities, to an extraordinary force of temptation. A city missionary has written to me, " I look on several parts of my district as breeding-places for prisons;" this is the concurrent testimony of all those who are best acquainted with the race before us; and how can it well be otherwise? Recollect the condition of these children; weigh their necessities, their moral state, the manner in which they have been brought up, the circumstances in which they are permitted to remain. Having no knowledge of right or wrong, except that which is begotten in some way or other by their fears; they believe that they have a right to prey on the whole world; " meum and tuum " depend not, in their estimation, on law or principle, but on the power to hold possession; their needs, so they conceive, giving them, not only a dexterity, but a claim, in appropriating the superfluities of others. Now, then, let me implore the House to consider the temptations to which poor children, thus morally provided, are exposed by the reprehensible carelessness of this commercial city; remember them living by their wits, hungry like ourselves, and not knowing, from one hour to another, whether they shall obtain anything for their sustenance during the day; look at the temptations which beset them on every side, temptations often commented on, and most justly, in the police courts, arising from the total want of care in the owners of property. I find, that of the felonies which were perpetrated last year within the jurisdiction of the metropolitan police, there were 814 cases of stealing tools, &c., from unfinished houses where they had been left by workmen without any care or supervision whatever; that the number of cases of stealing from carts and carriages which had been left without any one to look after them was 298; that the number of cases of theft from houses in consequence of the doors being left open by the most wanton neglect on the part of servants and masters was 2208; and that the number of cases of theft of goods exposed for sale at shop-doors—and hon. gentlemen will recollect how freely goods of all descriptions are so exposed, especially of all kinds of provisions, calculated to tempt the appetite of hungry children—of these cases the number was 2299. Now, every one of these felonies has increased in number, with the exception,—and this is a very curious fact,—with the exception of felonies of linen exposed to dry. These have considerably abated; and I hardly hesitate to assert that this has arisen from the establishment of public baths and washhouses, which enable poor people to wash and dry their clothes by a cheap and speedy progress, and keep them under proper care and supervision.

All these things tend to show the necessity of adopting a course that shall extricate these children from their present position, and save them from a return to it. I, therefore, seek to prove that they are of such a singular description as to be beyond any ordinary appliances, requiring a system of their own, unlike all other children in most respects; and in none more than in their habits of insubordination. Take, for instance, the scenes that invariably occur on the opening of a school in some new locality. I have heard teachers, who have undertaken to open such schools on speculation—I do not mean a money speculation, but by way of experiment—I have heard them describe the roaring and whistling, the drumming at the doors, the rattling at the windows, which signalize the commencement of the academical course. The boys, when admitted, oftentimes break everything, forms, slates, tables, intermixing their sport with occasional fighting. There is a school over the water well known, I believe, to the hon. member for Kinsale—when it was first opened, in 1846, there came four-and-twenty boys, all furnished with tobacco-pipes, who would neither learn nor dislodge, but kept possession of the room for several nights. The teachers waited with patience, trusting that they would soon be tired of their "lark," and go away, having left the school to those who desired better things. Their hope was fulfilled; others soon supplied their places; and now the school is in active operation, and is producing, thank God, most beneficial results. In another, the onslaught was of a sterner character; the teachers were compelled to barricade the doors, and escape through the windows over the roof. Such is the character of most inaugural meetings of these schools; a fortnight or more elapses, in general, before order can be maintained; nor can it ever be introduced without the highest exercise of patience in encountering obstacles so unpleasant and risks so peculiar. I heard from a gentleman, not long ago, who had himself officiated as a teacher, that he was once in charge of a class where a single boy was especially provoking. He bore it for a while, but at last could bear it no longer, and, seizing the boy by the neck, gave him a thorough good shaking. This passed off, and little was said; but in three minutes thereafter the teacher found himself prostrate at full length on the ground. The boy, it seems, determined to be avenged for the insult which he considered he had received, got upon the floor, and, passing between the legs of the teacher, suddenly expanded them, with a shout of joy; and then, having thrown the gentleman on his back, he returned to his seat. Now, had the gentleman given way to his anger, and punished the boy for this offence, the result would probably have been that the school would have been broken up; but, exercising a more correct judgment, he took no notice of what had occurred. He saved his dignity by assuming that he had fallen down, and the boy, having obtained his redress, was fully satisfied—the school is now in effective operation, and I believe the boy is become a diligent and obedient pupil.

Sometimes it has been necessary to call in the aid of the police to preserve a semblance of order. This necessity gave rise, in one instance, to a remarkable event. One of the policemen called in was himself a philanthropist, and also a bit of a scholar; and he thought that he should most effectually attain his end by taking a class; he did so, and then the whole school became like "the happy family," which may be seen any day in Trafalgar Square.

So great was the enthusiasm of the boys for the constable, that they gave him the title, which I believe he still retains, of "King of the Peelers." Now, you must bear in mind that these descriptions are applicable to the entire class; and that all who institute ragged schools must be prepared for similar events and situations —but if they are so resolved, and exhibit forbearance, sympathy, and real love for these pariahs of society, I hesitate not to say that they will reap a larger harvest than may be won from many schools, where the children have been trained to easier lives and in habits of constant indulgence.

Now look to another peculiarity which forms an obstacle in the way of those who would proceed by established methods. See their comparative attendance at different seasons. These children are not accustomed to ordinary rules; they have never been subjected to domestic discipline, and they have no notion of being forced. They may be invited, they may be soothed, they may be gained by attention; but in general they will have their own way. I find that summer is peculiarly attractive to them, and that it is difficult during that season to obtain an adequate attendance. They are drawn away to prowl about the country. Many of them go great distances in pursuit of something which they call pleasure, or they may call profit—their views and projects are best known to themselves—but, whatever are their motives, certain it is they are often drawn away in summer to great distances. I perceive, from a report of the comparative attendance at the school in the Broadway, Westminster, that the number of children who attend in winter is 200, while at the present season (June) the average attendance is not more than 40. This comparatively thin attendance arises also from the circumstance of the fine weather tempting them to remain in the streets to a later hour, begging or stealing, or selling the little articles they have to dispose of.

If such be their habits, the House will see that it is next to impossible to bind them down by ordinary rules, and make them conform to regulations which are salutary, and even palatable, to children accustomed to something of domestic discipline; the class has been newly discovered, and must be grappled with on a new system.

In confirmation of what I say, observe their migratory habits; how they shift from one part of London to another, and from the town to the country. In the report of the school at Broadway it is stated, that out of 507 boys admitted, very few who attended at the beginning of the year remained to the end of it. One of the city missionaries, stationed in Westminster, has assured me that one-fourth of the population in his district migrate every month.

Why, what can you do, with your ordinary rules and traditional methods, in the management of such people? Nothing—you must hold out to them some inducement to break their habits. Government, I must think, knowing the nature of this class, and knowing also that it has sprung from our neglect, and the neglect of our fathers, is in duty bound either to remove the temptations to which these children are exposed, or render them less attractive, or enable the youngsters, by the hope of recompense, to resist the temptations so freely thrown in their path. Their whole mode of life is perplexing, and defies all existing agency. Observe, they can come to the schools only in the evening. It is to no purpose to open a day-school, unless we also provide the food; and this addition inflicts a vast augmentation of expense. During the morning they are engaged in various avocations to obtain the sustenance necessary for the day; but this obligation alone is sufficient to take them out of the category of those children who can submit to regularity of attendance, and conform to canonical hours.

Now, Sir, to meet the exigencies of this case, the case of these many thousands of children, I have heard a variety of propositions; but I cannot concur in any one of them. I have heard it said, in the first place, that schools should be erected, and some system introduced of national education. But this cannot be undertaken, because the very instant any one proposes such a measure, the *vexata questio* is raised, as to how children should be trained—whether by a secular or a religious education, and, if by a religious education, what sort of religion; whether that of the Church of England or of a mixed character; and while we are discussing what we shall do on these questions, hundreds and thousands of the children are rising up into the ranks of thieves, and perhaps murderers.

Nor can we, at once, undertake to establish schools of this description. We must first consider a new element; we must consider the expediency and the practicability of not only teaching but feeding the pupils. It is a novel matter, and one of great importance.

I must again repeat, in reference to the proposition of erecting such schools, that we have no existing agencies by which they may be superintended and controlled. The Church has none: she is far too feeble amid the larger populations. The British and Foreign Society have none; the National Society is alike powerless. It is clear that they cannot be admitted into the schools already established; if they were so, their admission would be followed by the withdrawal of the "respectable" chil-

dren—such is the term. The parents of a better class would
shrink, and not reprehensibly, from the moral and physical contamination of these wretched outcasts.

It is next proposed, that grants may be made by the Privy
Council, and schools established, subject to an inspection. Now,
no doubt, if such schools were established, they would do a certain
degree of good; but it would be altogether inadequate to the evil
which prevails. In the first place, I do not hesitate to say, that it
would be next to impossible for Her Majesty's Government to
appoint an inspector capable of estimating the character and value
of all the difficulties and dilemmas to which these schools would
be exposed; they could never be conformed to his notions of discipline. And neither of these plans would meet the difficulty of
determining how these children were to be disposed of after they
are educated. We should still have the same mass of unemployed poor, still the same temptations, and still the same impossibility of resisting them. The third plan which I have heard
proposed is, the erection of a large barrack at some distance from
London, at which the great mass of these children should receive
their education. This is designated the hospital system. Now,
this has been tried to a great extent in Scotland, and has been
found most injurious, bringing up the children, as it does, in a
mode of life which is in no respect their mode of life in after
years; abstracting them for three or four years from all connexion with home, and from all domestic relations, and training
them exclusively within four walls. It has been found in all
instances—in the workhouse schools and elsewhere—very far
from answering the purposes for which such institutions are
established.

But I entertain another very strong objection to a wholesale
removal of the children from home, carrying them far away, and
shutting them up in some large receptacle. No doubt, in many
instances, it would be better if the children were removed from
their parents,—it would often be better if they had no parents at
all; but I must lay it down as a general rule that home discipline,
however imperfect, is of a beneficial character, and cannot be supplied by any other system employed elsewhere. We must also
recollect, that one great object of instituting these schools is to
produce a proportionate effect upon the parents of the children,
their relatives, friends, and associates. In most instances, it has
been found almost vain to attempt the reformation of adults by
direct efforts. It has been tried in various ways. In our prison-
discipline ingenuity is at a standstill to discover by what means
we can effect the permanent reformation of delinquents of riper

years. They have been found, in most instances, altogether inaccessible to the labours of the clergyman and the missionary. But very frequently an approach to them is open through the medium of the children. I could mention hundreds of instances where the example of children has brought the parents, by shame or precept, to habits of decency and order; and I feel confident that if we had the means of extending this system, and holding out the prospect of benefit to such parties from the reformation of their lives, we should be able to produce the most striking and permanent effects upon many abandoned localities within this vast metropolis.

Now, to meet the many difficulties I have referred to, there has been set up, at various intervals, the system of ragged schools. Many, I dare say, may take exception to the name. I will not detain the House by attempting to prove the value and efficacy of the title. It is sufficient to say, that I know many instances where the name, so far from being repulsive, has been attractive to that very peculiar class; and, though it designates those whom we receive, it does not always designate those whom we turn out. They are received ragged, but they are turned out clothed—they are received as heathens, and in many instances, I thank God, they go out Christians. Many such schools have been established, not only in London but in other parts of England. They have proved themselves, thereby, to be adapted to the necessities of the times; for the principles upon which they are founded recommend themselves to the judgment of those who are most conversant with the class. But to proceed; the number of ragged schools in London and neighbourhood are now about 60. The number of children who pass through them—including those who attend on Sunday—are estimated at 10,000. This is not the average attendance, because the greater number attend only on the Sabbath.

The position of these schools, and their mode of government, should next be stated to the House. They are generally planted in some miserable locality; we are fortunate enough, in a few instances, to obtain a good room; in one or two a room has been erected at the expense of some charitable person; in others we are obliged to rest content with converted stables, and such-like inconvenient places. They are opened, generally, every evening at six o'clock; the teachers are in some cases voluntary, in others they are paid. The children are taught to read, write, and cast accounts, and are carefully trained in the great precepts and doctrines of Christianity. The promoters of these schools have been beset by a variety of difficulties; they have been discouraged

by want of funds, and all those manifold and divers failures that
wait on every novel and infant institution; but they have, nevertheless, had greater success than they had at first presumed to
anticipate. They have obtained situations for many of their
pupils, and in no instance have any been dismissed for bad conduct in service. These schools are conducted altogether on a very
wide basis: the teachers consist of various denominations of Dissenters, as well as of the Church of England; and upon the committees Dissenting ministers and clergymen of the Established
Church unite in the most hearty co-operation. Nothing can be
more gratifying than to attend the periodical meetings, where all
ecclesiastical differences are sunk; and all are pleased at seeing
the plant thrive under their care.

An honourable member asks me "What is the religious teaching?" I reply, that all these schools are under local committees.
There is a central committee, of which I am chairman, and which
holds its meetings in Exeter Hall, but it imposes no conditions
upon those schools that are in union with it. We require no
more, but in this we are positive, than that the Bible should be
used in all its integrity. These meetings are held once a quarter,
for the purpose, among others, of collecting funds, as far as we
are able, and distributing them amongst the schools: but we leave
it to the clergymen of the Church of England and the Dissenting
ministers and other teachers to attend to the religious instruction.

We must take good care, in whatever we do for the advancement of this system, to do nothing that shall damp or discourage
the voluntary principle—but though it may not be damped, it
must be stimulated, as, unaided and by itself, quite inadequate to
the purpose. We must rely on the local agency of the various
districts, and the hearty and effective co-operation of the small
tradesmen in the vicinity; the office is at first so physically
offensive, and, for a long time, so morally disheartening, that
ordinary service is unequal to the task.

The system, however, must, as I have said, be stimulated—and
the proposition which I make to the Government is this,—That
the Government should agree to take every year from these
schools a number of children, say 1000—500 boys and the same
number of girls,—and transplant them at the public expense to
Her Majesty's Colonies in South Australia. When I make this
proposition, of course I do not do so in a dictatorial manner, and
if the Government only accede to it, they may vary it in detail
precisely as they please. I mention South Australia, because in
that colony there is at this moment the greatest demand for
labour. I propose, too, that the removal of the children to that

colony shall be the reward of good conduct, and that they shall have a certain amount of education; the test of that amount may be left to the Government, but of course with children of that class or condition the destiny for which they are intended must be looked to. It will not be necessary that the test should be of very high literary attainments. Nor do I wish to assign any particular period for them to be at the school,—so that they can fulfil the test imposed, I desire that their removal should be the reward of good conduct; this is all that can be required. The advantages of such a scheme will be indescribable. I am quite convinced, from all the inquiry I have been able to make, that it will produce a serious and permanent benefit upon the whole population of the country. When people see that their money will issue in something practicable, should these schools be instituted, and that the children will be decently trained, and afterwards removed from vice and temptation to some place where they may conduct themselves like honest citizens, they will contribute largely to establish many over the length and breadth of the metropolis—let us look then to the effect it will have upon the children themselves; miserable, ignorant, and forgotten as they are, those children, nevertheless, before they have passed three months at these schools, begin to aspire to better things. The right hon. baronet the Home Secretary was good enough to accompany me some time ago to one of these schools. It was during working time—but had it not been so, and had the children been at liberty to run about, I doubt not, that, knowing the dignity of my right hon. friend's station and the goodness of his heart, they would have beset him with applications to be sent to sea or to some one of the colonies. If, therefore, you will hold out to those children as the reward of good conduct that which they desire—a removal from scenes which it is painful to contemplate, to others where they can enjoy their existence,—you will make the children eager by good conduct to obtain such a boon. There are, be assured, amongst the children, guilty and disgusting as they are, many thousands who if opportunities are given them, will walk in all the dignity of honest men and Christian citizens.

But at present they are like tribes of lawless freebooters, bound by no obligations, and utterly ignorant or utterly regardless of social duties. They trust to their skill, not to their honesty; gain their livelihood by theft, and consider the whole world as their legitimate prey. With them there is no sense of shame; nor is imprisonment viewed as a disgrace. In many instances it has occurred that after a boy has been a short time at one of these schools he

suddenly disappears. At the end of a few weeks he comes back
to the very spot in the school where he sat when he was last there.
The master, going up to him, says, "My boy, where have you
been?" The boy answers, "Very sorry, sir, I could not come
before, but I have had three weeks at Bridewell." Now this has
happened repeatedly. Going to prison is with those children the
ordinary lot of humanity—they look upon it as a grievous act of
oppression, and when they come to school they speak of it as one
gentleman would tell his wrongs to another. But, in the course
of time, their hearts become alive to better things; knowing how
low they have fallen in the scale of humanity, they desire to be
removed to other scenes; and then it is that, if inducements are
held out to them to hope—and God knows what is the condition
of a human creature without hope—they would rise into the
dignity of man, and acknowledge the opportunity afforded to
them by the great goodness of Providence. I consider also that
much beneficial effect will be derived from the parents seeing that
something will be gained by the good conduct of their children.
Their motives must not be scanned too narrowly. Honourable
members should not judge them altogether by their own; these
parents, no doubt, think more of the temporal than the moral
welfare of their children, and will thus be influenced by temporal
considerations; it is, nevertheless, a step towards amendment, and
will, unquestionably, produce an extensive and healing effect.

But it may be urged, is your plan feasible? I reply, that it is a
practical proposition, and beneficial alike to the condition of the
colonies. Hear the evidence of Mr. Cuninghame, of Port Phillip,
before the Lords' Committee on Emigration :

"The want of labour is by far the greatest impediment to the
progress of the colony, either social or pecuniary. . . . Four
years have now elapsed, during which there has been scarcely any
emigration. In the year 1844 there were about 1400 people sent
out; but, with that exception, emigration has been at a standstill.
The result is, that not only is labour extremely dear, but it is
almost impossible to be got at all. The wool is worse got up, and
everything but wool-growing is at a perfect standstill from want
of labour. I have no doubt that from Port Phillip alone the value
of the wool has been deteriorated to the value of 40,000*l.* in
consequence of the deficiency of hands upon the last wool-clip
alone."

Further on the same witness said,—

"The colony will absorb many more than we could count upon
for future years. At present there is not merely a want of the
regular annual supply which is demanded by the annual increase

of both sheep and cattle, but there is a deficient supply of three years to make up. Many colonists have not built houses, nor fenced paddocks, nor made any improvements, owing to the want of labour. I think that, if 8000 statute adults were introduced into Port Phillip just now, the whole of them would be absorbed at good wages, and with abundant rations; . . . and that for three or four years to come 4000 or 5000 might be received each year."

I should be very glad if the Government would take these poor children and transplant some of them every year. I will not quarrel about the colony, for I am quite sure that under the right honourable baronet and the noble lord they will be fully protected. Mr. Cuninghame continued,—

" We can employ any species of labour, because shepherding is not an exhausting or fatiguing operation."

Exactly the labour for these children, and it is to this kind of work that I propose to send the lads who shall have exceeded their fourteenth year. As to the condition of the settled emigrants, the same gentleman also said,—

" Many instances have occurred of the change of labourers into proprietors. I believe that, amongst steady and intelligent men to set up for themselves after from five to eight years of labour is the rule; and to fail in doing so the exception."

In *The Times* of the 20th of May, 1848, I find the following extract from a letter dated Sydney, January 8 :

" You must strain every nerve to send us relief, for fully three-fourths of the 5000 emigrants now coming out will be instantly absorbed on landing, for domestic servants in Sydney, Melbourne, &c."

Observe, I do not propose to send them out under fourteen years of age. I have a statement which has been made to me by a gentleman who is well acquainted with the colonies. He says, that for every 1000 sheep three persons at least are required, with wages of 20*l.* a year and weekly rations of 10lb. beef, 12lb. of flour, 2lb. of sugar, quarter of a lb. of tea, and a house; thus at a station of 5000 sheep, fifteen men and boys would be required. Taking the numbers of farms and stations at 4000, and the number of the servants in the bush at 12,000, this would make at each station but three, not one-half of what is necessary. Three, then, to each station would take at once 12,000; if, then, 1000 were sent annually, it would be to each station only one every four years.

So much for the boys. Now it is perfectly clear we could dispose of females far more easily: the demand, indeed, for them as domestic servants is so great, that a gentleman told me that when he quitted the colony, as he came down to the shore to embark, he found a young girl who had just landed; and so eager were five gentlemen to engage her as lady's maid to their wives, that she, knowing how valuable her services were, refused to take less than 50*l.* a year. Now these poor girls, above fourteen years of age, whom we see standing at the corners of the streets, filthy and wretched, selling oranges, matches, and ten thousand other things, many of whom come every evening to the ragged schools, would be rejoiced at the opportunity of being sent to another country. When the House considers that the males in Port Phillip are to the females in a frightfully large proportion, how can they hesitate to believe that, if 20,000 of these miserable and distressed girls were transplanted to that settlement, they would at once be disposed of to advantage? And what does the House think is the excess in England of females over males, according to the last census? No less than 358,159. With such a disproportion, then, at Port Phillip, can you doubt, if you will thus undertake the proposition I suggest, that no difficulty will be found in disposing of all those young women, whom you will thus transplant from a life of misery to one of happiness and honour?

The Emigration Commissioners see no difficulty in the plan; they seem to think, so far as I am at liberty to quote them, that the scheme is perfectly practicable, and requires nothing to carry it out but a hearty determination. I trust that I shall not be met by an answer, that my proposition for these schools must be made for every other school where the poor may be educated, and so a system be begun of almost indefinite expense. In the first place, I have proved that these schools, and the children in them, are most peculiar—peculiar in their quality, and requiring a peculiar remedy. If you take, for instance, the whole average attendance of the children, which is about four thousand, and try it by the scale of crime and destitution I have mentioned before, you will conclude that, of that number nearly 1700 will have passed through the prisons, and 1800 will have lost one or both parents.

In the next place, I doubt not that, in a financial point of view, it is a real economy. I have here a letter from a most intelligent gentleman, Mr. Smith, the governor of the prison at Edinburgh; now, attend to his words: "In compliance with the request of the Committee of the Industrial School;" and here the word "industrial" recalls to my mind a part of our system to which I must allude. We have established, in some of these schools, industrial classes; and with the happiest effect. I am strongly of opinion that in every school where children are educated, who are hereafter to earn a livelihood by the sweat of their brow, some portion of the day or the week should be devoted to occupations of industry. Now, if it be desirable for ordinary children, it is doubly so for those to whom new notions must be imparted, notions that, when reclaimed from a lawless and wandering life, they will find industry to be both beneficial and honourable. These industrial classes have, in fact, obtained the greatest success; and labour, which in other situations is regarded as a penalty, is here considered as a recompense. In the school at Westminster we inculcate this both by precept and by practice; the children are received naked—naked certainly, unless the beastly rags about them can be dignified by the name of clothing—and they are told, when furnished with the raw material, " you shall learn to make your own things, and whatever you can make for yourselves shall be your own;" industry is thereby greatly stimulated—they are divided into tailors and shoemakers; the tailors make clothes for themselves and then for their companions, and the shoemakers return the compliment. But this is Mr. Smith's letter:—" In compliance with the request of the Committee of the Industrial Ragged School, that I would inform them what had been the effect of the schools on juvenile crime, it affords me very great pleasure to say, that the number of commitments to prison, of boys of 13 years old and under, was about 50 per cent. less in the three months ended March last than in the corresponding three months of the last year; and that I think this most gratifying circumstance is mainly to be attributed to the influence of the ragged schools.* It may be well for the public to know, that if 5*l.* a year be not paid for the education and maintenance of a little boy at the ragged school, 11*l.* a year will probably have to be paid for him at the prison in Edinburgh, or 17*l.* a year in the general prison in Perth."

Is the House aware of the costliness of crime to the country? Suppose, now, you vote 20,000*l.* a year for the ragged schools of the metropolis, or 100,000*l.* a year for the same throughout the whole kingdom; and this sum, remember, will elicit 200,000*l.* at least in addition, from private persons, public bodies, and benevolent societies—compare that grant of 100,000*l.* a year with the expenses of preventing and punishing crime; and see at once the true economy of the proposed plan. The expense of Parkhurst prison in the year 1847 was 14,349*l.*; of Pentonville, 18,307*l.* The total expense of prosecutions, removal, and subsistence of convicts formerly paid out of county rates is 348,000*l.* a year. I hear some

* Their establishment in Edinburgh is mainly owing to the exertions of the Rev. Thomas Guthrie, whose pious and eloquent " Plea for Ragged Schools," should be in the hands of every one.

one observe, " that item is for the punishment of adults;" why, to be sure, it is; but is it not in infancy that the seed is sown? is not the child the prototype of the man? but I anticipated such an objection, and I put, therefore, this question to some of the most experienced missionaries : "Does it frequently occur that a man, having reached the age of 20 years untainted by crime, afterwards becomes an established delinquent?" the answer was, "Rarely; in very few instances, except under the pressure of peculiar circumstances, do persons of that age betake themselves, for the first time, to evil courses." It is principally in childhood, no doubt, that vicious habits are formed, and take root; and it is in childhood that we must hope for successful prevention. But to return to the expense. The expenditure of county gaols for 1846 was 157,145*l.*; of county Houses of Correction, 160,841*l.* The rural police cost, in 1846, in those counties which had adopted it, 180,000*l.* The metropolitan police in 1845 cost 363,164*l.*; these, with other items, making a total of more than a million a year for the repression of crime. I do not ask for that sum towards the object I have in view; but I am sure, that if you vigorously attack the whole mass of juvenile delinquency, the mass of adult crime will speedily be reduced in a very striking proportion. There is one item of expenditure of 9600*l.* in prosecutions for coining, which is worthy of attention; for in these cases of coining and uttering bad money, children are almost exclusively employed. I am informed that there are more children engaged in fabricating and uttering base coin in the large towns of Birmingham, Manchester, and Liverpool, as well as London, than in almost any other way in which the revenue is cheated, and society injured; and this sum of 9600*l.* is nearly one-half of all that I require for the removal of two-thirds of the entire mischief!

Sir, I have not in the statement that I have just made to the House, enumerated the various cities and towns where a similar condition prevails of the labouring population. Suffice it to say, that in almost every densely inhabited district, you may discover similar evils and similar consequences—the details and arguments applicable to London are, in a great measure, applicable to Liverpool, Manchester, Glasgow, Edinburgh, Bath, and other large cities. In many of these towns ragged schools have been set up, and attended with the happiest results. One only I must specify, because no one, in handling the subject of these schools, may pass over the one established in Aberdeen, and the admirable exertions of Mr. Sheriff Watson. Here is a singular proof of full and unqualified success! The report for 1847 concludes : "The committee congratulate themselves and the community on the lightness of their labours. It is a remarkable fact that juvenile vagrancy has been entirely prevented, and juvenile delinquency greatly diminished by the sole instrumentality of the schools of industry, and the committee earnestly recommend the support of those crime-preventing institutions to the benevolence of the public. In every point of view, social, moral, and religious, they are deserving of countenance; they free the town and country of an intolerable nuisance, they increase the security of property by diminishing the number of depredators, they relieve the wants of the children of destitution, and, above all, they train these destitute ones to habits of decency and order, and inculcate that knowledge which, with the blessing of God, maketh wise unto salvation."

I do not assert that such a result is practicable in the metropolis; the surface is too large, and the population too various in its character and shifting in its habits, to admit of equal success; but in proportion and degree the same issue will be ours; the whole that we seek may lie beyond our reach, but something at least will be speedily attained.

It will be something to have rolled back the reproach from London that, in the midst of almost countless wealth, abundant professions and appliances of religion, with every facility, and lacking nothing but the will to benefit her children, she should have so long endured an exhibition of juvenile depravity and suffering, unexampled in the history of any state of equal importance and power. Should we fail to attain the summit of our hopes, we shall at least have wiped out the charge of indifference to such mighty duties.

It will be something to have conferred a benefit both on the colonies and the mother-country, by the transplantation of thousands of children untainted by crime, nay, more, trained in the habits of industry and virtue, from places where they seemed doomed to inevitable idleness, and consequently to misery and sin,—the transplantation, I say, to regions in rivalry for their labour, and abundant in assurances of reward. Thus they will bless alike the land of their birth and the land of their adoption; the boys, rescued from pernicious vagrancy, will rejoice in the fruits of honest labour; and the girls, not recovered, thank God, but saved altogether from prostitution, will walk in the happy and holy dignity of wives and mothers.

It will be something to have established a new principle of colonization; and no longer regarding it merely as the drainage of our gaols, or the outlet for the offscouring of the feeble, the mischievous, or the distressed, to hold it up as an object of ambition, the recompense of moral exertion. Governments bear the sword; they may also bear the olive-branch; they are sent for the punishment of evil-doers; but henceforward they may obey the apostolic precept, and be "for the praise of them that do well."

It will be something that the State, violating no principle, trenching on no right, yielding to no compromise, and incurring no unseen responsibility, will appear as resolute to prevent as to chastise the commission of crime. She will anticipate the gaoler and the hangman—and we, of the third and fourth generation, who are suffering justly the sins of our fathers, for we have made them our own, will, under God's blessing, take good care not to transmit them to our own posterity.

Lastly, it will be something that, leaving the higher and more ambitious speculations of commerce and politics, we have lent an open ear and a willing heart to the precepts of our common Saviour—gone into the highways and hedges, and dived into the foulest recesses of vice and misery, to rescue a host of naked, dirty, starving, and ignorant children, and drag them, in mercy, to the upper world, there, by God's grace, to thrive in the light and warmth of the everlasting Gospel. This will have been your work; and God grant that you may have your reward, in the contemplation of enlarged happiness, and in the harvest of a wise, united, and contented people.

---

Lord Ashley, in reply, observed that the House seemed to think that he had acted exclusively when he proposed only to include the metropolis; it was through extreme caution. His object was to make an experiment, and supposing that experiment had succeeded, no doubt it would be extended. His object was to get in the thin edge of the wedge, and then it was his intention to drive it well up to the head. The government and many honourable gentlemen had come forward in so generous a manner to support the proposition, that he thought that if he attempted to divide the House he should only take a hostile course, and convert into enemies many who would otherwise be coadjutors; he would therefore, with the permission of the House, withdraw his motion, but at the same time he would watch the government with jealous care, and take the liberty, both in and out of the House, to jog their memories.

The motion was then withdrawn.

---

NOTE. Subsequently a grant of fifteen hundred pounds was made by the government for the purpose of emigration. The result was most successful in all the cases selected.

## *Emigration and Ragged Schools.*

## HOUSE OF COMMONS,

### Tuesday, July 24, 1849.*

LORD ASHLEY rose to bring under the notice of the House the state of a portion of the juvenile population of the metropolis, and to move—

" That it is expedient that means be annually provided for the voluntary emigration to some of Her Majesty's colonies of a certain number of young persons of both sexes, who have been educated in the schools ordinarily called ragged schools, in and about the metropolis."

If he were asked why he had brought forward his motion at so late a period of the session, he must plead as his excuse his utter lack of opportunity to lay the subject before the House, owing to the interposition of other business day after day. But he nevertheless entertained a very strong desire that he should have it in his power to do so, not only on account of those whose claims he represented, but for the purpose of showing the House to what profitable use the small grant he had obtained last session had been turned, and the prospects of success their past experience might encourage them to cherish. He had another reason, besides, for pressing the subject on the attention of the House— that he was anxious to excite some interest, and perhaps discussion on the preventive, as contrasted with the reformatory, system. Prison discipline seemed a favourite topic for all writers and speakers ; and endless inquiries had been entered into with respect to the separate, the solitary, and the associated system of punishment, and with respect to summary jurisdiction and flogging, and confinement. But he thought that there was really a system preliminary to them all, and one which was economical and efficient. If he could show that the preventive system was not only economical and efficient, but also truly humane, he

* From " Hansard."

would show enough to rouse every well-wisher of the people to a sense of the importance of the subject, whether viewed with reference to policy or religion.

Last year he stated the number of that class whose interests he then attempted to represent at 30,000. He believed that estimate was very much under the mark. He then described the temptations to which they were exposed, and the great dangers which threatened society from the existence of that class. In the statement he should have to make that night, he would not be able to show any great improvement in these details. Any such improvement must arise from the application of another principle. So long as people were left in their present sanitary state, confined in courts and alleys, their dens and lurking-places—so long as they were crowded together in the sties from which they found it impossible to escape, even so long they could not hope for any improvement in the social and physical condition of the people. But what he wished to bring under the notice of the House was the increase of schools, the improvement of the pupils, and the well-grounded prospects for the future. He wished to show the condition of the metropolis; and for that purpose would state the number taken into custody by the metropolitan police in 1847, as contrasted with the number taken into custody in 1848.

In 1847, 41,479 males were taken into custody, of whom 8,405 were under 20 years of age, 3,228 between 10 and 15, and 306 under 10. In 1848, 42,933 males were taken into custody; of whom 8,776 were under 20 years of age, 3,604 between 10 and 15, and 312 under 10. The total increase in 1848 of males taken into custody was 1,454, of whom one half was under 20 years of age. But of those who had been taken into custody under 10 years of age—the class which chiefly attended the ragged schools—there had been an increase of only six. The whole number of males taken into custody between 10 and 20, a period of ten years, was 12,691; between 25 and 50, a period of 25 years, 18,591; only one-third more. But, looking at the number of those tried and convicted, there appeared a great disproportion. Between 10 and 20, the males tried and convicted were 1,237, whereas the males tried and convicted between 25 and 50 were only 1,059. The same rule prevailed in Manchester, to which he simply referred as a very large town, the returns being characterised by the same accuracy as those for the metropolis. There were taken into custody in Manchester 1,037 males between 10 and 20, and 2,157 between 25 and 50. But there were tried and convicted 165 between 10 and 20; 193 between 25 and 50.

Now, these returns showed the preponderating amount of

juvenile delinquency. They showed also the possibility of applying the preventive system. The crimes were perpetrated at a
period of life when the parties were open to the best influences,
and were most capable of receiving permanent impressions. It
was also clear that the seeds of crime were sown in early life, and
would not, if they were then rooted out, grow up into rank
maturity. Being anxious to ascertain the opinions of persons
best acquainted with the subject, he circulated among persons
having the charge of ragged schools, missionaries, and others,
this question, "Do many adult males become criminals for the
first time after 20 years of age?" From 43 committees he received the answer, "Very few." One said, "A small proportion,
and these chiefly through drunkenness and want of employment.
In London, many country people, and the Irish, become criminals
after 20 years of age, and those chiefly from the above-mentioned
causes." Another said, "I should say not one in fifty." Another,
"I believe that among the males of the lowest classes of society
hardly any become criminal for the first time after 20 years of
age." Such were the conclusions to which those persons were
led, whose opinion he had sought as being most conversant with
the circumstances of the poorer classes.

Now, what was the condition of those to whom he wished the
preventive system applied? That large class roaming over the
streets of London, in habits, manners, feelings, and pursuits
totally unlike anything with which people were acquainted in
ordinary life, formed a seed-plot for three-fourths of the crimes
of fraud and violence which prevailed in this metropolis; and
what he said of the metropolis he said of every great city in the
empire. A short time ago he was anxious to perceive with his
own eyes what was the condition of these people—what was the
state of their abodes, their lairs, their retreats for the night. He
and others perambulated the metropolis. They dived into its
recesses. The House would be surprised to hear what was the
condition in which they found those young people. Most of them
were living in the dry arches of houses not finished, inaccessible
except by an aperture only large enough to admit the body of a
man. When a lantern was thrust in, six or eight, 10 or 12
people, might be found lying together. Of those whom they
found thus lodged, they invited a great number to come the
following day, and then an examination was instituted. The
number examined was 33. Their ages varied from 12 to 18, and
some were younger; 24 had no parents, six had one, three had
stepmothers, 20 had no shirts, nine no shoes, 12 had been once
in prison, three twice, three four times, one eight times, and **one**

(only 14 years old) 12 times. The physical condition of these children was exceedingly horrible; they were a prey to vermin, they were troubled with itch, they were begrimed with dirt, not a few were suffering from sickness, and two or three days afterwards two died from disease and the effects of starvation. He had privately examined eight or ten. He was anxious to obtain from them the truth. He examined them separately, taking them into a room alone. He said, " I am going to ask you a variety of questions, to which I trust you will give me true answers, and I, on my part, will undertake to answer any question you may put to me." They thought that a fair bargain. He put to several of them the question, " How often have you slept in a bed during the last three years ?" One said, perhaps 12 times, another three times, another could not remember that he ever had done so. He asked them how they passed the night in winter. They said, " We lie eight or 10 together to keep ourselves warm." He entered on the subject of their employments and modes of living. They fairly confessed they had no means of subsistence but begging and stealing. The only way of earning a penny in a legitimate way was by picking up old bones. But they fairly acknowledged for themselves and others scattered over the town, with whom they professed themselves acquainted, that they had not and could not have any other means of subsistence than by begging and stealing. A large proportion of these young persons were at a most dangerous age for society. He had formerly met one very remarkable instance of a boy, past 17. He was struck at discovering that the boy knew the French language, and asked an account of his life. He said he had been in France at the time of the revolution, and had fought in the barricades. He and his mother had gone to Paris some four or five years ago. He there got into some employment, but as the political atmosphere became warm, he yielded to its influence, and being enticed by French boys, his companions, he joined in the general warfare, fought at the barricades, was taken prisoner, tried, sentenced to punishment, and, at the expiration of his sentence, shipped for England. There were hundreds and thousands of others in London, as capable of being employed for the worst purposes as the Garde Mobile of Paris. And therefore it was that, for the peace of society, no less than its honour, he would direct the attention of the House to the subject.

Again, what was the moral condition of those persons ? A large proportion of them (it was no fault of theirs) did not recognise the distinctive rights of *meum* and *tuum*. Property appeared to them to be only the aggregate of plunder. They held that everything which was possessed was common stock; that he who got most was the cleverest fellow, and that every one had a right to abstract from that stock what he could by his own ingenuity. Was it matter of surprise that they entertained those notions, which were instilled into their minds from the time they were able to creep on all fours—that not only did they disregard all the rights of property, but gloried in doing so, unless they thought the avowal would bring them within the grasp of the law? To illustrate their low state of morality, and to show how utterly shameless they were in speaking on these subjects, he would mention what had passed at a ragged school to which 14 or 15 boys, having presented themselves on a Sunday evening, were admitted as they came. They sat down and the lesson proceeded. The clock struck eight. They all rose and went out, with the exception of one who lagged behind. The master took him by the arm and said—"You must remain, the lesson is not over." The reply was, "We must go to business." The master inquired what business? "Why, don't you see it's eight o'clock. We must go catch them as they come out of the chapels." It was necessary for them, according to the remark of this boy, to go at a certain time in pursuit of their calling. They had no remorse or shame in making the avowal, because they believed that there were no other means of saving themselves from starvation. He recollected a very graphic remark made by one of those children in perfect simplicity, but which yet showed the horrors of their position. The master had been pointing out to him the terrors of punishment in after-life. The remark of the boy was—"That may be so, but I don't think it can be any worse than this world has been to me."

Such was the condition of hundreds and thousands. It was necessary for the peace of society that those horrors should be mitigated; but, looking to higher considerations, every one must feel the duty as well as the necessity which required that means should be taken to carry the knowledge of the Gospel to those classes. There were two modes of dealing with those cases; first, to wait till they committed crime, then to bring them to justice, and either transport them or confine them in gaol. The other was to take a preventive course, and anticipate the gaoler and the hangman by a system of wholesome discipline. It had been said in various instances that the case was a hopeless one, and there was nothing but punishment for such as these. He distrusted prison discipline altogether, taken by itself alone; he had no faith in it as a preventive, or as a mode generally of reforming individuals. Could hon. Members fail to observe how prison discipline had increased in severity of late years, and yet crime had not decreased in proportion? Nor could it decrease in proportion, neither would their prison discipline become effective for its purpose. That system might possibly become effective in certain cases—in the cases of those who had offended in wantonness, or who, on quitting gaol, had resources of their own, or friends on whom to rely. But, for the great mass of those who passed through the gaols, and who were afterwards discharged to recommence the struggle of life, what was usually known as the reformatory system had no effect beyond the walls. It was not his intention to question the utility of the institution at Pentonville, least of all whilst it had the advantage of the services of the present chaplain, of whose exertions for the reformation of offenders it was impossible to speak too highly. Pentonville Prison had produced some remarkable and gratifying instances of reformation; but in almost all those cases the parties reformed had found profitable employment in the colonies. To understand how prison discipline failed as a reformatory system, it was only necessary to reflect on the fate of a person committed to gaol. In the first place, there was the long detention before trial, followed in some cases by imprisonment after conviction. Now, it was well known that persons so circumstanced usually came out of prison ten times worse than they were when they entered it. The testimony of those who could speak with authority was conclusive upon this point. The chaplain of the Preston House of Correction said—

"In 1840, I stated that, whether led astray for a moment by bad companions, or assailed by overpowering temptations, or driven by distress and hunger, or trained to vagabond and thievish practices, and, in all cases, with a mind totally unformed by education and uninfluenced by religion, the child of 14, or 10, or even eight years old, is now turned into a yard or 'day-room,' tenanted by 40 or 50 older criminals. Once here, his terrors of a prison soon vanish before the levity and merriment of his new companions. He finds them great objects of admiration, and many are the plunderers who can relate the most attractive stories of successful and daring robbery. Excited by these tales, he soon becomes ambitious of imitating the heroes of them. He is instructed in the arcana of the dreadful calling which he has entered upon by some adept in the craft; and thus a few weeks, or even a few days before trial, have sufficed to convert the child, who, until the verdict pronounced at that solemnity, was accounted innocent in the eye of the law, into a hardened profligate, prepared and tutored for a course of iniquity, and determined to run it. I could furnish a hundred histories of misery and crime springing from the pestiferous society of the untried felons' ward."

It was notorious that in many of these prison yards the inmates were initiated into all the details connected with thieving. It was customary to have all the characters of a thieves' drama enacted by boys. This account was given by one of the youngsters : "We have," said he, "after five o'clock, our time to ourselves ; then there is the pickpocket, the gentleman, the lady, the policeman, and the magistrate. The gentleman walks about with a pocket-handkerchief hanging out of his pocket, and the lady, with her chains ; they then show us the best and newest way of doing the business." The chaplain of Pentonville Prison remarked that—

"It is not possible to convey to the mind of the reader any adequate idea of the extent of the corruption of mind, feeling, and character, or of the completeness of the education in crime, which goes on in the common gaols of the country, especially before trial."

Lord Denman was of the same opinion. In his evidence given before a committee of the House of Lords, his Lordship said—

"I am not reconciled to summary convictions, but I highly approve of frequent courts to try petty offenders of all ages promptly on the spot." . . . "As long, however, as juvenile offenders are mixed up in our gaols with adults, no effectual improvement can take place."

He heartily concurred with Lord Denman in his suggestion respecting the establishment of courts for the trial of petty offences, and in his objection to increase summary convictions, because he wished the punishment of crime to be as tedious and expensive as possible, being of opinion that no remedy would be applied until the grievance became intolerable. Now, even on the very youngest, the fear of imprisonment had oftentimes little or no influence ; true it was that the prospect of the first imprisonment was fearful to their imaginations, and this feeling would greatly aid the preventive system ; but the second had fewer terrors, and all in succession afterwards were less and less apprehended. Many, indeed, of the lads sought the prison as a refuge for their wants, pressed as they were by constant and hopeless necessity.

He would now for a moment draw the attention of the House

to what he conceived to be the various causes of juvenile crime. Their name was legion; but the first great cause was the example and neglect of parents. Next came the various temptations to which children were exposed. A fertile source of crime was the reckless exposure in or on the outside of shops of articles of value, and particularly of food, which presented an almost irresistible temptation to hungry children. The number of penny theatres was another cause of crime, and a still more fertile source of evil were the casual wards. No less than 42 thieves out of 150, whom he once examined, confessed that the commencement of their career of theft was attributable to the corrupting influence to which they had been exposed in the casual wards of various unions. Those wards might be necessary; but, nevertheless, it could not be denied that they tempted numbers of children to leave the houses of their parents; and, when once they quitted their homes, they oftentimes never again returned to them. In some cases the commission of crime might be attributed to an inherent spirit of wantonness, in others it was referable to want of education, in others, again, to want of employment, and in many instances to a combination of both causes. In a few cases, the commencement of a criminal career might be traced to oppression on the part of employers, and in some it was the result of absolute want. Now, he would assert that the preventive system was not only more economical, certain, and humane, but that it was the only one possible. The prison had failed; criminals were not reduced in number; or, if they were, it was by the operation of means that partook more of a preventive than a penal character. He would contrast the effects produced by the system pursued at Parkhurst and Pentonville Prison with those which proceeded from the scheme which the House of Commons sanctioned last year upon his recommendation. It was not his intention, he repeated, to deny that both the Parkhurst and Pentonville establishments had done good. But he wished to know in how many instances a permanently beneficial effect had been produced upon persons who, having quitted those places, had returned to their old haunts, and been driven to their old shifts to find employment. It was almost impossible, in the circumstances of the present day, for those convicted of crime, and bearing its brand on their forehead, to recover a position in society when driven to their old haunts and their old companions, exposed to their old temptations, and beset by their old necessities. The story which he was about to relate to the House would furnish the strongest evidence of the truth of that proposition.

In the course of last year he received an invitation from 150 of the most notorious thieves in London, asking him to meet them in some place in the Minories, and to give them his advice as to the best mode by which they might extricate themselves from their miserable way of life. He felt it his duty to accede to the request, and went to the place appointed, where he found, instead of 150, not fewer than 250 thieves assembled in a room. He entered into conversation with them, and addresses were made by several, the substance of which was, " We are tired of our mode of living; existence is a burden to us; we never know, from sunrise to sunset, whether we shall have a full meal, or any meal; we can get no employment—we have nothing but sorrow before us; give us your counsel as to how we shall extricate ourselves from our miserable position." He replied, it was a most difficult question to solve—that at the present day, so great was the competition for employment, that there were always three candidates for one situation—and that it was unlikely that a person who was stained by crime would be preferred to three persons of untainted character. Thereupon a man rose and said—

" What you say, my Lord, is most true. All in this room have made attempt after attempt to get into some honest employment, but we have found that our tainted characters beset us everywhere. My own case is a proof of this. I obtained a situation, and held it for five or six months. I was satisfied with my employer, and he was perfectly satisfied with me. One day there was a knock at the door; I opened it, and in walked a policeman. He asked for my employer, and, when he saw him, said, ' Do you know that you are employing a convicted felon ?' My employer said he was not aware of it, but the policeman assured him it was the fact, and then my master turned round, and dismissed me from his service. Thus I was driven back to my old courses, and I declare to God that the impossibility of obtaining employment compels me and many others to lead the lives we do."

Now, the reformatory system might succeed with discharged criminals if they were not pressed by actual necessity; but when they were placed in that position it was inefficacious, for in those circumstances human nature could not resist the temptation that overwhelmed them. He knew of one instance of a discharged offender triumphing over temptation; but he was a man of such determined character, that in order to persevere in the course of reformation which he had entered on, he endured the most wonderful privations—in fact, he lived the life of a martyr; but, by God's blessing, he ultimately overcame all difficulties, and was now in comfortable, nay, comparatively affluent circumstances. The scheme which the House sanctioned last year had produced as much permanent advantage at an expense of 1,500*l.* as could have been derived from the system in use at Parkhurst and Pentonville at an expenditure of 150,000*l.* or 200,000*l.* His scheme was to hold out a system of emigration as a reward of merit to a certain number of children attending the ragged schools. This scheme was doubly advantageous. It benefited not only those who emigrated, but those who remained, by inciting them to join the schools, and persevere in a course of good conduct, in order to qualify themselves for the reward held out. In this manner society, as well as the individual, was benefited. Can the same be said of any prison results? Has the reformation of any one prisoner been the signal for others without the walls to follow his example? A few extracts from letters written by some of the boys who had emigrated on the eve of their departure from England might prove interesting to the House. One boy wrote—

"I assure you, should it please God to spare my life and bless my industry, it is my intention not only to remit to England something for the support of ragged schools, but endeavour to stir up others to do the same."

Four of the best-behaved boys were presented with a suitable outfit and free passage from private sources, to the new colony of Moreton Bay, in Australia. The gratitude expressed by those lads, ere they embarked, was most pleasing; and before they left England, when it was clear that they would never see their benefactors again, they wrote the following letter to the committee:

"Gentlemen, We could not think of leaving England without expressing to you our most hearty thanks for all your care of us since we were admitted into the Refuge. We thank you for our protection, our education, and so worthy a master, and for our food and clothing. We hope so to behave as to comfort all your hearts. We may forget some we once knew; we never can forget the committee."

The following letter was addressed to him as chairman of the committee for the boys by three boys who had emigrated:

"Gravesend, April 8, 1849.

"We write to inform you we are arrived safe at Gravesend, and are quite well. We cannot express our gratitude to your

Lordship for your kindness towards us, especially when we reflect on our past lives. When Mr. Nash took us under his care, he promised he would never leave us, and he never did, but he often told us to you we were indebted for ragged schools. May God bless your Lordship, may God bless Mr. Nash, and every ragged-school teacher; and we beg one favour of you, that you will open more schools, such as Mr. Nash's Dormitory, at Westminster, for there are many poor boys that would be very glad to get in them; and we do promise, through God's grace, to conduct ourselves with the strictest propriety, and open a Sunday school in Australia. You said you would pray for us, so we will for you, every day of our lives, and tell the people in Australia what kind friends you are to poor boys. We are your Lordship's obedient servants."

Now, this was a sketch of their biography. One of the boys who signed the letter was aged 16; he had long lived in a pigsty, and was taken from it to the Refuge; he had been seen seven times in prison, and when rescued from his miserable position was resolved to commit such a robbery as would entitle him to the benefit of transportation. Another of the boys, aged 17, had lived all his lifetime by begging and stealing; he was connected with a gang of thieves in Duck Lane, and slept under carts and on the steps of doors. The third boy, aged 15, lived by begging and stealing; he had lived for days together on the rotten apples in the Borough Market. Perhaps the House would here permit him to read some extracts from letters written by emigrants who had arrived at Australia. A boy addressed his mother thus:

" Brisbane, Friday, December 22, 1848.

" Dear Mother—I write these few lines to you, hoping to find you in good health, as it leaves me at present. I have arrived with safety in the colony, after a long and wearisome voyage. I am in the depôt now, in Brisbane. I am engaged as a shepherd, or to be generally useful, to go to a place called Wide Bay, 120 miles further up the bush. The blacks are not very wild in the towns, but they are out in the bush, where they are wild; they catch kangaroos and eat them. Parrots and cockatoos are very numerous here; the natives will catch them for you, and give them to you, if you give them a piece of bread or tobacco. I forgot to tell you how much wages I am to receive; it is 12*l.* per year, and my rations and washing. I am very happy at present, thank God. So no more at present from your affectionate son,

" W—— S——."

A similar letter had been received from a boy named Flynn, who went out at the same time, who had also got a place to "mind sheep," as he called it, at 12*l.* a year, besides all his food, lodging, washing, &c. Another letter was in these terms:

" Ipswich, Moreton Bay, December 26, 1848.

"I have a good situation as a gentleman's servant. I have 20*l.* a year, board, lodging, plenty to eat and drink. I have had a merry Christmas of it. There is plenty of work for everybody. We were no sooner at the depôt than we were all hired."

One of the girls wrote—

"I found the country better than I expected it was. I like the place very much. All I wish is, that my sister Susan had come out with me. . . . My dear teacher—I am happy. . . . I have got a good place, for my mistress is more like a mother to me. Though I am thousands of miles from you and all my friends, yet you are always in my mind, and the old wall of the poor-school."

Contrast the moral and social condition of these children now with what it was. Those were samples of the effects produced by the emigration scheme. What had been the effect upon society at large? In order to ascertain that point, a series of questions had been proposed to the committees of various ragged schools in London. The questions were as follows:

"1. Has the plan of emigration acceded to last year by the government been the means of stimulating the increase of schools, and the attendance and order of the ragged class?"

The answer was unanimously "Yes." The next question was—

"To insure all the benefits that ragged schools are capable of conferring, is it not desirable that, wherever possible, the reformed vagrants should, either by employment or removal elsewhere, be kept from returning to their old haunts and companions?"

The answer was the same. Then the third question was—

"Do they, in general, desire one or the other?"

The answer was the same. He then asked—

"With such inducements, a fair provision of school-room, and an adequate supply of proper teachers, would there be any difficulty in obtaining the attendance of three times as many children as are now receiving instruction?"

The answer was uniformly that there would be no difficulty at all. He thereupon put this question—

" Would it therefore be practicable to grapple with the existing race, and so greatly reduce juvenile delinquency ?"

The answer was uniformly " Yes." By that the House might see the effect produced on society at large by this system; and when they considered that it was produced by a sum of 1,500*l.* only, he thought he had proved his point. It had effected as much good as their system of prison discipline with an expenditure of 200,000*l.* In relation to this point, he was very much struck by the testimony of one man who had given himself up to a vicious course of life; he visited one of the schools, and asked to be shown over it; after seeing it he said—" I approve of this very highly, and I shall subscribe a guinea a year." The answer was—" How can you do so ? we know what you are." To which he replied—" It is perfectly true : I know what I am; but if such institutions as this had existed when I was a boy, I never should have come to my present disgraceful condition." That was the testimony of one of the greatest thieves in the metropolis. Now, emigration was preferable to employment at home; first, because it abated the terrible competition of the present day; next, because it removed the young people far from their former haunts and temptations, and in another view, because they were thereby relieved from the infliction of excessive labour. They might depend upon it that one great cause of juvenile delinquency, where the delinquents had been in employment, was the excessive toil to which they were subjected, and from which they fled to dishonesty as their only resource. Two cases of that excessive toil had come to his knowledge, fair specimens of the whole apprentice-system. From the ragged school they had apprenticed a boy to a shoemaker. He (Lord Ashley) saw him the other day; the boy made no complaint; but, on inquiry, he found that the boy began work every morning at half-past five, and continued working until half-past ten at night. He said to the boy—" This is pretty severe; but I conclude you have the Sunday to yourself ?" The boy answered—" No; only Sunday afternoon, as I am kept at home to nurse the baby." That boy might resist the temptation, but 19-20ths of those who were so exposed would flee from their master's house and take themselves to an evil course of life. The other case was that of a little girl, who was also apprenticed. He found that she was engaged from four o'clock in the morning until ten or eleven at night; and so far from having Sunday to herself, she rose on that day at half-past five, and was engaged until half-past four in washing.

He wished now to consider the arguments for and against this proposition. One argument that he had heard against this scheme was, that if they did this for the children of the metropolis, they would be called on to do the same for the children of the other great towns in the country. That was perfectly true; but they might depend upon it that if they were to expend upon such a project 100,000*l.* a year, they would save ten times that amount in criminal prosecutions and penal expenditure. The next point was, that it would tempt the parents to neglect their children, and to abandon their duty to be performed by the State. He was of a different opinion. In the first place, a very large proportion of those children had no parents at all. He desired the House to observe that fact. In the second place, not a small proportion of them were the children of convicts; and, in the third place, the parents of many of the children were so poor that it was next to impossible they could make any provision at all for them. He would read an extract from the last report published a short time ago by the London City Mission :—

" The poverty of those who avail themselves of the benefits of this institution (Glasshouse Yard) is such, that the average number of articles brought by each washer is less than seven, even when the family apparel is included ; and the matron has frequently to lend them dresses to wear while they wash those they take from their backs. Their poverty is indeed such, that Mr. Bowie, a surgeon in the east of London, says, ' I have seen women toiling unremittingly to wash their own and their children's clothing, who had been compelled to sell their hair to purchase food.' "

Now, would they dispose of those children by sending them to the workhouse ? Let them consider the result of such an arrangement. The number of children of that class roaming about London exceeded 30,000. The number of children in the unions in England and Wales already amounted to 56,000 ; and if they added this 30,000 to that number, they would fail in the object they had in view, and throw an intolerable burden on the ratepayers. But suppose they did that; was a workhouse system of education such as would give them more confidence in the success of their undertaking ? He was not going to speak disparagingly of the unions, many of them were most excellent, and he was sure that so long as the administration of the poor-law was under the care of the right hon. gentleman the President of the Poor Law Commission, everything would be done to render the management of all unions as excellent as it could be. But the result of the education at the workhouse, when the children quitted the unions, was most calamitous. Not one in fifty, he believed, occupied that situation in life which they would wish it to occupy, morally or socially. As a proof of that, he would read the following report of the guardians of Marylebone, which appeared in the *Times* of the 11th of July instant:

"Hitherto the system of education," says the report, "has been quite unsuccessful, which may be thus demonstrated:—From July, 1840, to July, 1849, 326 female inmates, between the ages of 13 and 20, have been provided with 896 situations from the workhouse, being an average of nearly three situations to each.

"There were 46 who left the school at the age of 13; 103 at 14; 72 at 15; 44 at 16; 18 at 17; 20 at 18; 12 at 19; 11 at 20; Total 326. Of these 89 are now leading abandoned lives; 20 have had illegitimate children that have become chargeable; 37, after having had several situations and outfits, have emigrated; 10 are married; 1 passed; 7 dead; 10 are receiving relief either in or out of the house; 45 are supposed to be in service; 99 nothing certain is known; 8 taken out by friends. Total 326.

"Of the boys, only one class could be traced, namely, those who had been apprenticed to the captains of vessels in the merchant service. From 1843 to the end 1847, 137 youths, from 15 to 18 years of age, left the workhouse and engaged themselves in the sea service, as above described, and of these 83 returned and became subsequently chargeable."

The fact was, that the workhouse system was, of all, the most ill adapted for training children of that class for the service to which they were to be devoted; and therefore he should hope they would not think of consigning them to the workhouse, with a view to advance their morals, or better their condition. They looked, perhaps, for a remedy in the general amelioration of society: they were right; but they must wait a long time; and meanwhile they had a positive evil of great magnitude to grapple with, and the question was, how they should encounter it? Would they leave those 30,000 children as they were? If they did, they could not be surprised if they grew up in habits of fraud and violence, and became the subjects of the judges and transportation.

Let him describe the hopeless condition of those children. He had examined several of them. He asked them, did they ever seek for employment? Their answer was, "Repeatedly." But let it be remembered that they were generally in an utterly filthy condition, covered with vermin, with hardly any clothes to their bodies, wholly unable to read or write, not having, in fact, the least elements of knowledge; and the consequence was, that their application for employment was met with such answers as these: one would say—"How can you ask for employment in this filthy state; go and get new clothes." That was, in fact, a rejection, for the wretched children had no means of getting clothes, and only got their food by picking up scraps, begging, and stealing. Another would ask, "Can you read or write?" The answer was, "No;" and the reply followed, "How can you come here without knowing how to read or write?" But how could the children learn, when they had no school to go to—when they had no opportunity of acquiring the first principles of knowledge, sacred or profane? How, then, obtain a subsistence? The necessary, the inevitable consequence was, that the children were driven to crime and hopeless ruin. He wished the right hon. gentleman the Home Secretary would tell him how he, as responsible for the peace of the country, would address himself to this evil? How would he, in his high office, attack the mischief? Now, what was their (the ragged-school) system? They received the children in the evening, in their rags, and at their own hours. They addressed themselves to their habits, feelings, and propensities, and bent themselves for a while to their irregular habits, until they could bend the children to their better principles; he asserted that, in no one instance, had the parents been induced, by such expectations, to abandon their children. Was the inducement strong enough? Did it exonerate them from the charge? When they took the vagrants into the ragged school, and held out the hope of emigration, it was coupled with these conditions—conditions required of every candidate for emigration from the government grants, or from any fund under the control of the Chairman of the Ragged School Union :—

"Sound health; regular attendance for at least six months in a ragged school; the ability to write a sentence from dictation; to work the four single rules of arithmetic; to read fluently; to repeat the Lord's Prayer and the Ten Commandments, showing a comprehension of their meaning, and answer a few simple questions on the life of our Saviour. To these must be added a certificate of regular attendance in some industrial class for at least four months, or a competent knowledge of some handicraft, or practical occupation, which would serve as an equivalent for such industrial training."

Now, along with all this, the child must be maintained, and maintained too, during the process, by its parents or guardians; they must bear their share in effecting the reformation, in preserving the good conduct, in supplying the necessities of the young

candidates; and, so far from being tempted to the crime of desertion, they had been oftentimes themselves reformed by the
process.

And now, Sir, revile the system, and criticise it as they may,
these ragged schools have been, and are, the sole means whereby
religious and secular knowledge is imparted to the thousands of
a race sunk, whole fathoms deep, in destitution and suffering.
This is decidedly the opinion of that intelligent gentleman,
Mr. Tufnell, the government inspector of schools, who was
engaged to examine the young pupils or candidates for emigration. You vote 100,000*l.* a year for the purposes of education;
you might, so far as these miserables are concerned, vote one
hundred pence; they cannot receive any portion of your bounty
—they cannot be accommodated to the system of your National
and Borough Road schools. What other means exist? We
have now 82 schools, full 8,000 children, 124 paid, and 929 voluntary teachers, of whose services I cannot speak with adequate
gratitude and respect. In weariness and painfulness, and with
every form of self-denial, they surrender themselves, body and
soul, to this noble cause, hoping to excite in others a kindred
sympathy. But they are not successful; the sympathy with the
cause is lamentably small, and especially from those who should
be the very first in every work of charity and religion. There
are, thank God, some glorious exceptions; we owe much to a few
active laity, some pious clergy, and a munificent lady, who has,
alone, sustained nearly one half of our expenditure. But it is
manifest that we must not confide in private benevolence; it has
the power, but not the will, to contend with the evil. It is then
to the House of Commons that we direct our attention, in the
hope that the Legislature will take up the duty that individuals
seem to reject. I can hardly appeal to your feelings, because you
appear to me to lie under an obligation to consider the case of
these desperate sufferers. "Their enemies drive them into the
sea, and the sea throws them back upon their enemies;" and yet
they are immortal spirits, as precious, body and soul, in the
sight of God, as the very best among us in this august assembly.
I commit, therefore, the issue to the representatives of the
kingdom, believing that they will not gainsay, by their actions,
what so many of them profess with their lips, when they pray
that "it may please God to defend and provide for the fatherless
children, and all that are desolate and oppressed."

LORD ASHLEY shortly replied. He denied that he had spoken
disparagingly either of the discipline, or its effects, of the Park-

hurst or Pentonville establishments. On the contrary, he had expressly stated that these institutions had produced great reformatory effects; but they had produced these effects only in those cases in which work was provided for their discharged inmates in this country or in the colonies—not in the cases where the convict at the close of his period of imprisonment was thrown upon the world again to re-fight the great battle of life. He had to complain of the statement made by the hon. Member for the city of Oxford, who had just sat down, which was in fact quite a perversion of what he (Lord Ashley) had wished to convey. He had never praised the ragged schools because no discipline was maintained in them. What he had said was, that at the outset the habits of the children were so wild and lawless that no discipline could be preserved, for, say the first fortnight or three weeks. But he had added, that the general result was, that the children were soon tamed down, and brought under regular habits of discipline, and he could answer for it that, in a vast majority of cases, the scholars of ragged schools were as orderly, as attentive, and as much attached to their masters as were the pupils of 19-20ths of the British and Foreign or the Borough Road schools. As he saw that there was a strong feeling in the House against the proposition which he had submitted to them, he felt that it would be indecorous in him to press it to a division; and he would, therefore, without further trespassing on the time of the House, at once withdraw his motion.

The motion was then, by leave, withdrawn.

*Lodging-houses for the Working Classes.*

## HOUSE OF COMMONS,

### April 8, 1851.*

Speech on moving for leave to bring in a Bill to Encourage the Establishment of
Lodging-houses for the Working Classes.

Lord Ashley had now to bring under the consideration of the
House a subject very homely in appearance after the stirring
questions that had so lately agitated the public mind, but one
which he thought he should be able to show was of vital importance to large classes of the community. Twenty years ago it
would have been necessary to state many principles, and urge
many arguments; but now he believed it was necessary merely
to state the evil and indicate the remedy; he wished simply to lay
before the House the experience of himself and others in regard
to the subject—one which he had studied for several years, and
in reference to which he could say that a very great existing evil,
pressing upon a large portion of the labouring community might
be removed, and that without establishing institutions of an
eleemosynary character.

He would first call the attention of the House to the condition of
a large part of this urban population, looking upon it as stationary
and as migratory. To begin with what might be called the stationary population, those who were living in houses, not removing every
week or night by night from one lodging-house to another, but
permanently settled. A return made in 1842 gave the following
result of a house-to-house visitation in St. George's, Hanover
Square, reported to the Statistical Society :—1,465 families of the
labouring classes were found to have for their residence only
2,174 rooms; of these families 929 had but one room for the
whole family to reside in, 408 had two rooms, 94 had three, 17
four, 8 five, 4 six, 1 seven, 1 eight; the remaining three families
were returned "not ascertained." If this was so in one of the
best parishes in London, what must be the condition of the over-

* From "Hansard."

populous and more needy parishes in the east of London? Now, this return said nothing of the condition of a great many of the residences of the working people, in which there was not one family in a room, but two families, three, four, and, as he had himself seen, five; four occupying the corners, and the fifth the middle of the room. To look first at the moral aspect of the subject. In these rooms there were grown-up persons, male and female, of different families, or the same family, all living together; in these rooms every function of nature was performed. How could decency be preserved? Education was impossible; pernicious example was ever before the child. Who could wonder that in these receptacles nine-tenths of the great crimes, the burglaries, and murders, and violence, that desolated society, were conceived and hatched? Or, if the physical state of these people were considered, what must be the condition of dwellings with 8, 10, 20, or 25 persons, or even more, living in a single room? Nothing produced so evil an effect upon the sanitary condition of the population as overcrowding within limited spaces: and if people were in a low sanitary condition, it was absolutely impossible to raise them to a just moral elevation. Their general state of health and capacity for work reduced, they must be brought upon the parish and the general charity of the community. Here was a very remarkable statement of the evils of a system existing now over the surface of this metropolis and all our large towns; it was an exemplification of the effects of living in a crowded atmosphere. In the report of the London Fever Hospital for 1845, of one particular room in an establishment it was said—

"It is filled to excess every night, but on particular occasions commonly 50, sometimes from 90 to 100 men are crowded into a room 33 feet 9 inches long, 20 feet wide, and 7 feet high in the centre. . . . The whole of this dormitory does not allow more space, that is, does not admit of a larger bulk of air for respiration, than is appropriated in the wards of the Fever Hospital for three patients."

What was the consequence? Why, that considerably more than one-fifth part of the whole admissions into the Fever Hospital for that year—no less than 130 patients affected with fever—were received from that one room alone. The experience of the Board of Health went to the same point. The horrible desolation in the children's infirmary at Tooting was found to arise principally from enormous numbers being crowded in small ill-ventilated apartments. A similar case occurred, about the same time, in Hackney, in a charitable institution where the parties were well cared for, well fed, well warmed, well clothed, surrounded by a district in which there was not one death; and yet the mortality in that establishment amounted to no less than 10 or 15 per cent. of the inmates, simply because they were put in ill-ventilated and closely-crowded apartments. Such was the condition of the stationary population: this was what might be seen by any one who would take a walk into the more crowded parts of the metropolis. How was it with the migratory population—those who flitted from one lodging-house to another, and were perpetually moving? Here was a report made by one of the city missionaries:

" In my district is a house containing eight rooms, which are all let separately to individuals who furnish and re-let them. The parlour measures 18 ft. by 10 ft. Beds are arranged on each side of the room, composed of straw, shavings, rags, &c. In this one room slept, on the night previous to my inquiry, 27 male and female adults, 31 children, and two or three dogs, making in all 58 human beings breathing the contaminated atmosphere of a close room. In the top room of the same house, measuring 12 ft. by 10 ft., there are six beds, and, on the same night, there slept in them 32 human beings, all breathing the pestiferous air of a hole not fit to keep swine in. The beds are so close together that, when let down on the floor, there is no room to pass between them; and they who sleep in the beds furthest from the door can, consequently, only get into them by crawling over the beds which are nearer the door. In one district alone there are 270 such rooms."

The statement went on to say—

" These houses are never cleaned or ventilated; they literally swarm with vermin. It is almost impossible to breathe. Missionaries are seized with vomiting or fainting upon entering them. 'I have felt,' said another, 'the vermin dropping on my hat like peas. In some of the rooms I dare not sit, or I should be at once covered.'"

These were some of the worst instances. But, though they were the worst instances, it must be recollected that these houses were the receptacles of thousands. He hoped the House would forgive his going into these details, because the conclusion he desired to enforce was not to be proved by argumentation, but by an induction of facts, the collection of which was the result of much inquiry and long investigation. He was sorry to say the state of things he had described was not confined to London. It prevailed in many parts of the kingdom, and in almost all the great towns. The following was an extract from a report of

Mr. Rawlinson, an inspector of the Board of Health, being a communication from a clergyman in Dover:

"From a ministerial experience of thirteen years, first in a parish of 7,000 souls, then in a parish of 20,000, and now in a parish of 10,000, I am perfectly satisfied of the close connection subsisting between the sanitary and moral condition of our poorer classes. At Fulham, Maidstone, and Dover, I found, without any exception, the worst demoralization in the worst constituted dwellings and neighbourhoods, the one being traceable from the other directly as effect from cause. I affirm, in conscience, that to raise them while they live in such places and under such circumstances as they do now, is impossible. No sense of decency or self-re ect can struggle against the difficulty; and the chief for of our pastoral ministrations is rendered nugatory. I may add, that I have very rarely met with a parish priest, accustomed to minister in a large town, who has not fully felt the same conviction. The relieving officer for Charlton stated—' There are 650 houses, or rather substitutes for houses—hovels. The whole parish is one receptacle for filth. In reference to Barwick's Alley, where there are about fifty separate small huts, built in steps, one over the other, against a steep hill-side, there are but three privies attached, and there is only one very dirty draw-well to supply the whole neighbourhood with water. The horrid state of this alley is beyond description.'"

Birmingham was in the same condition; so were Manchester and Leeds. He could make that statement from his own personal experience, having examined Manchester from one end to the other. Morpeth was worth mentioning, because, being a small town, it afforded a very fair sample of what occurred even in small places. Of these, there was scarcely one in the kingdom where a measure of the kind he proposed ought not to be brought into operation. Looking to Morpeth, the inspector said—

"In Lumsden's Lane I found lodging-houses dirty and crowded, one of which was over a large ashpit, the same where the woman had died of cholera. At the head of Lumsden's Yard there are also open middens and privies, the drains from which pass under the adjoining cottages."

And he went on to describe a place called Bell's Yard. He proceeded:

"This state of things surrounds the poor inhabitants with a surface of visible filth, and also keeps them in an atmosphere of foul gases, where the seeds of disease most readily ripen. Fever, according to the medical evidence, is almost constant in these places; and cholera, as shown, is first developed in such rooms as that over the privy and ashpit situated in Lumsden's Lane. This undue crowding is as destructive to the property as to the health of the poor inhabitants. The wet and damp retained by the middens generate rot, and the surface filth is trodden into the houses, the cleansing of which is consequently neglected, and the result is rapid decay. If a labouring man is compelled, for want of better accommodation, to reside in such tenements, he loses his health, loses his labour, and the owner cannot obtain payment from a family reduced to pauperism, and so he loses his rent."

Such was a state of things which was frequently found to exist, and hear the consequences. A labouring man came to a town where employment was to be had when he was in the prime of life, from 25 to 35, and capable of making 15s., 20s., or 25s. a week. It was necessary he should take a lodging near the place where his work was carried on. The tenements he had to choose from were many of them in ill-drained, ill-ventilated neighbourhoods, and of the filthy description already mentioned. From these, however, he was compelled to make his selection. What was the result? The result, as appeared from the testimony of city missionaries and ministers of all denominations, was that of hundreds and hundreds of these men, who came in the prime of life to a town in search of employment, it was found, ere long, that their health was broken down, that they came on the parish, that they sank into the grave, and that they left their wives and families a permanent burden on the community. Now, the following graphic description of the lodging-houses in Morpeth was furnished by the town-clerk:

"The table will show the narrow space afforded to each, but it can give no idea of the actual state of the rooms, or the scenes they exhibit. Those that offer beds have these articles of luxury filled with as many as can possibly lie upon them. Others find berths below the beds, and then the vacant spaces on the floor are occupied. Among these is a tub filled with vomit and natural evacuations. Other houses have no beds, but their occupiers are packed upon the floor in rows, the head of one being close to the feet of another. Each body is placed so close to its neighbour as not to leave sufficient space upon which to set a foot. The occupants are entirely naked, except rugs drawn up as far as the waist; and when to this is added that the doors and windows are carefully closed, and that there is not the least distinction of sex, but men, women, and children lie indiscriminately side by side, some faint idea may be formed of the state of these places, and their effect upon health, morals, and decency. Fevers prevail, and the sick ward of the workhouse is filled with typhus in its worst form from these places."

A gentleman, who had taken a great interest in the examination of towns, with a view of obtaining some remedy for the existing evils, gave an account of a part of Leeds, in which he stated that in a yard he inspected—

" was a house containing one room, with one bed in it, and no fewer than eight persons were found occupying it. In the same yard was another house, comprising two rooms, and containing three beds, and 31 persons were occupying them, giving an average of more than 10 persons to each bed. In that yard there were several other houses, in which three, four, or five persons occupied each bed. In a semicircle, drawn in a radius of about a quarter of a mile, they found 222 such lodging-houses."

What wonder, then, that typhus fever greatly prevailed? that the medical officers reported that it mainly had its origin in the low lodging-houses of the town? Again, another from Bradford writes:

"In some of these cellar-dwellings, of about four yards square, there were collected sometimes 20 persons, some in beds, some on the floor; some naked men and women together: children with the smallpox in the midst of them. One of these lodging-house keepers had been fined a few days before for having taken in so many. 'Sir,' said he, 'what is to be done with these people? there are not houses for them; can I let them lie in the street?' 'I am told,' said his informant, 'that supposing Bradford to contain 60,000 people, at least one-fourth are at this moment thus lodged.'"

He should mention only one other place in London, with the purpose of showing the absolute necessity that existed for some remedy similar to that which he contemplated; because it was right that the House should know the effect that clearances and alterations, made with the view of beautifying the metropolis, had on the accommodation of the working classes. When the great thoroughfare of New Oxford Street was opened, a great number of wretched dwellings were cleared away, and no provision was made for the accommodation of those inhabitants who were displaced, so that while the formation of that street added to the beauty of the town, it had the effect of exaggerating the evil that pressed on the humbler classes. There was a district in Bloomsbury called Church Lane, one of the filthiest that existed in the metropolis, and one of the most unsafe to visit, from the constant prevalence of fever. It was examined in 1848 by the Statistical Society, whose committee stated in their report that it presented—

"a picture in detail of human wretchedness, filth, and brutal degradation. In these wretched dwellings, all ages and both sexes, fathers and daughters, mothers and sons, grown-up brothers and sisters, the sick, dying, and dead, are herded together. Take an instance: House No. 2, size of room 14 feet long, 13 feet broad, 6 feet high; rent 8s. for two rooms per week—under-rent, 3d. a night for each adult. Number of families, 3; 8 males above 20; 5 females above 20; 4 males under 20; 5 females under 20; total, 22 souls. Landlady receives 18s. a week; thus a clear profit of 10s. State of rooms filthy."

Now, the average number of persons in each house in Church Lane was 24, in 1841; but when an examination took place in the end of 1847 the average was 40 persons to each house; and he desired particularly to direct the attention of the House to the fact that the parties who had swelled those numbers were people displaced along that line of street occupied now as New Oxford Street, displaced in consequence of the formation and beautifying of that thoroughfare. When great improvements were in progress it was a matter for consideration whether provision ought not to be made for the accommodation of those removed, not only for their own sakes, but for the sake of the community, who were exposed to peculiar danger from the confluence of many persons into places which fostered typhus and cholera. Now, to give a summary of the state of the country, he would mention that the inspectors of the Board of Health had examined 161 populous places, the aggregate population being 1,912,599; and he might safely say that, without exception, one uniform statement was made with respect to the domiciliary condition of large masses of the workpeople—that it was of one and the same disgusting character.

It was therefore to meet such a state of things that he asked leave to bring in a bill which should be as nearly as possible a transcript of the Baths and Washhouses Bill. That measure had not been fully worked out in all respects, as he trusted it would be; it was coming slowly into operation; but where it had been applied it had conferred a boon on the people, of which the benefits were incalculable. The provisions of the bill he now asked leave to bring in would be—1, That the act might be adopted in certain boroughs and parishes; 2, that the council of any borough might adopt the act, the expenses to be charged on borough funds; 3, that on requisition of ten ratepayers, churchwardens might convene a vestry to determine whether the act should be adopted, but the resolutions would not be deemed carried unless two-thirds voted for it; 4, that, when the act was adopted, the vestry should appoint commissioners for carrying the same into execution; 5, that the overseers levy, as part of the poor rate, such sums as the vestry should deem necessary; 6, that vestries of two or more parishes might concur; 7, that town councils and commissioners might erect lodging-houses, or adapt buildings, or purchase existing houses; 8, that if lodging-houses were considered unnecessary, or too expensive, they might be sold with the approval of the Treasury; 9, that the council and commissioners might make by-laws, subject to the approval of the Secretary of State, and also fix charges, subject to an appeal to the Poor Law Board; and, 10, which was a necessary provision, that no person receiving parochial relief should be allowed to be a tenant. This bill he proposed to be altogether permissive, and not compulsory; it was desirable to follow, in this respect, the precedent of the baths and washhouses.

He might now state from some experience of the model lodging-houses what good effects they had produced. Nothing was more remarkable than the cheerfulness with which the rents were paid. By an accurate or rigorous system, by not allowing rents to fall into arrear, the greatest punctuality was observed, equally beneficial to the parties who let and the parties who paid. Another advantage was the freedom from disease. There was a very remarkable statement by Dr. Duncan, an officer of the Board of Health, writing from Liverpool, with reference to the effect which even a registration of lodging-houses had attained :—

" In a certain number of registered lodging-houses, the history of which has been traced, there occurred annually, before registration, which involves supervision, prevention of overcrowding, and attention to cleanliness, 150 cases of fever. During the late epidemic there occurred in these houses only 98 cases of cholera, while the total cholera cases in the town were to the fever cases of the preceding years referred to as two to one. So that cholera after registration was only in the proportion of one to three as compared with fever before registration."

The Model Lodging-house in George Street, Bloomsbury, was within a stone's throw of Church Lane. The ravages of cholera in Church Lane were dreadful; in the model buildings in George Street, Bloomsbury, not one person died, and there was only one case of diarrhœa, which speedily yielded to medical treatment. There was another benefit. The wages the people earned they kept. These were not expended on medical relief or the beershop.

The accommodation offered in these houses held out inducements to remain at home; the possibility of cultivating some of the better part of man had been the means of reforming many in these establishments. These parties said, "The wages we earn we now keep." It was impossible to go among them without hearing the liveliest expressions of gratitude. One who visited the Model Lodging-house in Streatham Street would see the advantage to children, who had a large open space for play, instead of running in the streets and forming evil associations. Some objections had been stated to the system. First, it was said an increase of rent was a consequence which working people would not be able to bear. Assuming an increase, he was convinced they would be able to bear it, from the greater health they enjoyed, and the greater activity and diligence they would be able to bestow on their work. In many instances a working man was calculated to lose by sickness about 30 days in a year. At 1s. 6d. each day, the loss would be 2l. 5s., which was a vast deal more than any increase of rent for superior accommodation. He would say, besides, there was no increase of rent, but a diminution, and with that an adequate profit. It was stated that—

" The average rent paid in Snow's Rents, Westminster, ' a vile place,' was, in 1844, 2s. 4½d. per week per room. The people employed in the docks pay from 1s. 6d. to 3s. per week for single rooms, which for filth and disgusting appearance were such wretched hovels as defied giving a fair description of them. The single men pay in the lodging-houses 1s. 6d. per week for half a bed, and 2s. for single beds, several sleeping in the same room, wanting in comfort, cleanliness, &c."

Another statement was, that the apartments rented by the London Dock labourers were at 2s. to 4s., the average being 3s. per week per room. Another person said—

" As near as I can judge, the average price paid per week for the wretched rooms occupied by the lowest poor in the vilest neighbourhoods is about 2s. 6d. To make up this rent the apartments are crowded to the greatest excess."

What was the rent in the model lodging-houses? In George Street, Bloomsbury, every man had a compartment to himself, with a bed, chair, and space for all necessary movements. For that compartment he paid 4d. a night, exactly the same payment demanded from him in the worst and most disgusting locality. That house yielded a clear profit of 6½ per cent. on the money invested. Then houses of three rooms, with every accommodation and a constant supply of water, were given at a rent equal to that exacted for one room elsewhere. The rent varied, according to

the position of the rooms, from 3*s*. 6*d*. to 7*s*. An artisan, with
25*s*. to 30*s*. a week, might take a house at 6*s*. or 7*s*.; those making
less, a house at 4*s*.; but they received every accommodation for
the same sum that they paid for one disgusting room, which often
had to be shared with another. Then it was said these matters
ought to be left to private speculation. He should much object
to that. Private speculation was very much confined to the
construction of the smallest houses of the lowest possible description, because it was out of those the most inordinate profits could
be made. Private speculation was almost entirely in that
direction. Then private speculators would not undertake these
houses, for to make the lodging-house system work well there
must be constant and vigilant superintendence. Again, at that
particular time there were many advantages for the construction
of model lodging-houses. First, the reduction of the duty on
bricks had greatly facilitated the operations. It was a reduction
of 15 per cent. to the consumer. On the entire cost of the house
in Streatham Street it was about 3 per cent.; but when the hollow
brick was brought into use for houses of moderate size, a saving
would be effected of no less than 25 per cent. He wished also to
bear testimony to the great value of reduction of the window
duty, and wished the Chancellor of the Exchequer were present
to hear the result of the experience obtained by those interested
in the model lodging-houses. The Streatham Street house contained suites of apartments for fifty families. If these suites were
separate dwellings, there would be no window tax; but, being
under one roof, window tax might be demanded to the amount of
between 60*l*. and 70*l*. a year, adding 25*s*. a year to the rent of
each set of apartments. The removal of the window duty would
permit a reduction of rent from 7*s*. to 6*s*. 6*d*., and so on.

Now, the present proposition violated no principle. These
houses were self-supporting. What had been the result of some
years' experience? The Society for Improving the Condition of
the Labouring Classes had expended 20,750*l*. in building and
fitting up these new piles of model houses, and 2,250*l*. in improving, adapting, and fitting up these ranges of old dwellings,
making together an expenditure of 23,000*l*. The net return on
the same, after deducting all incidental expenses, including those
of management and ordinary repairs, averaged 6 per cent.; or on
new buildings, 5½ per cent.; on old, 12 per cent. They had kept
one house as a curiosity, and as an illustration of the exorbitancy
and intolerable profits levied by the low lodging-houses. It was
a small house, on which the profit was not less than 30 per cent.
There could be no doubt that, from many of the houses a much
larger profit was obtained. By the removal, too, of single houses

in some localities, much might be done to promote a better circulation of air, and improve an entire district at a very cheap rate. It would, moreover, be very desirable to remove impediments in the way of associations to be formed with limited liabilities; but the expense of a charter was now an insuperable obstacle to the formation of all societies.

He was anxious the House should take up a matter which had excited the interest of all civilized Europe; from parts of which, as well as from America, letters had been received, asking for the plans and reports on the subject. He was certain that he spoke the truth—and a truth which would be confirmed by the testimony of all experienced persons, clergy, medical men, all who were conversant with the working classes—that, until their domiciliary condition were Christianised (he could use no less forcible a term), all hope of moral or social improvement was utterly vain. Though not the sole, it was one of the prime sources of the evils that beset their condition; it generated disease, ruined whole families by the intemperance it promoted, cut off or crippled thousands in the vigour of life, and filled the workhouses with widows and orphans.

Let this be taken as a proof: in the time of cholera, in the Model Lodging-house in St. Pancras there were 500 persons under one roof. In a small court, called Peahen Court, in Bishopsgate Street, there resided 150 persons. Mr. Grainger, the inspector, went over that court, and reported to the committee that, if the cholera did break out there, the consequences would be frightful. Three days afterwards the cholera broke out on that spot. In the Model Lodging-house not a single person died of cholera. In Peahen Court there were 7 deaths; and in one day 12 orphans were thrown on the workhouse. He found that the number of widowers, widows, and orphans, in 95 unions caused by the cholera was—widowers and widows, 628; orphans, 1,689; total, 2,317. In Bradford there were 27 widowers and widows, and 82 orphans; total, 109; in Leeds, 35 widowers and widows, and 73 orphans, 108; Lambeth, 81 widowers and widows, and 234 orphans, 315; West Bromwich, 34 widowers and widows, and 86 orphans, 110; Wolverhampton, 27 widowers and widows, and 68 orphans, 95; and most of these became permanently chargeable on the workhouse. But what cholera did suddenly and openly, fever did slowly and secretly. The cholera slew its thousands, but fever its tens of thousands; and, if they doubted the fact they might have full evidence of it, within ten minutes' walk of the magnificent palace that was now being built for the Houses of Parliament.

His prayer was, for leave to bring in a bill to remove some of the fatal impediments that prevented the free exercise of the activity and vigour of the working classes. They had never sufficiently tested either the will or the capacity of those classes, who, from a variety of circumstances, had been placed in a condition very disadvantageous indeed to the exercise of all their energies. He saw no reason why the working people of this country should not equal, if not surpass, in physical prosperity their brethren of the United States. Their wages were enormous, but their expenditure, in a great measure owing to their sanitary condition, was wild and extravagant. Mr. Porter, of the Board of Trade, had published a work some time ago, called *Self-imposed Taxation*, and in that work he said that the expenditure of the working classes in this realm, in the consumption of three articles that might be abstained from entirely, or in a great degree, namely, spirits, beer, and tobacco, amounted to not less than 57,000,000*l.* a year. Imagine that sum expended in wholesome food, clothing, education, and the improvement of dwellings; and could any one say that the moral, social, political, and religious condition of a responsible and immortal being would not be exalted in the scale of society? He could not believe they would fail in their efforts. He felt assured that God would bless such efforts, directed, as they would be, to the advancement of the social, moral, and religious well-being of a very large portion of the human race.

He desired to add the closing remark, that it must be well borne in mind that it was as necessary to pull down as to build: if these foul and dark receptacles were left standing when their inmates were removed, thousands arriving in London from the country, or from other parts of the city, would flow into them, and perpetuate the vice and wretchedness which disgraced and endangered these localities.

---

Lord Ashley a few days afterwards introduced a bill for the registration and inspection of common lodging-houses—houses where individuals or families were received by the night. It was accepted without any preliminary remarks, it being generally known and acknowledged that the state of them, both morally and physically, was most pernicious.

Both bills passed into laws—the first, being limited by the House of Commons to towns of a population of 10,000, has been adopted in one place only, in Huddersfield.

The other has been very operative throughout the kingdom, and has received the amplest testimony from the police and medical men in every district.

*Religious Liberty in Turkey.*

## HOUSE OF LORDS,

FRIDAY, MARCH 10, 1854.

MY LORDS,

A few days ago there appeared, in the public papers, a document purporting to be a manifesto from the Emperor Nicolas, which contained this portentous statement: " England and France have sided with the enemies of Christianity against Russia combating for the orthodox faith."

My Lords, it is not surprising that all should feel such an imputation as this, nor out of place here that some notice should be taken of it. England and Europe demand an explanation; and those who have been called to bear a part in the administration of the religious societies of this country and the Continent can give, and are prepared to give, a most direct contradiction to the assertions of the Czar; and dropping, in this case, the term " enemies" or " friends" of Christianity, and looking only to the results, we will undertake to prove that Turkey has of late done everything to advance, and Russia everything to retard, the progress of Christianity among the nations of mankind.

But first a word as to these famous negotiations. I do not believe that, from the very outset, there was on the Russian part a particle or an atom of sincerity. If my noble friend, the Secretary of State for Foreign Affairs, had been an angel of light, he would not have been able to bring the negotiations to any other issue; the predominant desire in the mind of the Czar was the absolute, though virtual, rule over the Turkish empire. This is manifest in his arrogant assumption of a personal right of protection of the Christians in the East, and in his haughty rejection of the efficient protectorate offered by the four powers; a most ample guarantee, if protection to the Christians had been his only object of solicitude. That this was evident to my noble friend after the production of the Menschikoff note, may be inferred from the tone and style of the despatches which followed it; documents which, I must say, have conferred no small honour on the government, and have added not only to the dignity, but to the literature of the country.

Now, my Lords, the Emperor of Russia is not the first man who laid to our charge the imputation of an unholy alliance with infidels and Mussulmans. He took it at second hand from an accomplished Member of the other House, merely adding, by way of a cordial to himself, that he was combating " in defence of the orthodox faith !" It is really astonishing that a gentleman of the sagacity and knowledge of Mr. Cobden should have regarded this question as though an alliance of Mahometans and Christians were a thing unprecedented in Christian annals. He talked as if the history of India had never been either written or read; as though we had never formed, as though we were not actually executing now, alliances offensive and defensive with heathen powers in those countries; and as though we had not been allied, not very long ago, with these same Mahometan Turks to recover possession of Egypt. My Lords, there is a wide difference between an alliance with any power, heathen though it be, to maintain the cause of right, justice, and order, against the aggressions even of professing Christians, and an alliance for the development and aggrandizement of that power. Law, order, and justice, are things so sacred in the eye of God, that they must be respected, whoever be the recipients of them. It is not a question here, whether the Turks, as such, shall continue to reign at Constantinople; it is no question here, whether we shall uphold a Mussulman empire, as they say, " in its dotage :" Turkey is the battlefield, and the Turks the objects of these great principles. But the true question at issue is, whether we shall assert the rights of a weaker state, maintain the independence of nations, and endeavour to assign a limit to the encroachments of a power that seems bent to darken all that is light, and subjugate all that is free, among the nations of mankind.

My Lords,—I have no particular sympathies or antipathies for either of the parties engaged in this struggle. I wish that we were well rid of them both—that the Russians were driven to the north of Archangel, the Turks to the east of the Euphrates; but since we are compelled to make a choice; since we must declare for either one or the other—let us see whether there are no alleviating circumstances in the course we have adopted; whether we have not judged rightly to prefer, as I most heartily do, the Turkish to the Russian autocrat—the autocrat that has granted such great facilities to the advancement of Christianity and civilization—to the autocrat who denies them in his own dominions, and who would deny them still more fiercely should he ever become, by our neglect, the master of those noble provinces that he so ardently covets.

My Lords,—It is my deliberate conviction that this is a long-conceived and gigantic scheme, determined on years ago, and now to be executed, for the prevention of all religious freedom, and so ultimately of all civil freedom, among millions of mankind.

But first allow me, in a few words, to describe the gradual growth, during the last twenty years, of wealth, intelligence, and civilization among the Christians of Turkey. I do not deny that there have been occasional outbreaks of Mussulman bigotry, but they have been local, not general; the result of some momentary fanaticism, and not authorized, nay, controlled, by the government. The truth is that the great enemy of the Christian in these countries is not the Turk, but the Christian himself. A very large proportion of the torture, the spoliation, the imprisonment that has taken place, has been inflicted by Christians upon Christians, and principally stimulated by the Greek priesthood, with the view of retaining dominion over the laity of their flocks. But to proceed—I desire to show the progress of the last twenty years. First, the diffusion of the Scriptures during that time has been almost incredible. Now, whatever may be the private opinions of any one with regard to the Bible, no one will gainsay this assertion—that the diffusion of it has ever been the precursor of lasting civilization and free institutions. Wherever the Bible has free course, and is freely admitted into the minds of men, there you will be sure to see the development of knowledge, of progress, and of wider and nobler aspirations.

It was stated last year, in a speech by Mr. Layard, in the House of Commons (and the statement has since been confirmed by the American missionaries), that there are more than forty towns and villages in Turkey (subsequent inquiry has raised them to fifty) in which there are distinct congregations of Protestant seceders from the Greek communion. I use the term " Protestant," because it is a term of their own choosing; I should have preferred their other designation, Gospel Readers, because we should thereby have avoided an apparent admixture of the Roman Catholic question—there is, however, here nothing of the sort.

There are, besides, among the Armenians, both in the capital and in the provinces, a large multitude heartily disposed to the new doctrines, and waiting only for opportunity or protection to stand openly among the seceders. Twenty-five years ago not a single Protestant could be found among all the natives; and now there are more than sixty-five regular Protestant teachers in Turkey, and fourteen Protestant schools in Constantinople alone! What then was the consequence of all this?—improvement in social and moral position; vigorous desire among the laity to emancipate themselves from the thraldom of the priesthood; much resistance by the hierarchy; and, thank God, much success with the people!

Now to what is it all ascribable? I affirm, to the singular and unprecedented liberality of the Turkish system: free scope is there permitted to every religious movement; no hindrance is ever experienced except from the Greek or the Armenian superior clergy. Not only in Constantinople, but in all the provinces, associations for religious purposes are openly recognized and permitted. Printing-presses exist at Constantinople, at Bucharest, and other great towns, where we print the Scriptures in every Oriental tongue, including the Turkish, for circulation among the Turkish people. There are forty depôts for the sale of the Bible in Turkey; and at this moment we have a host of colporteurs and native agents perambulating the provinces, reading the Word, and distributing the Scriptures, "no man forbidding them."

Now contrast this with what is permitted or prohibited in Russia, and draw your inference as to what we have to expect should these awakening provinces fall under the dark and drowsy rule of the Czar. No associations for religious purposes are tolerated in Russia;—no printing-presses are permitted for printing the Bible in modern Russ, the only language understood by the people!—no versions of the Scriptures are allowed to cross the frontier except the German, French, Italian, and English. Not a single copy, I repeat, of the Bible in the modern Russ, in the vernacular tongue, can gain access into that vast empire; and it is believed, on the best evidence, that not a single copy has been printed, even in Russia, since 1823, in the tongue spoken by the people! No colporteurs, of course, nor native agents to enlighten the gloomy provinces; no depôts for the sale of the Scriptures; no possible access to the Word of God!

But here is a restriction which seems incomprehensible. The Emperor has within his dominions a concentrated population of Hebrews, amounting to nearly two millions:—not a single copy of the Scriptures in the Hebrew tongue is allowed to enter Poland for the benefit of this people. I am told that this is refused with even greater severity than the importation of the modern Russ. I called it incomprehensible, but on reflection it is not so: it springs from his fear of the smallest particle of light and life on the feelings and faculties of men, and especially this energetic and wonderful race. But if this be so; if this be the spirit that governs the Emperor in his own dominions, do you think that he will manifest a different spirit should he once, by right of conquest, get possession of these regions, in which he discerns the dawn of liberty and the rights of conscience? I cannot doubt, and no one can doubt, that so far as lies in man, the rising provinces of Turkey would be crushed to the level of the internal provinces of Russia!"

But Russia and this "orthodox faith" are not more favourable to missions,—not missions, be it remarked, to disturb the Greek Church,—but missions to the wild and ignorant heathen of her own dominions, the outskirting provinces of her own empire, where the people are sunk in idolatry and the grossest darkness. Even thither no missionary is permitted to go; and to this hour we believe that no mission has been sent from the Greek Church to supply the places of the expelled foreigners. How methodical, how systematic is all this! The Moravian Brethren—and your Lordships know well the order, decency, discipline, and vital Christianity of this admirable body—the Moravian Brethren laboured for many years among the Calmuc Tartars between the Black and Caspian Seas. About three hundred converts had been gathered together, but the missionaries were forbidden to baptize any one of them, on the ground of an old law of the Church that "no heathen under Russian sway shall be converted to Christianity and baptized but by the Russian Greek clergy." This mission was therefore abandoned.

The Scottish Missionary Society began a mission in Russian Tartary in 1802—their operations were widely extended. A Mahommedan convert of high standing was baptized by the missionaries, upon which the authorities commenced a series of vexatious restrictions and annoyances, which compelled the society to relinquish its operations, and, after more than twenty years' labour, and a large expenditure, to withdraw just at the time they were beginning to reap some little fruit of their exertions.

The Basle Missionary Society opened a mission among the Tartars, on the confines of Persia, and laboured first in the Persian dominions. Meeting with opposition there, they removed into the Russian territory about 1823, where they continued about ten years, until they received orders to quit the imperial domains, and the missionaries retired to other fields of labour.

The London Missionary Society undertook a mission in Siberia, on the frontiers of Chinese Tartary. They were countenanced by the Emperor Alexander (mark this, for we shall soon see a contrast between the Czars), and joined by several Russian missionaries. But in the year 1841, after twenty years' expense and toil, this mission was suppressed, by an order from the Russian synod; this mission, on the frontiers of China, at the extremities of the empire, to the veriest heathen in the midst of darkness, ignorance, and vice, was suppressed, on the liberal and Christian ground, that "the mission, in relation to that form of Christianity already established in the Russian empire, did not coincide with the views of the church and the government!"

Now, in contrast with all this, take the course and policy of the Turkish government. It has given full liberty—and it has observed what it has given—to Christian missionaries of Europe and America, whether Protestant or Roman Catholic, to carry on their operations to any extent, by preaching, by the circulation of the Scriptures, by printing establishments, by living agencies; it has issued edicts of toleration; it has announced its will to protect every one in the exercise of that religion which he may conscientiously profess. I say again, as I said at the outset, that we have nothing to do with the motives of these powers: it may be bigotry on the part of the Russian; it may be indifference on the part of the Turk—I look only to the results; and there you have every facility on the one side, and every obstacle on the other, to the progress of all that is good, and worthy, and desirable, for the human race.

What then, my Lords, was the issue? A great development of knowledge and liberal sentiment, enlarged hopes and aspirations of the Christian population; but redoubled violence and persecutions by the clergy against the laity, backed by the Russian consuls. Here are samples of the character and conduct of the Greek priests! "In Turkey, the dignitaries of the Greek or orthodox Church (the 'orthodox faith' of the Imperial manifesto) exercise, in some degree, the powers of civil magistrates. The abuses of the Greek hierarchy," said Lord Stratford, "as well in the exercise of civil authority, as in the management of temporalities, are notorious."

This shows the character of the Greek Church in Turkey; and, to understand it well, there is no necessity to read more than the correspondence relating to the condition of Protestants or Seceders in Turkey, from 1841 to 1851. The letters of 1844, from

Consul Wood, himself, I believe, a Roman Catholic, speak with indignation of the cruelty and intrigues of the Greek clergy; and he adds these significant words :—" The Russian consul-general of Beyrout has sent his dragoman to the authorities of Damascus to persuade them to assist the Greek Patriarch in recovering his flock!"

Other instances follow. Mr. Wellesley wrote to Lord Palmerston in 1846—" The promises of the Armenian Patriarch, that the penalties should not affect the civil rights of the seceders, have been violated. They are falsely accused of crimes, charged with imaginary debts, turned out of their houses. The Patriarch possesses the right of banishing any Armenian from one part of the Sultan's dominions to the other."

This is the state of things which the Emperor of Russia is determined, if it be possible, to perpetuate over the whole body of the laity in communion with the Greek Church. We trace, step by step, the efforts of Lord Stratford, then Sir Stratford Canning, to obtain for the Christians of the East liberty of conscience and independence of action; and we trace also, step by step, the interposition of the Russian government to prevent such concessions. The records of the Foreign Office are full of such facts. I do not ask my noble friend to rise and confirm what I say, but I defy him to contradict me.

Now, the disposition of the Russian government began principally to be manifested in 1844. In that year the Consul Wood wrote to Lord Aberdeen :—" The menaces of the Russian consul-general, supported by the unreserved declaration that he would protest against every proceeding which tended to the encouragement of the professing Christian Protestants, coupled with the subtle intrigues of the Patriarch, &c. &c." On this Lord Aberdeen, writing to Sir Stratford Canning, says,—" As the Russian government have expressed an earnest desire that the English authorities should be instructed to abstain from taking any part in the conversion of members of the Greek Church to the Protestant faith, . . . I have conveyed to the Russian government an equally explicit desire that the Russian consul-general should be restrained in his over-zealous exertions in favour of his co-religionists in Syria." This is very good: here we have the testimony of the noble Earl, then at the head of Foreign Affairs, to the vexatious, persecuting, intermeddling activity of the agents of the Czar to harass the Greek laity.

The papers then proceed to detail the efforts of successive British ministers to procure the public recognition and protection of the Protestant Seceders from the Armenian Church at Constantinople, and for all the Protestants. The first step is a single sentence in a general proclamation; "Metropolitans and dignitaries shall not use force or injustice to their co-nationals;" then follow cases of oppression given in detail, in many of which the Patriarch is the chief agent. Lord Aberdeen again declares that "remonstrances must be made against religious persecution;" the Armenian Patriarch promises to protect the Protestants at Hasbeya from violence, and breaks his promise. Lord Palmerston then takes up the correspondence, and transmits to Constantinople a memorial from the Free Church of Scotland, and puts the question wholly on the rights of conscience. The Honourable Mr. Wellesley writes to Lord Palmerston, and recounts the violence still perpetrated against the Protestants—by whom? by the Turks?—no such thing: by the Christians, by the clergy, by the bishops and archbishops themselves. "It is true," he says, "that Sir Stratford Canning, before his departure, obtained the promise of the Armenian Patriarch that the penalties attending excommunication should be limited to the spiritual condemnation, and should not affect the civil rights of those who came under its ban. Yet not only is this promise constantly violated, but other means of annoyance have been found." Mr. Wellesley proceeds and suggests the "incorporation" of the Protestants for their protection. He points out, however, the difficulty which would inevitably arise in obtaining such a measure—and what is that? —why, these are his own words, "the fear of offending the Russian government"—this ever-watchful defender of the "orthodox faith!" Lord Palmerston, nevertheless, continued to urge on the minister at Constantinople a perseverance in the measures proposed.

Next comes a memorandum from the Turkish Minister for Foreign Affairs, affirming these principles; then Lord Cowley obtains a vizierial order of toleration. Lord Palmerston transmitted a copy to the late Archbishop of Canterbury and the Bishop of London, who acknowledged it, as well they might, "with great satisfaction;" the Bishop of London terming it "a valuable concession to the rights of conscience!" To be sure it was; but when have we received such a boon from Russia? When has Christianity been thus set free in the Muscovite dominions?

But here is the climax; here is the final point of aggravation! Sir Stratford Canning obtains a charter of Protestant rights, under the signature of the Sultan, which he thus characterizes:— "Religious liberty, and exemption from civil vexations on account of religion, are now secured to all the Protestant community;

and the example of its members may, with God's blessing, operate favourably on the relaxed morals of the Greek and Armenian clergy."

Allow me, now, a few words to show what led to this happy issue—this charter of the liberties of the Eastern Christians.

"In the latter part of January of the year 1846, the full vials of hierarchal vengeance were poured out upon the heads of the defenceless men and women in the Armenian Church who chose to obey God rather than man. They were summoned, says the narrator, before the Patriarch, one by one, and peremptorily ordered to subscribe their names to a creed, which had been prepared for the purpose, on pain of the terrible anathema, with all its barbarous consequences. In the course of a week or so they were ejected from their shops and their business; men, women, and children, without regard to circumstances, were compelled to leave their habitations, sometimes in the middle of the night, and go forth into the streets, not knowing whither they should go, or where they should find shelter. The bakers were prohibited from furnishing them with bread, and the water-carriers with water. Parents were forced by the Patriarch to cast out even their own children who adhered to the Gospel, and to disinherit them."

What, I ask, could the fanatical Turks have done worse than this? But it proceeds:—"The Patriarch and his party resorted to every species of oppression:" they had, it appears, neither pity nor scruple; lack of power, but no lack of will, to decapitate their co-nationals. The brethren were reviled, spit upon, and stoned: some were cast into prison, and anathemas sounded against all for several Sundays throughout the churches.

"It was at this crisis," continues the narrative, "that the bitterness of persecution was arrested, from a quarter whence such an interference might have been least expected. The Turkish government interposed to stay the tempest of ecclesiastical fury, and protected the incipient reformation. The Armenian Patriarch, summoned before Redshid Pasha, the Minister of Foreign Affairs, was charged by him to desist from his oppressive course." By whose influence was this? By the influence of Sir Stratford Canning, whose noble and persevering efforts, the writer affirms, to secure in Turkey liberty of conscience, are above all praise. "It matters not with him," says Dr. Dwight, the American missionary, "by what name the victim of persecution is called, or to what nation or denomination he belongs—whether he be Jew or Greek, Mahommedan, Armenian, or Roman Catholic. This noble philanthropist is always ready to fly to his relief, and his influence is very great. The Lord has used him (he justly continues) as an instrument in bringing about as great changes in this land as we have ever seen in any part of the world ; and the recognition of the principle by this government, that Protestant Rayas can live in this country, and pursue their lawful callings, and at the same time worship God according to the dictates of their conscience, is not among the least of these changes."

My Lords, — I should be sorry to mention the American missionaries in the East without uttering a passing word of respect and admiration for their most noble exertions. Whatever may arise hereafter for the benefit of the Oriental Christians, a very large portion of the honour, and I trust, too, a very large portion of the happiness, will fall to the lot of those praiseworthy men, our missionary brethren from the United States.

" From this period," the narrative concludes, " the principle of toleration in connection with the Turkish government has been steadily advancing. The Sultan, in a speech delivered at Adrianople during the year 1846, openly declared that difference in religion is a matter that concerns only the consciences of men, and has nothing to do with their civil position."

The exertions of Sir Stratford Canning were unceasing, and they reached at last their grand consummation. He obtained from the Sultan an imperial firman, whereby the Protestants were placed on the footing of the ancient established Christian communities. All previous documents had been vizierial, only local and temporary in their application; but this Charter of Protestants is imperial, and stamped with the Sultan's cypher.

Hear its important words :—

" To my Vizir, Mohammed Pasha, Prefect of the Police in Constantinople.

" When this sublime and august mandate reaches you, let it be known that hitherto those of my Christian subjects who have embraced the Protestant faith have suffered much inconvenience and distress. But in necessary accordance with my imperial compassion, which is the support of all, and which is manifested to all classes of my subjects, it is contrary to my imperial pleasure that any one class of them should be exposed to suffering.

" As, therefore, by reason of their faith, the above-mentioned are already a separate community, it is my royal compassionate will that, for the facilitating the conducting of their affairs, and that they may obtain ease and quiet and safety, a faithful and trustworthy person from among themselves, and *by their own selection*"—mark the words—" should be appointed, with the title of '*Agent of the Protestants*,' and that he should be in relations with the Prefecture of the Police." My Lords, here is at once emancipation from the political power and tyranny of their priests! emancipation from the power and influence of Russia, whose instruments they are!—a recognized status, a recognized independence, a declaration and assurance of the rights of conscience! The grant was indeed of indescribable importance.

But it goes further, and adds practice to principle: "You will not," says the document, "permit anything to be required of them, in the name of fee, or on other pretences, for marriage-licences or registration. You will see to it, that, like the other communities of the empire, in all their affairs, such as procuring cemeteries and places of worship, they should have every facility and every needed assistance. You will not permit that any of the other communities shall in any way interfere with their edifices, or with their worldly matters or concerns, or, in short, with any of their affairs, either secular or religious, that thus they may be free to exercise the usages of their faith.

"And it is enjoined upon you not to allow them to be molested an iota in these particulars, or in any others; and that all attention and perseverance be put in requisition to maintain them in quiet and security. And,"—now, my Lords, attend to this,—"*in case of necessity, they shall be free to make representations regarding their affairs through their agent to the Sublime Porte.*"

They have, therefore, a distinct agent, an officer, a representative selected by themselves, to carry their grievances to the very fountain of authority. Thus the political power of the priest was crushed, and with it the hopes and machinations of Russia!

Here then is the whole truth; the secret of the whole movement! the origin and the object of the Emperor's fears! The danger had become imminent; the thing was creeping from under his hand. The circulation of the Scriptures, the growth of Christianity, the rights of conscience, are the resistless preliminaries to freedom of institutions; these provinces are conterminous to his own; no quarantine, no cordon sanitaire was of any avail—and how, then, put out the light that had begun to burn so brightly? Nothing was left for him but the Menschikoff note, and the imperious proposal of the "status quo ab antiquo." And why "ab antiquo?" why these simple words, apparently so natural and so harmless? Because, had the Sultan been entrapped by this demand, had he yielded but a hair's breadth to menace or persuasion, then at one fell swoop would have been cancelled every effort of the British ambassador for twenty years; the decree of Redshid Pasha, the firman of the Sultan; the independent position of the Seceders annulled, the rights of conscience subdued, and the whole mass of the Greek laity thrown back under the thraldom of the priestly tools of the autocrat of Russia.

Do we wonder now, my Lords, at the imperial hatred of Lord Stratford de Redcliffe? do we wonder at the Nesselrode calumnies? Has not that great and good man, year by year, and day by day, dogged the steps of Russian tyranny? has he not detected their plans, and enabled us to expose this colossal conspiracy against the nascent civil and religious liberties of the fairest portions of the habitable globe, and of fourteen millions of the human race?

That these are the sentiments of the reigning Emperor, and this his policy, may be gathered from a brief comparison of himself with his predecessor. The Emperor Alexander was a very different man; and those who read the history of the two will speedily perceive the difference. The Emperor Alexander did all in his power to repress the bigotry of the Greek Church; the Emperor Nicholas has done, and is doing, all in his power to stimulate it for political purposes and his own aggrandisement. In the reign of the Emperor Alexander, there was the most free, unfettered action for the labours of the Bible Society, as much as even in England itself. The Emperor gave his personal sanction and aid to it. He issued an order that all letters on the business of the society, as well as the Bibles and Testaments, should be transmitted, free of charge, to every part of the empire.

He gave, moreover, a house; and added fifteen thousand roubles for the expenses of adaptation to the purposes of the society.

He formed the Moscow Bible Society, and announced it in this most remarkable passage—remarkable for any man, but singularly so from one of his great power and station:—" I consider," he said, "the establishment of Bible Societies in Russia, in most parts of Europe, and in other parts of the globe, and the very great progress these institutions have made in disseminating the word of God, not merely among Christians, but also among heathens and Mahometans, as a peculiar display of the mercy and grace of God to the human race. On this account I have taken on myself the denomination of a member of the Bible Society; and I will render it every possible assistance, in order that the beneficent light of revelation may be shed among all nations subject to my sceptre!" These are great and glorious sentiments.

He died; and in 1826 the Emperor Nicolas ascended the

throne; and what did he then do?—He suppressed, by an ukase, the Russian Bible Society with all its branches; suppressed every privilege granted to religious societies; and brought back that Cimmerian darkness of the human intellect and the human heart that he seems to prize so highly.

Has Turkey, I ask, done anything of the sort? Has she not, my Lords, in the last twenty years, allowed more to the progress of liberty and truth, than Russia, in the whole of the famous nine hundred years that the Emperor boasts as the present age of the alliance between the Sclavonic nations and the Greek Communion? Undoubtedly she has; and this inference cannot be gainsaid— that, if the Sultan had been less liberal towards freedom of religion, less considerate of the rights of conscience, there would have been no Menschikoff note, and no invasion of the Principalities.

But now, my Lords, though these are not the matters for which we undertake the war, we may rejoice that we are not engaged in upholding a state of things adverse to all amelioration, and subversive of all liberty and truth. I trust that out of our present policy we may extract some good to be felt to the latest generation—I trust, nay, I am quite sure, that my noble friend, the Secretary of State for Foreign Affairs, will complete what in his despatches he has so admirably begun, and support Lord Stratford in the largest demands for the civil and religious rights of the Christians in the Ottoman empire. I trust that this country, looking to a prosperous issue of the conflict, will consider the basis of a lasting peace, how best it can restrain inordinate ambition, assist the independence of weaker states, and dam up the floods of barbarism. The forbearance and reluctance, my Lords, manifested by the allied powers of France and England in all their strength, have conferred incalculable service on the present cause, and on the hopes of expanding civilization. It has secured you the sympathies of the country, the sympathies of Europe, and the sympathies, too, of that people with whom I trust we shall ever be allied—our brethren in the United States! It has done much to prevent the recurrence of such an evil; it has shown that war is a solemn, fearful thing; and that, while permitted to us in our fallen state, it may be resorted to only in the last extremity—not in the gratification of passion or revenge— but as a deliberate act, to assert the rights and liberties of men and nations. Seeing then, my Lords, that we have entered on this conflict in no spirit of ambition, covetousness, or pride, but for our own defence, and in the maintenance of great principles which concern alike all the races of mankind, let us have no fear for the issue; but, offering a humble and hearty prayer to

Almighty God, let us devoutly trust that His aid will not be wanting to bless our arms with success, and a speedy peace, in this just and inevitable quarrel.

------

The newspapers of the 11th, the day following the delivery of this speech, contained this remarkable passage, from the St. Petersburg Journal of 18th February:—

"Since the year 1829, his Majesty has followed with earnest attention the march of events in Turkey.  The Emperor could not close his eyes to the consequences of changes which, one by one, have been introduced into that state.  Old Turkey has disappeared since the Turkish government has sought to plant institutions diametrically opposed to the genius of Islamism, and to the character and customs of Mahometans—*institutions*, more or less *copied from the type of modern liberalism.*"

The object of his policy is hereby manifested.

## *Young Men's Christian Association.*

Manchester, Tuesday, March 25, 1856.

Delivered at the Tenth Annual Meeting of the Manchester Young Men's Christian
Association.

THE Earl of Shaftesbury, who presided, said : Ladies and gentlemen, and young‑men of Manchester,—It is a matter, I assure
you, of much gratification to me, that I may present myself
to you without the formality of an introduction, for, although
not connected with this great city, I am, I believe, no stranger to
you—having been connected at various times with many of its
most important interests. I feel, therefore, a very peculiar
pleasure in coming before you on the present occasion to take
the chair, and join with you in thanks to Almighty God for the
signal prosperity with which He has blessed the Young Men's
Christian Association of this great city of Manchester.

Now, I will begin by rejoicing with you, not only in the prosperity
of the institution we now commemorate, but in the wide extension and diffusion of similar associations in London, and in
almost all the great towns of this vast empire. And I rejoice
because these institutions are singularly adapted to the exigencies
of the times; nay, I may say that they are indispensable to the wants
of the age in which we live. Not that they are to be regarded as in
themselves sufficient, or as the only indispensable institutions, because I have had experience enough—and so have you had experience enough—to know that every succeeding day requires many
and various agencies to bear upon the great mass of evil that surrounds us, and to enable us to address ourselves to the great
amount of duty that requires our interposition : and to suppose
that any one association, or any one department of effort could
stand alone without the combination and assistance of all the
rest, is as if the mouth should say that it did not need the
eye, or the arm say it did not need the co‑operation of the

foot. We must be banded together, and give the right hand of fellowship to all who, in different careers, are addressing themselves to the same objects as ourselves; for, when you have all strained your utmost energies, to the last gasp of your effort, the work will be still incomplete, and there will still be an incredible amount of labour to be performed.

But that the importance of these institutions is in harmony with the character and exigencies of the time in which we live, must be manifest to all who consider the purpose for which they were founded. Are they not for the purpose of bringing within the pale of morality and Christian knowledge the thousands—I might say the tens of thousands, ay, I believe the hundreds of thousands —of the young men of the British empire;—young men who are to be hereafter our capitalists, our bankers, and our tradesmen, and who are to do much to determine the character and condition of the country in which they live;—whose disposition, whose knowledge, whose Christian feeling must add much to its internal heart, and, in their outward efforts, add much to the external honour of the country that has given them birth? Now, gentlemen, in all that I say, and in all that will be said,—in all that is said anywhere, on this subject, and in all that is done, we proceed upon the grand, undeniable assumption that you are immortal and responsible beings. I have no sympathy, and you have no sympathy, with those who erect capital and all its results into a divinity, who hold obedience to its dictates to be a duty, and its acquisition to constitute the first and almost the sole requirement of the human race—I say, who erect it into a divinity and worship it with ten times more intensity than they do the God that created them. I look upon you and address you as immortal beings, sent, all of you and each of you, to fulfil a part in the destinies of this world, and to join with your brethren in the great march towards eternity. And if we be such beings, why, then, is it not manifest that we cannot labour with too much earnestness, we cannot devote too much time, we cannot give too much effort, nor can we too much weary heaven with prayer, that institutions like this may be spread over the whole surface of the land, and endeavour to drag within their net —the net of the Gospel—every young man who is brought into these departments of industry—departments of industry honourable for himself, for his relatives, and for the kingdom at large.

I know it is said that we are apt to magnify the present at the expense of the past, and, sometimes, even of the future; but there is no necessity that we should enter into any comparison to find whether the present state of things is better or worse than the state of things through which we or our forefathers have passed. The actual condition of things is quite sufficient for our contemplation, and more than sufficient for all our combined energies; and I would ask any one who hears me, or any one who may read what occurs in this room, if ever there was a time in the history of mankind when the perils to which young men are exposed were more fearful, more abundant, and more various than they are at the present moment?

Well, now, just let me pass in review a few of those evils that beset young men,—and not young men only, but that beset us all, even those of mature age, but especially young men—on account of their excitability and deficiency of experience. First of all, take the unprecedented magnitude of all the great cities and of all the towns of this vast empire; consider the temptations, consider the difficulties, consider the obstacles, consider the impulses, consider everything that can affect the appetite, that can allure the sense, and that can benumb the consciousness of responsibility, and you will see what is the state of things within them, in their fearful exhalations operating on the physical and moral condition of the great mass of our population. Look, too, at the diseased activity of commerce—nobody, I hope, will misunderstand me and suppose that I intend to speak in disparagement of commercial effort—but everybody who has observed our world of trade will admit that there has been, that there is, and that there may be again in tenfold proportion, a diseased activity of speculation that carries on people as in a whirlwind, giving them neither time to see nor feel, and wafting them, as it were, against their wills to an issue they would deprecate; and all this, because they suffer themselves to be carried on by the stream, along with which they must go until they are thrown over the waterfall into the depths below. Consider the unceasing recklessness, the unceasing competition among both small and great, in things large and minute, of one town with another, of one trade with another, one shop with another, one man with another;—it is this system of competition which produces the most serious effects upon those who are witnesses of it, and, in some measure, the subjects of it, and who are themselves afterwards to be placed in positions in which they will probably enter into competition in the same spirit of their early experience. Consider again—and here is a matter of deep and solemn import, and I trust I shall give offence to none when I speak of it,—but I will speak of it because I know it to be that which has produced the deepest and most deleterious results on the minds of young men engaged in warehouses and similar establishments—I speak of that conventional morality, or, if you please, that conventional immorality, that is found in so many of the establishments of this great empire—establishments in which the worse is made to appear the better cause, the worse the better article ; in which the customer is to be seduced in a variety of ways—and in which the persons who are so to seduce and deceive are the young shop-people, taught by the more experienced superintendent—taught, in truth, by the one who is to gain the whole profit, how he is to serve his master's turn in the present instance, and his own in time to come. I need not dwell on this longer ; I am speaking to persons who know the details of it much better than I do, and I merely mention it because it is corruptive of all moral and religious principle, and, if not checked in the outset and qualified by the effects arising from associations such as this, will tend to involve the trade of England in one general denunciation of corruption and dishonesty.

Again, look at the facilities for indulgence of every kind that are offered to young men in this great aggregation of human life ; look at the facilities that are offered to them for concealment, if they desire concealment ; and look at the sanction that is offered to them by numbers, if they are shameless enough to avow their profligacy. These are great temptations, which require more than an ordinary amount of principle and of grace to withstand. They are met at every corner ; they are met at every moment of the day ; and no ordinary force is required of effort and association to resist the overwhelming influence of these combined temptations. Again, I very much think there is no slight amount of mischief arising from that long detention—I know not whether it has been ameliorated here ; it has been to some extent in London, but by no means to an extent commensurate with the evil—that long detention of young people of both sexes to late hours in the shops and warehouses. I believe this practice to be productive of the very greatest mischief ; it lowers the whole physical system by over-toil, and it lowers simultaneously the moral taste and appetite, and destroys in them every desire for what is wholesome, leaving only the desire for what is most stimulating and sensual. Hence it is, I regret to say, that by these very means the young men so occupied are addicted to profligate habits and to low amusements ; hence it is that all those places of resort, which I will not designate, are crowded ; hence it is you have in such demand the low theatre, and vile literature, and everything that is most alluring to the diseased sense. The body is wearied, and the spirit deadened, which otherwise might have been employed in matters such as this before us now, tending to reform, elevate, and dignify the personal character—and therefore I see, and I believe you know here, the immense value of what is called the early closing system. It has been to the young of deep and permanent service, for upon those who have been subjected to its benefits it acts and reacts in a beneficial way; it is an admirable movement, and is an inducement to those who may be disposed to allow their young men to join in these associations, because it shows that a good preparation is made for the vacant hours that are given them; and it is a good argument against those who will not do it, because it shows that the movement, if rightly carried into effect, will produce those results that we have just now indicated. I believe that the early closing movement, if extended over our large towns, accompanied by such associations as this, would go very far indeed to remove many of the evils of which we complain, and very greatly to elevate the character of the young men employed in those establishments; and I should be very glad to know that, simultaneously with that, we had, not only for those young men, but also for the whole operative class, the assignment every week of a good half-holiday. In what way can you improve the observance of the Sabbath so effectually as by giving a time for amusement and repose on every Saturday afternoon? And I maintain that all those who have concurred with me in opposition to the motion of Sir Joshua Walmsley for opening places of amusement on the Lord's Day, are bound to go along with those who entertain the opinion that I do—that if we refuse to give them that form of recreation on the Lord's Day, we are bound to do what we can to give them some form of recreation on some other day.

There is another and a very serious view of this question. The large mass of those young men who are thrown together without any parental or superintending care are not in a condition to stand against the fearful examples that are brought before their eyes. Is it not too often the case that they see in those who employ them an inordinate desire to be rich, or at least to have the appearance of being so? The desire to be rich is not illegitimate, and may be restrained; it is not necessarily productive of immoral effect; but to be constantly witnesses of endeavours to deceive the world,—to be constantly witnesses of various schemes, artifices, and tricks by which the person with scarcely wealth enough to pay his way day by day, tries to palm himself off on the world as a capitalist, and to attract all the respect and confidence due to a man of capital,—I maintain that such a teaching to young men is so pernicious that I cannot but augur from it the most unfortunate results. Young men, again, are brought

away at so early a period from their homes to live in the houses
of strangers, and altogether away from parental care, that,
unless they are strongly imbued with moral principles, or fall
into good associations, they become inevitably the victims of
temptation.  Perhaps this is not, by contrast, so great an evil
now as it was some time ago; for none can notice the progress
of the mind and feelings in the present day, from the highest
to the lowest, and from the most wealthy and exalted down to the
poorest labourer, without observing that the authority of the
parents and of home has greatly diminished.  It certainly is a
growing evil, and I know not how it can be modified or checked,
except by the pouring out of God's grace and a larger embracing
of the doctrines and practices of Christianity.  But, nevertheless,
even supposing the young men were not withdrawn from parental
care, and had such a home as I should desire for them, that
alone is not enough.  As young men grow up and advance
into the years of manhood, they will ask—and I do not blame
them for it, it is natural, and proper if duly regulated—they
will ask for associates out of doors, for companions of their
own age—something beyond the parental dwelling.  It is in
the order of nature and providence that it should be so; but due
preparation should be made for it.  What we want to do is not
to interfere with the conditions of society within the precincts of
their own homes, but to enable them to meet with safe friends,
instead of being left in the midst of gulfs and whirlpools, and
in the high road to perdition.

To ventilate, then, and drain the moral atmosphere, good
and wise men have founded associations such as this, of great
and inestimable value to the young; and depend upon it, that
those who have founded them, and those who carry them on,
are the best friends you ever had, both for your temporal
and eternal interests.  If in this association you choose to look
for it, you will find guidance and friendship, and wholesome
counsel in religious and even in secular matters; and you will
find in it what you all need—it is in nature that you should need
it—you will find countenance and sanction for any feeling of
piety you may exhibit, for any good works you may resolve to
perform.  As, in the other course, numbers give a sanction to a
profligate life, so, in this course, by the happy effect of communion,
numbers will give a countenance to virtue, and enable you to go
forward in your way rejoicing, and not be driven from the battle
of honesty and virtue by the sneers and jeers of those who
hope, by the means of ridicule, to turn you from the path of
rectitude.  This institution, in our social system, is like the

Lord's Day, in our religious system; it is something rescued from ignorance, something rescued from toil, something rescued from avarice, and something rescued from sin, to be devoted to the great and high purposes of advancement, to the glory of God, and to the welfare of the human race.

Now, too, this association forms to young men a legitimate, a strong, and a real corporation, so to speak, for mutual strength and mutual advice, for mutual counsel and mutual aid. You young men, be assured of this, are in a great measure the architects of your own fortunes; under God's grace you may achieve great things; but remember these things must be done by yourselves —they cannot be done for you. We may counsel and advise, and we may lend a helping hand; but everything that is good and lasting, everything effective and true bearing upon your condition, must, in fact, be effected by yourselves; and keep in mind this truth—which I love to urge as an argument to the great mass of the operative class, and it is equally true in principle in some degree to you, my friends—that if you wish to maintain your condition, if you wish to improve your condition—but I revert to the first—that even if you wish to maintain your condition, you must do everything in your power to elevate yourselves—personally, morally, singly, and collectively. Remember this—nothing so invites attack and oppression—whether it be on a nation or on a class of the community—nothing, I repeat, invites aggression so much as the degradation of that class or nation. On the other hand, an elevated moral condition —whether it be in the working man, or whether it be in a people or a kingdom—that elevated condition, that moral bearing, repels aggression. And of this I am quite sure—I speak of you as a body—that if any effort should ever be made to deprive you of the privileges you now enjoy, it will be only when you have departed from the high tone of thought and of action which you have now adopted. On the contrary, by persisting in the course you have begun, and by still going forward to the higher degrees of excellency, you will not only prevent encroachment, but you will take from those who may have desired or thought of it, not only the power, but even the desire, to make the experiment.

Now, these associations, moreover, have very great intellectual advantages, and this is a matter well worthy of consideration in the present days—when we see so many young and ardent spirits, so many young men desirous of knowledge, and possessing, I doubt not, so many fine abilities, and so many earnest and honest hearts—it is a matter for great consideration, I repeat, at the present day in what way we can feed the intellectual appetite, and turn it to the best account for the individual himself and for the community to which he belongs. I think that you cannot do better than cultivate your intellectual faculties by the highest literature and the best history that you can attain. Your intellectual faculties are a part of yourselves, and belong to you as much as your souls belong to you; but they must be cultivated in subordination to the more noble part—and all in reference to the great object for which you are sent here, which is not for any work of time, but for a great work—the preparation for eternity.

But in advising you to cultivate your intellectual powers and to betake yourselves to these intellectual studies, which will form so noble and delightful a recreation after your work-hours, and which will place you as high as you ought to be in the social scale among your fellow-men, yet allow me to speak a word of counsel, and say that these things—good and great as they are—are not without their hazards at the present day. I will omit altogether many temptations to which you might be exposed, many of which must be manifest, and will only draw attention to one, and that for a few moments. I said that in these days, intellectual pursuits, however great and good in themselves, were not without their hazards; and the truth is, that these intellectual dangers appear to me to be in our time the great and dominant evil—the great master mischief, from which we have to apprehend the most fearful results. There is a plausible, a specious, a captivating kind of scepticism now abroad, pretending in many instances great reverence for religion and almost for holy writ—pretending a great show of piety, and endeavouring to reconcile several difficulties in the Scriptures and in revelation by eliminating all that is most repulsive to what is haughtily called the intellect of man. Two great objects seem to divide the attention of the people of the present day—the love of gold and the adoration of intellect; but that adoration of intellect is in no small measure guided by the love of gold—the worship of intellect being the worship of that power that gets money or money's worth. This may be the history, in frequent instances, of this new cult, the adoration of the intellect; but it is not always so, for many are governed by their passions and their feelings—they are governed by vanity and self-conceit and arrogance, by the love of distinction, and a spirit of implicit obedience to the supreme majesty of science. I regret to say it, but this evil to which I have just alluded is no longer confined to a few, and those comparatively obscure people; no, it begins now to be promulgated at our universities; it begins to appear in our great literary works; it has got hold of ministers and dignitaries of the Church of England; it has got hold of some of the most able and distinguished of the Nonconformists; it has got hold of the ministers of the Presbyterian church; and such is the state of things, that I believe at no time were the young men of this country in greater peril than they are now from the character of those principles that are widely enunciated; for the mode in which they are propounded is gratifying to their taste, and is flattering to their vanity. Your age, my good friends, I say it with all deference, is just at that period when you are most subjected to influences such as these, because you are in the heyday of life; you have not had the experience that has fallen to the lot of persons of maturer years; you are carried forward with a great desire for distinction, and you think (such is the infirmity of youth)—you think that to differ from those who have gone before you—to differ from the received opinions of the mass of mankind, shows a great superiority of intellect and power of discernment, and places the young and rising generation very far in advance of their fathers and forefathers. It is the most stimulating food that can be offered to the appetite, and you catch at it because it costs you little trouble to acquire, and administers more favourably than anything else to secure the means of an occasional display; but recollect the words of Bishop Horne: "a trifler," said he, "may state in three lines what it may take a learned man thirty pages to answer." You may read the three lines, but you may never have the patience or the opportunity to read the thirty pages. The doubt will have entered into your minds and may never be shaken off; and even if you hesitate to plunge at once into the depths of infidelity you will go on your journey with a millstone round your neck, and be greatly retarded in your march to immortality. Let me advise you, then, that all your reading be of a practical and nutritious nature; avoid mere speculations as much as possible. If you were men of learned leisure and profound acquirements, I should not speak to you in this way, because I should say that it might be possible, were you troubled by doubt in the morning, that the length of your study and researches during the day might remove the doubt before the evening. If you have but a little time to spare, let that little be devoted, not to handling curious and unprofitable questions, but in taking that line which is most conducive to your professional progress—to that which is most practical in its results; because, bear this in mind, although there are mysterious and speculative doctrines in the Christian religion, Christianity, as applied, is absolutely and essentially practical. Now, I rejoice to learn from the report that has been read to us this evening, that almost every member of this association is a Sunday-school teacher, and you could not possibly have given to me a single fact that would more completely have proved its paramount value, one that would more completely have proved that you had entered into the full spirit of your union, than by showing that your Sabbath days are given, not to idle discussions or to the indulgence of doubts, but to a course that will determine your own characters—and that a happy course—for the remainder of your lives, by feeding the lambs of Christ's flock, and by endeavouring to advance your Redeemer's kingdom, and, in that, your own hopes of eternal blessedness.

Amidst, then, all these difficulties and dangers, what security can you seek for your belief? I believe there is but one, and that is to take the Bible in all its openness and simplicity—to take it in its plain, straightforward meaning, to sit down to it with the docility of a child, and receive the Scriptures as a tender-hearted and obedient infant would receive its teaching at the knees of an affectionate mother. Accept and obey the language of St. Paul, where he thanks God for the simple piety of the Thessalonians, because, says he, "when ye received the word of God . . . ye received it not as the word of man, but as it is in truth, the word of God;" and I know of nothing that is more impressive, more striking, or more delightful, than to see men of gigantic understanding and profound attainments sitting down to the study of Holy Writ with all the docility of children in an infant school. I need not allude to the names of men or women, of whom you have often heard it said, that they accepted and obeyed the principles and precepts of Christianity. I do not allude to such names as those of Locke and Newton—they received Christianity, it is true, but they squared it, in some measure, to their own notions—I speak rather in reference to such men as Drs. Chalmers and Abercrombie, the "beloved physician,"—men of unrivalled power of mind, and of deep and extensive knowledge, who received the Scriptures with infantine simplicity and joy, and who never found themselves so learned, so happy, so satisfied, or so elevated, as when they listened to the word of God, and listened to it with the affectionate attention of obedient and loving children. Mark well the words of that good old man, the Rev. Mr. Wilkinson, who for so many years officiated at the church near the Stock Exchange, and who day by day called many of those men engaged in the ardent pursuit of wealth away for an hour to listen to his eloquence, and to the divine and simple precepts that fell from his tongue. And when past his eightieth year, and on the brink of the grave, what did that good old man declare? Why, said he, " after sixty years of service, and sixty years' study of the Scriptures, and everything that could give a help to the knowledge and pursuit of the sacred records, I have never been able to get beyond the prayer of the publican, 'Lord be merciful to me a sinner.'"

Now, one word more. I have asked what is your security for your belief, and I have stated that I believe it to be in the devout and simple reverence of the word of God, as indeed it is. And what is your security for your own conduct? I believe that it lies here—a deep, earnest, solemn sense of direct and individual responsibility in every man and woman born into this world. I know no sentiment that so tends to exalt, and at the same time so tends to humble the human heart, as does the sense of direct and immediate responsibility to Almighty God. If you consider yourselves in relation to man, and consider the duties you owe to your fellow-men, the purpose for which you were sent on earth, the duties you have to perform—to defend the fatherless, to plead for the widow, to enlighten the ignorant, to solace the suffering, to spread the knowledge of God among those who know it not, and to give a helping hand to all in need—if you have ever before you that sense of responsibility to man, will it not tend to urge you forward in the daily discharge of that duty? and if other men were to place these principles perpetually before them, would it not urge them forward also in the discharge of their duties towards you? Now, look higher; regard yourselves in the light of responsible beings to Almighty God, and see how it lifts the whole mass; and though you may still continue to regard yourselves as units among the many millions, yet you are units to every one of whom God has given gifts of which sooner or later you will be called upon to render an account. I cannot conceive of anything that will tend more to regulate your conduct, govern your hopes, and exalt your desires, than the sense of individual responsibility. Ay, it has also this good effect—have you not often heard many persons exclaim, when urged to do some good in their generation, "Why, what can I do? I am a poor insignificant person; it is not in my power to do good to any one; I must hold on my course, because I am utterly powerless." If such a person was governed by a sense of deep responsibility to Almighty God, that person—be it man or woman—would perceive that he has been sent into this world for some purpose, and that purpose must be fulfilled—that he has been endowed with gifts to carry it into effect—and that, if that be not done, a frightful and fearful account must be required in the end. The more I think of it the more I am convinced this is the best guarantee for your conduct; and I rejoice to inculcate it on the mind of every one who listens to me, whatever may be his destination in life. When you come to stand before the great judgment-seat of God, the responsibility of every one—of the sweeper of the crossing, the shopman, or the excavator, will be just as certain and minute as the responsibility of Queen Victoria, who sits upon the throne of England.

And now let me conclude by an earnest and hearty appeal to you young men of Manchester that you would rise to the position, the dignity, and the calling of British citizens and Christian men. You will be exposed to many and various trials in your course through life, many existing in the present, many to arise in the future. I doubt not that difficulties of all kinds, a few of which I have endeavoured to indicate, will arise in tenfold abundance in these the latter ages of the world. You have but one security—a single eye to the service of Almighty God. Let that be your cloud by day and your fire by night; thus will you realise at the last the blessed words of God's holy book, and ascertain, in your own individual experience, that "the path of the just is as the shining light that shineth more and more unto the perfect day."

## *Sanitary Legislation.*

SOCIAL SCIENCE CONGRESS OF 1858, LIVERPOOL.

LORD SHAFTESBURY, as President of the Health Section, concluded his address by remarking :—

These are some of the evils; of the remedies for them, many may be accepted, many rejected, but all should be investigated; for, I say it without presumption, that the things we state from the platform are founded on experience, and what we propound is no longer matter of experiment. The operation of the Public Health Act has shown, in Ely, that the town might be nearly as healthy as the country; it shows a marvellous reduction of mortality, to 17 in the thousand, when the mortality of rural districts around it amounts to 21 in the thousand. It is the same in Croydon; and in Liverpool, I am informed—greatly to your honour, and this adds no little to your responsibility—that your sanitary arrangements save 3,700 lives a year as compared with former times. I do not mean to say that the very highest sanitary arrangements in towns will bring health and life to the same standard as the highest arrangements in country districts; but I assert the great improveability of urban life, and the abatement of much suffering among dense populations. Surely that is a matter for deep and solemn consideration; and ought we to be tranquil when we are told that the preventible mortality in this country amounts to no less than 90,000 a year? Let us say, to be within compass, 40,000; that is, four lives an hour. Again, I assert, here is a matter for solemn consideration. Now, we may be told by some that these things are but in the course of nature, and we ought not to interfere; on such we will turn our backs; we will not listen to such a representation. We may be told that these things are costly, and require financial effort, and the people are not ready to undertake the expense; but we may safely say that it is disease that is expensive, and it is health that is cheap.

There is nothing that is so economical as justice and mercy towards all interests—temporal and spiritual—of all the human race. If we be told that spiritual remedies are sufficient, and that we labour too much for the perishable body, I reply that spiritual appliances in the state of things to which I allude are altogether impossible. Make every effort—push them forward—never desist—lose not a moment—but depend upon it that in such a state of things you will in the end be utterly baffled. But when people say we should think more of the soul and less of the body, my answer is, that the same God who made the soul made the body also. It is an inferior work, perhaps, but nevertheless it is His work, and it must be treated and cared for according to the end for which it was formed—fitness for His service. I maintain that God is worshipped, not only by the spiritual, but by the material creation. You find it in the Psalms,—" Praise Him, sun and moon, praise Him, all ye stars of light." And that worship is shown in the perfection and obedience of the thing made. Our great object should be to do all we can to remove the obstructions which stand in the way of such worship and of the body's fitness for its great purpose. If St. Paul, calling our bodies the temples of the Holy Ghost, said that they ought not to be contaminated by sin, we also say that our bodies, the temples of the Holy Ghost, ought not to be corrupted by preventible disease, degraded by avoidable filth, and disabled for His service by unnecessary suffering. Therefore, all that society can do it ought to do, to remove difficulties and impediments; to give to every man, to the extent of our power, full, fair, and free opportunity so to exercise all his moral, intellectual, physical, and spiritual energies, that he may, without let or hindrance, be able to do his duty in that state of life to which it has pleased God to call him.

---

Note.—This extract has been inserted in order to meet the argument, at that time very prevalent, that all physical efforts were vain, nay, almost worse, and that moral remedies alone could be applied.

## Literary Institutes for Working Men.

SWINDON, NOVEMBER 22, 1859.

Delivered at the opening of the Swindon Literary Institute.

THE Earl of Shaftesbury said: Ladies and Gentlemen,—
Although I have the honour of being known to you, and although
many of you are known to me, this is the first occasion that we have
ever met together; and I am exceedingly glad of the opportunity
which is thus afforded me of expressing my respect for you
personally, and the great desire which I have to promote institutions such as that which you are this evening met to inaugurate.

The statement which has been made by my hon. friend on my
left has fully explained the objects and the mode intended to be
pursued in the conduct of your institution, and I do not know that
anything further is required of me; but as I have come down here
this evening, you will, I suppose, expect that I should make a few
supplementary remarks, and give you my own experience of
similar institutions in other parts of the country. These institutions may be taken as one of the most remarkable signs of the
times in which we live. There are, in the present day, many
signs of a healthy and many signs of an unhealthy character.
There are signs of fear, and there are signs of comfort, and there
are signs to make men think. But I hold that the signs which
have brought us here this evening are among the most healthy
of them; because, observe—we are not met here to inaugurate
a new theatre; we are not met here to celebrate the opening of a
new gin-palace; we are not met here to rejoice that another
casino has been added to the number of those which already
devastate society; we are not met here to do that which is worse
than all the other evils which have been laid open before the
people—we are not met here to inaugurate a new racing ground;
but we are met to celebrate the opening of an institution, which

*may* be perverted, but which, by God's blessing, may be rightly turned to the moral, the physical, and the spiritual improvement of hundreds of the inhabitants of this town.

With these views, I am not a little distressed to find that this institution has already been made a subject of difference. To-day my son brought me a paper, in which he showed me a letter stating that some little jealousy existed between Old and New Swindon, on the supposition that one institution would injure the other. Now this is great nonsense, to say the least of it. My belief is that in two such towns as Old and New Swindon there is ample room for both; and if I may judge by my drive to-night from the station hither in Mr. Brown's open carriage, I can hardly suppose that the operatives and mechanics of Old Swindon, however ardent for literature, would be disposed to take a walk to the New Town during the dark and wet winter evenings. My belief, therefore, is, that although the offer of New Swindon may be very generous, it is an offer that will never be accepted. On that account I say there is ample room for both institutions; and let the only rivalry between them be, which can do the greatest amount of good and prevent the greatest amount of evil. But I am sorry to say that another difference prevails besides that to which I have alluded. I am afraid that some have conceived—most erroneously—that institutions such as these are not consistent with religion, and they think that no institution can exist unless it is openly and professedly founded upon a religious basis, and that basis one of a clear, definite, and doctrinal principle. Now, I should be prepared, were it necessary, to contest that point; but let us pass to an observation of the actual state of things. There is a great tendency throughout this country, among the masses of the people, to seek the means of intellectual improvement and intercourse. That desire, in itself, is a right one, and one which ought to be cherished. I cannot hope—and no man living can hope—that such a desire and taste should be moulded strictly in accordance with his own views and opinions. He must know that the tendency of the working classes to seek information is strong, undeniable, and irresistible; and the wisdom of every man will be this —not to oppose himself to the tide which is rushing in, but to see if he cannot turn that tide into a channel where it will flow safely, without bursting its banks, and doing injury to everything around it. My idea is that we should endeavour to control the tendency of the age, not by prohibition, but by infusing into the minds of the members of institutions like this that spirit of true judgment and self-control, which will make such institutions beneficial to the public and harmless to those who belong to them. In this sense I deeply regret that any opposition of this kind should be raised. In some parts of the country mechanics' institutions have, I am aware, fallen into disuse; but in other parts—such as the West Riding of Yorkshire—they have produced the best moral and physical effects; and no spiritual mischief whatever, so far as we can see, has resulted from them; whilst among the working classes members of such associations are to be found as sound, good, hearty Christians as in any part of her Majesty's dominions.

Such being the case, and admitting that these things cannot be resisted, we should consider in what way we can make them most conducive to the public benefit, and your scheme, I think, is a good one for the purpose. I heartily approve a system of classes. I am glad also to find that you intend to have a library. That will, if rightly conducted, be of very great value; but you must consider well—and here will lie a great deal of your safeguard—you must be careful as to the books admitted into your catalogue. I would advise you to lay it down as a rule, that your committee (who will, I presume, be the judges of the books to be admitted) should, as far as possible, exclude all simply controversial works: that they should make a selection of the best works of history and general literature; and, recollecting that your body will be composed of persons differing in religious, in political, and in private opinions, you should, in the formation of your library, consider as much the feelings as the tastes of those who are admitted among you. One of your greatest difficulties will lie in the selection of what are called works of fiction—many of which are, in their general character, most detestable. To say that you are to exclude altogether works of fiction would be preposterous, because by so doing you would exclude works of unspeakable service to the human mind; but I am talking of those milk-and-water, drivelling, weak, nauseous, profligate, sensational works of fiction, which turn the mind from sober thought and transplant many who read them from the society in which they are placed into a world of diseased imagination. All this, therefore, requires to be carefully weighed. Recollect, I do not say to you exclude all works of fiction—I do not say to you repress all works of imagination. On the contrary, I maintain that the imagination should be fed and cultivated. Imagination, when rightly used, will bring oftentimes comfort to the human heart. It is a quality given to us by God, not to be extirpated, but to be well directed; and if the committee keep this in view, you will, I trust, co-operate with them in making such a selection of books as will elevate the mind, and lead you from that description of washy and worse than useless trash to which I have alluded. [His Lordship then went on to observe that he hoped the library would not only be a library to those who frequented the rooms of the institution, but also a lending library, so that the men might take home the books and read them to their wives and families.] I want (said the noble Earl) to counteract the tendency which there is in all institutions of this kind to abstract people from the duties and the comforts of domestic life and induce them to lead a life of self-indulgence, to the exclusion of those who ought to participate in their recreations. In the use of these books, I wish to have the system such that the wives and children of the men may share in the benefit of the study which will be carried on by means of the library; and such an arrangement will have an admirable effect upon society, because it will tend to carry on and perfect the education of the people generally. No greater mistake, I maintain, ever occurred than to suppose—as many people do—that education ceases at the period when a child leaves the school. Education goes on to the very end of life; and you will ever find that the education the most effective and the most lasting is that which a man gives to himself. It is very well at school to receive from tutors and governors the elements of knowledge; it is very well to learn there the use of the weapon which is put into our hands; but be assured that the department in which a man excels—that in which he is able to rise to affluence and distinction—be it whatever it may—must have been acquired by his own exertion, and the adaptation of study to his peculiar bent of mind. Here, then, is the advantage of an institution like this—that it enables a man to select the course of study for which he has the most peculiar liking, and by bringing his mind to bear upon the particular acquirement for which God in His goodness has given him a special adaptation, either to qualify himself to adorn the station in which he is, or raise himself higher in the social scale. The State, no doubt, may provide certain means to set men in the right path; but actual education must be acquired by a man himself—it must be done by his own efforts—by his own intellectual vigour; and there are no means by which the truth can be carried into any man's mind, if that man will not himself go nine-tenths of the way to receive it. A few years ago there was great repugnance to the education of the people. We found men in this country—men who passed for wise statesmen— who thought that nothing was more perilous to the public peace than the knowledge of reading and writing among the people. But others there were who took a different view; and the working people themselves manifested so strong an impulse that it became impossible to resist the influence, and popular education made great strides.

And now let me ask what mischiefs have arisen to this great land, with its mighty millions, by this march of education? Let me ask what mischief has arisen from the admission of the sons and daughters of toil to some of the benefits of intellectual attainment? You have heard from Mr. Foote that a great many young men in this place, who used to pass their time at beershops, or perhaps in more mischievous places, have already evinced a desire to be admitted as members of the institution, and that in all the gatherings the greatest order and decorum prevail. But what you see here, you may see throughout many districts of the land. What is it that has brought the population of the great towns of Lancashire to a feeling of loyalty and obedience to the law, never before surpassed in this kingdom? There is, I believe, at this moment throughout England a greater degree of loyalty and industry, and a better understanding between the employer and the employed, than ever before existed in this country or in any other country in the world. And what is it, I ask, that has brought about this happy state of things? If it is not altogether owing to education, at any rate it proves thus much—that the extended education of the people is not antagonistic to such an issue; nay, further, that it will only exist under the continued education of the people and the enrolment of many of them in such institutions as this, by which they will be brought into habits of study, of diligence, and of order. Acquirements like these are by no means incompatible with labour; and the converse is true, that labour is by no means incompatible with such acquirements. On the contrary, in a great majority of cases, it will be found that the man who devotes himself the most steadily to his labour can give most attention to those intellectual pursuits which soften society. Take the man who has done an honest day's work. He is fatigued, no doubt; but if he has done a fair day's work—and such as every honest man in this country would do—and no more than a fair day's work should be required—I say that having performed such a day's work, he would have ample strength remaining for intellectual labour. By the blessing of God, we are so formed, that when we are tired of one pursuit we can oftentimes turn with vigour to another. The great Sir Matthew Hale, after spending a long day upon the bench, would retire to his room in the evening, and there recruit his mind and strength by solving a variety of problems in algebra; and I remember that the learned and illustrious Robert Southey had so much on his hands, that it was only by change of study and occupation that his mind was sustained for work; and, refreshed by this means, he was able to do in one day more than others could accomplish in five. In his room he had a number of desks, each one devoted to a different subject of study; and when wearied with one subject he went to another, and in this way, enjoying refreshment at every change, he was able to do more than any man who gave his whole time from first to last to one single topic. And so it may be to you. Having given your day to labour, you will find that you retain sufficient strength to devote a part of the evening to intellectual pursuits. Men can find time to go to the gin-palace, and there spend their substance in riot and filthy conversation; and why cannot they devote the same time to the reading room, and to matters which will be of permanent benefit, and from which they will carry away with them a mind well stored, instead of racking pains in the head, and diseased livers, and the eternal ruin which awaits all those who frequent the beerhouse, the casino, and the racing ground? I indeed much wish that you, my good friends at the other end of the room, would enter with all your hearts and minds into the contemplation of what may be called the dignity of labour. We have all our various callings in life. You are called to labour with the sweat of your face, and to earn your livelihood by daily toil. Others, like myself, have been placed in a different situation; but be assured that, in the sight of thinking men, and in the sight of that God who made you, there is no difference between us. There may be a difference in our temporal position; but a Great Day is coming when the true level will be seen, and when it will be found that the man of great wealth, and the man who has been called to what the world regards as great things, will undergo as strict a scrutiny as the poorest, and that he only will be the truly great man who, with humbleness, with truth, with simplicity, and with honesty, did that which he was called to do—who, in the faith and fear of God, endeavoured so to regulate his own life and the lives of those who were dependent upon him, that they might go through the world advancing the honour of their Maker's name, and contributing to the welfare of those among whom their lot was cast. I know that there are many who are ambitious—that there are many who are desirous to rise in the world—I know that there are many who come to institutions like this because they are anxious for distinction— because they wish to acquire here the usage of wit, of eloquence, and other means by which they may raise themselves above their fellows and lay hold of the great prizes of life. Now I do not say to any one of these—think no more of rising above your

station : be content where you are; but I would say to all—be
wise, be thoughtful, forecast these things before you dash into
a career which may be irrevocable, and which may end in ruin.
All can strive; but recollect it is only a few who can win; reflect
upon the cruel disappointment which awaits those who, having
left their safe and sober calling, rush into a pursuit for which
they are unfitted, and who, foiled in the object which they
have in view, find themselves wholly unable to return to the point
from which they started. This one thing is certain, that the
great majority of mankind must continue at the level on which
they were born. But is that a degrading thought? Is it a
thought which should bring despair, or shame, or sorrow to the
heart of any man who rightly considers it? I ask you, are there
no opportunities near at hand for you to improve your condition,
and yet remain within the sphere in which you live? Are there
no means open to you of doing good in your generation? Have
you not houses to rule? Have you not children to be trained as
citizens and as patriots, and, above all, as citizens of that enduring
city which "hath foundations, whose builder and maker is
God?" Remember what was said by one of the wisest women of
antiquity to her son, a man of great aspirations, who complained
that the town in which he was born was but a small place and
unlikely to produce a due effect upon the world. My son (she
answered), recollect that that little city has been allotted to you,
and it is your duty to protect and to adorn it. Little families
have been allotted to you, my friends : it is your duty to protect,
to adorn, and to elevate them : it is your duty to train up your
children in the way they should go. And here is a truth for
your contemplation; be assured that the greatest man that ever
lived, whether in the command of armies or in the roll of empires
—whether by his thrilling discourses he may have been able to
stir up whole senates—to drive men to madness or calm them to
repose—I tell you that those men who fill all history will not at
the last great day receive higher honour, or be more accepted in
the sight of Almighty God, than the honest Christian,—than the
sons and the daughters of toil; inasmuch as " God seeth not as
man seeth, for man looketh on the outward appearance, but the
Lord looketh on the heart."

*Religious Service in Theatres.*

---

# HOUSE OF LORDS,

## Friday, Feb. 24, 1860.

---

Speech on the motion of Lord Dungannon to call attention to the performance of
Divine Service at Sadler's Wells and other Theatres by Clergymen of the
Church of England on Sunday Evenings; and to move a Resolution, that such
Services, being highly irregular and inconsistent with Order, are calculated to
injure rather than advance the Progress of sound religious Principles in the
Metropolis and throughout the Country.

My Lords,

However unwilling I may be to address your Lordships on
this or any other subject, I believe that, as I am certainly the
only culprit in this House, and as I have been one of the principal
movers in originating these services, your Lordships will naturally
expect me to give you some information on this subject. I rise,
therefore, not to justify, but to explain; although I should have
thought that even the superficial knowledge which everybody
must have of the condition of this metropolis, and the difficulties
and dangers which beset society here, would have been quite
enough to have carried conviction, and have satisfied any reasonable mind. But if your Lordships desire it, and will bear with me,
I will state the motives which have actuated myself and others in
this movement, the mode in which it has been conducted, and the
results which we have attained.

Now, the first argument urged against these services is, that
between them and the associations connected with a theatre there is
an utter incongruity. Well, I admit that the case is an abnormal
one, and I am not going to find fault with those who feel startled
by the proposal to hold religious services within the walls of a
playhouse. It is natural that such a feeling should be entertained; and, indeed, I myself have shared it to a certain extent.
In deference to this feeling we have done everything in our power
to procure other buildings in which these services might be performed. The necessity to do something for the vast multitudes

in the east and south of London was overwhelming; and minute inquiries were made for any large rooms or open spaces in which Divine service could be celebrated. Nothing of this sort, however, could be found, and we were therefore compelled to hire theatres, as being the only places fit for the reception of any large body of people. My Lords, among the masses to whom religious services are altogether unknown, who are rarely or never visited, the greatest possible repugnance is found either to church or chapel—to anything, in short, which bears the least appearance of a registered place of worship. I have heard many of these people say, over and over again, that they never had been inside any place of worship, and that they never would enter one so long as they breathed. Possibly such a prejudice may in time be overcome, but meanwhile we have to deal with it. Now, there are music-halls which might have been hired, although not so capacious as the theatres; but these places were rejected because, in almost every instance, they are connected with taverns; and it was apprehended that great mischief would follow if those who were expected to attend were brought into any such connexion. But before going further I will notice one of the most monstrous assertions I have ever heard. Surely that may be called monstrous which is quite inconsistent with truth. The noble Viscount said that ginger-beer bottles were opened, and oranges cried during Divine worship, just as during the theatrical performances. Now, having myself attended some of these services, I can solemnly deny any such statement. What might have been going on outside the walls, of course I do not know; but I can quote statements made by clergymen and nonconformist ministers who have attended these ministrations from the first of January down to the present time, in order to show that nothing could have surpassed the order, decency, and attention of the persons present. I have myself attended three of these places, in each of which there were 3,200 people of the lowest description; and during the whole of my experience I have never seen a body of men so attentive to the great truths that the preacher addressed to them.

I do not deny that the associations of a theatre are to a certain extent incongruous with such services; but is it more incongruous than for a Christian missionary to enter a heathen temple, defiled, as it may be, by every impure and cruel rite, and there announce to the listeners the truths of the Gospel? Many a minister of the Church of England is compelled during his ministrations to go into the worst places, and exercise his sacred functions even at the death-bed of a prostitute in a brothel; but, as he is engaged

in his duty, the place becomes sanctified by the duty he performs.
Surely the noble Lord is passing the most complete condemnation
—it is he, not I—on all those that go to a theatre on a week day,
when he says that a theatre is so foul that it is impossible to
entertain in it a high and holy thought; that the Word of God
cannot be preached there even on a Sunday without desecration,
and without casting a stain on the character of a minister of the
Church of England. If, then, theatres be such foul places, even
on a Sunday, and with religious services, what must be the condition of those who enter them on a week day, when they must be at
the very depth of foulness and secularity!

[Lord Dungannon denied that he had stated what the noble
Lord attributed to him. What he had said was, that there was a
class of persons of a serious character who objected to what
passed in theatres, extending even to immorality, and he had
asked whether those persons could approve public worship in
those places on Sundays. He had never said it was impossible
for well-disposed persons to go to theatres, nor had he found fault
with those who went to them.]

The Earl of Shaftesbury said, I understood the noble Lord
to say that a theatre was a place where even on Sundays no holy
sentiment could be felt, and I justly inferred that if that be the
case on Sundays, it must *à fortiori* be far more so on week days.

Now let me point out what is the true history of this movement.
Those who are really acquainted with the state of a great portion
of the people of this country, and particularly of the metropolis,
have long beheld it with dismay and apprehension. I believe I
may state without fear of contradiction, as the statement is
founded on minute inquiry, that not two per cent. of the working
men in London attend any place of worship whatever. In the
inquiry before their Lordships' committee on church-rates, Dr.
Hume, of Liverpool, gave the following evidence, which, bad as it
is, gives a result more favourable than for London.

" Do you think, he is asked, that the active progress of irreligion
is one of the phenomena that now surround us ?—If your Lordship
will allow me to read a few numbers, I think those will speak for
themselves. In Southwark there are 68 per cent. who attend no
place of worship; in Sheffield there are 62; in Oldham, 61½; in
Lambeth, 60½; in Gateshead, 60; in Preston, 59; in Brighton,
54; Tower Hamlets, 53½; Finsbury, 53; Salford, 52; South
Shields, 52; Manchester, 51½; Bolton, 51½; Stoke, 51½; Westminster, 50; Coventry, 50. I have taken 34 of the great towns of England, embracing a population of 3,993,467; and 2,197,388, or 52½ per

cent. of the population of those towns, attend no place of worship whatever. The population is growing very rapidly in our large towns, and religion ought to grow with at least equal rapidity, but is not doing so. Our population in England is rapidly increasing; but it is still more rapidly becoming a town population. In 1851 we had 9,000,000 in towns of 10,000 people and upwards, and only 8,000,000 in smaller towns, in villages, and in rural districts; and at the close of the present century I believe that 70 per cent. of the gross population will be seated in large towns. Therefore, if our large towns are left to themselves, practical heathenism must inevitably soon outgrow Christianity."

Listen to the statement of a city missionary in Lambeth. These are mere representative instances, samples of what is generally prevalent:—

" At 1 o'clock the public-houses open, when it is no uncommon thing to see more than 100 men waiting for the opening of the three gin-palaces at the Marsh Gate, and in the evening to find these places full of men and women, who feel themselves more at home here than they do in their wretched apartments. The New Cut is as notorious for its places of amusement as for its Sabbath-breaking or its drunkenness. The penny gaff, or Olympic Circus, still exists, and there is reason to fear it is doing a world of mischief. No respectable person goes, so they have it all their own way, and corrupt the minds of youth without rebuke. The Victoria Theatre is well attended. The company may be seen standing at the doors about four o'clock. They are almost exclusively the dirty poor,—the working people such as we visit. Astley's, the Surrey Theatre, and the Bower Saloon are all very near the district, as well as many concert-rooms of a low character. The district is notorious for vice. Granby Street, Waterloo Road, is the chief place for fallen women in this neighbourhood. In this street and the next there are supposed to be more than 100 women who live on the wages of iniquity. They are not so wretched in their appearance or their homes as are those at Westminster, nor are they so accessible. The women who keep the houses do all they can to keep me from speaking to the inmates. It is at the doors of the houses that I have my interview with them. In describing the state of the district, the depravity of the juvenile population must not be overlooked. It is at the Sunday-evening ragged school that much of this is seen. The conduct of many of the youths is abominable; their language is outrageous, and cannot be repeated. Human nature is seen here

in some of its darkest shades. But for the ragged school things
would be worse with this class than it is."

Evidence may be multiplied without end. Here is the opinion
of the Rev. Mr. Weeks, whose testimony no one could gainsay :—

" The late incumbent of this district, the Rev. Mr. Weeks, has
been recently appointed Bishop of Sierra Leone, where he was
before for many years a missionary of the Church Missionary
Society. He was for years incumbent of the district, and, after
gaining much knowledge of its condition, and the habits of its
population, he remarked in a printed statement which was issued
by him, 'I can testify that the moral and religious condition of
St. Thomas, Lambeth, will bear no comparison to that of Sierra
Leone, on the west coast of Africa, with which I was connected
as missionary for twenty years.' We mentioned in our introduc-
tory remarks, that St. Thomas's district had at present no church.
Contributions have been for many years collecting for the erection of one. And it is a remarkable fact, as illustrative of the
heathenish condition of parts of London, even as compared with
the distant parts of the globe to which foreign missionary societies
send labourers from England, that 29*l*. 14*s*. 6*d*. has been contributed from native congregations in Sierra Leone towards the
proposed new church for this part of Lambeth."

My Lords, I maintain that, in order to know what is the condition of the people, it is necessary to go among them, not only by
day, but by night, and to visit them early and late in their dens
and recesses. It is necessary to see them under all their conditions and in all their phases if we desire to become acquainted
with their precise character, to examine their peculiar habits,
and, as it were, their natural history ; and I defy any one who
has penetrated into their retreats not to come back in terror,
dismay, and shame at finding that among a great number of
people in this country there should exist a state of things so
perilous and so disgraceful. Not but that the special religious services of the last two years have produced good fruit ; and when
the noble Viscount taunts me with my early prediction, and says,
that great benefit has not arisen from those services, I reply that,
regard being had to the means which the promoters of the movement have had at their disposal, they have come up to, and even
exceeded our expectations. By a letter to myself from the
incumbent of one of the largest parishes in Southwark, it appears
that nearly 100 artisans from that parish had gone to Exeter
Hall, because they liked the style of the service there ; and what

was the result? why, that, instead of being absentees from the parish church, a large proportion had become habitual attenders on Divine worship. This is the way the leaven works; and if a taste for God's Word is thus excited in men's minds, they will settle down by degrees either as members of the Church of England or of some one of the Nonconformist bodies.

Another and very material fact to be borne in mind, is the peculiar character of a large portion of the people of London. Considerable numbers are nomad in their habits: not less, perhaps, than 50,000 or 60,000 persons in the metropolis are in an almost constant state of motion, seldom being stationary for more than two or three months. The statement in my hand proves the migratory life, either from taste or necessity, of the population:—

"The missionary," says one witness, "has been for the long period of 15 years labouring in the district, and certainly not without result, although that result would doubtless have been more apparent but for the migratory character of the people. He estimates that of the 600 families visited by him, about 300 annually remove."

Again, the books of a school in —— district showed that, with an average attendance of 380 scholars, there has been an average of 340 new scholars every year.

"I have to deplore," says another, "constant changes of residence on the part of the people. Often the missionary had no sooner obtained a footing in a house than its occupiers removed. In one street, on going round, he had found all gone;" and yet let it be remembered that the city missionary must revisit the whole of his district once every five weeks.

But the most remarkable evidence received on this point came from a most amiable and efficient minister, the Rev. Albert Rogers. That gentlemen stated:—

"As the late incumbent of Regent Square Church, the district attached to which contained about 10,000 souls, of whom some 6,000 or 7,000 were poor, and having laboured among them during a period of nearly seven years, I am capable of forming a very decided opinion respecting the habits of the lower classes. I had labouring with me between 30 and 40 district visitors, one or two curates, and three lay agents, and their unanimous testimony was to the effect that our united efforts for the good of the poor, and especially of the poorest, were almost paralysed in consequence of their roving character. Repeatedly whole streets in the lowest parts of the district have been cleaned out of their inhabitants, and a new colony has arisen in it in the course of a few weeks. Some houses were occupied by thieves and prostitutes, who generally have no certain dwelling-place. Our schools suffer in proportion to the roving habits of the parents of the children, and it would not be difficult, from the statistics of the schools in London, to prove the migratory character of the poor."

Now, these migratory habits of the people render it impossible to bring to bear upon them the ordinary parochial machinery of the Church. Moving, as they do, from one point to another, it stands to reason that in this manner, at least, they can never be reached. But something must be done, and that speedily; for although matters have greatly improved within the last twenty years, and are still improving, yet the state of things is of the most fearful description. I am speaking correctly when I say that, although the regular depredators and thieves of London— those who live by perpetual breach of the law and nothing else— may not, according to the inquiries I have made, exceed the number of 3,000, yet there is a large floating class of the most dangerous description in the metropolis, who get their daily sustenance by jobs of all kinds, small trades, and by picking up money here and there, not in a violent or fraudulent way, but of whom it may certainly be predicted, that if there should be, from any cause, but a momentary suspension of order and authority, they would, to the number of 100,000, be let loose upon the property and lives of the inhabitants; and sure I am that their terrible excesses would throw the riots of Nottingham and Bristol into the shade. A moment's sight of the populace when aggregated in Houndsditch, Petticoat Lane, Rag Fair, the New Cut, and other such places, would be better for proof than whole volumes of reports, and endless speeches founded upon them. No evidence, however full, no language, however strong, is adequate to the truth. It must be seen, and felt, and tested, by personal contact with the people themselves.

Such are the classes whom I and my friends desire to soften and to render amenable to order and civilization. They must be won, and for that purpose resort must be had to everything that is true and legitimate. For this purpose I rejoice to say that many Churchmen and Nonconformists have joined together in a common effort. The question now is, Shall these vast masses be left in ignorance, or shall they be brought in this way to a knowledge of the truth? Is the evil of thus opening the theatres comparable to the evil of abandoning the people to total darkness? I may be told that a committee of your Lordships' house, appointed at the instance of the Bishop of Exeter, has produced a very admirable report, recommending a variety of measures for the diffusion of religion.  Very true; but, in the first place, I doubt whether that project will ever be carried into effect; and in the next, I am not quite certain that, if carried into effect, it will be in any degree successful.  The old prejudices will still continue against church and chapel.  But your Lordships have been told by the noble Viscount that there is church and chapel room in many parts of London sufficient to contain the largest congregations. It is not so in fact, but let it be so for the sake of argument. How will that overcome existing prejudices ?  In the first place, the preacher may not be attractive; yet these wild and irregular people must be conciliated; and in the next, the church or chapel may be at too great a distance from the abodes of the poor. Reference has also been made, by the noble Viscount, to the city churches; but the city is entirely denuded of its population on Sunday, and, in many parts, even on the week days; the churches are surrounded by tenements converted into warehouses, and even if the clergymen could compel the people to attend Divine service, their congregations would never exceed 40 or 50 persons each.  The city churches are altogether useless for missionary work.

My Lords, I must maintain that in an endeavour to bring these poor people to a knowledge of sacred things, we must have no little regard to their habits, their feelings, and even their preju- dices.  They are men of like passions with ourselves, of the same capacities for virtue and vice, for time and for eternity.  It is by our neglect, and by the neglect of those who preceded us, that they have been reduced to their present condition.  We have given them no help in matters where it was impossible that they should help themselves; we have permitted every physical and moral mischief to grow up around them, tainting both body and mind by their poisonous influences; and it is not for us to censure, or ignore, the weaknesses that our own misconduct has created.  We may not treat them with indifference, and say that, unless they conform at once to our rules and systems, they shall receive nothing at our hands.  Why, consider, there are many who dislike to show their faces during the day.  It is a fact that the after- noon services are never so well attended as those in the evening; and for this reason, that many of these unhappy beings are so filthy and so ill-clad that they are ashamed to come out in the light and expose themselves to the public gaze.  They creep forth under the shadow and shelter of night, and thus occasionally attend the evening service.

But there is a lower stratum of humanity still; and this, too, must be reached. We cannot stop in what we have begun; and we are resolved to go deeper and deeper, and use every legitimate and every available appliance for the purpose of spreading a knowledge of God's truth among the destitute and outcast population of London. My Lords, I assert that it is not the locality that can desecrate the word of God, but it is the word of God that consecrates the locality; and here is a proof! The noble Viscount has spoken of disorderly scenes in one of the theatres. There has never been any disorder. When the people, unaccustomed to such things, entered, for the first time, and took their seats, there may have been a great deal of bustling about; but I defy the noble Viscount to produce a single human being who will venture to say that he was present during the time the services were going on, and saw or heard anything that would have been objectionable in the most devout and pious congregation ever assembled within the walls of a church. Now for the proof of what I have asserted! At the opening of Sadler's Wells on the 1st of January, a most indefatigable and admirable clergyman of the Church of England officiated—the Rev. Mr. Owen—well known during the fury of the cholera at Bilston. What was his description of the conduct of the people? The adults, he said, entered the building quietly enough; but about 500 or 600 boys in the upper gallery made considerable disturbance by shuffling their feet and calling out to one another. Before the services began Mr. Owen rose, and, addressing the boys, told them he had come to do them good here and hereafter; that if they would be quiet and listen to what he had to say, he should thank God for their presence; but that if their object was to create a disturbance he entreated them to leave the place. From that moment to the close of the services, which lasted an hour and a half, "you might," to use the words of Mr. Owen, "have heard a pin drop." Was that no triumph? Was there here no moral discipline?—no hope for good and lasting effects? The services began with a plain hymn, then a chapter of the Bible was read, then an extempore prayer was put up by the minister, then another hymn, and then a sermon. Must we not regard it as a great moral victory, that a minister of religion, by simply announcing to a motley crew that he had come to preach to them the word of everlasting life, had persuaded 2,500 persons—the mass of them unaccustomed to any religious services whatever—to sit quietly for an hour and a half, and listen to the glad tidings of the Gospel? At the Victoria Theatre there occurred a remarkable scene. A well-known man was going in. One of the policemen present said to a city missionary, "You should not admit that

**person**; he is one of the most dangerous men in the district, and will make a terrible disturbance; it will take four of us to carry him to the station-house." The missionary allowed the man to pass. His conduct throughout was admirable; and next morning the missionary called upon him at his own house, and the man suffered him to read the Bible and offer up a prayer. Was that no triumph? Was there here no prospect of better things? Had not clergymen and Nonconformist ministers described in touching language the good impressions they had seen produced? The experiment, in fact, has been attended with wonderful and encouraging success. This letter, dated the 6th of February, which I have received from Sir Richard Mayne, will show how the people have behaved themselves in circumstances so trying and so novel :—

"Before answering the inquiry in your letter I thought it best to make special inquiry on the subject. I have now the satisfaction to acquaint you that the people attending religious worship in the theatres and public places mentioned in the memorandum have conducted themselves with great propriety. There has not been cause for the police interference on any occasion."

On the 23rd (for I was desirous of having the latest information), Sir R. Mayne again wrote :—"The conduct of the people continues to be most decorous. I have been able to reduce the number of police on duty at each of the places since my letter to you of the 6th of February." He had reduced the number of constables at our theatres; and yet at that very time he had sent, of necessity, sixty policemen in full uniform to attend the services and keep order at St. George's-in-the-East!

Again, I say, was that no triumph—was nothing gained there? Was the contrast, though painful, not instructive? Is it nothing to find that if we only speak to the people in a kind, straightforward, sincere, open, and earnest manner, we may govern their affections, and keep them in obedience and good order? My Lords, what the people of England want is, not patronage, but sympathy; the bringing of heart to heart, the acknowledgment on the part of persons of all conditions, of all degrees of wealth, that they are men of like passions with themselves, with the same hopes, the same aspirations, the same fears, and the same destinies. If any Prime Minister of England, and those associated with him in the government, will only show that sympathy, especially in its highest and most solemn form, the people might be led like a flock of sheep.

The question will naturally be asked, What are the numbers of those who have engaged in these services, and upon whom so happy an influence has been exerted? Observe, my Lords, it is not in a single instance only that good effects have been produced, nor have audiences been attracted by the mere novelty of the thing. These services have been going on since the 1st of January, at five different theatres during the first five weeks, and at seven since last week. The total number of people who attended at the seven houses which were open on Sunday last was 20,700; and allowing, for the sake of argument, a deduction of 10 per cent. for people coming from mere curiosity, there would still remain 18,630 persons who had come to hear the Word of God, and who had never before frequented any places of public worship. I am aware of the assertion that these people do not belong to the lowest class, which has never yet been reached, and that these services only serve to withdraw good folks from the churches and chapels they ordinarily attend. But this has been disproved in the most emphatic manner by the experience of all those who have been present at any of these celebrations. I do not deny that there is a still lower class than that which has hitherto come to these services, a class which we shall have much difficulty in reaching; but we have, I maintain, most certainly got at a very low class indeed by means of this movement. A city missionary writes:—

"I have been really astonished at the multitude of persons who are attending these services out of very low neighbourhoods, and who previously altogether neglected public worship."

The incumbent of St. Matthew's, St. George's-in-the-East, a young minister, who has been very zealous in going about among the poorer classes, and has acquired much experience of their character, states:—

"I have preached at the Obelisk in Southwark, in Ratcliff Highway; I have preached for two seasons on the steps of the Royal Exchange; and last Sunday I preached at the Garrick Theatre. The place was densely crowded by persons of a class I never before got at."

Mark these words, my Lords, "never before got at," from a person so conversant with these classes.

"I have carefully inquired," he adds, "from the city missionaries, and I find that their meetings are better attended, a deeper religious feeling pervades them, and their access to the homes of the people is much more easy."

Another experienced clergyman says:—

"These characters, and such as they, do not, and will not, attend the ordinary ministrations of the Word of God in church or chapel. They have an aversion to cross the threshold of a place of worship, where they think their appearance would be a subject of remark."

The same testimony is borne by the Rev. Newman Hall, the distinguished minister of Surrey Chapel, who states that the class of people who attend the special services are just those whom we are most anxious to improve. But let me read to your Lordships, in illustration, two short letters, giving an account of these celebrations. They are well worthy of attention. The first is from a very eminent Nonconformist minister, the Rev. Mr. Graham :—

"In connection with the united committee," he writes, "I preached in the Victoria Theatre last Sunday evening to a great concourse of people. The assembly was of the most heterogeneous character, but the great body of the hearers were evidently such as never enter a house of worship, and never would, except the Gospel sought them in such places as those in which it now can get them to assemble. When we entered the theatre the assembly, especially in the galleries, was noisy and confused, and cries of 'Tom' and 'Bill' and 'Jack' were frequent and loud; but before the service had proceeded ten minutes all were as orderly and attentive as in most religious assemblies. Indeed, before the close of the sermon, all was deeply solemn and still. I mingled with the multitude as they issued from the service, and had an opportunity of more closely observing their bearing and grades. They appeared to be drawn from the lowest stratum of London population, such as the Great Master would have had compassion on as sheep scattered and without a shepherd. Nowhere in the three kingdoms, during a ministry of nearly twenty years, have I ever preached to an assembly of my fellow-men that seemed more deeply to need the preaching of the Gospel of holiness and peace. In none of the special services have I felt myself so much in place as an Evangelist as preaching to those who are in every sense 'the poor.' The spirit of Christian union in these services makes them, I think, especially telling."

What can be more descriptive, what more touching, than this narrative? The other is from the Rev. Mr. Acworth, the vicar of Plumstead, and is of equal value :—

"When I officiated," he says, "at the Victoria Theatre, the theatre was so crowded that it was found necessary by the police to shut the door before the time of service. The congregation consisted almost entirely of working men. The hubbub that existed ceased the moment I asked the dense congregation to unite in prayer; but from the few voices that joined in repeating the Lord's Prayer, I judged that the larger portion of them had little or no acquaintance with it. After singing a hymn I preached, for nearly three quarters of an hour, upon Moses lifting up the serpent in the wilderness. On giving a narrative of the life and miracles of Moses, and of the lifting up of the serpent as typical of what our Saviour had suffered to obtain for us eternal life, I was listened to with the most extraordinary attention, as if the subject had never been heard of before. I had had a considerable prejudice against going into a theatre; and it was only the strongly-expressed opinion of laymen who had studied the character of our London population that induced me to undertake the service. The best answer to my prejudice was the appearance of my auditory. During a ministry of thirty years I never entered so much into the feelings of the Author of our religion, who 'when He beheld the city wept over it.'"

These statements I can confirm by my own personal experience, having myself attended at the Victoria Theatre on three successive occasions. The audience each time numbered no less than 3,200 persons, so closely crowded that a straw could not have been placed between them. From the beginning to the end of the service no assembly could have been more orderly, more attentive, more apparently devout, and more anxious to catch every word that fell from the preacher's lips. On one of the occasions, so solemn and touching was the discourse of the preacher, and so moved were many even of the wildest and roughest present, that when, after the "Benediction," they rose to leave the building, they went so quietly and solemnly that you could hardly hear the sound of a footfall. Surely no one can deny that a deep and solemn impression is made on the minds of those people: it is found that many come to the services week after week; and can it be doubted that we are by degrees spreading a leaven throughout the whole population? We only want, I am confident, more extended machinery, and more numerous opportunities, to produce a really living and lasting effect upon those large masses.

Now, there can be no mistake as to the character of the assembly. At one celebration of the service the men mustered in proportion to the women as nine to one, and on another occasion as seven to three. I asked a person who happened to be present, and who is conversant with the character of the people in the

neighbourhood, and knows most of them, both by calling and by
name, to give me some idea of the sort of people who were
gathered together. The man replied that there were 3,200 present
he was certain, because he was expert at such calculations, from
having to count the people in the theatre; and of that number
2,000 belonged to the class called "roughs"—the most violent,
disorderly, and dangerous of all the men in that very quarter.
This man lifted up his hands in amazement when he saw how
quiet was their demeanour. He had expected uproar and even
danger, and he frankly said he could not comprehend how those
two thousand wild, unruly fellows behaved themselves so well.
And certainly it is a very remarkable thing, and a great moral
result, that so many men of such turbulent character and disorderly habits should have been got to listen patiently and quietly
for an hour and a half to a religious service, an occupation so unusual, and, as we might have supposed, so distasteful to them.
Do you inquire as to the fruits? A report is weekly made to the
committee for conducting these services as to the character of the
audiences on these occasions, and the effect produced. These
reports are one theme of congratulation and expression of thankfulness from those who have taken part in them, that they had
been permitted to enjoy an opportunity of making known religious
truth to thousands and tens of thousands, who, except for this
instrumentality, would have gone to their graves without a
knowledge of the God that made them, and of the Saviour who
died for them.

But it is said that the issue of holding these religious services
in theatres is to draw away the congregations from other places
of worship. Happily, the fact is just the reverse. I hold in my
hand the testimony of several clergymen and Dissenting ministers of the districts around these theatres, who unite in saying
that there has been no abatement, but rather an increase, in the
numbers of their congregations. They state, and it is reasonable
that it should be so, that many of those who had attended these
services had been so impressed by what they had there heard,
that they had become regular attendants at the churches or
chapels of the neighbourhood. Now, if there is a human being
who is well acquainted with the working people of the metropolis
it is the Rev. Joseph Brown, rector of Christ Church, Blackfriars.
Mr. Brown's parish is included within one of the most awful
localities in the world. I wish that your Lordships would go there
and spend a little time in that and similar neighbourhoods. You
would thus do a great service. It would be time well spent.
Proofs such as this, of interest in the welfare of the people, of a

desire to know, and, if possible, improve their condition, tend to
harmony and good-will among all classes, the preservation of
order, and loyalty to the crown. I remember, in one of my walks
in the east of London, an intelligent working man said to me, " I
hear that there are very fine folks at t'other end, with such fine
carriages and horses; why don't they come here, and see what we
are a-doing on? We are worth thinking on, for we are many."
He spoke the truth: they are " worth thinking on ;" and it is to
recover a treasure so valuable, and bring them back to the communion of Christian life, that the present labour is bestowed.
Now, Mr. Brown, whose church is near the New Cut, says that
his afternoon service is not affected by the services in the Victoria
Theatre, and he even recommends a morning service therein for
the benefit of the tens of thousands who are to be found in the
New Cut on Sunday morning. In the New Cut, like Petticoat
Lane and Rag Fair, on Sunday, are thousands of persons, many
of whom pass the day playing at skittles, at pitch-farthing, and
in almost every crime; and it is hoped that some of these, at
least, may be enticed into the playhouse to listen to the Word of
God. However abnormal these services may be, good cannot but
follow the collection of 20,700 of these persons to hear the Gospel,
many of whom would otherwise be in the highways and the
streets, having no other occupation than to break the Ten Commandments from first to last. The Rev. Newman Hall, minister
of Surrey Chapel, says: "My church was quite full with an
attendance of 2,500 prior to the services. There has been no
diminution since." The Rev. R. Robinson, of York Road Chapel,
states: "I am happy to say that the attendance at the chapel
has suffered no diminution whatever since the opening of the
Victoria; even the young have not been drawn away." The
Rev. Hugh Allen, the rector of St. George's, Southwark, writes:
"None of my church services have been at all diminished, either
in number or interest; and I have no hesitation in saying that
these special services at the theatres, so far as they have come
under my notice, were attended principally by the class of persons
for whom they were instituted, and the attention given to my
preaching there was as solemn and as marked as ever I witnessed in
any church." Of the services at Sadler's Wells, the Rev. Daniel
Wilson, of Islington (a well-known name), says: "I am not
aware that the congregations attending any of our churches in
this locality have been affected by the special services." The
Rev. Robert Maguire, of Clerkenwell, observes: "My congregation in Clerkenwell Church has not been in the slightest degree
affected by the theatre services." The Rev. A. M. Henderson, of

Claremont Chapel, testifies: "My congregation has not been lessened." The Rev. H. Ingram, of Pentonville Chapel, also: "My evening congregation has improved rather than diminished since the opening of Sadler's Wells. On the evening of the special services we were crowded." With respect to the services at the Garrick Theatre, Whitechapel, the Rev. T. Richardson, incumbent of St. Matthew's, Pell Street, to whom I have already alluded, says: "My congregation has increased ever since I preached at the Garrick, and the increase has been from the lowest orders." The Rev. R. H. Baynes, incumbent of St. Paul's, adds: "These services have in no way affected my evening congregation, though my church is not more than three hundred or four hundred yards from the theatre." This is an important fact. The Rev. W. Tyler, Mile End Chapel, says: "We are still always full." The Rev. C. Stovel, Commercial Road Chapel, says: "If anything, the evening attendance has improved." The Rev. J. Markwell alone writes: "I must say that the congregations of an evening at St. James's, Curtain Road, have, since the service at the Britannia Theatre, Hoxton, fallen off greatly; still would fondly hope that God will own and bless these extraordinary efforts for the conversion of sinners." But here I may remark that the congregations assembled at the Britannia Theatre are of a somewhat superior class, and though consisting of persons who are not frequenters of places of worship, are not composed altogether of the wild and destitute beings who flocked to the other theatres. Who can entertain a doubt that these services are producing a considerable benefit by small means—an enormous church and chapel extension at a small cost? The argument against them, and it is the only one, is, that there is something unpleasant in the association. I do not deny there is something abnormal in these services, something that is unpleasant. But the Right Rev. Archbishop has put the case truly and well when he says, that "while on the one side there is a natural and legitimate sentiment, on the other there is principle." It is so; for what do those who object to these services give in exchange, what do they offer in the present most awful necessity for doing something? Suppose that an appeal be made to the country for church accommodation, and that the country should in time respond to the appeal, would the response be equal to the demand? I was told by the late Bishop of London that, when an appeal was made to the public for twenty additional churches for the metropolis, by the time the money was collected, and the churches were built, the population had increased in a far greater proportion than the churches would contain, and the arrear remained the same as before. Now, suppose the House should adopt the resolution, and suppose the services should in consequence be discontinued, what is to be done meanwhile? Years must elapse before this great scheme of church accommodation, even if adopted, could be carried into effect, and hundreds of thousands would go to their graves in utter ignorance of all saving truth, and contributing while they live to the disgrace, dishonour, and insecurity of the country.

My Lords, hard things have been said of the ministers of religion who have taken a part in these services. I have a totally different view; I cannot too much commend them. I feel bound and rejoice to bear my testimony to the conduct of the Nonconformist ministers in this matter. Some of their most eminent men have joined this movement with hearty zeal. The noble Viscount says that we are endangering the Church. Just the reverse. I believe that the movement of which this is a part has done more to strengthen and perpetuate the Church than any other cause; and the clergy of the Church who have participated in these services have gone far to rivet the hearts of the people to the Establishment. But there has been some talk of an inhibition to stop these services. Now, first I doubt the legality of such an inhibition; and I, for one, am prepared, if an inhibition be issued, to test its legality. I question whether any human being or any law has the power of preventing a clergyman in his capacity of a Christian citizen from performing that great duty, the salvation of souls, in season and out of season, at all times and in all places, to any who may be disposed to hearken. I hold in my hand a short letter from a clergyman of the Church of England; and here I may remark that many other clergymen of the Church are coming forward to join in this work—it speaks the sentiments of a large body who feel that principle in such a work is paramount to every other consideration. The writer says—

"I presume the right of Christian men to exhort an ungodly multitude, wherever found, ought not to be interfered with; and it was only as a Christian man that I addressed the multitude in the Garrick Theatre. I wore no ecclesiastical dress, and used no part of the Church service."

He well asserts the right of the clergy, and shows that it is exercised with moderation and judgment.

My Lords, you must perceive the rising struggle to preach the Gospel among this mighty mass of human beings. Can you be indifferent to it? I ask whether you are prepared, as members of the Church of England, to see the Church stand aloof, and the

whole of this movement given up exclusively to the Dissenters ?
Will you say to these destitute and hungering men, " We can do
you no sort of good. Come, if you like, to Episcopal churches
and chapels, and there you shall be preached to in a stiff, steady,
buckram style. We will have you within walls consecrated in
due and official form; otherwise you shall never hear, from us at
least, one word of Gospel truth ?" Are you prepared to admit
that the Church of England, despite the pressing and fearful
necessity, is bound so tightly by rule, and rubric, and law, and
custom, that she can do none of the work ? Will you say, " We
have not a sufficient force of clergymen; we have not churches
or chapels; we have no money to ordain and support the ministers
of religion ?" In that case the people who are benefited by these
services will reply, " Let the Nonconformists, then, do the work,
but let the Church of England take up her real position as the
Church of a sect and not that of the nation; she has been applied
to and found wanting, and let us follow those who have called us
to the knowledge of the truth." My Lords, I believe it will be
found that those who have been awakened to religious impressions
by ministers of the Church of England will connect themselves
with the Church, and that those who owe those impressions to
Nonconformist ministers will join Nonconformists. But whatever may be the case in this respect, I trust your Lordships will
not be heard to declare that no minister of the Church ought to
take part in this great movement, and fatal would it be if, for
any reason, our clergy were to withdraw from it. I have great
respect for the Nonconformist body. Among them I have many
affectionate and valued friends; but I have a sincere attachment
to the Church of England. I dread to see that Church lose one
particle of its influence or power, or shrink from what I believe
to be its sacred duty. I rejoice to see the friendly rivalry that
exists between the clergy of the Church and Nonconformists, in
relation to this great work; but I, for one, will not surrender to
them the right, the comforts, the privilege, and the joy, of
evangelizing the masses of the people. My Lords, you are asked
to pass a resolution. The resolution, if passed, cannot have the
force of law in reference to this movement: it would be just so
much waste paper, and no more; and not being backed by public
opinion could have no influence out of doors in checking or
impeding us; the only effect it could produce would be to rouse a
strong feeling of indignation or sorrow. I hope the noble
Viscount will not go away with the notion that this is a movement
in which the middle classes take no interest. The middle classes
of the present day are much better informed than those of a

former generation. They know that the safety of their lives and property, and the preservation of public order, depend on their having around them a peaceful, happy, and moral population; and they feel that the course now being pursued is one which, by the communication of Christian truth, will mainly conduce to that issue. I implore your Lordships not to adopt this resolution; but whatever may be the decision of the House, I feel myself bound to say—and I am speaking, I know, the sentiments of those with whom I am associated—that, by the blessing of God, we will persevere in the course which we have begun, so long as we have breath to speak and materials to work upon.

---

The foregoing speech on the question of "Religious Services in the Theatres of London" was published soon after its delivery, in obedience to the wishes and representations of several of my friends, and of others who took an interest in the subject. I now append as a note the substance of what I then prefixed to it as a preface.

In setting before the public one of the many schemes devised for the benefit of the working population, I must avail myself of the opportunity thus offered to call attention once more to the master-evil which surrounds and depresses them. There are many forms of ill, no doubt, and many remedies that may be applied—in these days we need great variety of effort, and equal variety of agency—but one evil predominates over all, and by its action and reaction is daily dragging the people down to lower depths of degradation.

The domiciliary state of whole legions of our fellow-citizens has been with me, for some time, a subject of observation and inquiry; and I do not hesitate to assert that it lies at the root of nineteen-twentieths of the mischiefs that we seek to redress. Not only the actual dwelling, but the situation of it, the character, physical and structural, of the locality, whether it be street, or court, or alley, or some deep, dark, and poisonous recess, never penetrated except by its own wild and unknown inhabitants, must be included within the term "domiciliary state;" and in these places —low, narrow, with a death-like dampness, impervious to light or air (the work of greedy speculators, uncontrolled by law)—are aggregated all the fearful influences that breed evil and neutralize good, whenever it seeks to establish a footing among these neglected classes.

Fever and disease of every kind prevail; a poor standard of physical strength, the result of the fetid atmosphere they inhale by day and by night, deprives them of power to do able-bodied work; while loss of energy and depression of spirits drive them to seek life and support in vice and intoxication.

Their modes of existence are sometimes diametrically opposite. A large mass is found in the perpetual din and whirl of close-packed multitudes. A smaller, in the remote and silent retreats of filth and pestilence (through which no thoroughfare passes), dwells in a kind of savage solitude, seldom emerging by day from their hiding-places, and rarely visited. But whether in great or small numbers, whether in the most active or the most tranquil quarters, all are equally shut out from the possibility of domestic life. A dozen families in a single house, though barely sufficient for two; as many individuals of both sexes and of all ages in a single room, the common and only place for cooking, washing, sleeping; the want of fresh air, the defect of water, of every decency, and of every comfort, give proof enough. We need not wonder why the gin-shop and the tap-room are frequented; why the crime of incest is so rife; why children are ragged and ignorant, and the honest dignity of the working man's home degraded or forgotten. These poor people, by no fault of their own—for they did not create the evil, nor can they remedy it—are plunged into a social state which is alike dishonourable and unsafe to our common country.

The main mischief of this condition of things lies in the counteracting power, nay, the almost insuperable barrier, it presents to all efforts for amelioration. These efforts, nevertheless, must be made; no good may be left unattempted; against hope we must believe in hope, and endeavour, though the mass be inaccessible, to rescue individuals. A few, by God's blessing, will be reclaimed, and many, no doubt, will be comparatively humanized. This is the object of the special services; and were they accompanied by a simultaneous improvement of house and home, we might be sure of seeing and feeling the beneficial effects of religious principle, of extended education, and of the revived sanctities and joys of domestic life; we might then urge, with effect, the foundation and use of the collateral helps of savings-banks, sick funds, mechanics' institutes, reading-rooms, lectures, coffee-clubs, mutual improvement societies, working men's Christian and other associations, with every institution for proper recreation or profitable knowledge. Such efforts as these will then have an open field, which now is denied them.

It must not be supposed that, with all these facts before the public, no attempt has been made to devise some means of remedying, or at least of abating, the evil. Better drainage has been established in many places, and with beneficial results. The effects, however, of drainage will be but small where ventilation is impossible, and while the structural condition of the buildings and localities, made worse by the overcrowded masses within, is so vile and pestilential. Experiments of model lodging-houses of all kinds, for married couples, for single men, for single women, have been instituted. The principle of them has been most satisfactorily proved, in the moral and physical improvement of their inmates; and, were the financial returns equivalent to what has been gained in health and character, we might hope for a general extension of the system. But unhappily the price of land and the cost of building in the metropolis are so high as to forbid any remunerative employment of capital, unless by such an increase of rent as would be intolerable to the working classes.

The Common Lodging-house Act has introduced many arrangements of health, comfort, and decency for a large portion of the people, which they thankfully accept and acknowledge. One or two short statements will be a sufficient proof. The policemen engaged in the inspection immediately after the passing of the Act report : " So abundant was the vermin, that repeated changes of clothes were necessary ;" " that the evils existing in the lodging-houses were beyond description. Crowded and filthy, without water or ventilation, without the least regard to cleanliness or decency, they were hotbeds of disease, misery, and crime."

Take an instance : " In one room, ten feet square, wherein three persons would be allowed by the regulations now enforced, seven men, nine women, and one child were found huddled together in a most filthy state ; the bedding dirty beyond description ; no partitions or ventilation ; and a few minutes before the visit of the officer one of the females had been confined."

Now, observe the effect of periodical inspection by proper authorities : " The accommodation," says the Report of 1857, " given in registered houses consists of clean beds and bedding ; well-ventilated and lime-washed sleeping-rooms ; well-cleaned kitchens ; plenty of water for all purposes ; sinks drained and trapped to the common sewer wherever such is available. The mixing of the sexes is carefully avoided, except in rooms used as sleeping-rooms by married people, where partitions of solid material secure the privacy of each couple.

" Property thus registered is improved in every respect, and its value greatly increased. The amount paid for lodgings in these houses since their improvement is not greater than heretofore.

" In the houses thus registered in the metropolis good accommodation was provided at the time of registration for 42,370 persons; deducting the number in the houses closed, the actual accommodation is for 28,000."

But the general effect over the whole country cannot be stated more clearly than in the report from Wolverhampton :

*Wolverhampton, June 9, 1853.*

I HAVE to acknowledge the receipt of your letter of the 6th instant, and, to reply to the questions proposed, viz. :

*Q.* How many common lodging-houses in my district ?

*A.* Two hundred.

*Q.* How many persons frequent them annually ?

*A.* Males, about . 340,000
Females, about . 171,000

Total . 511,000

*Q.* Do keepers object to inspection ?

*A.* They do not.

*Q.* Are the rooms and beds any cleaner since inspection ?

*A.* Very much so.

*Q.* Is there less or more of vice and sickness ?

*A.* Much less vice and immorality, in consequence of the separation of the sexes who are unmarried. There has not been a case of fever or contagious disease since the Lodging-House Act has been in force, viz., July, 1852.

*Q.* Is the Public Health Act beneficial or otherwise?

*A.* I think it most beneficial, especially as regards the Irish houses, which are of the lowest class, and which were in a most filthy and disgusting state, but since they have been brought under the regulations of the Lodging-Houses Act, they are now clean and wholesome.

I beg to say, that out of the number of houses given (200), about 150 are Irish houses, and keep what they term regular lodgers : still the act has been carried out as far as practicable.

I am, &c.,

(Signed)      RICHARD BENNETT,

*Inspector of Lodging-houses.*

Yet these results, happy as they are, reach only a certain portion of the population in London, and principally those of a wandering and unsettled existence. The far larger portion, for which we should desire the possibility of attaining to the honours and comforts of domestic life, are untouched. Their numbers are more than tenfold those of the migratory class; and they are lodged in tenements which, by an evasion of the spirit of the act and under the fiction of being private dwellings, contain, probably, a greater amount of filth, vice, and disease than could be found in any other capital. Their inspection and regulation would be both just and feasible ; but, under the plea that " Every man's house is his castle," dirt, crime, and fever are permitted to reign without observation or control.

Doubtless there are still many dismal sights in the metropolis, enough almost to beat one down with despair. And yet the state of things in the present day, as contrasted with that of some thirty years ago, is decidedly favourable. The various agencies brought into operation during that period have not been without fruit, for many, who have not come directly under such influence, have been partially civilized by the example of their fellows ; and scenes of atrocious savageness and indecency, which were often recorded to me when a young man by the chief police-officers of that day, would now be beyond the imagination of even the most depraved.

But we must not trust to this improvement as, in itself, certainly and necessarily permanent. There are signs of an incipient return to a former condition of things ; and every one who cares for the character of the people of England must endeavour to put down the attempted revival of the prize-ring, not only by law, but by public opinion.

Of one point I feel perfectly sure, and it is one which gives us much hope. A great deal of the destitution and misery that we see is not inevitable and inherent. It is the result of sickness and intoxication, and these are, to an enormous extent, the result of the sanitary condition of the people. Here they cannot help themselves ; the obligation is ours. Give them fair play ; and they will be both willing and able to earn sufficient wages to keep their families in comfort and honour.

To aid the progress of the general improvement is the object of these special services. No one contemplates them as a permanent system : our desire is to fell the trees, to clear the jungle, to remove impediments. We hope to bring thousands of our ignorant and neglected brethren to think about Christianity. Having learned it, they will, we trust, pursue it; and, rising above their attendance at the theatre, attach themselves to the Church of England, or some one or other of the recognized and established forms of worship.

Their humanizing effects are already manifest in the language, manners, and appearance of those who frequent them. This is no wonder; for matters of such deep and vital interest can never be altogether without their fruits. With many it may be transitory; with a few it may be lasting; but utterly ineffectual these services cannot be: and, surely, we may fairly say of them, without fear of disappointment, as Southey said of the music of church bells, that "however it may fall on many unheeding ears, it never fails to find some that it exhilarates, and some that it softens."

S.

## Indian Irrigation and Inland Navigation.

### HOUSE OF LORDS,

#### FRIDAY, JULY 5, 1861.

Speech on moving that an humble Address be presented to Her Majesty to assure Her Majesty that this House has regarded with great satisfaction the Progress of Public Works in various Parts of India; and to beseech Her Majesty that, with a view to confer further Benefits on that Country, She will be pleased to take into Her immediate and serious Consideration the Means of extending throughout it, as widely as possible, the best Systems of Irrigation and internal Navigation.

MY LORDS,

It will be necessary for me to bespeak the indulgence of your Lordships, and to request your consideration of the subject which I have now the honour to bring before you. It is a subject which has been discussed a good deal lately in writing and at public meetings; and I should not have ventured to direct your Lordships' attention to it had it not been for two recent events of supreme importance. I refer to the famine which has desolated so large a part of India, and the revolution which has broken out in the United States of America. The famine proves unmistakably the defect of irrigation; and the revolution shows the great hazard to which we are exposed in depending almost entirely on a single source for the supply of cotton. It is not my intention here to put India in the place of America, and to say that we might safely be dependent on India alone for our cotton supply; I indicate it only as one great source. The subject, confessedly, is worthy of serious reflection, inasmuch as from 4 to 5 million mouths (workpeople and their families) throughout the country look for their daily bread to a constant supply of that article; and, therefore, while recognising West African and Australian sources for a portion of our supply, we may for present purposes confine our consideration to what may be produced by the territory of India. Neither is it my wish to enter upon the inquiry whether the famine might have been prevented, or the short supply of cotton foreseen. The fact is, the evils are before us, and we have to deliberate what can be done to avert the recurrence of such formidable mischiefs.

The two great requisites of India are irrigation and inland navigation—irrigation for the purpose of fertilizing the soil, and inland navigation for the purpose of carrying away the produce. In India we want canals for traffic as well as fertility ; for unless the ryot has a pretty good assurance that he can easily transport the crop to a place of sale, he will not cultivate the soil; and it has often happened that, lacking the means of transport, a great abundance has been to him a burden rather than a benefit.* Here let me remark that, in any proposition we may make for the purpose of extending inland navigation, we are not, directly or indirectly, acting in antagonism to the railways. Railways must subsist in India; and it is certain that the more you improve the country and increase the wealth of the people, the better will be the prospect of the railways. But, whether the railways be remunerative or not, we may fairly say of them that the great development of Indian resources has been coincident with the expenditure on the works, and the partial opening of those undertakings.

Now, India is particularly adapted to the purposes of irrigation. Not only is there a vast quantity of water both for flow and for store, but the conformation of the country offers but few engineering obstacles. An irrigation system has prevailed for many centuries in India. It was undertaken upon a large scale by the native princes. They have set an example which we ought to follow. They have laid down the true principles upon which to provide for the necessities of the country ; and it is for us, with our greater scientific knowledge, to carry those principles into effect. No one can doubt the extent of the irrigation system who has read an extract from *Reports on Public Works at Madras in* 1853 :—

" The mere mention of the number of works (*i. e.*, works executed under native princes) would give no just idea respecting them, as they vary so greatly in size and value, but we may

* " The wheat, corn, and flour of Ohio, Illinois, Iowa, Missouri, is carried 1,500 and 2,000 miles by *river, lake,* and *canal* to the port, and exported to Europe, while the same articles grown in India at one-third of the cost *rot upon the ground,* 200 or 300 miles from the coast, for want of an outlet. I have known rice to be actually unsaleable at a distance of only 60 miles from a port."—Capt. Haigh's Report on the Navigation of the Godavery. Parliamentary Paper, H. of C., Feb. 6, 1860, sec. 21.

notice tanks and channels in fourteen of the chief Ryotwar irrigated districts. They number 43,000 in repair, and 10,000 out of repair. The estimated amount of capital invested in their construction is 15 millions sterling."

The reporters go on to make this strong and just observation :—

"An examination of this list of works suggests humiliating reflections. The ancient rulers of the country, with resources of science and skill immeasurably inferior to what we can command, raised those numberless magnificent and valuable works. . . . They are due to the enlightened intelligence of princes whom we are accustomed to style barbarians."

Surely it is our duty—in possession, as we are, of far greater scientific knowledge and far greater means of executing such works than the native princes—surely it is our duty to the vast country over which we have assumed dominion, to do everything in our power to carry into effect whatever will conduce to the general welfare of the population. Does any one now doubt the value of irrigation ? All objections to it were admirably disposed of in the Report of the Commissioners.* Let any gainsayer consider the great deficiency of water at times, the character of the soil, and the words of Dr. Watson,† asserting that not only water but river-water is indispensable; and the value of irrigation in India cannot be questioned. In his admirable lecture on cotton in India, Dr. Watson says,—

"Irrigation is essential not merely as bringing water, but also organic matter, and certain, though small, quantities of salts, such as gypsum and common salt."—A new, but unanswerable, argument in favour of such works.

My Lords, they suffer in India as much from excess as from deficiency of water—as much from deluges as from droughts ; and therefore a great part of the irrigation must be by constructing, according to the system of the native princes, large tanks, in which the excess of water during a period of fall is stored, and is dealt out by distributing-channels in periods of drought ; and, moreover, dealt out in sufficient quantities to render rivers and large canals navigable which in time of drought would otherwise be pretty nearly, if not altogether, dried up. In this way, I am told, water may be so distributed as to keep not only the surface of India in a constant state of

---

* Report of Public Works, Madras, sects. 295 *et seq.*
† Dr. Forbes Watson, M.D., Reporter on Products of India.

irrigation, but the canals also, and rivers, navigable by boats. It is by the use of their internal waters that the Americans have made those rapid strides which are the wonder of the present generation : but we have advantages in India which the Americans do not possess. By the distribution to which I have alluded—by storing the water in tanks, and by pouring it out at proper times—we may render the rivers of India navigable during twelve months in the year, whereas in America the rivers, being exposed to hard frosts, are, generally speaking, not navigable for more than nine months out of the twelve. Inland navigation, moreover, is peculiarly necessary and peculiarly adapted to India. The watercourses are most easy to arrange or construct. The canals may be easily and cheaply kept in repair. They are best adapted to carry heavy burdens at a low cost, and yet insure a return of the largest possible revenue upon the cost of their construction.

Now, having all these advantages, what is the use which has been made of them by various successive Governments? This report on Public Works states :—

" In general it may be affirmed that the greater part of the flood waters of our rivers are turned to no account, and vast bodies of water flow annually to the sea which might be made use of to fertilize hundreds of thousands of acres, to feed a vast population, and to add enormously both to the wealth of the people and the revenue of the government."\* In speaking of the canals, the reporters say—and the remark, though made in reference to the native princes, is equally applicable to the British government :—

"Still less use was made of the canals of irrigation, though many of them were well adapted for water-carriage during six or eight months of the year."

We will say nothing just now on the almost equal neglect' for many years at least, of roads and highways. But ought we not to direct our attention more especially to these important matters of irrigation and canals, when we know that it is from the deficiency or excess of water in one way or other that has arisen the greater part of the evils which have afflicted India—its famines, its pestilences, its fevers,

---

\* " As canals for irrigation have been found to be prejudicial to the public health in Northern India, we may here state that such a result has never been met with in this Presidency."—*Madras Papers*, p. 5.

I have been informed by a gentleman of experience, that many of the irrigation works in Northern India are of faulty construction.

and all the consequent sufferings? It is impossible to have a stronger proof of this than in what has taken place in respect to the great Ganges Canal, which runs through a country particularly in need of the agency of water. When it was constructed it was left unfinished; the distributing channels were not connected with it, and it did not, therefore, perform all the purposes for which it was intended. There is no man living who has more to complain of than that great engineer Sir Proby Cautley. He was the engineer of that work, and he achieved a considerable part of it, but a material part was left uncompleted; and the consequence was that the Ganges Canal, for a considerable time, was always quoted as a proof of failure and a strong argument against the introduction into India of the canal system. But what is the present state of things? Let us see what its effect has been, even in its incomplete state, and while deficient in distributing channels. P. Moss, Esq., the Assistant-Secretary to the Government of the North-West Provinces, says:—

" The beneficial effect of the canal during the past season cannot be over-estimated."

What then, my Lords, would have been its results had the full design been wrought out?

And Captain Turnbull, the Superintendent-General of Irrigation, states:—

" Had there been no canal there would have been no crop on broad lands which are now covered with wheat and other cereals in large abundance."

Observe, too, this remarkable calculation, made by Captain Turnbull:—

" According to a rough calculation, 339,243,840 lb. of grain have thus been supplied to the market during the recent calamitous season, and, as each pound is an ample quantity for one man daily, or, perhaps, one woman and one child daily, this would be equal to the maintenance of 644,718 men, 464,718 women and children for a whole year; while it will also have produced fodder sufficient to keep from starvation the cattle of the districts through which the canal has passed, and has probably saved the government from making remissions of land revenue to the amount of 180,000*l.* or 200,000*l.*" He adds, as well he may, " It cannot fail to produce a very great impression on the minds of the people who will thus have been saved from starvation and misery, and to make them happy and contented." How, then,

after this, can we wonder that the Secretary should close with—
" His Honour feels sure that it will be both policy and good
economy to push on this magnificent work to completion with the
utmost vigour, even though at the risk of some present financial
inconvenience ?"

Now, consider what an extent of country needing a supply of
water has been saved by this work; and you may see what would
have been its position without it, by looking to what is the state
of those lands which are beyond the reach of the system. Look,
on the other hand, to districts afflicted, in times past, by the other
extreme. Take the delta of the Godavery. This formerly was
deluged by floods, but now, by the works carried on there, it has
become a habitable, profitable, and safe country. But the
greatest triumph of all that may be achieved by irrigation, and
by opening canals, is to be found in the district of Rajamundry,
the wonderful work of Sir A. Cotton. I beg your Lordships to
listen to these results, and see how a small expenditure will
produce mighty benefits, and in a short space of time too, and
how it is that the most remunerative economy at the present
moment is to lay out—I will not say a large sum, but even a
small sum, to realize these enormous profits. The revenue of
this district of Rajamundry has increased within the last year
45,000*l.*; the exports in 1860 were 500,000*l.*, being an increase of
180,000*l.* over the previous year. The bullion imported by the
people, now becoming quite a commercial people, but who were
formerly among the most abject and impoverished of India,
amounted to 190,000*l.* The total increase of the revenue is
175,000*l.*, being an increase since the works began of no less than
90 per cent., and the profit on the expenditure has been 40 per
cent., which is mainly attributable to the works. Pray, give
particular attention to the benefits which have been derived from
the works on the canal, and you will see that, while in 1852-3 the
number of boats passing down to the seaports was no more than
752, in 1860, a period of eight years only, it had risen to 15,000;
and the tonnage of the boats has on an average been fully double.
Not having any personal experience of India, it is not possible
for me to describe adequately the benefits which this canal has
conferred on that district; but I have heard from persons who
lived there that it has been tantamount to its regeneration. But
your Lordships may, to some extent, judge of them when you
consider that it was formerly a district traversed by muddy
streams and narrow channels altogether impassable, and that it
is now traversed by this great canal, over which pass no less than

15,000 boats in the course of the year. A letter which has just
been received contains a most remarkable statement as to the
advantages which these works have conferred on Rajamundry.
The writer says, speaking, in the first place, of another district :—

" Nothing is more probable than that this tract of country may
this very year be visited with famine for want of those works.
As it is, even at this moment a great part of the Madras Presidency is on the very verge of famine; rice is selling at 1*d.* a
pound—from two to three times its ordinary price, indicating
most terrible sufferings among the poor. In Rajamundry, on the
other hand,—now observe this,—where irrigation works are in
operation, the price is just half what it is in other districts, and.
while the people are entirely free from all such pressure, they are
exporting probably more than 80,000 tons this year to relieve the
suffering provinces."

So that your Lordships will see that under the operation of
these irrigation works Rajamundry, which was formerly one of
the most desolate and miserable districts, has not only become as
wealthy as I have described, but is actually exporting produce
to other provinces. What a proof is here of the value of easy
communication! See the important advantage of this canal,
that it brings food tolerably within the reach of the people.
Formerly, in some cases they would have to travel from 300 to
400 miles in search of food, where now it is brought almost to
their own doors.

There are not wanting other strong proofs of the value of these
works, and of the necessity imposed on the government of India
of doing all that in them lies to promote undertakings which so
materially advance the welfare of the people of India. In the
Appendix Z to the papers of 1853 there is a very striking and
suggestive statement of the result of expenditure on irrigation
works in the 14 years from 1836 to 1849. Within those years
the works were carried on in 39 places; on one point the profit
was 77 per cent., on another 91 per cent., on another 197 per
cent., on another 259 per cent.; but the average profit on the
whole, taking bad and good together, was 69½ per cent.; and I
am told that if the results were brought down to the present
time they would give a still larger return. On the other hand,
let us see what has been the effect of neglect and omission; and
first let me call your attention to the famine which took place
some years ago in Guntoor, which lies on the south bank of the

Kistnah river, and has an area of 4,700 square miles. In the report on the state of that district we read:—

" The large number of ruined tanks in all parts of the country indicate that formerly the extent of irrigated land was considerable; at present it is only 4 per cent. of the total cultivation."

Here is a country which had formerly enjoyed the advantages of a system of irrigation. It has suffered fearfully, the tanks having been allowed to fall into disrepair, probably under the native princes, but which were not restored when the British government obtained possession of the territory. The number of ruined tanks, however, shows what the native princes had done, and what they, after the experience of centuries, considered necessary for the welfare of the country. The famine broke out, and vast numbers of persons migrated in search of food. No fewer than 200,000 perished by starvation and fever; and the total loss to the zemindars, ryots, and the government, was estimated at above 2,250,000*l.*; all of which might have been prevented by a little providence and the expenditure, at the right time, of not a fourth part of this sum. But what is the condition of Guntoor at this moment? Mr. Bourdillon—whom everybody acquainted with India must know as a gentleman most capable of giving information on this matter—was asked as to the present state of Guntoor. He replies:—

" The works on the Kistnah were suspended by the mutiny, and works of distribution very partially executed." Nevertheless, see what his reply is as to the present state of Guntoor:— " You ask whether Guntoor is more safe from famine than it used to be. No doubt it is, and why? My Lords, because two talooks "—that is villages or districts—" are partially watered from the Kistnah. The dams are complete," he says, " but the channels for them are wanting, though the cost would be small, and the addition to the revenue immediate."

The cost small, the return large and immediate! Are such truths to pass unheeded by the governing powers? This work is not completed; nevertheless Mr. Bourdillon says that by the irrigation of these districts the production has been so raised as to be not only sufficient for the people themselves, but enabling them in some measure to supply their neighbours. Instances to show the necessity of attending to the distribution of water for the prevention of floods are equally numerous and striking. In Cuttack alone, by neglect in this matter, there were, during a period of twenty-three years, seven years of inundation, and two of very severe inundation; and in 1855, in the Muddea district alone, forming but a small part of the delta of the Ganges, a single flood destroyed no less than 22,000 houses, 8,000 persons, 40,000 cattle, and 20,000 acres of crops, worth at the very least 320,000*l.*—all preventible!

I come now to the Godavery, to which it is right that your Lordships should give more than ordinary attention. The full navigation of the Godavery would open, perhaps, the finest cotton district in the whole world. "The valley of the Godavery"— this is the report of Captain Haigh—"has an area of 130,000 square miles, or about four times as large as Ireland." The population of the valley is estimated at 8 millions, and this valley alone contains a cotton-field larger than that of America: America having but 4 million acres under cultivation—an area not much larger than that of Yorkshire. The products of this district are various and abundant. There is wheat unsurpassed by any in India in quantity and quality; Indian corn, millet, peas, beans, rice, sugar, hemp, oil, seeds, chilies, safflower. But there are two products of especial value at the present time—I mean flax and cotton—to which I will return by and by. Yet this mighty country, capable of such immense products, and of meeting almost every demand which could be made by Great Britain, is pretty nearly locked up by defective means of transit, and through the want of canals, of railways, and of every means for the easy conveyance of goods. What a discouragement this is to production may be conjectured from the fact that the time occupied in the conveyance to Bombay or Calcutta of goods on the backs of bullocks—which is the only mode of conveying the products of the country to different ports—is two months. I need hardly say that when goods are conveyed on the backs of bullocks they are exposed to great hazards, being subject to the influences of weather, to bad roads, and, perhaps, to be plunged into the rivers which it is necessary to cross; and thus the quality of the article is much deteriorated, while the cost per ton upon the cotton or the flax would be about 160*s.* How splendid an opening would be secured by the improvement in the navigation of the Godavery may be judged of from the description given by an engineer who has surveyed the district :—

"The river (says Captain Haigh) runs for 100 miles through the finest cotton-fields of India, and may be said to direct its course in a very direct line from the chief cotton centre to Coringa, the best and safest port on the eastern coast." Another authority, speaking of the Godavery, says, "The river, with its numberless tributaries, may one day become the Mississippi of the Indo-British empire."

Now the estimated cost of rendering this river navigable for 473 miles, so that goods might be conveyed down to the port, from the port into the interior, is 292,000*l.*, being at the rate of 618*l.* per mile; and if the works were rendered more complete, so as to make the transit still cheaper, the estimated cost would be 360,000*l.* And what would be the result? Why, that the cotton, instead of spending two months on the backs of bullocks, and exposed to every hazard, would go down in boats to Coringa in eight days, and that the cost per ton, instead of being 160*s.*, would be only 24*s.* This great result would be obtained with the small outlay of public money I have mentioned; and when you consider the great interests which are at stake both in India and in England, there can surely be little hesitation as to the course to be pursued so as to open the finest fields which can be found for the cultivation of flax and cotton, for the export of Indian products, and the import of British manufactures.

But I cannot altogether omit another point, the consideration of which will show how many services would be performed and how many interests consulted by rendering the Godavery navigable. In the first place, it must be regarded as a military work. Colonel Balfour, the Inspector-General of Ordnance, observes on " the large pecuniary saving which will ensue not only in the conveyance of stores, but in the preservation of human life by reducing the risks that now attend our soldiery during long marches." He adds most truly, " European lives in India are now more valuable than ever." Colonel Balfour gives details to show the saving which might be effected by opening up the Godavery:—" The march from Masulipatam to Nagpore is very circuitous, and traverses one of the most notoriously deadly jungles in India. The march occupies, I believe, a month and a half. It might be reduced to seven days by the river."*

Thus, instead of sending the troops, whether European or

---

* In the debate it was urged that I had not made any reference to the Bombay and Nagpore Railway, which it is expected will be open in two or three years. I certainly did not, and for the reasons given in the extract which follows from the Reports by Captain Haigh, sect. 19 :—

" But the complete failure of this expensive system of conveyance, and its utter unsuitableness to the circumstances of India, become more strikingly apparent, if we compare the condition of Berar with its railroad to the valley of the Mississippi with its rivers, and see what is the proportion which the cost of carriage bears to that of production in each case. I suppose this is a fair comparison, and an important one, America being the great competitor of India in the supply of cotton.

native, from one place to another by a tedious and fatiguing
march of six weeks through a most unhealthy country, they
might be sent in a week by the river. Despatch, health, humanity,
and policy, would be alike consulted. Then, a saving would be
effected in the transport of stores. " On that line," says Colonel
Balfour, "the transport of stores and cart-hire alone amounts to
18,000*l.* per annum;" which 18,000*l.*, let me observe in passing,
would more than cover the interest of the 360,000*l.* to be expended
in opening the communication.

Again, there is another point materially affecting the welfare
of the natives and the revenue of the government. The Indian
government derives a large revenue from the salt-tax. Whatever
may be the objection to such a monopoly existing in such an
article, the fact is that the price exacted by the government under
its monopoly at the place of manufacture does not by any means
constitute in itself an onerous tax. The great pressure upon
the natives arises from the difficulty of transporting the salt
from the place of manufacture into the interior. The Indian
government clears, by its monopoly, on every ton of salt two
pounds sterling. Now, wherever salt is cheap—that is, wherever

---

" A ton of cotton is carried on the Mississippi from Memphis to New Orleans,
800 miles, for five dollars, or 1*l.*, or at the rate of 0·30*d.* per ton per mile; to
Mobile, by a very inferior river, 400 to 580 miles, at 0·60*d.* per ton per mile.

" In India, cotton will be carried from Berar to Bombay for 5*l.* 6*s.*, or 2¾*d.* per
ton per mile.

" The two cases may thus be stated:—

| | Cost of Production per lb. | Cost of Carriage to Port, 470 Miles, per lb. | Ratio per Cent. of Cost of Carriage to Cost of Production. |
|---|---|---|---|
| | *d.* | *d.* | *per cent.* |
| AMERICA .. .. | 3½ | −⅑ | 3½ |
| BERAR .. .. | 1 | 0·57 | 57 |

" So, by way of helping the ryot in his competition with the American planter
we provide him with a means of conveyance which makes the expense of carriage
to market twenty times as heavy a charge on the cost of production as it is in
America! And not only so, but we are in a fair way of actually adding to his
existing burdens, by making him contribute to the support of the very road which
is of so little value to him; for it now seems almost certain that this Bombay and
Nagpore line will not pay its own interest.

" Is such a communication suited to India, and is it likely to make Manchester
independent of America?"

it can be bought at a small advance on the cost at the pans, it is estimated that every native of India consumes annually about 20 lb. But the price of salt—and this shows how severe must be the pressure upon the people in the interior—the price of salt in Nagpore, Berar, and generally throughout the Deccan, is 6*l*., 7*l*., 10*l*., and even 16*l*. per ton. Here, then, in consequence of the high price, it is estimated that the natives do not consume more than 8 lb. per head. The cost at the pans is raised to the consumer, by the difficulty of transport, from three to six-fold; but the opening of the navigation of the Godavery would reduce the cost to one-fourth of its present amount. Now, my Lords, if salt is a necessary in this country, how much more is it a necessary in the sultry climate of India! and how important then it is to reduce the cost of so essential an article! In effecting this, by reducing the cost of transport, you benefit yourselves and the natives alike; for the result would be that, at a very moderate computation, in this one district alone, the government revenue would be increased by 64,000*l*. a year. Calculate hence the financial results of similar facilities in all the salt factories, and we shall see that the Indian exchequer would be replenished; and great advantage would be simultaneously conferred upon the entire people.

Now, it has been doubted whether India possesses great capability of production. I will show you what are those capabilities of producing; and first, as to cotton and to quantity of it. A high authority states that as much cotton is wasted in India as the whole quantity grown in America. At the present moment there are, according to the calculation of Dr. Royle, under cotton cultivation in India about 24 million acres. The number of the population that is clothed in cotton, from the Himalayas to Cape Comorin, must be estimated at probably 200 millions. Then see the many purposes to which cotton is turned by them; it is used for almost every purpose to which textile fabrics can be applied—for ropes, tents, saddles, stuffing, carpets—for almost everything. Guzerat, Broach, and adjoining districts, forming hardly one-hundredth part of the surface of India, will this year give us one-third of the ordinary supply we receive from America; but why? Because Guzerat has the ports of Gogo and Surat, and other small ports. Dharwar will probably do as much, as soon as the port of Sedashevagur shall have been completed, and the ninety miles of railway to connect it with the producing territory.

I have stated what is the producing power of India as to quantity; now look at its capability as to quality. I have

spoken with many gentlemen on this subject—among others to
Mr. Bazley, himself a cotton-spinner, and on this subject one of
the highest authorities ;—he states that, with all the imperfections, Indian cotton is at present equal in quality to 75 per
cent. of what is now required for the fabrics we manufacture.
But it may be asked what guarantee have we that India will
produce the finest sorts to compete with the American supply ?
Hear Dr. Forbes Watson on this head. He states, in his valuable
writings, that in Dharwar the cultivation of American cotton
is increasing at the rate of from 30,000 to 40,000 acres a year ;
that the acreage last year under this kind of cotton was 180,000 ;
and the quality of the crop is quite equal to the New Orleans,
or the American cotton. Then take the article of flax, which
is becoming one of great demand and necessity in this country :
one sample of Indian flax imported last year was valued at 64*l.*
per ton, and the Punjaub and other districts exceed, we are told,
Russia in the capability of producing it. And I wish your Lordships to weigh this important consideration,—that when we
talk of cotton in India we are not talking of a new cultivation
which we are going to introduce for the first time : we have not
to clear the land, or send the seed, or teach the people what they
have to do : they have cultivated cotton for many centuries ; all
that they require are roads, canals, the means of transport and
communication, markets, easy access to ports, and vigilant pur-
chasers. Give India these, and her productiveness, both as to
quantity and quality, will far exceed all our expectations. But
until we do give those facilities of transport, some of the most
rich and fertile regions of the world will remain altogether impoverished and useless.

Again, it has been asked whether India is capable of producing
speedily, and according to our wants. Just look, my Lords, at
such a statement as this—first, of jute, an article of great importance, and particularly so now in Dundee, there were imported
from India in 1841, 3,000 tons ; but in 1859 the quantity imported
was 53,000 tons. Take then the article of wool—in 1852 there
were imported from India about 5,000,000 lb. ; in 1860 the
quantity imported was upwards of 20,000,000 lb. And observe,
as a proof of the energy of the people, that the greater portion of
this wool was brought on camels' backs from distances varying
from 200 to 600 miles. Down to 1851 the largest quantity of
linseed imported from India in any one year was 6,000 tons ; in
1854 it had increased to 35,988 tons ; in 1855, owing to the
Russian war, it rose to 66,687 tons ; and in 1859 it was 96,000 tons,
or nearly equal to the supply from Russia and all other countries

combined.* I cannot but direct attention particularly to this point. If the Russian war did so much to stimulate the production of linseed, what may not the revolution in America be expected to do for the production of cotton? That event is likely to deliver us from our perilous habit of depending on a single country for our supply, to relieve us from much hazard and annoyance, and, above all, from that incubus on the hearts of hundreds of thousands—the necessity of purchasing the produce of slave labour. The cotton grown in India will be grown by free labour; and this issue, I believe, will go further to abolish slavery in America than all our writings, speeches, and combinations.

Having thus shown the capability of India to produce, I now wish to show its capability to consume. In 1851 the value of the cotton manufactures, including twist and yarn, imported into India from Great Britain, was 5,220,194*l.*; the value of other articles was about 2,022,000*l.*, making a total of 7,242,194*l.* The proportion, therefore, in reference to the rest of the world, of British cotton manufactures taken by India at that time was 18 per cent. In 1859 the value of the cotton manufactures taken by India from Great Britain was 14,713,812*l.*; the value of other articles taken by India was 5,131,108*l.*, making a total of 19,844,920*l.* The proportion of British goods, therefore, taken by India, relatively to the rest of the world, was in 1859 more than 30 per cent. But 1859 may be considered a year of forced export; look, then, at 1860, and it appears that India took British cotton goods to the value of 12,000,000*l.*, and other goods to the value of 5,000,000*l.*, showing a total value of 17,000,000*l.* Now, all this shows a wonderful progress; and we must bear in mind that it has been made in spite of all kinds of difficulties—of war, of the mutiny, of the difficulty of transport, of deluge, of drought, of famine and pestilence. Yet, so great are the resources, so strong the elasticity of India, that, notwithstanding all her obstacles and all her dangers, India has nearly reached the point of being our best and safest customer.

Another doubt has been expressed as to the character of the people, and whether they will respond to the efforts we may make in their favour; it is said they are generally listless and idle, requiring another people to think and act for them. But let us see how the stimulus of gain and self-interest acts on this

---

* A very experienced gentleman has furnished me a note on this point. He says:—" Linseed is much more easily carried than cotton; but it is a remarkable fact that the increase in exports of linseed and rape-seed is from those districts which, by reason of their proximity to the coast, and other carriage-facilities, are now furnishing large extra supplies of cotton."

population. In Dharwar, where the American cotton is grown, it has been found necessary to introduce the saw-gin, it being an instrument particularly adapted to cleansing purposes. The government set up a factory for these machines ; and so great became the demand for them by the ryots, that the manufacture was, for the sake of despatch, transferred to this country. These machines cost from 11*l*. to 16*l*. each, and yet the natives have already purchased them to a considerable amount—about 12,000*l*.; and they expend on an average in this manner about 2,500*l*. yearly. And this has been done by the ryots themselves, of whom it has been said that no stimulus can induce them to look beyond the day. The fact is, my Lords, I believe we have been governing India for nearly a century, and have never yet arrived at a proper estimate of the character of the people. They are, I believe, a people eminently commercial, active, and intelligent. It may not be a very amiable consideration, but it is, I believe, a true one, that, if you only make it clear to the ryot that a thing will pay, as the phrase is, there is nothing on earth, or below it, that the ryot will not at least attempt in the hope of money. I have been told that persons will travel hundreds of miles, carrying on their heads the articles they have to sell; and should they succeed in obtaining the profit of a few rupees, they believe themselves amply rewarded for their trouble. Now, with respect to the cultivation of cotton in Dharwar, there can be no doubt that, if you open to the people a certainty that they shall obtain a speedy and fair payment for their productions, no effort will be spared on their part to supply the demand. In that way we can, I am assured, open a great field without having recourse to the objectionable system of advances. Nothing, it is clear, can be worse than such a system. It is most injurious to the man who makes the advance, inasmuch as it produces a despotic and domineering habit, while it leaves the ryot in a state of dependence, and wholly deprives him of any character of manliness and self-respect.

I cannot conclude the instances which I have ventured to bring before your Lordships' notice, without adducing one which, more strongly than any preceding, proves the immense advantage resulting to the country from works of irrigation and internal communication. I will take two districts, Cuttack and Tanjore, which are of about equal size, both situated in deltas of great rivers, and both of equal fertility. The revenue from Cuttack is 85,000*l*., while that from Tanjore is 470,000*l*. The land in Cuttack is worth 30*s*. per acre, but in Tanjore it produces 5*l*. Cuttack has by far the best natural supply of water ; and yet in

twenty-three years there have been three years of famine, four
years of drought, seven of inundation, two of severe inundation,
and only seven of moderate seasons. During that period there
was expended yearly in Cuttack upon waterworks 2,400*l.*, and in
Tanjore 11,600*l.* ; and yet in these two countries of equal natural
advantages, the aggregate excess of revenue from Tanjore over
Cuttack during the twenty-three years was no less than 6,970,000*l.*
To what, I pray you, is this to be ascribed ? Is there no argument
here for public works ? Here is a very important paper, a report
of the Madras Board of Revenue to the Madras government in
1859. The reporters, although just and true, are not over-partial
to Sir A. Cotton's plans; and thus this paper, dispelling as it
does all doubts of accuracy, shows unquestionably the character
of what has been done. They say :—

"The Board now approach the third branch of the subject, the
cost of the two Coleroon anicuts, and the net amount of revenue
which they have yielded to the State. The sums expended on
these works, and the percentage which the net profit yielded by
them bears to the original outlay, underwent careful scrutiny by
the Department of Public Works and the Mahramut Commissioners, and the result at which they arrived after examining the
bills and revenue statements was that for an outlay of 21,738*l.*
the government have received a clear gain of 412,052*l.* in sixteen
years, or a profit of 118 per cent. per annum."

My Lords, here is the deliberate opinion of those gentlemen,
arrived at after most careful consideration. What more could be
desired ? I have heard it said of Sir A. Cotton's works that his
estimates were always exceeded by the actual cost. That may be
so ; but then it is also true that, in all instances, the expenditure
has been followed by enormous and almost fabulous profit ; and
that, with such results, he may have sometimes made insufficient
estimates, can hardly be regarded as much of a reproach. It has
also been said that most of his works have been carried out in the
deltas of great rivers. That is, no doubt, true ; but if all the
deltas of India were brought into the same condition as that of
Tanjore, the revenue of the empire would be now nearly double
what it is, and the people proportionately flourishing and secure.
When Sir A. Cotton first set his schemes on foot, he was told
they were impracticable ; but now that he has carried them to
completion, he is told, with equal assurance, that the results are
incredible !

Now, after what I have stated as to the success of such works,
can your Lordships wonder at the favourable opinion which has

been expressed by those authorities who are most acquainted with the facts? Lord Dalhousie, in a despatch to the Court of Directors, wrote—

" Everywhere I found evidence of the wonderful effect produced by irrigation, wherever the means could be obtained ; everywhere I found lands of vast extent, fertile properties, now lying comparatively waste, but wanting only water to convert them into plains of the richest cultivation ; and everywhere I found among the people the keenest anxiety to be supplied with that by which alone they could be enabled to turn their labour to good account."

I find in a speech delivered by Lord Stanley in 1859, himself at one time Secretary of State for India, the following statement :—

" With regard to the public works in India, I have seen some doubt expressed whether the returns from these works were accurately given. I have since gone through the figures and verified them from official documents, and I find they are strictly accurate." The noble Lord was speaking of these very works in Tanjore.

The Hon. W. Elliot, a member of the Council of Madras, says :—

" In irrigation-works the physical impediments are generally few and easily met, the returns are sure, always considerable, often immense ; they have increased the wealth of the inhabitants in a remarkable degree; and with property the people have acquired habits of independence, a desire for knowledge, and for the extension of useful schemes of every description."

Sir C. Trevelyan, in a report upon the state of Madras in 1859, states that—

" Works of irrigation create new value by an immediate and positive process, with a profusion of which there is no other example. They add from three to six fold to the annual productiveness of the land. This is better than the annexation of new territory. . . . The natives are encouraged to a life of peaceful industry."

It is, indeed, far better than annexation ; for if only one-tenth part of the Presidency of Madras were cultivated after the fashion of the districts I have mentioned, it would more than double the revenue and quadruple the comforts of the people. The words of Dr. Johnson might be realized ; there would be " the potentiality of growing rich beyond the dreams of avarice." A large addition would be made to the exchequer; and that, not only without pressing hardly upon those who contribute to the revenue, but with an increase of their resources. We should improve the condition of the people in all senses. We should enable them not only to meet the demands of the government, but also to become large consumers of British manufactures, thus benefiting our own countrymen and adding to the well-being of our own people. In whatever light we consider this question we cannot fail to be convinced of its deep and lasting interest. If we regard it financially, we see the means of largely increasing the revenue, and at the same time extending the means of those who furnish that revenue. If we regard it commercially, we see benefits on both sides; we perceive the means of stirring the industry of Great Britain to the greatest extent, and, at the same time, of enabling India to return to us by her produce what we require in exchange for our manufactured goods. Politically it is of manifest importance that we should adopt all measures that may add to the contentment and happiness of the people, and thereby give honour and security to our rule. If we regard it morally, is it not, I would ask, a great matter that the natives of India will be induced to look with favour upon the laws, the language, the civilization, and the religion, of a race of men who exhibit such powers of science, and turn them to such high and beneficent purposes? I have heard that, in one of the improved districts, it was said to a missionary, " Until you Christians came among us we never had anything of this kind." By elevating socially the condition of the people we create feelings of independence and self-respect. Instead of a servile, down-trodden race, they will become able to assert their rights, to exercise their privileges, and to stand erect in the dignity of free men.

My Lords, when the late famine broke out in India, the people of this country properly and liberally subscribed to relieve the distress. It was right and humane to do so; but I venture to say that if a sum equal to that contributed for the relief of the famine had been expended, in earlier days, upon the construction of works, it would have prevented that calamity, and have rendered those districts fertile and productive for many generations to come. My Lords, what do we not owe, in the position we occupy, to ourselves and to British India? By the seizure of the territory, we have assumed the many and various responsibilities of empire. By the conquest—no doubt the beneficial conquest—of the country, we have torn from the natives all means of improving their own financial condition, of regulating their own internal concerns, or of advancing, unaided, their own interests. Our duty, then, is clear. But, above all, we owe these efforts, in gratitude and obedience, to Almighty God, who has been pleased to place under the rule and protection of Queen Victoria the most magnificent empire that ever yet figured in the annals of mankind.

———————

The facts in the foregoing speech, founded on high and indisputable authority, will, I am disposed to believe, convince the people of Great Britain that, by the judicious and diligent application of science to the soil and waters of India, we shall, under God's blessing, not only advance our own interests, but greatly mitigate, if not altogether prevent, the horrors of drought and famine in that country.

*Legislation on Social Subjects.*

---

# SOCIAL SCIENCE CONGRESS OF 1866.

---

Delivered at the opening of the Congress.

LADIES AND GENTLEMEN,

Having already fulfilled the respective offices of a Vice-President, and President, at two of the meetings of this Institution, if I be asked a reason of my reappearance on the present occasion, the answer thereto will be very simple.

First, Lord Stanley, who had been appointed to the distinguished honour, was called away to exercise his high talents in the discharge of the duties of Secretary of State for the Foreign Department; and,

Secondly, Lord Brougham, who has so often and so powerfully occupied this chair, pleaded, in refusal, the increase of age and infirmities, desiring some little repose after his brilliant and laborious services. However deep our regret, the appeal was irresistible; and the committee, though sure that it was difficult to find a successor, and impossible to find a substitute; and while convinced, moreover, that the noble Lord, differing from so many men who at times are able, but not ready, and at others, ready but not able, would here be, as usual, both ready and able in any effort of science and intellect, gave way upon the point, and followed his judgment rather than their own.

By this time the session was very far advanced; most persons of note had quitted London—the choice was necessarily limited; and the request was addressed to myself, with which I complied, because, although weary from labour and other causes, and, in many respects unfit, I wished to show that I had not forgotten, and that I never could forget, the people of Lancashire.

We are now about to celebrate our tenth anniversary, and we may be summoned to show cause why our existence should be prolonged—we may hear that the questions are exhausted, and the perpetual repetition of the same details is wearisome and useless. But let it be observed, that the repetition of the same details is not in the same places, and before the same audiences; and, even if it were so, there steps in the language of the Apostle, "to write the same things to you, to me, indeed, is not grievous; but for you it is safe:" safe, because we speak of things which come home to every man's life, and almost to every man's bosom, things which cannot be neglected, if ignorantly, without danger, and, if wilfully, without both danger and crime.

It is true, no doubt, that we have given to the world several volumes of transactions, abounding in most valuable reports of our discussions and proceedings. They are rich in argument and facts on all the subjects embraced in our programme; and were the curious and the sympathizing disposed to study them, we might be spared, for some time at least, any further efforts in this direction. But such is not the case; and we must trace it to a spirit, at all periods strong, but peculiarly so in our own generation, a love of things, actually or apparently, new. An old thought, an old fact, an old inference, dressed up in a new garment, and presented in a fresh light, has all the charm of novelty, even to minds well conversant with the subject; and hundreds, no doubt, who would shrink from the dull and solitary pursuit of facts diffused through numerous and bulky octavos, are fascinated by the human voice in the delivery of eloquent addresses, or in the lively, vigorous, and profitable discussions that follow so frequently on the close of the several papers.

But, though we have old subjects, see how constantly we are aided by new men—and herein lies one great advantage of our system. Latent science, latent zeal, latent energy, latent intellect—latent, through diffidence, want of opportunity, or subject-matter—are brought to the light of day before your assembled congress. Each one who has contributed an essay, or taken part in the deliberations, returns to his home, and becomes recognized as a centre of influence and practical knowledge. Thus the spirit and power of active service are widely diffused, silently working in times of health, but prompt and loud in times of disease; and I cannot but attribute, under God's good providence, the suppression of the late epidemic, in no small measure, to the larger views, the readier knowledge, the greater capacity for imposing discipline, or submitting to it, and to the faculty, so recently and so advantageously exhibited, for immediate and effective co-operation among functionaries and volunteers, professional and unprofessional persons—all which issues have sprung from the exhortations we have uttered, the lessons we have given, the facts we have adduced, the proofs we have instituted, and the healthy and enlightening circuit, as it were, of our Judges of Assize, who go forth, year by year, to set at liberty a legion of physical and moral truths, long and hopelessly despised or imprisoned by the ignorance or indifference of our forefathers.

It is said in many quarters, " the Congress has exhausted the subject, but nevertheless it has devised no cures." The second part of the sentence thus refutes the first, for the whole thing then remains to be done. So far from having exhausted the subject, we have barely penetrated the outer crust, nor will our real difficulties diminish, as in the physical sciences, with improvements of knowledge. It is impossible for us to lay down our formulæ, as in chemistry, astronomy, and geology, to be obeyed, and relished, the moment they are reduced to actual demonstration. In our pursuits, the moral and physical elements are closely, intricately, and inseparably, combined. We shall, probably, break up, this very session, having established to our heart's content, and that of all thinking people, the necessity and practicability of many things, essential to the bodily and mental welfare, nay, safety, of millions—all to be set aside or ignored, as the phrase is, with some honourable exceptions, by vestries, boards of guardians, and every form, pressure, and kind of single or associated proprietors.

To pause, however, in our career would, on the part of science, be a pusillanimous confession of defeat; but, on the part of humanity and morals, it would be a resolution no less perilous than disgraceful.

Nevertheless, some care is required in the opposite direction; I may be wrong, yet I cannot but suggest a little hesitation before we embark on questions that are simply political or imperial. I have been urged to lay before the Congress, irrigation in India, bribery at elections, treaties with foreign nations, and many other points of a similar character. But, first, I have no wish to see our gatherings converted into Parliaments; and, secondly, we have enough on hand to demand, and to occupy, the activity of at least two-thirds of a generation.

The President of the day is, I conclude, expected to say a few words, in the nature of a charge to the Jury, on the several subjects to be handled in the various sections. For my own part, I approach not a few of them with fear and trembling, feeling, in my ignorance, that the " safest eloquence concerning them is my silence;" and that in matters of law, the first here on the list, we unprofessional persons are tempted sometimes to take a commonsense view of the question; and then we are sure to be wrong. So, leaving the important principles and graver details to the enlightened and distinguished men appointed to this department, I will simply notice one or two heads that have fallen occasionally under my own observation.

A great and startling problem is proposed, " What are the best means of preventing infanticide ?"  I am glad that the subject is introduced, and that the Congress scouts the assertion made, I regret to say, not very long ago, by two eminent persons, that to institute such an inquiry, was to institute a libel against the women of England.  The crime has attained to formidable proportions, and may not, in decency, be disregarded.  We have not yet sufficiently examined and methodised the many various and complicated causes that lead to the perpetration of it by interested agents, or the palliation of it before juries.  My own opinion is, if I may venture to say so, that, in a state of the population where infant-life is not, as in vigorous and growing colonies, of high marketable value, the law will do but little.  The bill of last session, which did not pass into an act, offered one excellent provision ; and a strict registration of all reputed to be still-born might give us some further security.  But we must not rely upon statutes.  The nostrums of some reformers are unfit to be discussed ; and I hope that, without much weightier arguments, we shall place very small confidence in foundling hospitals.

The coroner's court is a most valuable and ancient institution ; and every one will acknowledge how many admirable men we number among its officers.  But still, we may ask whether the proceedings are not oftentimes slurred over to the miscarriage of public justice, particularly in cases where no public excitement has preceded the inquiry.  We may ask, too, whether the substitution of a fixed salary for a fee does not, in many instances, virtually prevent the establishment of an inquiry at all ?

Are we right—I put the question with diffidence before men so skilled in jurisprudence—to exhibit such extreme, and almost inviting, lenity towards crime and violence, in some instances, simply because the parties are young ?  Is it wise ? is it just, to encircle property with such severity of protection, and visit offences against the person with comparative indifference ?  It may be so ; but the public would be glad to hear the reasons from high and competent authority.

The subject of education will be so well handled by our liberal and enlightened friend, Mr. Bruce, and his coadjutors, that comment of mine on its principles and practice would certainly be superfluous, and might, besides, be considered arrogant.  But I cannot refrain from a few words of gratitude and joy, when, by the blessing of God, I review the past, and compare the state of the infantile population in factories, collieries, mines, and other trades, with that which "shocked our eyes, and grieved our hearts," some five and thirty years ago.

Thanks to a merciful and Almighty Providence, we have learned, and learned by happy experience, that labour, manual labour—the lot which He has, in His wisdom, assigned to the vast majority of our race—is not incompatible with the highest moral dignity of man. Thousands, nay, tens of thousands, under the limitation of the hours of toil, are receiving a sound and effective education; the young by frequenting the schools, the adults, both male and female, by the improvement of their opportunities to advance in moral, domestic, and literary acquirements.

The alternation of work and study, in due succession and relief, the half-time system, as it has been called, is alike healthy and fruitful. The mind is not depressed by the labour, but the labour is invigorated by the refreshment of the mind. Do we not all feel the principle of it in ourselves? Its practical and most blessed effects we see in all the mercantile occupations governed by the provisions of the Factory Acts. We see it in numberless industrial schools in London and elsewhere. If you doubt the assertion, study the reports of Messrs. Baker and Redgrave and their efficient officers, the sub-inspectors: study it in the reports of Messrs. Chadwick and Tufnell in their accounts of the Metropolitan Scholastic Establishments.

A short time back the excellence of the system came before my eyes in a very prominent way. I visited the Potteries in company with Mr. Inspector Baker, to whom we owe so much, so very much, of this successful issue. I need not describe to you the bodily and mental degradation, in former days, of that neglected district, the state of the places of work, the dust, the insupportable heat, the prolongation of toil through the day and through the night, the utter ignorance, the gross immorality, with all the evils that attend on a defiance of the material and spiritual laws of nature. They are all set forth at large in that true bill of indictment against the English nation, the five Reports of the Children's Employment Commissioners. But how is it now? Though the test has, as yet, been only partially applied, the scene is changed. Two thousand children are at school on the half-time system; and two thousand children are thus exhibiting the results of mercy, consideration, and love. The evidence of the teachers who knew them before, and who know them now, is wonderful and heart-stirring.

The half-timers are equal, nay, oftentimes superior, to the whole-timers, that is to say, those who study and work surpass those who study and do no work at all. Of this we had a forcible proof in the past year, when the half-timers of the several schools distanced the whole-timers in the race of competition, and, in almost every instance, carried off the prizes. The reason is obvious; the character of their toil demands accuracy, precision, constant, unwavering attention, and prompt obedience; everything must be seized at the moment, because nothing can be recovered. Unbroken, unwearied after moderate toil, they bring their habits with them to the school: and the discipline of pots and pans, humble as it may appear, is found to be nobly instrumental to the acquisition of letters and learning.

"I was opposed to the measure," said one of the intelligent schoolmasters; "but a few months have given me a totally different view. Formerly as I went through the streets, I heard nothing but oaths and cursing, blasphemies and obscenity, from children of the tenderest years. But now I hear nothing of the kind; the boys touch their caps, and the girls drop their curtsies, and all try to exhibit affection and respect."

This I can confirm by personal observation. When I went into the schools, and talked to them of their books, of the course they had begun, of the hopes they entertained, and of the thraldom from which they had been delivered, their eyes sparkled with confidence, freedom, and joy; and I blessed God—who could help it ?—and I blessed the Legislature, and I blessed the employers, and I blessed the schoolmasters, and in my satisfaction I blessed everybody, for the glorious sight I had been permitted to witness.

All, however, is not achieved. There is much land yet to be won. "Let not him that putteth on his armour, boast himself like him that putteth it off." I appeal to you on the behalf of fourteen hundred thousand children, women, and young persons, still under the slavery of cruel and oppressive trades, who are, to this hour, without the pale of legislative protection.

But while I leave the remainder, I must dwell for a moment on the abomination of the brickfields. Let the hardest heart that can be found in England visit those spots, and if he be not moved, he must at least be ashamed of his sex and of his country. There the female seems to be brought to the lowest point of servile ignorance and degradation. Hundreds of little girls, from eight to eleven years of age, half-naked, and so besmeared with dirt as to be barely distinguishable from the soil they stand on, are put to work in these abodes of oppression. Bearing prodigious burdens of clay on their heads, and in their arms, they totter to and fro during many hours of toil. When I spoke to them, they either remained aghast with astonishment, or ran away screaming, as though some evil spirit had appeared to them. I could not restrain my indignation, nor can I now, at this wicked scorn of female rights, this wicked waste of female excellence and virtue. Mothers and wives they can never be, in the high and holy sense of those words; and yet, were they trained to decency and truth, might there not be found some to equal the priceless heroism of Lady Baker, or the Christian intellect of Mrs. Stowe?

Is it possible in Manchester (Manchester, so high and proud that she professes to have a school of her own) to pass, without notice and rebuke, another terrible phase of human suffering? The law has already denounced the crime and cruelty of the system of climbing-boys. Why, then, is it still found in so many cities and places boastful of their wealth and civilization? Which of all our national sins is more atrocious, more degrading, and so little justified by the plea of necessity? The evidence cannot be stated here; it is recorded at large in the Commissioners' Reports. But this fact I will adduce for your consideration. When England, a few years ago, took a high and noble tone in denouncing American slavery, an accomplished and zealous lady of the Southern States, alluding, in a tale called " Tit for Tat," to the wretched chimney-sweepers, upbraided us with our hypocrisy that, while we had so much sympathy with the blacks, we had none whatever for our own white children. America, God be praised, has purged herself of that foul stain. Let us be as forward and as true; and let not the young republic put the ancient monarchy to shame and confusion.

The subject of the education of children in the agricultural districts is one of more difficulty, not in reference to the principle, but in respect to the method and details. The want of the agricultural children is not so much a better education, as that a longer period should be devoted to it. Many persons of experience have known children very well taught up to seven or eight years of age, then called away to daily labour, and, in consequence, so unmindful of their former studies, as by the time they are sixteen or seventeen to have wholly forgotten almost the very letters of the alphabet. The introduction here of the half-time system is neither necessary nor practicable; it is not necessary in the sense of overtoil, unhealthy occupation, or danger to life or limb; and it is not practicable, for the children do not work, as in manufactures, congregated in large masses. They are separated in twos and threes at considerable distances from each other,— the places of labour are far remote from their school and their dwellings, so that the whole day would be expended in effecting the exchange of the students and the workers. The evening classes, with some exceptions, are hardly a supplement to this defect, for, during the fine months, the lads prefer the open air; and when the winter has set in, the heavy rains, the bad roads, the long distances, and the dark nights, and, where a separation cannot be effected, the dislike of the adults to be found with the youths in the same place of study, all back up and aid the general indifference to books and learning.

Yet the question must be wrought out. I have myself a plan, which, I admit, will require trouble, will cost a little money, and may, after all, prove a failure. I may be exposed to severe criticism, but it is worth a trial. I should propose two sets of lads, each to work and study on alternate days. I propose it simply as a principle, to be subjected to many modifications in practice. At any rate, while we keep this class in view, let us go forward with the other, and not listen to the resolution, as illogical as it is cruel, that nothing shall be done to relieve the miseries of the children in trades because there is a defective education for the children in agriculture.

Essential, and, indeed, indispensable as is the section on public health in any meeting of our Congress, it need not be dwelt upon in an opening address. The subject has excited a deep and general interest. Almost all the causes of mischief have been dived into, and brought to the surface; and remedies of various kinds have been suggested for their cure. The Legislature, too, by the act of last session, has declared that a wider activity must be exercised by the government, and larger powers be confided to it. But there are yet two points on which the executive is nearly impotent, and those of the greatest consequence to the labouring poor—the wretched supply of water, and, in the widest sense that can be given to the term, the adulteration of food. Let us hope, and let us work, in this very Congress, that another year may not elapse without an effectual abatement of these monstrous inflictions.

But the master-evil which nullifies every effort for the benefit of the working people, which leaves us no rest, and on which let us take good care that the public also has no rest, the evil that embraces and intensifies all the others, the hot-bed of pauperism, immorality, disease, and drunkenness—drunkenness alternately the cause and consequence of disease—the evil that is negative in preventing every improvement, and positive in maturing every mischief, that lies at the root of nineteen-twentieths of the corruptions that beset our social state, and forms the crowning abomination of the whole, is the domiciliary condition of many thousands of our people. But we must look not only to the

pestilential character of the actual dwellings, but to the unventi-
lated, fever-breeding localities in which they stand, the dark,
damp, and narrow alleys never visited by a ray of the sun or a
breath of fresh air.   To describe these things is impossible.
They must be seen, smelt, tasted in person.   Dirt and disrepair,
such as ordinary folks can form no notion of; darkness that may
be felt; odours that may be handled; faintness that can hardly
be resisted, hold despotic rule in these dens of despair.   There are
hundreds where there should be tens; and thousands where there
should be hundreds.   The overcrowding is frightful, it disgusts
every physical and moral sense; and the more so when we see it
as a growing, not a declining, evil.   The numberless displace-
ments, past, present, and to come, fill the poor people, and us too,
with terrors and perplexity.   And, as though this were not enough,
the countless hosts in London ejected from their homes, and endeavouring to find shelter in dwellings already occupied, and abounding with life far beyond every limit of decency, health, and comfort, are encountered by some 40,000 immigrants annually, who
are seeking the same accommodation, and contribute, along with
other causes, to heap family upon family in these bursting
tenements, to lower the rate of wage, and yet raise the rate of
rent, for the great mass of the unskilled labourers.

Is there no remedy for this ?   None that I can see, except a new
fire of London to sweep away all these filthy regions that must be
destroyed to be improved, and then a vast and liberal contribution
from all sorts and sizes of men to erect the city on a basis of
health and humanity.   Four-and-twenty years of experience in
the matter have led me to no practical conclusions on a large
scale.   We have built model lodging-houses; and so far as they
go, they are a blessing to the people.   But "what are they
among so many?"   They yield every return that a mere
philanthropist can desire, but, financially, nothing that could
tempt the large capitalists, who seek a remunerative investment
for their money.   The price, too, of land is rising mightily; and
the great increase of wages among carpenters, masons, and brick-
layers is a very heavy addition to the cost of building, and, by
consequence, to the amount of the rents.   Houses are springing
up around the cities, it is true, but they are altogether for workmen of large weekly receipts.   Suburban villages are proposed
with penny trains, but the objections made to them are endless,
principally by the women, who assign to me very sound and
business-like reasons for refusing to quit their ordinary abodes :
and, indeed, were they to do so, the public weal would be little
served thereby, for the filthy tenements (unless a wholesome

system prevailed to pull down in proportion as you build up) would instantly be seized by a herd of occupants, and all the mischiefs be perpetuated, and probably increased. It is necessary, moreover, that many classes of skilled workmen should have their dwellings within hourly reach of their principal and of each other. To these the suburban village and the penny train are of small use; nor, in truth, to any but those who have fixed hours, fixed places of work, and good and certain wages. To the labourer who lives from hand to mouth, hunting around for a job, hanging about the docks, the yards, the shops, the courts, always uncertain of the amount of his gains, and sometimes uncertain of any receipt at all, " rising early and late taking rest," the railways and the residences are utterly worthless; and yet these classes are the vast majority of the ill-housed population. For these, our model buildings have done nothing, and can do nothing; no one of the schemes hitherto propounded, no one of the bills submitted to Parliament holds out even the shadow of a promise. Suppose it be ordained that tenements shall be built; it follows, of course, that they must be constructed with everything that health and decency requires. But who of this class of the people will be able to meet even the lowest rate of the new weekly payments for family houses? And if constructed on a plan of single rooms— the utmost that these casual labourers are able to afford—we shall perpetuate, by law, a system of life subversive of every moral and physical obligation.

I will refer to but one mode among the many which have been devised for the amelioration of this state of things. A society, of which I am president, has executed several works in the way of the adaptation and conversion of existing tenements. Single houses, or entire courts and alleys have been repaired, whitewashed, and ventilated—drains have been fitted to the main sewers, pavements laid down, and a due supply of water provided. The accommodation, no doubt, is not equal to that which is given by new buildings; but many of the happy issues are obtained by it, and the benefits are effected at about one-seventh of the cost of fresh constructions. This plan, though qualified to effect improvements on a large scale and at a cheap rate, has not, I am sorry to say, found many imitators : but hear the result in a single locality. I had long coveted a court in a sad part of London, because I knew it to be a hot-bed of fever, violence, and immorality. One house alone had produced twenty-two cases of fever in twelve months. At last, by the liberality of a widow lady, I obtained possession of it. The society went to work, and achieved its purpose. Turbulence and disease were banished. The medical man of the district writes, "fever is unknown in this once pestilential court;" the police officers assure us that, whereas in former days the constables never dared to enter it but in twos or threes, they now rarely find it necessary to go there at all. And the whole of this has been done in such a way that the inmates enjoy a vastly increased accommodation, with no increase of rent; and the society receives upon its outlay a return of at least nine per cent.

Such, amidst abundant advantages and blessings, is the social state, in things material, of many of our fellow-subjects.   We need not, however, dwell longer on these details,

> " Quis aut Eurysthea durum,
>  Aut illaudati nescit Busiridis aras ?"

But may we not lift up our eyes a little above the level of laws and regulations, codes and edicts, and see whether there exist not motives of action, motives of universal impulse, of greater power, and more adapted to the wilful individuality of the present times ?  Is there nothing in the human heart, in the human intelligence, in the human consciousness, to which we may appeal, to beget a higher and happier public opinion, in which we might, as it were, " live, and move, and have our being ;" not as a substitute for statutes and enactments, but to inspire, direct, and govern that which statutes and enactments can never reach ?   Is it vain to hope that common sense may, hereafter, exercise, not an absolute, perhaps, but a wider influence among civilized peoples, and teach them that, nationally and internationally, men do not dwell securely, and thrive, by the misery and degradation, but by the welfare and honour of each other ?   It may be vain ; but it is not vain, in gatherings such as these, to proclaim the truth, to discuss its practical character, to cherish and desire it. And yet I am aghast, when I observe that, in all the exhibitions at home and abroad, compounded of the products of the various regions of the earth, rifles and cannons, swords and torpedoes, with the manifold munitions of war, occupy a broad space in the temples professedly devoted to art and science.  I ventured a similar remark at the Statistical Congress of 1862; and the same thought has been stated in the present year by that eminent engineer, Mr. Hawksley, who seems to think that the great bulk of the inventive and mechanical faculty is, for the moment, directed, almost exclusively, to refine and perfect every instrument of destruction.  I do not say this in any craven spirit of submission to foreign nations, or that we should make ourselves naked before our enemies—out upon such a notion !—but simply to express a wish that they would listen to our appeal, and entertain thoughts as far remote as our own from insolence or aggression.

Does the Atlantic Cable teach us nothing? Has a merciful Providence established an intercourse between two nations of the same race, with kindred institutions, and common interests, only that we may hear of "wars and rumours of wars," give, or receive, orders for every military service, hurl defiance at each other, and pervert that which was intended for our peace into an occasion of falling? This mighty result of intellectual and moral power has begun its career with mutual words of congratulation, friendship, thankfulness, and joy. May no other spirit ever pass along its wires; and may "it lead the rest of its life according to this beginning!"

But turn to contemplations more purely national—why are our colonial fellow-subjects, when they visit our shores, nearly strangers in the land, and find not hospitality at every corner? Do we despise their loyalty, depreciate their affection, or shut our eyes to their mighty future? Very far from it. Our neglect is the result of ignorance; and we lose, by listlessness and inattention, the happy means of binding together all regions under her Majesty's rule with a reciprocal esteem and regard, conducive alike to the dignity and freedom of the children, and to the honour and benefit of the mother-country.

But this is applicable, with no less force, to our fellow-subjects from the East. India is making prodigious' strides, not only in material but moral progress. Her sons come hither from every presidency and every province; they enter our colleges, inns of court, and schools of science, in preparation for professional career in their own country. They dash boldly into competitive examination with the European, and not unfrequently carry the day. In sense, justice, policy, in the spirit of Christianity, are these men to be overlooked? Attentions shown to them in England strike a chord that thrills through the whole of Hindostan. Their manners and conversation are graceful, their thoughts high, and their views of the blessings of the British rule sagacious and solid. It is from this rule that they foresee the welfare of their fellow-millions. "Abolish polygamy," said a number, as they stood around me; "educate our women, raise them in the scale of life, and make them what all women should be." I ask you, was not this "social science?" Have we announced, shall we announce, the Gospel alone excepted, a greater truth for the comfort and civilization of mankind?

Surely, we may have a larger sympathy, a demeanour less cold and formal, expressions more genial and cheering, with more of our common nature, towards those who live in our service, or whose labour we employ, or whom among the poorer classes we may visit at their homes, or meet along the road. We read in the book of Ruth that Boaz said to his reapers, "The Lord be with you; and they answered him, The Lord bless thee!" The sentiment may ever be in our hearts, though the practice of it must be regulated by opportunity.

To enunciate, diffuse, and enforce such views, we must look to the aid of the most portentous engine that ever existed, the public press, an engine with such unprecedented capacities for good or evil, that it can hardly be regarded as a simply human power. It is idle, I think, to assert that its influence is less than in former days. The influence of the press, in all its various forms and ramifications, of journals, pamphlets, and periodicals, has increased, is increasing, and can never be diminished. Doubtless social science has some business here; how we may act I cannot say; but what we should desire is to see the press intrusted to the stoutest intellects, the highest morals, and the truest hearts in the country. The spring-tide of self-confident democracy is now nigh at hand; and I see no other hope save this (and it is a feeble one) for national and individual liberty, for external and internal peace, and for the grand, though homely issue of "Live and let live." But the editors of the British journals (and let me include those marvellous men, the body of the reporters) have never been deaf to the claims of humanity and justice, to cries such as those which are sent forth from these halls—nor will they be so now, when we appeal to them to do that which no statutes, no edicts of Privy Council, nor Acts of Parliament can achieve, to reprove, rebuke, exhort, with all vigour and perseverance. Public opinion may lead to good laws, or supersede the necessity of them, and so avoid the abundant variety and complication of enactments which eventually break down, or fall into disuse by their minuteness and extent. Is it not a frightful condition of things that, here in the nineteenth century, we are compelled by disclosures which astonish and shock the inmost conscience, to demand, year by year, of the Legislature, protection for tens of thousands of women and children of the tenderest age, against a system of physical and moral suffering and degradation, such as reduces all past "history to an old almanac?" And is it not frightful when we consider that the vast proportion of these intolerable tribulations to which the children are subjected are in all cases permitted, and in many cases inflicted, by the parents themselves? The law has stepped in and rescued many; the law will again step in and rescue many more; but I tremble, I confess, for the efficiency and permanency of any machinery, that is "cabined, cribbed, confined," by the union of money interests, perverted natures, and the mercenary belief that godliness is gain, and therefore gain must be godliness. Turn your thoughts to the numerous females, some 600,000, engaged in the various departments of dress, from the royal milliner to the most abject sempstress. Their sufferings have oftentimes excited the deepest emotion. Restrictions and regulations are demanded. But in this matter who can invent them? And, if invented, who can enforce them? A more considerate spirit, a more enlarged sympathy, and a profounder and more practical appreciation of "do as you would be done by," would stay the cries of these unhappy victims, and leave our legislators but little to do.

Turn your thoughts also to this fact, and weigh it well. These terrible sorrows, to a great extent, do not spring from the necessities, but from the luxuries, of man; the luxuries not of the rich alone, but of every class from the peer to the labourer. Read the tales of woe of those who toil on the apparel of the wealthier circles; nor omit the records of the needlewomen and the slop-shops; read the almost incredible narratives of all the disease and death that taste and the love of show inflict on children and females in the manufacture of lace, in straw plaiting, in cheap jewellery, in artificial flowers, in button-making, and a hundred other callings. The mass of the people at large, and not a select few, maintain the demand for these adjuncts and embellishments of human life.

I do not say this in a vain hope, or even with a wish to restrict the tendencies of the age and introduce a new science of political economy. I only implore you, in your meditative moments, to reflect how far such things are necessary, and whether by thoughtful and convenient arrangements, while the enjoyments of the consumer will not be stinted, the happiness of the producer may not be very greatly advanced.

It is now time to conclude. But there are some, I fear, who will reply, that I have entered on a high flight of speculation, and have left terrestrial difficulties too far below. Nevertheless, "it is good for us to be here." It is good for murmuring man to see how much of the misery that he suffers, or inflicts, is due to himself, and how little to the decrees of a merciful Creator. It is good for him to see how the principle of self-control is the grand principle of all social and individual freedom; that the sense of responsibility to God and his fellow-man, whether it be in the sovereign on the throne, or the labourer at the plough, is the source of all that is virtuous and dignified, and considerate and true.

Neither is there any hope of attaining excellence, unless our aims be directed by the highest standard. "Be ye, therefore, perfect, even as your Father which is in heaven is perfect." Surely, this was said by our blessed Lord rather to elevate the efforts and the prayers, than to declare the actual powers of fallen man. And have we no guide? When at night we lift up our eyes, and contemplate the peace and splendour of the host of heaven, how each one is conforming to the law of its nature, and, as it were, rejoicing to subserve the universal order, we recognize an omnipotent, yet gentle principle that demands, and receives, a willing and exact obedience. When we turn our thoughts to the globe on which we dwell, we see, in all the works of the great First Cause, the same invariable principle. It ruled at the Creation, has prevailed throughout all time, and will bless the countless ages of eternity. It is the law of kindness and of love, the law that—

> " Lives through all life, extends through all extent,
> Spreads undivided, operates unspent."

Here, then, is the law for our ardent, but humble imitation. It is rich in promise, joyous in operation, and certain as truth itself. Of such a law how can we speak but in the noblest language that ever fell from the pen of uninspired man, "Of this law there can be no less acknowledged, than that her seat is the bosom of God, her voice the harmony of the world: all things in heaven and earth do her homage, the very least, as feeling her care, and the greatest, as not exempted from her power; both angels and men, and creatures of what condition soever, though each in different sort and manner, yet all with uniform consent, admiring her as the mother of their peace and joy." *

* *Hooker's Eccles. Pol. Book I.*

# Refuges for Homeless Children.

WILLIS'S ROOMS, APRIL 11, 1866.

At the anniversary meeting of the " Refuges for Homeless and Destitute Children."
Lord Shaftesbury in the Chair.

THE Chairman prefaced his remarks by saying that he would
not detain the meeting by any lengthy preliminary observations,
because this was not an ordinary anniversary of the refuges in
Great Queen Street and elsewhere, but he had to propound to
them another scheme with the view of extending this good work,
and for the purpose of gathering a greater number of the poor
homeless and destitute children of this great metropolis. Neither
would he detain them by referring to the report, beyond the
remark that, when they came to regard this matter in all its
bearings, and when they came to consider how more than hopeful
was the reclamation of these wandering and wretched children,
when they heard of the great triumph that had been attained,
when they heard of the thousands that had been rescued from
the streets, brought into the home, and taught to obtain an
honest livelihood, and when they considered also that in proportion to their numbers the failures and disappointments had been
so few, they must come also to the conclusion of the vast benefit
of these refuges, and that the work was one which commended
itself to the heart of every good Christian.

He thought, when they looked at the report, and saw what had
been done, and when they considered, in reference to the progress
which this work had made, and how little countenance and
support had been given to it at the outset, they would allow that
some thanks were due to the master mind that instituted and
effected the whole matter; but while his modest and invaluable
friend, Mr. Williams, was reading the report, the meeting would
not have gathered that it was Mr. Williams himself who was the
founder of the refuges, and that it was to his zeal, intelligence,
and activity that their success was mainly due. In this institution
small beginnings had been developed into large operations, and
in laying before them another development of the same system,
he hoped it might be attended with as great success as had

marked all their operations hitherto. What they now purposed
to do was this: they desired to obtain a ship from the government, and have that ship moored in the Thames, and to convert it
into a training ship, where large numbers of these poor destitute
boys might be instructed, with the view of drafting them into
the commercial or royal navies. Now how came this project to
arise? The meeting would no doubt recollect a supper that was
given to these wild, wandering lads, the wandering vultures of
the metropolis, for so he might call them. About 400 boys were
invited; they conformed to the ordinary usages of society, and
were admitted by tickets. About 150 were present, the others
were not present, not because they disregarded the supper, nor
because they had any doubt of his friend, Mr. Williams, but,
as some of the boys themselves explained it afterwards, "We
thought it was a trap." Others, more practical, were afraid that
"they would get lots of jaw and nothing to eat." The object
of this supper was to ascertain from the lads themselves accurate
statements of their natural history, accurate statements of their
own views, and how they lived and how they slept—to obtain, so
far as was possible, an account of their true position in the world.
Only a few preliminary words were required. They answered all
the questions readily and truthfully. "Now, boys, we want you to
tell us the truth; we only desire your good, and you have no need
for concealment." And they heartily promised that if they were
assisted they would do their best to earn an honest livelihood.
The next day from fifty to sixty of these boys presented themselves for admission at the refuges, and Mr. Williams took them
in. Now, hear the first result. They had then been in the
refuge in Great Queen Street since February; and he could say
from personal knowledge of the matter, backed by the assurances
of Mr. Williams and other gentlemen who knew more of it than
himself—although he had attended at the refuge two and three
times in each week—that the conduct of these boys was so
remarkable that nothing but ocular and other unquestionable
testimony could have led him to believe that such an issue could
have been arrived at in so short a period. His friend, Mr.
Williams, would correct him if he were wrong when he stated a
large proportion of these children had neither father nor mother;
many were left with one parent, and that one of a most dissolute
character; they had received no education, some not so much as
that received in an occasional attendance at some night ragged
school. They had been accustomed to sleep in dry arches, in old
iron rollers, or any place in which they could nestle; and many
of the boys were clear in their assertions that for years they had
never been inside a bed. Brought into the refuge, put to study,

and put to work, he (Earl of Shaftesbury) had no hesitation in saying that they were not to be surpassed by any sixty boys in the entire metropolis. They were diligent in the extreme, they went to their employment cheerfully, and, what was more remarkable, they let no foul words escape their lips, and there was no quarrelling among them. It happened one day that the excellent superintendent of the refuge was confined to his bed by an attack of pleurisy; the whole of that large number of boys were in consequence left without any control, excepting the old cobbler, whose post was in a remote corner; and yet when he (the Chairman) went there, without notice, he found them in the greatest order, carrying on their work, going regularly to the schoolmaster with their day's task, and steady in the course of all their operations. Not a single disturbance, not a single act of rebellion, not a single act of misconduct had to be reported, and so well pleased was he (Earl of Shaftesbury) with the conduct of the boys that he called them together, and said to them, "Boys, this is the best thing I have ever seen. We put you here, we gave you a good chance, and now we see that we can trust you;" then a general shout of "Yes, you can." These incidents were stated to prove to them that it was not true, as was sometimes urged, that such lads were utterly incorrigible, and must be left to the ordinary operations of the law. Only introduce, he proceeded, the great law of human love and kindness, and more good will be effected than by any other agency, and the service rendered to these poor little outcasts would be a good measure pressed down and running over. No doubt they had all read the experiences of an "Amateur Casual." They would recollect a character in that history who was called "Punch," a terror to the whole place, "prigging" the casuals' clothes, and gibing and chaffing every one. "Punch" was denounced by every one as incorrigible, but "Punch" was an inmate of the refuge, and "Punch" was equal in intelligence, activity, and obedience to any of the other boys. "'Punch,' my boy," he said to him one day, "will you be a man?" "Yes, sir." "Will you set a good example?" "Yes, sir." "Punch" kept his word, and being older than the rest, became a model to his comrades.*

Now, the proposition he had to bring before this meeting was, that a ship should be moored in the Thames, for the purpose of receiving a greater number of these wild lads. It was not necessary to enter into the various propositions for the general treatment of these boys at certified industrial schools. He was not prepared to say one word against these institutions; he only

---

* This lad is now gone out on emigration, full of honesty and diligence.

regretted that there did not exist a sufficient number of them. The principle on which these schools were conducted was not one suited to the work they had in hand. A magistrate by committing a lad to one of these certified industrial schools destroyed the whole pith and the whole spirit of the voluntary principle, which induced the boys to come to these refuges. The great secret of the success of these refuges was the voluntary principle upon which they were founded; the boys were not forced, they came of their own accord, and this accounted for the self-imposed order and good conduct that generally prevailed in them. Take a society called the Marine Society, which was carried on pretty nearly for the same purpose as that proposed for their training-ship. He (Earl of Shaftesbury) had no doubt of its being a most excellent establishment, but its rules were very stringent. To obtain admission to it certain conditions were to be complied with, one of which demanded the boy to produce the certificate of his father's death—an utter impossibility in the case of many of them, seeing that they had lost their parents while very young, and before they had reached an age to enable them to understand the nature of these events. To provide then these for outcasts there was the simple proposal for a training-ship. And why a ship? For this reason; a ship could be obtained and kept in order at a much less expense than the hire of houses or large rooms, at very high rents, to accommodate 400 boys. Again, the directors would have more influence over the boys when away from the streets and afloat on the water, and such an abode would be more beneficial to the health of the boys themselves. But here came another reason, and one too of the very greatest importance. There could not be any doubt existing in the public mind as to the great necessity in our commercial and naval services of a number of well-trained and good-disciplined lads, as the stock of our future seamen, and such lads would thus furnish a supply to the two services. Was it not a fact that a great portion of our ships left our ports manned by crews for the most part foreigners? Was it not a fact that on board the ill-fated ship, the "London," there were no fewer than forty Dutchmen in the crew, of whom it had been said that as soon as the storm began these men went below and got into their hammocks? Would that have been the case if the crew had been composed of well-trained and properly-disciplined English sailors? Would they not have stood fast to their work in the hour of peril? This training-ship would improve the tone of our naval services, and introduce a class of well-trained lads who had chosen for themselves a life on the water.

Take another consideration—look for a moment at the awful

number of wrecks that annually take place on all our coasts. The loss of property by these wrecks every year was estimated at not less than 4,000,000*l.*, in addition to a sacrifice of from 2,000 to 3,000 able-bodied men. A very great proportion of these wrecks arose from the ignorance or the indiscipline or the inability of the crews. Were it possible to introduce a better class of sailors into the services, what an enormous amount of property would be saved to this country! The property, perhaps, they could afford to lose; but how afford to lose 2,000 or 3,000 able-bodied men every year? who might be a defence to their country in the hour of need, and whose loss will never be estimated until the day when it cannot be supplied. They must, moreover, be aware that in the life of a sailor none made such good sailors as those who had a predilection for the sea. A man, if he had been forced to sea, whether he were an officer or a seaman, seldom turned out a real man to the service; his thoughts were always elsewhere; and, in fact, he was more fit for any service than the one he had been placed in. Now, it did so happen that these lads had a great predilection for the water,—they had a positive affinity for it; and, he would undertake to say, if any one were to visit those boys, and ask them what calling they would like best, a great majority of them would reply " why, go to sea." Others of the lads might emigrate to distant settlements, and the instruction given them on board the ship would not, in that case, be thrown away. It was of great importance to the welfare of Great Britain that those who emigrated to her Majesty's colonies should be men of good character and well disciplined. It brought credit to the country; and late events had convinced them that the greater the number of good emigrants the Canadians could get, the greater would be the blessings that would accrue to us and also to the settlers in that colony.

He thought he had so far succeeded in placing clearly before them the object the Committee had in view. The government had given them a ship, but it was given on the consideration that the society should bear the whole expenses of fitting it up and keeping it in proper repair. The cost of fitting up the ship would be about 3,000*l.*, and the sum required for its proper maintenance would be about 6,000*l.* a-year, so with this sum annually, and with 3,000*l.* to start with, they believed they would be able to accommodate at all times 400 boys, and prepare 200 in every year for the commercial and royal navies.

He (Earl of Shaftesbury) knew that this was a good sum of money, and he knew also that persons now-a-days were apt to regard everything in a commercial aspect, and were anxious to get the best interest for the money which they had expended;

but he must add that, if this question were considered in a commercial aspect, it had many things to recommend it. Was it no return to know that every year there would be the means of rescuing from the violence, cruelty, and crime of the metropolis, 200 destitute lads? It was not in their power to abolish all the vice and misery of London; but it was in their power to greatly limit the operation and power of crime by addressing themselves to the juvenile population. The meeting had smiled just now when he spoke to them about "Punch," and they might smile still more when he told them that he propounded the following question to one hundred thieves. He asked them, if societies such as this could only get hold of the large mass of the juvenile population of London, and place them under a system analogous to that which they proposed to inaugurate that day, what would be the effect produced on their profession? The answer given by each declared that a work like that would strike a heavy blow and great discouragement to their calling; that it would destroy the seedplot of the rising generation of young marauders. This happy result would be partially attained by the adoption of the proposition which he had laid before them, and which would only involve an expenditure of 3,000*l.* at starting, and an annual income of 6,000*l.* With this income they would be able to supply the commercial and royal navies with two hundred lads each year, and enable them always to accommodate four hundred boys in the homes. Whether the proposition would succeed he could not venture to predicate; he was sure it was a proper object for their attention, and one that commended itself to the heart of every one. He knew that there were already many calls upon the charitable, and he knew also that many contributed to religious and charitable works, not only according to their means, but beyond their means. But he appealed to that large body who had grown rich by the advancement and increasing prosperity of the country, and who never contributed of their wealth to any purpose beyond their own enjoyment. He asked them to deliberate whether they would not extend a helping hand to some of these castaways from all hope of a comfortable or decent life. It was stated the aggregate private income of this country now exceeded annually 500,000,000*l.*, and it was to the holders of this immense wealth that he now made his appeal, and he did so by all the claims of religion, of Christian charity, and upon personal, political, and social interests. He trusted the response would be a liberal one; but whether they succeeded or not, the committee and Mr. Williams would have the satisfaction of knowing that though they had not achieved the good they had sought, they had at least made a great and noble effort.

# Homeless Boys of London.

BLACKWALL, TUESDAY, DECEMBER 18, 1866.

Delivered at the inauguration ceremony of the " Chichester " Training Ship.

NOTE. This speech will be better understood if prefaced by a short extract from the statement previously read to the meeting by Mr. Williams, the Secretary to the Refuges for Homeless Boys.

My Lord, Ladies, and Gentlemen, in consequence of certain revelations made by a gentleman who spent a night in a casual ward of one of the London workhouses, where boys of tender age were found mixing with the vilest men that could be found in the kingdom, it was deemed advisable that an effort should be made to rescue these juveniles from the contaminating influences of these casual wards. On the 14th February an invitation was given to the boys accustomed to sleep in the casual wards of London, and other nightly haunts, to come to supper at the Boys' Refuge, Great Queen Street. Nearly 200 accepted the invitation, and the meeting will not soon be forgotten by those who came to see and hear. After supper the boys were assembled in an upper room of the refuge. The hearts of the spectators were much moved at the forlorn spectacle before them, and many friends were so touched at the sad condition of these immortal beings that it was impossible with some to restrain their tears, while other ladies and gentlemen then present were seen making every possible effort to prevent their feelings being manifest. Quietness being gained, the noble Chairman, the Earl of Shaftesbury, questioned the lads in a kind and affectionate manner, with a view to ascertain their mode of life, and what could be done for their future welfare. Among other questions put by the noble Lord the following was one—If a ship were moored in the Thames, how many of you would be willing to go on board? In an instant a shower of hands went up, to signify that they were all willing to avail themselves of that opening. As a practical matter resulting from the supper, nearly sixty of the boys were received into the refuge within a week from that time; but the applications for admission were so numerous week by week that a determination was come to to make an effort to provide for 400 of these poor boys. The scheme was this:—1. To retain 100 boys in the refuge in Queen Street; 2. To establish a

" training-ship," where at least 200 more boys might be educated and trained to a seafaring life; 3. To hire or purchase a country home, with from 60 to 100 acres of land, where 100 more boys might be trained to agricultural pursuits. Shortly after the supper the Earl of Shaftesbury applied to the Lords of the Admiralty for a ship to be used as a training school; and after a correspondence with the authorities of the Admiralty, under the late and present government, as to the completing and fitting up of the ship for the purpose for which it was to be used, it was finally agreed that the hull of the vessel in which we are so comfortably housed to-day should be handed over to the committee, and that they should be allowed to draw from the dockyard masts, sails, and other stores required for completing and fitting up the ship, to the value of 2,129*l.* 15*s.* 8*d.*, the committee undertaking to pay that amount in nine months' time. This was the only arrangement which could be made at that time; but it is hoped that Sir John Pakington will, on the meeting of Parliament, use his influence to relieve the committee from the payment to the government of this sum of 2,000*l.* When the committee obtained possession of the ship, in October last, they lost no time in getting the works in hand; and it is their very pleasing duty here publicly to mention that immediately the matter was laid before Mr. Henry Green, that gentleman, in his usual generous and benevolent way, at once kindly offered to do all the work required to complete and fit up the ship at cost price. For this benevolent act the committee are most grateful, and beg thus publicly to tender him their warmest thanks. The committee also beg to tender their sincere thanks to W. M. Bullivant, Esq., for certain parts of the rigging supplied by him at cost price. The vessel is now complete, and we are gathered here to-day to inaugurate her as a training-ship for the homeless and destitute boys of London, and to seek the Divine blessing on this noble effort, which must be looked upon as one of a national character, for whether it is viewed as a means for rescuing the waifs and strays of this great metropolis, or as a means for supplying the diminution of seamen so generally felt in every port of our country, the work which is established this day must prove beneficial to the country at large; and when it is remembered that this is the first training-ship established in the River Thames for this class of boys within the present century, the committee cannot but be thankful to Almighty God that they have been the humble instruments in setting on foot so great a work. There are at the present time 160 boys in the refuge. From this number fifty have been selected as the first members of the happy family who shall take possession of this new home. Fifty more could easily be added to the number from the present inmates of the refuge, but until the funds for the maintenance of the boys are contributed, the committee feel they must not increase their number beyond fifty, as it is their wish to avoid getting into debt, even though it be for the food and clothing of these poor homeless boys. But the committee have every confidence that this effort will be thoroughly appreciated by the public, and especially by all who are interested in keeping up our naval and merchant services, and they trust that it will not be long before the committee have funds subscribed to support the 200 boys for whom provision is made in this vessel. The boys will be under the control of the commander, Captain A. H. Alston, R.N., a gentleman of great experience and of sincere Christian principles; and every care will be taken that the lads will not only be initiated in all that is necessary to fit them for a seafaring life, but the religious and secular instruction they will receive will be of that character, and that only, which will fit them for performing their duty to God and their duty to their fellow-men. As soon as the ship leaves this dock, which will be shortly, she will be taken down to Greenhithe, and there moored, that being the spot appointed for her destination. The committee had hoped they would have been able to have established the " Country Home " for 100 boys as well as this ship, but at present nothing has been definitely settled on this point for want of funds. One gentleman has promised 1,000*l.* if the scheme can be carried out. In conclusion, the committee would just mention they are not expending all their energies on boys. The wants of destitute girls are ever before them. Besides the Boys' Refuge in Great Queen Street and this training-ship, the committee support two homes for girls, each containing 40 inmates, and they trust that these helpless ones will not be forgotten this Christmas. In addition to all the refuge operations the committee manage and support five day and six night ragged schools, wherein upwards of 1,000 poor children receive gratuitous education. The committee, therefore, earnestly appeal for funds for the ship as well as all the other works of usefulness they have in hand.

The noble Chairman then said that it being so very desirable these proceedings should be brought to an early close, he should confine himself to an expression of his delight and gratitude at seeing so large an assembly on the present occasion, notwithstanding the distance from London and the time of the year. He thought it betokened a great amount of sympathy and feeling; and he could only pray to God that that sympathy and feeling might be reduced to practice, and that it might favour and support this institution through all the difficulties and trials which it would have to encounter. The statement made by his friend Mr. Williams—and here let him say that the name should remind them how deeply they all were indebted to the talent, the energy, the principle, and the indefatigable zeal of that gentleman—the statement which that gentleman had made had sufficiently explained to them the origin and purpose of this institution. He would only just support it by his own experience in saying that what Mr. Williams had asserted as to the character of these lads, the condition in which they had found them, and the condition of mind and body in which they were now, was within the mark; and he (Earl of Shaftesbury) did not hesitate to say that the movement which they were making was by no means an experiment; the thing was a positive certainty. It had already been proved that if they would take out of the streets of London all these homeless, most friendless, and most destitute lads, polish them gently, and apply the hand of skill and affection, they would turn out to be diamonds—and diamonds, too, as clear and as bright as had ever adorned the most splendid crown. Let them look at these boys;

some of them were now present. He did not like generally to praise a lad to his face; but here he must speak out the truth, because it was an argument in their favour, and in favour of this institution. The Committee took these boys from the streets indiscriminately, from the very haunts of crime and misery—they took them at hap-hazard, some sixty, seventy, or eighty a day. These boys, before coming to them, were living in the midst of sin —they did nothing but pilfer, and live by their thefts. What had they made them? They had, by God's blessing, made them the reverse to what they formerly were. He (Earl of Shaftesbury) said without fear or hesitation that 160 boys never came together who were so docile, so happy, so industrious, and so full of promise, as those on whose behalf they appealed that day. Therefore let him repeat that this was no experiment—it was a positive certainty; let them prove it by gathering in these boys from the lanes and alleys of their crowded city, let them take this waste humanity under their fostering care, and they would be found to reply to all the efforts put forth in their behalf, and they would grow up to reflect honour on the blessed old mother-country. He would not enter into the assertions, called arguments, used against this institution, for there were really no such things as arguments against it. There was a great deal of argumentation, but that was quite a different thing. Nevertheless, persons had been found to raise objection against this institution, and it was said that resort must be had to the industrial and certified schools. Now, if objectors would show him where these schools were, in number sufficient for a population near upon three millions, he would willingly consider the question; but after a minute search, and after applying every microscope, they could find but two industrial schools in the whole of London. Well, whenever the industrial schools were to be found in adequate force to meet the wants of the population, then he (Earl of Shaftesbury) would discuss their merits or demerits—but at the present time, while others were deliberating, shall we not act? While others were deliberating and considering what were the best means to remedy the evil, would they not do all in their power to provide a home and education, and a means of livelihood to these homeless and destitute children, and thus be the means, under God's grace, of saving many souls from death, and many bodies from misery? He (Earl of Shaftesbury) must confess that he could not speak without indignation of what he had read in a letter addressed to the *Times* newspaper, coming as it did from an official and Government Inspector, who of all men should be the most careful in ascertaining the truth

of what he said. He (Earl of Shaftesbury) found a Government
Inspector coming forward in opposition to this movement, and
making a statement such as he had read in the *Times*, and he
did not hesitate to say that it was a false and abominable calumny.
This gentleman argued that these refuges were not entitled to
support, inasmuch as they took no care of the children after they
left their roof. Was that so? He asked him to name the refuge
where this was the case. Was it so with the one with which his
friend, Mr. Williams, was connected? Was it not rather a fact—
and he (Earl of Shaftesbury) would answer for all the refuges
and ragged schools with which he was connected—that the care
exhibited for the children, not only while within the schools, but
when they had left their roof, was that of a tender, solicitous, and
high-principled parent? When these boys left the schools it was
not true that they took no further care of them—they did what
they could for them. in the way of getting them situations, and
they encouraged them to come to them at any time for their
advice and support; they did, in fact, everything they could, and
so long as they were able, within the short term of human power,
they watched these poor boys, as it were, from their cradle to
their grave. They might ask, perhaps, why had they chosen this
mode of educating these boys—why train them for a seafaring
life? His answer was, that wherever they went—from the banks
of the Thames to the furthest northern point of the metropolis—
if they only put the question to one of these ragged and forsaken
lads whether he would like to go to sea, he would invariably
answer, " Yes, that I should; it is just what I want above other
things." On the occasion to which their secretary had alluded,
when he put this question to the boys, they did not merely
put up one but two hands, so anxious were they to show their
willingness to be on the water. That was the first reason why
they had suggested this mode of education—the hearts of these
boys seemed set on a seafaring life; and it was the truth that
without a boy set his heart upon the sea he would never turn out
to be a good sailor. And, moreover, old sailors would tell them
that if a boy once set his heart upon a seafaring life he would do
but very little good at anything else. Again, he held it to be a
matter of vital importance to the welfare of this country that they
should have a supply of good, intelligent, and well-conducted boys
for both the royal and mercantile marine. The royal navy could,
in a great measure, take care of itself; but their mercantile
marine needed great improvement, and this improvement could
only be effected by their merchant ships being manned by men who

would submit to discipline, and who were possessed of the principle of self-control. Let them look at the number of wrecks every year upon our coasts, and out on the open seas; and he had no hesitation in saying that 99 cases of every 100—and he said this, he believed, in the presence of shipowners and ship-captains—arose out of the indiscipline and the drunkenness of the men. Was it not a scandal and a disgrace to the honour of this great maritime power, whose sole security and only defence was in its navy?— was it not, he asked, a shame that the largest proportion of our mercantile marine should consist of foreign sailors? It was desirable, and essentially necessary, that they should do all in their power to provide fit men to man their ships—men of intelligence, men of good discipline, men of good conduct, and men who would value everything that was dear to an Englishman—the common defence of his territory and the character of his institutions. But it was not sufficient that they should be simply aware of the importance of having such a class of men as he had described for their mercantile marine; they ought to do something to obtain this class; and from this ship they might supply this part of the service with 200 boys every year, fully capable of undertaking the duties, and gathered from the wandering lads of London. They must, moreover, also look well to the conduct, the character, and the principle of the shipowners. They must see that the ships to which these boys were consigned were provided with due accommodation, and that there was everything necessary for the health and morality of the men. It was absolutely necessary that these two things should go together, if they wanted to improve the character of the mercantile marine. He (Earl of Shaftesbury) could foresee the time, notwithstanding the great and present difficulties, notwithstanding the vast multitudes that throng around, and which must make us stand aghast to view the amount of misery and crime that now abounds in the midst of us, he could foresee the time when by the application of zeal, and the multiplication of institutions like this, the population of England, instead of becoming a curse, would become a blessing. And it would also be proved that, with our millions of people, there were none too many for all the necessities of this great country. And, above all, they would give a sound, religious, Christian education to these boys, who would be sent to all ports and harbours of the world, by their good conduct removing whatever was now a blot upon the honour and name of the country. Instead of bringing drunkenness, disorder, and disgrace into our navy, our vessels would in future be manned by intelligent, well-conducted, and good-disciplined men—the character of the English sailor would no longer be such that it should be said of him that he was of all those afloat by far the most profligate. The boys educated on board this ship would show quite the reverse of this; they would show to the whole earth what the British nation really was, and what it would continue to be; and they would enable us to repeat with certainty, with joy, and with assurance, the words of the hymn that had just been heard:

> " Through every land, by every tongue,
> Let the Redeemer's name be sung."

## Clerical Vestments Bill.

## HOUSE OF LORDS,

TUESDAY, MAY 14, 1867.

THE Earl of Shaftesbury.—In rising to move the second reading of the bill which is now before your Lordships, I think
there is no occasion for me to remind the House of the necessity
that exists for passing some measure on this subject.    The
question has been so long before the public, and has given rise
to so much agitation throughout the country—we have had so
many remedies proposed for the evils that exist in connexion
with this matter by the clergy, the bishops, and the laity, that I
think it must be apparent to every person that some remedy
must be adopted to check certain practices that are now prevalent.
It has been stated that I have been somewhat hasty in this
matter.  But, my Lords, this is a matter which has been long
considered by the country.  I have long had it before me.  I
propounded this measure to your Lordships in the month of
March, and it is now the 14th of May before we come to the
second reading.  Subsequently to my propounding it, it was
proposed that a Commission should issue to take into consideration all matters connected with Ritualistic practices; nevertheless,
I thought it my duty to persevere with the measure.  I offer no
impediment to the Commission; but there happens to be one part
of Ritualistic practice which has created so much alarm and
dissatisfaction among the community, which has so disturbed
men's minds and consciences, that I am of opinion that no delay
ought to be allowed to intervene before the matter is discussed,
and some remedy at least attempted.  Now, the remedy I wish to
propose is not by introducing any innovation.  What I maintain
is, that these Ritualistic practices are a great innovation on the
system and conduct of the Church.  Yet I do not meet innovation
by innovation, and so make matters worse.  I wish to see the

usage and practice of the Church ever since the period of the Reformation, which has been sanctioned by experience, which has given contentment and satisfaction to our forefathers, our fathers, and ourselves—I wish to see that usage embodied in an Act of Parliament, and that statutory effect may be given to the usage of this country which has now subsisted for more than 300 years. To effect this purpose, I take the spirit and, in great measure, the words of the 58th Canon, and engraft them on the bill now before your Lordships. Although there may be a slight alteration in the words, yet in principle and details the spirit of the canon is preserved.

It will be my duty, I fear, to detain your Lordships by reading a certain amount of documentary evidence, because I am anxious to prove that the law and authorities are on our side, from the Reformation down to the present day—to justify the course I pursue, and show that what I propose to enact has been the law of the Church of England, recognised in past times by all her great prelates and divines, recognised at the present moment by the two Houses of Convocation, and, I believe, by the great body of the clergy. To show that what I propose has been the law of the Church from the earliest period, I must first recite the rubric in the second Prayer Book of Edward VI., of 1552:—

" And here it is to be noted that the minister at the time of Communion, and at all other times of his ministration, shall use neither alb, vestment, nor cope; but, being archbishop or bishop, he shall have and wear a rochet; and being a priest or deacon, he shall have and wear a surplice only." (" Liturgies of Edward VI., Parker Society Ed.," P. 217.)

This was the statute law of the Church, as enacted by Cranmer, Ridley, and other Protestant martyrs. In the time of Queen Mary the statute was repealed; but on the accession of Elizabeth power was given to her Majesty to issue advertisements that should have the nature of law. In 1564 Strype says (" 3 Strype's Parker," P. 65):—

" The Advertisements arose in this way : the Queen directed her letter this year (1564), in the month of January, to her Archbishop, requiring him, with other Bishops in the Commission for Causes Ecclesiastical, that orders might be taken, whereby all diversities and varieties among the clergy and laity, as breeding nothing but contention and breach of common charity, might be reformed and repressed, and brought to one manner of uniformity throughout the realm."

The result was that in 1565 Queen Elizabeth issued her Advertisements in respect of the ornaments of the ministers, one of which ("Sparrow's Articles," 124) was as follows:—

"That every minister saying any public prayers or ministering the Sacrament, or other rites of the Church, shall wear a comely surplice with sleeves, to be provided at the charge of the parish."

Now follows the recognition (and it is worthy of great attention) by the prelates in their Injunctions and Visitation Articles, that the surplice was the only dress of the minister between the time of the issuing of the Advertisements of Queen Elizabeth and the passing of the Canons of 1604. Parker, in his Visitation Articles in 1569 ("1 Cardwell, Doc. Ann.," 356), inquires :—

"Item, whether your priests, curates, or ministers do use in the time of the celebration of Divine service to wear a surplice prescribed by the Queen's Majesty's Injunctions, and the Book of Common Prayer, and whether they do celebrate the same Divine Service in the Chancel or in the Church, and do use all rites and orders prescribed in the Book of Common Prayer, &c., and *none other*."

Sandys, Bishop of London, in his Injunctions, 1570, orders the clergy in all Divine service to wear the surplice. Grindal, Archbishop of York, in his Injunctions for the province in 1571, directs ("2 Strype's Annals," 6) the clergy—

"At all times when ye minister the Holy Sacrament . . . . and other Divine service in your parish churches and chapels, ye shall when ye minister wear a clean and decent surplice with large sleeves."

At the same Visitation, Archbishop Grindal orders the churchwardens and ministers to see that—

"All vestments, albs, tunicles, stoles, phanons, pyxes, paxes, hand-bells, sacring bells, censers, chrismatories, crosses, candlesticks, holy water, stocks, fats, images, and all other monuments of superstition and idolatry, be utterly defaced, broken, and destroyed." ("Grindal's Remains," 124.)

Again, the Archbishop, in his Metropolitical Visitation in 1576, inquires—

"Whether you have in your parish churches and chapels all things requisite for the common prayer and administration of the sacraments, specially the Book of Common Prayer with the new calendar, . . . . and a large decent surplice with sleeves. Whether all and every antiphoners, mass books, . . . . all vestments, albs,

&c. . . . . be utterly defaced, broken, and destroyed? Whether your pastor do wear any cope in any parish church or chapel?" (Pp. 157—9.)

Now, observe, my Lords, that here another authority interposes —the authority of the University. Dr. Caius, in 1572, was charged at his College with Romanizing. Strype ("1 Strype's Parker," 399) says—

"For that he had a kindness it appears in his private reservation of abundance of Popish trumpery, which he might think could come in play again; and so that, out of good husbandry, preserved them to save the College the charge of buying new furniture for the chapel. But, in the year 1572, all came out, for the fame hereof coming to the ears of Sandys, Bishop of London, he wrote earnestly to Dr. Byng, Vice-Chancellor, to see those superstitious things abolished. Byng could hardly have been persuaded that such things had been by him reserved; but, causing Caius's own company to make search in that College, he received an inventory of much Popish ware, as vestments, albs, tunicles, stoles, manicles, with other such stuff as might have furnished divers masters at one instant. It was thought good by the whole consent of the heads of the houses to burn the books and such other things as served most for idolatrous abuses, and caused the rest to be defaced, which was accomplished the 13th of December, 1572, with the willing hearts, as it appeared, of the whole company of that house."

My Lords, I continue the episcopal testimony. Archbishop Whitgift, in 1584, required—

" That all preachers and others in ecclesiastical orders do at all times wear and use such kind of apparel as is prescribed unto them by the Book of Advertisements and her Majesty's Injunction." ("1 Cardwell Doc. Ann.," 468.)

In the same year, in the Visitation Articles for the diocese of Chichester (*sede vacante*), he asks—

" Doth your minister in public prayer wear a surplice, and go abroad apparelled as by her Majesty's Injunctions and Advertisements is prescribed?" (" Strype's Whitgift," 243.)

Piers, Archbishop of York, in 1590, follows, and (Robertson 97) asks—

" Whether all copes, vestments, albs, tunicles, . . . . and such like reliques of Popish superstition and idolatry be utterly destroyed and defaced?"

Now, my Lords, I request you to observe the agreement between the Canons of 1571 and the Canons of 1604. The Canons of 1571 and the Canons of 1604 recognise the surplice with the hood as the only dress for the minister during the time of public prayers, being in strict accordance—let not this escape attention—with the second Prayer Book of Edward VI. and the Advertisements of Queen Elizabeth. The Canons of 1571 contain the following order :—

" No dean, nor archdeacon, nor residentiary, nor master, nor warden, nor head of any college or collegiate church, neither president nor rector, nor any of that order, by what name soever they be called, shall hereafter wear the gray amice, or any other garment which hath been defiled with like superstition; but every one of them in his own church shall wear only that linen garment which is as yet retained by the Queen's command, and also his scholar's hood, according to every man's calling and degree in school." (" 1 Cardwell, Synodalia," 115, ed. 1842.)

And Canon 58 of Canons of 1604, which is embodied in the bill, requires—

" That every minister saying the public prayers or ministering the sacraments or other rites of the Church, shall wear a decent and comely surplice with sleeves, to be provided at the charge of the parish. And if any question arise touching the matter, decency, or comeliness thereof, the same shall be decided by the discretion of the ordinary. Furthermore, such ministers as are graduates shall wear upon their surplices, at such times, such hoods as by the orders of the Universities are agreeable to their degrees, which no minister shall wear being no graduate, under pain of suspension. Notwithstanding, it shall be lawful for such ministers as are not graduates to wear upon their surplices, instead of hoods, some decent tippet of black, so it be not silk."

This canon, my Lords, is essentially the same as the rubric in the second Prayer Book of Edward VI. and the Advertisements of Elizabeth, and in strict accordance with the Injunctions and Visitation Articles issued by the Archbishops and Bishops since the passing of the second Act of Uniformity of Edward VI. Let me now draw your attention to the recognition by prelates of the use of the surplice after the Canons of 1604, and before the enactment of the present Prayer Book in 1662.

Bishop Cosin, in 1627, inquired in the articles for the Archidiaconal Visitation of that year, whether—

" The minister doth observe all the orders, rites, and cere-

monies prescribed in the Book of Common Prayer in such manner
and form only as is there enjoined, without any omission, or
addition, or alteration whatsoever? (He was not a Bishop at the
time.) Whether in the time of public and Divine service, . . . .
and at all other times of his ministration, when any Sacrament
be administered, or any other rite or ceremony of the Church
solemnized, use and wear the surplice without any excuse or
pretence whatever; and doth he never omit the same?" ("2
Cosin's Work," 19.)

Observe, now, the recognitions by prelates of the use of the
surplice after the enactment of our present Prayer Book. Bishop
Cosin, in his Visitation, October, 1662—I may here observe that
this eminent Bishop is ranked by all as among the very highest
authorities of the Anglican Church—the Bishop—

" Requires the surplice to be worn with the habit by the
ministers at the reading or celebrating any Divine office; and
asks whether the lecturer read service, and that in a surplice;
and whether, in lecturing, he used the ecclesiastical habit appointed for all ministers of the Church."

Archdeacon Harrison (on the " Rubrics," 175) has the following
note upon the word " habit :"—" This is obviously the gown." To
proceed, Archbishop Frewen, in 1662, in his Visitation Articles
for the diocese and province of York, asks, " Have you a decent
surplice for your parson, vicar, curate, or lecturer, to wear in the
time of public ministration? Doth he read the Book of Common
Prayer, &c., and doth he wear the surplice while he performs that
office, or other offices mentioned in the Book of Common Prayer?"
In 1670, Laney, Bishop of Lincoln, in his Visitation Articles,
inquires, " Doth your minister, at the reading or celebrating any
Divine office in your church or chapel, wear the surplice, together
with such scholastic habit as is suitable to his degree?" And, in
1674, Bishop Fuller, the successor of Bishop Laney, makes the
like inquiry as his predecessor. In 1670, Archbishop Sheldon
requires of his clergy " an exemplary conformity in their own
persons and practice to his Majesty's laws and the rules of the
Church, . . . . and that in the time of such their officiating they
ever make use of and wear their priestly habit, the surplice and
hood." (" 2 Cardwell, Loc. Ann.," 328.) Dr. Owtram, Archdeacon
of Leicester, inquires, in 1676, " Have you a large surplice for the
use of your minister in his public administrations?" And, in
1679, Bishop Barlow in his Visitation Articles of the diocese of
Lincoln, inquires, " Have you a fair surplice for the minister to
wear at all times of his public ministration provided at the charge

of the parish, and doth he make use of the surplice when he reads Divine service or administers the sacrament?" ("Harrison," 178.)

And here, my Lords, I ask you, can we have a more uniform, more connected "catena patrum"—(catena is the word, I believe, in the present day) than this which I have just concluded?

But I will now call attention to what has taken place in more modern times, in reference to the dress of the ministers. In the Lower House of the Convocation of the Province of York the following resolution, seconded by the Dean of Ripon in a powerful speech, was adopted in March of the present year:—

"Whereas certain vestments and ritual observances have recently been introduced into the services of the Church of England, this House desires to place on record its deliberate opinion that these innovations are to be deprecated, as tending to favour errors rejected by that Church, and as being repugnant to the feelings of a large number of the laity and clergy; and this House is further of opinion that it is desirable that the dress of a minister in public prayer, and the administration of the sacraments and other rites of the Church, should continue to be the surplice, academical hood (or tippet for non-graduates), and the scarf or stole, these having received the sanction of long-continued usage." ("Dean Goode's Speech in Convocation.")

This resolution was passed unanimously by the Upper House, and was carried by 23 to 7 in the Lower House.

And here I think it right to bring under your Lordships' notice a declaration of the American Bishops, in March, 1867—the testimony of the Episcopal Church in the United States, identical in creed and discipline with our own. Your Lordships will not fail to see the value of it. The declaration of the assembled bishops is as follows :—

"And we, therefore, consider that in this particular national Church, any attempt to introduce into the public worship of Almighty God usages that have never been known—such as the use of incense, and the burning of lights in the order for the Holy Communion; reverences to the Holy Table or to the elements thereon, such as indicate or imply that the sacrifice of our Divine Lord and Saviour, 'once offered,' was not a 'full, perfect, and sufficient sacrifice, oblation, and satisfaction for the sins of the whole world;' the adoption of clerical habits hitherto unknown, or material alterations of those which have been in use since the establishment of our episcopate—is an innovation which violates the discipline of the Church, 'offendeth against its common order, and hurteth the authority of the magistrate, and woundeth the consciences of the weak brethren.' "

I will now close this part of the subject by reading to your Lordships the opinion of the Province of Canterbury. The resolution passed by the Upper House of the Southern Convocation in February last stands thus :—

" Resolved,—That having taken into consideration the report made to this House by the Lower House, concerning certain ritual observances, we have concluded that, having regard to the dangers (1) of favouring errors deliberately rejected by the Church of England, and fostering a tendency to desert her communion; (2) of offending, even in things indifferent, devout worshippers in our churches, who have been long used to other modes of service, and thus of estranging many of the faithful laity; (3) of unnecessarily departing from uniformity; (4) of increasing the difficulties which prevent the return of separatists to our communion—we convey to the Lower House our unanimous decision that, having respect to the considerations here recorded, and to the rubric concerning the service of the Church in our Book of Common Prayer, to wit,—' Forasmuch as nothing can be so plainly set forth but doubts may arise in the use and practice of the same, to appease all such diversity (if any arise), and for the resolution of all doubts concerning the manner how to understand, do, and execute the things contained in this book, the parties that so doubt, or diversely take anything, shall always resort to the Bishop of the diocese, who, by his discretion, shall take order for the quieting and appeasing of the same, so that the same order be not contrary to anything contained in this book; and if the Bishop of the diocese be in doubt, then he may send for the resolution thereof to the Archbishop '—our judgment is, that no alterations from long-sanctioned and usual ritual ought to be made in our churches until the sanction of the Bishop of the diocese has been obtained thereto." (" Dean Goode's Remarks," &c.)

This resolution is quoted to show the opinions entertained by the prelates of the impropriety and danger of these Ritualistic observances, not by any means in approval of the remedy they propose. And I now come to the bill, which I ask your Lordships to read a second time. The object of the measure is simply, as I have said before, to give statutory effect to the principle of the Canon of 1604, which has had the effect of governing the system of the Establishment from that time to the present, and of securing peace and harmony among our communion. I do not know what objections are entertained to the bill, beyond two or three unimportant criticisms. The first is that the bill touches but one point. That is true, and the reason is because it is the only point on which there is really any legal doubt. There is no doubt about incense, lights, and other points, but there is a doubt about vestments; and therefore it is the subject to which the attention of Parliament should be more immediately drawn. It is the one point which of all others most disturbs and alarms the minds of the laity, which is the most prominent, which strikes the eyes with the greatest force, and goes the deepest into the hearts and convictions of the people. This is the reason why I thought that no time should be lost in submitting a bill on the subject to your Lordships; and, should your Lordships not think proper to adopt it, some other measure might be proposed more acceptable to the House. The next objection is one taken to the provisions of the bill. I have received numerous letters in reference to the measure; but I do not think the objections expressed in any of them go beyond mere matters of the smallest detail. Great care has been taken, in preparing the bill, to make nothing lawful or unlawful which is not so at present. Any alterations as to matters of detail can be made in the committee, but they would be so small and slight that were they not made it would not be of any importance. I am censured, too, for proceeding by law. Why, my Lords, law, or fancied law, is the cause of the whole mischief, and by law alone it must be removed. Again, the proceeding by way of Commission has also been urged as vastly preferable. But your Lordships are now aware that the promised Commission did not precede the bill, but that the bill preceded the Commission; and it was not until the bill had been some time on the table of the House that a Commission was suggested. I frequently consulted many of the Right Rev. Prelates in private, and showed them the bill. Little or no objection was expressed to the course of proceeding I proposed to pursue, and many of them gave me very strong hopes that they would support the measure, considering it a great boon to the Church. If a Commission had been proposed some three years ago it might have been expedient to leave the subject to the investigation of such a body; but to abandon an attempt at legislation now, in consequence of the promise of a Commission, of which we know neither the terms nor the members, and thereby to hang up the question for a considerable time, would cause great dissatisfaction to the country; and in the meanwhile the state of things which has created, and which is still creating, so much discontent would go on increasing without check or hindrance. By such a course you would be doing for the extreme Ritualistic party the very thing they would most heartily desire. I cannot give a better proof of my assertion than by reading an extract from one of their recognized and authorized organs, by which you will see that this is the policy which they most earnestly labour to accomplish. The value which they attach to delay may be gathered from the following passage, which I take from the " Church Times " :—

" In the meantime our counsel to our friends is, in homely phrase, to make their hay while the sun yet shines. Every church that adopts the vestments renders their abolition a great deal more than proportionately difficult. We have no hesitation in saying that if the ornaments rubric were only carried out in every church where it would be acceptable, our position would be impregnable."

And hear, in confirmation of their policy, a book of the highest possible authority among them—a book full of amazing learning, but learning, no doubt, of a most useless character—here is a statement which completely harmonizes with the astute system thus counselled by the " Church Times " of making their position impregnable. The " Directorium Anglicanum " assures us that there are already " 2,000 churches which have lights on the altars," the result of secret and gradual advancement. " His brevibus principiis, via sternitur ad majora."

I think I have now shown your Lordships that some necessity exists for legislation, and that the line which I propose is founded on precedent, tradition, long and unbroken usage, on the content-ment and satisfaction of the people, the peace of the Church—in short, on every consideration which tends to maintain unimpaired throughout the kingdom the blessings of civil and religious liberty. I must, however, ask your indulgence while I detain you a little longer. I am anxious, having disposed of the legal aspect of the question, to inquire whether we are not standing on the brink of a system which, if extended, may lead to the subversion of the Church of England itself, and bear along with it political evils tending to shake the existence of the empire. There are so many points illustrative of that view that it would be unpardonable in me if I did not advert to one or two of them for the purpose of conveying conviction to your Lordships' minds. Here is one point, which has, I confess, filled me with considerable alarm. A short time ago a very remarkable book was published, called "The Church and the World; or, Essays upon the Questions of the Day;" and I observe, on referring to an authorized work, called " The Chronicle of Convocation," June, 1866—a work analogous, so far as the proceedings of that body are concerned, to " Hansard," for parliamentary debates—that an event took place in the Upper House which I should like to state to your Lordships. The Bishop of Oxford, on the occasion to which I am referring, said—

"I have now to present to your Grace and this Upper House of Convocation a book which has been forwarded to me under cover, directed to the Upper House of Convocation. I have not read the book myself."

I can well believe, my Lords, that the Right Rev. Prelate had not read it, for if he had done so he would, I am sure, have been one of the first to repudiàte its contents. The title of the book was, he added, " The Church and the World," and when he had presented it the Bishop of Salisbury rose, and, speaking in more precise language, said—

"I think we ought to present our thanks to the author of this book. I have read a good many of the essays contained in it, and they are most able. Although persons may differ from its conclusions, I am sure that everybody who takes the trouble of reading the work will find a great deal of matter in it admirably well put together."

Now, my Lords, I have read the greater part of this book, and in my humble judgment I never opened a book more disloyal to the Church, to the Bishops, and, I may add, to the truth. I will, with your Lordships' permission, give you one or two specimens of the character and purpose of this publication. To begin. We have said, my Lords, that the Ritualistic system adopted in many of our churches has altogether changed their Protestant character, and given to them the appearance of Popish places of worship, so as scarcely, and oftentimes not at all, to be distinguishable from those of the Church of Rome. Well, that being so, one of the essays in this book contains the following passage :—

"Anglicans are reproached by Protestants with their resemblance to Romans ; they say a stranger entering into a church where Ritual is carefully attended to might easily mistake it for a Roman service. *Of course he might*" (listen to these words, my Lords, *of course* he might) ; "the whole purpose of the great revival has been to eliminate the dreary Protestantism of the Hanoverian period, and restore the glory of Catholic worship; the churches are restored after the mediæval pattern, and our Ritual must accord with the Catholic standard. . . . Ritual, like painting and architecture, is the only visible expression of Divine truth. Without dogma, without any esoteric meaning,

Ritual is an illusion and delusion, a lay figure without life or spirit, a *vox et præterea nihil.*" (P. 212.)

The book urges also the celibacy of the clergy. A whole essay, indeed, is devoted to the object of demonstrating that the unmarried state is the highest state of human existence. It urges, moreover, the revival of religious confraternities, while one of the essays proceeds to contend that the Church ought to be assimilated to the theatre.

"Managers," it says, "have constantly been compelled to make gorgeous spectacle their main attraction; and a splendid transformation scene or a telling stage procession will draw crowds night after night, even in the absence of any theatrical celebrity. Hence a lesson may be learnt by all who are not too proud to learn from the stage. For it is an axiom in liturgiology that no public worship is really deserving of its name unless it be histrionic."

Here, my Lords, we have it declared that the simple worship of the Almighty as hitherto observed in our churches is now to be converted into a histrionic display, and that the house of God is to be turned into a stage, where gorgeous processions are to take the place of spiritual service, and religion is to be turned into a glittering drama. Again, the following passage approaches very close to the adoration of the Virgin :—

"The veneration of the blessed Virgin I perceived to a certain extent really exalted our Divine Lord, by showing the dignity attached to everything connected with the incarnation; and that Protestants misunderstand it because they practically degrade Him to the level of a saint, and then of course are shocked at any human creature being compared with Him."

In another essay we have the value and necessity of the confessional vigorously asserted. It contains a remarkable statement, which purports to be written by a lady, who gives details of what took place when she, a young girl, went to confession without the sanction of her parents, her confession occupying six hours. She adds—

"Years have passed since then, days and weeks of severe suffering, mental and bodily, but never anything that can be compared to those hours and the weeks that followed them, and I know that I can never pass through anything worse on the earth side of the grave."

She goes on to say how absolutely indispensable confession is, and she assigns this as her reason—

" Many persons think that their sins confessed in secret to God are fully confessed. *I believe it to be a most fatal mistake.*"

Now, was there ever before, my Lords, a doctrine such as this sanctioned by the approval of a Protestant Bishop? Was there, ever a doctrine so calculated to found, and maintain, a system of sacerdotal tyranny? That no intercourse can take place between a man and his Maker, without the intervention of some priest, weak and fallible as himself, is a dogma as false as it is revolting. Yet these are but samples, and those not the most violent and extreme that might be quoted from this book. Surely it is a sign of the times that such avowals have been befriended by Episcopal authority.

And now, my Lords, can we wonder at results such as I will now put before you? Can we wonder at a narrative such as that which is extracted from the "Church Review" of the 18th of November, 1865, describing the scenes that occurred at the church of St. Lawrence, Norwich, a few days before, with reference to the dedication of a cope :—

"The Church of St. Lawrence, Norwich.—On Sunday last an unusual ceremony was witnessed at this church. A cope had been purchased by a Cambridge undergraduate, and, at his wish, was presented and duly dedicated to God's service in a particularly impressive manner. The usual procession of choir and priest entered the church for evensong, headed by the crucifer. At the rear, immediately before the thurifers, the cope was carried by the deputed person who acted for the donor; the priest went to the altar accompanied by the thurifers. At the bottom step of the sacrarium the cope was presented to him with these words :— ' Reverend Father, in the name and on behalf of the donor, I present this cope for use by the priest in this Church of St. Lawrence on all fitting occasions.' The priest received it with these words :—' We receive this cope to the glory of God and for use in this church of St. Lawrence in the name of the Father, and of the Son, and of the Holy Ghost, Amen.' The priest then duly presented it on the altar and incensed it, after which suitable versicles, responses, and a prayer were used. Then the priest was vested in the cope and remained so until after the Magnificat. The cope is of rich gold and white brocatelle, with crimson orphreys and hood."

My Lords, I suspect a frugal mind, as well as a devout heart, in this narrative, for it added—

" The cope was supplied by Mr. R. L. Bloomfield, and is the same as shown at the Ecclesiastical Art Exhibition at Norwich."

The stories of this kind in reference to our churches and chapels might be largely multiplied, and notably I might call your attention to the Church of St. Raphael's, Bristol. Now, this cope is, after all, but a very servile imitation of the Holy Coat of Treves; still, that coat, miserable as it was, excited very great commotion throughout many parts of Germany. It is, indeed, our interest, no less than our duty, to mark the extremes to which these things are carried, and the necessity that they should be checked. At this moment there are very many men, of great ability, great zeal and learning, all engaged in an endeavour to promote and fix in the hearts of the people this Ritualistic system. And, to prove my position, I must advert to a book of the highest authority with the Ritualists, which shows the great lengths to which they have gone, and, beyond dispute, to which they intend to go. The work which I am about to quote is the "Directorium Anglicanum," a work of authority; and it thus lays down the mode of worship which, the writers assert, ought to be observed in the Church of England. It says—

"Ritual is the expression of doctrine, and a witness to the Sacramental system of the Catholic religion."—Very well, to begin with.

The various vestments are also described, and the times and seasons at which they are to be worn thus pointed out:—

"The order of the many-coloured vestments :—White, from the evening of Christmas Eve to the Octave of the Epiphany, &c.; Red, Vigil of Pentecost, and all other feasts; Violet, from Septuagesima to Easter Eve, &c.; Black, Good Friday and public fasts; Green, all other days."

From this your Lordships will be able to see the advanced position of the Sacramental system occupied by a portion of the clergy. Now, follow a few of the orders and injunctions for the administration of the Sacraments :—

"The greatest care should be taken to avoid the sacrilege of allowing the smallest particle to fall from the ciborium or pyx, &c.—It is impossible to communicate persons (who put their faces on the floor or kneel away from the cushion) without the greatest danger to the blessed Sacrament.—After the Consecration prayer, it is most desirable that no person passes before the blessed Sacrament, without genuflecting, bowing, or some token of reverence. [Is not this, my Lords, an act of adoration ?]—Let the priest test it by his minister, who will taste both the wine and water. But the priest himself ought not to taste it, . . . . . (but) pour a drop on his hand, rub it with his fingers, and smell it. . . . If it is too watery, he must not use it unless he knows that the wine exceeds the water. He shall fetch a breath, and with one inspiration shall say,—' *Hoc est enim corpus meum*,' so that no other train of thought shall intermingle with (the words). Again, he should never take the chalice at one draught, lest, by reason of the impetus, he should unadvisedly cough ; but twice or thrice he should take it warily.—Before mass the priest is not to wash his mouth or teeth, but only his lips from without, with his mouth closed, as he has need, lest, perchance, he should intermingle the taste of water with his saliva.—If, after having communicated of the body, he shall have the water already in his mouth, and shall then for the first time perceive that it is water . . . . . it is safer for him to swallow than eject it; and for this reason, that no particle of the body may be ejected with the water.—If a fly or spider, or such like thing, should fall into the chalice, after con- secration, it should be warily taken out, oftentimes diligently washed between the fingers, and then burnt, and the ablution, together with the burnt ashes, must be put into the piscina." (A laugh.)

My Lords, I do not quote these things to provoke laughter; far from it. Strange and abhorrent as they may be to our Protestant feelings, there are many earnest, though deluded, minds that hold and teach them, and of such it is far from my wish to speak with contempt. The book then goes on to say—

"If the consecrated host . . . . slip from the priest's hands into the chalice . . . . he ought not to take it out of the blood, but proceed in making the sign of the cross, and other matters, as if he held it in his hand.—If the Eucharist has fallen to the ground, the place where it lay must be scraped, and fire kindled thereon, and the ashes reserved beside the altar. In a similar case we (Ed. *D. A.*) should put the ashes down the piscina.—If any of the blood be spilled upon a table fixed to the floor the priest must take up the drop with his tongue, &c., and he to whom this has befallen must do penance 40 days." (Observe, my Lords, the constant repetition of the word "blood," showing the identity with the Roman system.) "If any one, by any accident of the throat, vomit up the Eucharist, the vomit is to be burnt and the ashes reserved near the altar, and if he shall be a cleric he must do penance 40 days, if a bishop " (I call the attention of the Episcopal bench to this) " 70 days, if a laic 30 days."

Well, my Lords, are we then to return to the burdens that neither we nor our fathers were able to bear ? Are we to be subjected to a system of Ritualism which, if merely for decoration, is childish and irreverent; but which, if symbolical of the deepest mysteries of our faith, amounts to blasphemy? Will your Lordships take the trouble to look at the Preface to the Book of Common Prayer, and read that part of it which explains why certain ceremonies were retained and certain others were rejected? You will see a reference to the fact that there the great St. Augustine complained of the intolerable yoke of ceremonial in his times, and spoke of the condition of Christian people as being worse in that respect than that of the Jews. The paragraph goes on to ask if St. Augustine had lived in those days what would he have said at seeing such a multiplication of observances? Said! why, would he not have said that our Protestant worship is a worship in spirit and in truth, and that it recognises only so much outward observance as is necessary for reverent and decent devotion? This state of things is, beyond denial, tending to Popery, and such is the assertion of many of our prelates; and unless it be checked it must issue in Romanism! Speaking in Convocation in February, 1866, the Bishop of Llandaff said—

" This has been called a Romeward movement, while others have denied that it is so. I cannot but consider this a Romeward movement, and a very rapid movement."

What says the Bishop of St. David's?—

" Nothing, in my judgment, can be more mischievous, as well as in more direct contradiction to notorious facts, than to deny or ignore the Romeward movement."

And here I cannot hesitate to call your Lordships' attention for a moment to an ancient writer, whose words are curious, as showing how identical are the policy and action of those who now seek to bring back Popery with the action of the men who 300 years ago were opposed to the spirit and principles of the Reformation. In " Cardwell's History," in reference to the Conference of 1559,—

" Gualter, it states, also the friend and colleague of Bullinger, writing to the Queen's physician early in the year 1559, and alluding to the attempts at comprehension, entreats that they would not hearken to the counsels of those men who, when they saw that Popery could not be honestly defended nor entirely retained, would use all artifices to have the outward face of religion to remain mixed, uncertain, and doubtful, so that while an Evangelical Reformation is pretended, those things should be

obtruded upon the Church which will make the returning back to
Popery, to superstition, and to idolatry very easy."

Mark these last words, "The return to Popery, superstition,
and idolatry very easy." In 1867, 300 years after, listen to the
same designs, the same hopes, the same facilities. The whole
scheme is set out · in the "Church Times" of March 30, the
acknowledged organ of the Ritualistic party :—

"The address of Dr. Pusey" (says the journal) "to the members
of the English Church Union at their last monthly meeting is one
of considerable significance, and fraught with most important
lessons for the present time. It is, simply, a formal declaration
of war—war against unbelief, against coldness, against timidity,
against all which goes to make up that form of religionism which
dignitaries call safe, and the 'Times' calls English. *War, then, it
shall be.* But, that point once settled, the question is, *What shall
be the tactics by which the campaign shall be conducted?*

"The advice of Dr. Pusey is this : Let no further advances be
made for the present, but all attention be concentrated in *fortify-
ing the position already attained,* and in completing the military
education of the Church's army. This is the method by which
Russia has pushed her way so steadily and permanently into the
far East."

Observe, my Lords, the dexterity and astuteness with which
they press everything into their service.

"A fort is erected in the enemy's country, with clear lines of
communication back to the basis of supply. A village of soldier-
colonists gathers round the fort, and civilians follow where a
market springs up. When the post has been Russianized it
becomes, in its turn, the base-line of operation, and another fort
is thrown out some score of miles in advance, and the process is
repeated, until, as we have seen, Khokan, Bokhara, and the
neighbouring territories are in a fair way to be as Sclavonic as
Kazan and Perm. But two rules are inexorably maintained. No
fort is erected at a dangerous distance from the base-line, and no
non-combatants are allowed to be the pioneers of colonization.
Exactly identical with this should be our policy.

"*Churches like St. Alban's, Holborn, and St. Lawrence's, Norwich*"
(observe this, my Lords, the Church of the Holy Cope!), "books
like the 'Altar Manual,' the 'Priest's Prayer Book,' and the
'Church and the World'" (bear in mind the title of this book),
"fairly represent *the most advanced post yet reached* by the
Catholic Revival in England. THEY ARE NOT THE ULTIMATE

GOAL." (What is it, then, my Lords?) "Why, THE FINAL AIM, WHICH ALONE WILL SATISFY THE RITUALISTS, IS THE RE-UNION OF CHRISTENDOM AND THE ABSORPTION OF DISSENT WITHIN THE CHURCH."

Here, then, my Lords, is the true object avowed—the subjugation of all Christendom, viz., body, soul, and spirit, to sacerdotal dominion. The journal proceeds:—

" This, then, is the thing to do. Let the advanced posts remain as they are. Let each of those which is a little behind, and only a little, gradually take up the same position, and let this process be carried on (only without haste or wavering) down to the last in the chain. *Let a gradual change be brought in.*"

I beseech your attention, my Lords, to the quiet and secret progress—

" A choral service, so far as Psalms and Canticles are concerned, on some week-day evening, will train people to like a more ornate worship, and that which began as an occasional luxury will soon be felt a regular want. Where there is monthly communion, let it be fortnightly; where it is fortnightly, let it be weekly; where it is weekly, let a Thursday office be added. Where all this is already existing, candlesticks with unlighted candles may be introduced. Where these are already found, they might be lighted at evensong. Where so much is attained, the step to lighting them for the Eucharistic Office is not a long one. Where the black gown is in use in the pulpit on Sundays, let it disappear in the week. The surplice will soon be preferred, and will oust its rival. It is easy for each reader to see how some advance, all in the same direction, can be made, and that without any offence taken."

The resistance of our forefathers in the days of Queen Elizabeth has given us a Protestantism of 300 years; may the resistance in the present day assure to us one of no less duration!

And now it may be asked why a layman should deal with this question. My Lords, I will tell you at once why I have undertaken the duty of bringing this subject under your notice. For a very long time the laity of the Church of England have been looking for assistance in every direction. They have turned to the clergy—they have turned to the bishops. They have been answered by charges and exhortations; but nothing effective has been done for their relief—and this is the answer why the laity have resolved to take the matter into their own hands. They think, moreover, that the bishops require the assistance of the laity, and they have determined, with them, or without them, to make every attempt in their power to remove this abuse from the fair face of the Established Church. In common with many others, I was, I confess, alarmed in no slight degree at what occurred in the early part of this year (in the month of February). The Most Rev. Primate had put out an invitation to the bishops of both provinces to meet at Lambeth in order to discuss various important subjects connected with the Established Church. In the *agenda* paper there was, however, no mention of Ritualism, the question of all others most sharply agitating the people of England. I believe I am correct—and if not the Most Rev. Primate will set me right—in saying that some of the bishops of the Northern Province declined to attend the Conference proposed to be held at Lambeth because Ritualism was not on the list of the *agenda*.* In addition, my Lords, I must say that I myself had been deeply moved, and the laity likewise had been moved, by certain declarations made by the Bishop of the diocese in which I have the honour to reside. In these declarations strange powers were claimed, powers as great and absolute as were ever claimed and exercised by any of the priests of the Eastern and Western Churches. Convinced that matters were approaching a fearful issue, I consulted with many of my lay friends, and we agreed that an effort should be made to test

* In the course of the debate, the Bishop of Carlisle made the following explanation :

His Lordship stated that in the episcopal gatherings at Lambeth, in the springs of 1865 and 1866, the subject of Ritualism had been brought forward and discussed. He was not at liberty to enter further into particulars ; but this he might say, that, owing to certain causes, no decision had been come to on either occasion. When, with his usual courtesy, the Most Reverend Prelate summoned the Bishops to Lambeth in February last, he was surprised and pained to find that this pressing subject was altogether absent from the list of topics to be considered. On this he wrote to his Grace, stating his reluctance to be present at the episcopal conclave under such circumstances. This elicited a kind note expressing regret at this decision. On this he attended, out of respect to his Grace, the first meeting, which was but preliminary, and lasted for a very few minutes. On learning from the remarks of his Grace that the decision to ignore Ritualism was still in force, he retired when the prelates dispersed to attend on her Majesty at the opening of Parliament, and did not return to the episcopal gathering. The Right Reverend Prelate then expressed an earnest hope that their Lordships would give a second reading to the bill before them, and referred to the existence of an organised conspiracy which, with a consistency of purpose, a perseverance of action, and a fertility of resource worthy of a far better cause, was carried on in order to restore the system of Popery in this country, and effect what had been called " the subjugation of an imperial race."

the feeling of the laity on this subject. A large county meeting
was accordingly held; and nothing could give a stronger proof
of the extent to which the people of England were animated
and resolved. I did not know until I had received accounts from
many parts of Dorset that the farmers could be so painfully
excited as they were by these Ritualistic observances. I should
not like to repeat the language used on this subject; it was,
indeed, of the strongest description; and no one could hear it
without feeling that if these practices are continued the farmers
of England, instead of being, as they always have been, the
friends, will become the bitterest opponents of the Established
Church.

Now, in regard to this bill, I heard on high authority that
there was nothing to be objected to it, except on the ground that
it had not proceeded from the decisions of Convocation. My
Lords, I am bound to express the deep respect I feel for the
individual members of Convocation of both Houses. But collectively I do not feel the same respect for their opinions and judg-
ments; and, for this reason, that Convocation represents only
the clergy, and those only most imperfectly, while of the laity
there is not a shadow of representation. I believe that no Convocation is of any value that does not contain the laity as well as
the clergy. In the American Episcopal Church of the United
States the laity form the majority of their assemblies; and when
I was in Paris a few days ago I had the benefit of a conversation
with a bishop of that Church, and learned from him that the laity
formed a large part of the governing body. Without them, he
added, Convocation would not get on at all; but with their aid
the Church in America had been greatly extended, and would
continue, he believed, being extended far beyond its present
limits. Another objection I urge to the supremacy of Convocation is that the Convocation of Canterbury does not include the
province of York. Yet that province contains the very pith and
marrow of the whole empire. The province of York contains the
diocese of Chester, which includes the great town of Liverpool.
It includes the diocese of Manchester and the whole of Lancashire
the Archbishopric of York, and the diocese of Ripon, and the whole
of the West Riding of York, the diocese of Durham with the
whole of Durham and Northumberland, and the diocese of
Carlisle, including the whole of Cumberland and Westmoreland.
If the bill had proceeded from the Convocation of Canterbury,
which generally assumes to be exclusively Convocation, it would
have proceeded from the weaker of the two bodies, and from a
body which, as I have said already, does not represent the

laity at all, and most imperfectly represents the whole body of the clergy.

My Lords, I hold that this is essentially a question for the laity. I will never cease to proclaim that it is not for the bishop and the minister to settle between themselves the order of the service, or what vestments are to be worn, but that it is for the great mass of the congregation to determine whether they will go on in those usages which their fathers have practised for 300 years. It is not for the mere majority of the congregation to determine what changes shall be made, but for the congregation at large; and even then it must be done consistently with the law of the land. What are the minority to do? Affected conscientiously, they cannot continue to worship in a church where these Ritualistic practices prevail. And whither can they go? Must they seek in their necessity another place of worship? Doubtless they must, and such has been the smart and ready counsel of a bishop, who preferred to give such advice to the judicious exercise of influence and authority in the suppression of harassing innovations.

I know, my Lords, that a great difference has grown up between the Ultra-Ritualists and those denominated the High Church—a greater difference, perhaps, than there is between the High Church and the Low. I am not about to speak with disrespect of those who belong to these two bodies. The High Church, I acknowledge, contains many wise, good, and learned men. I have ever expressed my admiration for the virtues, talents, and learning of the head of that party, Dr. Pusey. The Ritualistic party also, no doubt, contains men of sincerity and learning, who think by what they are doing they are conferring a blessing upon the Church and the country. I admit it all. But we must consider the effect of the system they are introducing. It is alienating many of the devout and faithful members of our communion. In some it is producing a state of complete indifference, and an opinion that there is little or no distinction between the Church of Rome and the Church of England. Others are averted altogether from the Church, and are going over to the Nonconformists. Congregations are broken up in all parts of the country, and numbers are on the point of being added to the ranks of Dissent. There are noble peers here present who could tell you of three or four churches in their neighbourhood being completely emptied of their former people. See the effect it is producing among many of your best friends—those who have been faithful to the Church in circumstances of difficulty and danger. I will allude to that powerful body the Wesleyan Method-

ists. I have many friends among them, and I know that they
have been accustomed to cherish a warm attachment to the
Church of England. I can tell your Lordships, however, that a
great change is coming over their hearts and minds. With
regret, but conscientiously, they hesitate not to declare that if
these observances continue and are allowed to extend in the
degree in which they are extending, there must be a complete
change of policy, leading, as a matter of deep conviction, to help
in destroying the Church of England as a rag of Popery. There
is at all times a large body of Dissenters who desire, as a question
of principle, the abolition of the Establishment, and in a time
of difficulty and distress it may go very hard with our ancient
system if to this active society there be added allies drawn from
our former friends and supporters. My Lords, it is quite certain
that if the present state of things continues, if no vigorous
attempt be made to repress these practices, and show that the
Church of England is yet prominent in all her purity and all
her truth, another Reformation will begin in this country. But
that Reformation will not be like the last; it will not descend
from the heads and come down to the people, thus bringing with
it episcopacy and all its orders; but it will ascend from the
people to the heads, and may land us perhaps on the platform
of Geneva. There is testimony to this among persons of great
experience and well acquainted with the present aspect of ecclesiastical affairs. Canon Blakesley, speaking in Convocation,
declared his opinion—" That if we look the country through, you
will find that it has been more Puritanized by those practices
than Romanized." I believe that to be true; and that if you beget
in the people the spirit of the old Puritans you will also see in
them the action of the Puritans; and that the Establishment, if
once uprooted by their assaults, will never regain its first position.
Hear also an eminent Nonconformist, Dr. Vaughan, the author
of one of the ablest treatises upon Ritualism which has yet been
published :—

" The success of the Ritualists (says Dr. Vaughan) hitherto
has been in corrupting the members of the Church of England,
not in making converts from beyond her pale."

And so it is, my Lords. They have brought none to the
embrace of the Church of England, though they have driven
many over its border, and have tarnished the simplicity of the
faith of many who remain within it.

Let me close this statement with an extract from the Charge of
the Bishop of St. David's, one of the most acute, profound, and

exhaustive documents which I have ever read—one remarkable alike for its learning, wit, power, and sound defence of the purity of the Church of England. The Right Rev. Prelate, taking exactly the same view which I have ventured to take, says, among other things—

"I believe that in most neighbourhoods the number of those who are attracted by the revived Ritual bears a small proportion to that of those who dislike and disapprove it, even if they are not shocked and disgusted by it. And I strongly suspect that those who take pleasure in it do so mainly, not on account of its superior sensuous attractions, but because it represents a peculiar system of opinions."

But listen to these weighty remarks :—

"The Committee of Convocation, in a passage of their Report, remind us that the National Church of England has a holy work to perform towards the Nonconformists of this country. If the innovations which offend many, I believe I may still say most, Churchmen, are peculiarly obnoxious to the Nonconformists of this country, it is not simply as innovations, but because they present the appearance of the closest possible approximation to the Church of Rome. And the danger on this side is far greater than that which is suggested by the language of the Report. It is not merely that we may make fewer converts from the ranks of Dissent, but that we may strengthen them by large secessions, perhaps of whole congregations, from our own."

"Perhaps!" why, my Lords, the evil is already in full action. He proceeds :—

"And the danger—if I ought not rather to say the certain and present evil—does not end there. These proceedings both tend to widen the breach between us and Dissenters, and to stimulate them to more active opposition, and furnish their leaders with an instrument which they will not fail to use for the purpose of exciting general ill-will toward the Church, and weakening her position in the country."

My Lords, it cannot be denied, nor do I wish to disguise the fact, that, in dealing with these things, we are dealing in a large measure with the symptoms and not with the root of the disease. We may take away the altar, and yet leave the spirit that erected it. We may take away Ritualism, and yet leave Sacerdotalism. No doubt this is true. This is the weakness of all repressive laws; but still we must subdue these external abuses, and, while seeking other means to purify the source of the mischief, endeavour to turn to the best account the powers committed to our hands.

And now, my Lords, in concluding, having thanked you most heartily for the courtesy and patience with which you have listened to me, allow me briefly to say a few words in reference to myself on this occasion. I have at various times been called by various appellations. Perhaps your Lordships will hardly believe that I have sometimes been termed a High Church bigot, while at others I have been described as an irreverent Dissenter. I think neither of those appellations can be fairly assigned to me. It has ever been my heartfelt and earnest desire to see the Church of England the Church of the nation, and especially of the very poorest classes of society, that she might dive into the recesses of human misery and bring out the wretched and ignorant sufferers to bask in the light, and life, and liberty of the Gospel. I have ever desired that in a country, such as our own, where, under freedom of thought and freedom of action, Dissent must ever be found, the Church of England should extend the right hand of fellowship to those who, though they differ from her in matters of discipline, agree with her in the grand and fundamental doctrines of the faith, and so advance the great interests of our common Christianity. I have ever desired that the Church of England should in her wisdom, her piety, her strength, and her moderation be a model to all the nations of the earth. It has ever been my most ardent desire that in all the great dependencies of this vast empire the Church of England should be powerful and beneficent—that in the east and in the west, in the north and in the south, and in all the regions of the earth, wherever the English name is heard or English rule is obeyed—in profound gratitude to Almighty God, and in affectionate reverence of their common mother, her children should rise up and call her blessed. This, I know, is the earnest prayer of every one of your Lordships, and may God give it a prosperous issue!

*Agricultural Gangs.*

## HOUSE OF LORDS,

### April 11, 1867.*

The Earl of Shaftesbury, on rising to bring under the notice of the House the Sixth Report of the Commissioners relating to the Agricultural Gangs, said,—

I have no intention of troubling your Lordships at any great length, particularly as I know that a debate of considerable importance is going on in the other House; but, having given notice some time ago of my intention to bring this subject under your Lordships' notice, although I have been forestalled by a motion made in the House of Commons a few nights ago, yet I think it my duty to show, as briefly as I can, that this House has not been unmindful of the welfare of the agricultural community, and that the charge made against the landlords, that they evinced no interest with regard to their poorer tenants, was altogether unfounded. Two years ago I had the honour of bringing this subject under your Lordships' notice, and, I believe, I was the first person who drew attention to it. I then moved your Lordships to present an address to the Crown, praying for the appointment of a Commission to inquire into the subject of the employment of children and young persons in various trades not protected by the Factory Acts, and that that Commission should also take into consideration the system of agricultural gangs. The report of that Commission was made a very short time ago, and I wish to read a few extracts, in order to show your Lordships what the system really is. The Commissioners say—

"The system of 'organized' labour known by the name of 'agricultural gangs' exists, as far as the Commissioners have been able to ascertain, almost exclusively in the following counties:—Lincolnshire, Huntingdonshire, Cambridgeshire, Norfolk, Suffolk, and Nottinghamshire. There are a few instances of the employment of these gangs in three other neighbouring counties,

* From " Hansard."

namely, in the counties of Northampton, Bedford, and Rutland. They are not found over the whole of any of these counties, but are distributed irregularly through various parts of them, in obedience to local circumstances. All organized agricultural gangs consist of the gang-master, a number of women, and young persons of both sexes. The Commissioners, in designating 'young persons,' adopt the definition of the Factory Acts, namely, those between 13 and 18. Children of both sexes from the age of 6 to 13. The 'organized gang'—the subject of the present inquiry—is called in some districts the 'public gang,' in others the 'common gang,' in some places it is called the 'jobbing gang,' elsewhere the 'travelling gang.' The numbers in each public gang are from 10 or 12 to 20, 30, and 40, very rarely above 40. But the most common, because the most manageable number is about 20, employing in the whole about 7,000 boys and girls, from six years old and upwards. In addition to the 'public gangs' there are also many 'private gangs,' employing full 20,000. The 'public gang' master is an independent man, who engages the members of his gang, and contracts with the farmer to execute a certain kind and amount of agricultural work with this body of slaves. The 'private gang' is a small gang, seldom exceeding 12 or 20, similarly composed, but in the farmer's own employ, and superintended and directed by one of the farmer's own labourers. The unanimity with which the public gang system is condemned in consequence of its injurious influences on the moral character of those subject to it is all but entire throughout the whole evidence. The number of persons who are able to speak well of the system under its moral aspects, as far as they have witnessed it, is very small indeed. The rest, with an earnestness of expression which testifies to the sincerity of their convictions, are evidently deeply impressed with the desire to call attention to the great amount of moral evil connected with the system, and to urge the consideration of some mode of improving it. A great part of the work consists in making or keeping the land in a fit state for the growth of crops by cleaning it from weeds of all kinds, and may be included under the description of weeding; 'knocking,' or spreading, and putting in manure are sometimes added. Thinning or 'singling' turnips and mangold wurzel is a work of the same nature as weeding. The work also includes the putting crops into the ground, as by setting potatoes and dropping seed for dibblers, treading corn on light soil, &c. The work also includes the getting in of certain crops when ripe, *e.g.* pulling turnips and mangolds or beet, pulling flax, and sometimes peas, instead of their being mown; picking up potatoes when dug or turned up;

also gathering garden produce in market gardens of fruit and vegetables. The turnips or mangolds when pulled have also to be topped and tailed."

As an instance, take the following, which is recorded by Mr. Savage:—

" Mrs. Antony Adams, labourer's wife, Denton, Huntingdon-shire,—' In June, 1862, my daughters, Harriet and Sarah, aged respectively 11 and 13 years, were engaged to work on Mr. Worman's land at Stilton. When they got there he took them to near Peterborough; there they worked for six weeks, going and returning each day. The distance each way is eight miles, so that they had to walk 16 miles each day on all the six working days of the week, besides working in the field from 8 to 5 or 5½ in the afternoon. They used to start from home at 5 in the morning, and seldom got back before 9. They had to find all their own meals, as well as their own tools (such as hoes). They (the girls) were good for nothing at the end of the six weeks. The ganger persuaded me to send my little girl Susan, who was then six years of age. She walked all the way (eight miles) to Peterborough to her work, and worked from 8 to 5½, and received 4*d.* She was that tired that her sisters had to carry her the best part of the way home—eight miles, and she was ill from it for three weeks, and never went again.' "

When a system like this exists, it is obvious that the Legislature ought not to hesitate a moment in applying a proper remedy for the evil. The Report goes on to say—

" The dress of females collects wet much more than that of boys or men, and even if they are at work does not dry nearly so quickly. The workers are often waiting about for long intervals with wet feet and their clothes soaked through up to their knees or waist, or higher, doing nothing but waiting till the weather or the crop is drier. Children, from being shorter, are wetted by the crops higher up their bodies than elder workers, though not worse off as to rain. The gang-workers, as a rule, are the poorest of the labouring class, and many of them are badly fed, shod, and clothed, and have very small means of making a change of clothes when they return home. Not only rain, but even in fine weather the dew makes the crops very wet, some much more so than others, and the higher the crop the more are the workers exposed to this wet, and females, owing to their dress, much the most. Hence they are often soaked through up to the knees or waist, and children even higher, and have to squeeze or wring out their petticoats, and even take them or other parts of their dress off and hang them up to dry. A young woman entirely crippled

with rheumatism, which she got soon after going into a gang at
11 years old, says, ' We have had to take off our shoes and pour
the water out, and then the man would say, " Now then, go in
again." ' It is suggested by a competent person that, if the employment were placed under regulation, one of the several rules which
it is suggested should be endorsed on a licence to be required
from the gang-master should be, ' No girls to be permitted to enter
high wet corn in weeding.' "

In my opinion, my Lords, no female at all should be engaged in
this injurious and disgusting employment.  To say nothing of the
moral considerations involved, there is not a medical man who will
not tell you that the most critical period of a woman's life is that
between 11 and 13 years of age.  That is the time when a change
in her constitution takes place, when maladies are most easily
contracted, and when the female child requires to be watched with
the most parental and minute care.  Children at that tender age
are nevertheless exposed, as we are told, to all the inclemencies
of the seasons, with every malady that besets humanity, and yet
no hand is stretched out to rescue them from their miserable condition.  I shall next proceed to read to your Lordships the evidence
of Dr. Morris, of Spalding, who says—

" I have been in practice in the town of Spalding for 25 years,
and during the greater portion of this time I have been medical
officer to the Spalding Union Infirmary.  I am convinced that the
gang system is the cause of much immorality.  The evil in the
system is the mixture of the sexes in the case of boys and girls
of 12 to 17 years of age under no proper control.  The gangers,
as you know, take the work of the farmers.  Their custom is to
pay their children once a week at some beerhouse; and it is
no uncommon thing for their children to be kept waiting at the
place till 11 or 12 o'clock at night.  At the infirmary many girls
of 14 years of age, and even girls of 13, up to 17 years of age, have
been brought in pregnant to be confined there.  The girls have
acknowledged that their ruin has taken place in this gang work.
The offence is committed in going or returning from their work.
Girls and boys of this age go five, six, or even seven miles to
work, walking in droves along the roads and by-lanes.  I have
myself witnessed gross indecencies between boys and girls of 14
to 16 years of age.  I once saw a young girl insulted by some five
or six boys on the road side.  Other older persons were about 20
or 30 yards off, but they took no notice.  The girl was calling
out, which caused me to stop.  I have also seen boys bathing in
the brooks, and girls between 13 and 19 looking on from the
bank."

Listen now to the evidence of the Rev. Mr. Huntley, the rector of Binbrooke, who says—

"Turning to the moral side of the picture, all is blank. The benefits of education which charity has provided are thrown aside by the parent. The young being occupied in manual labour from morn till night, the village school is comparatively denuded of scholars. In room of moral and religious teaching, children are auditors of obscene and blasphemous language, while also exposed to the most profligate and debased examples, thus completing the first stage of ruin. Progressing from childhood to womanhood, the girl is brought up without experience in the management of domestic affairs, and it is no wonder that when the duties of servitude and married life are demanded of her she is ignorant of both. There is not one extensive occupier of land, nor one sober-minded person throughout my parish, who does not denounce the gangs as destructive to the morals of the poor." Then we have the evidence of Mr. Richard Greenwood, a farmer, who tells us—

"I never employ a common gang. The common gang is very bad indeed. There is a reason for them when children can't be got otherwise, but I think that they could, if they tried, in many cases. I don't think that work is done much cheaper by the gang. I think the gang system is full of evil. There are great girls and boys of 14 to 15 years of age among them, and there is always something wrong going on. It does not matter who the ganger is; where there is a lot together, he has a control over them all. I have counted 20 to 25 in the gangs that come from Binbrooke. The only advantage to the farmer is that it saves him the trouble of seeking the children. Half the girls from Ludford have been ruined by going out. I think that farmers would not be at all losers by girls not going out to work at all."

That is the testimony of a man who farms 1,000 acres; but I now adduce the evidence of some mothers whose opinions on this subject are entitled to the greatest weight. A very intelligent woman, named Rachel Gibson, says—

"I can't speak up for any gangs; they ought all to be done away with." Most heartily I say "amen" to that. "My children shan't go to one if I can help it—*i.e.*, as long as I and their father are alive, I hope, if we can keep them; one is seven, one five. I believe that I am the same as many other people about this. There are a great many mothers who send their children into gangs who would not if they could help it, and they say so. Nothing comes amiss to children after they have been in them, no bad talk nor anything else. I know that a child, if brought up in a gang, is quite different from what it would have been if brought up otherwise; you would soon know that it had been out, especially if you were to talk to it. Gangs might be very well for boys, but never for girls. I did not go myself till I was 17, and could take care of myself. The coming home is the worst part; that's when the mischief is done. There never was any good got out of gangs, neither in talk nor in the other way, and they never will be kept as they should. I don't think it proper that women-kind should go into the fields at all, in gangs or not, though I have done both. There would then be more in the houses to mind them. Harvest work is different; you are not under a gang-master, except that sometimes the tying has been done by a gang, and at harvest much more money can be made; a woman may make 2s. 3d. in a day, and that comes nice to any one. But other work is different. I should just have liked you to have met that gang coming back this afternoon, with their great thick boots and buskins on their legs, and petticoats pinned up; you might see the knees of some. A girl whom I took in to live, because she has no home to go to, came back to-day from the gang all dripping wet from the turnips. If you don't feel any hurt from the wet when you are young, you do afterwards, when you are old and the rheumatism comes on. Girls wear a pair of buskins to keep them from the wet. It is hard work when you have to wring the tops of turnips and mangolds up, and often makes blisters on the hands."

Here are the views of another mother as to the working of the system—

" What I say is, these gangs should not be as they are. There are so many girls that they make lads at a loose hand—*i.e.*, leave them nothing to do. Then there is the girls coming home at dark; that is when the job is done. The gangs are drafted off, two (*i.e.*, workers) here, three there, and so on, so that the gang-master cannot look after them, and is not to blame. I have gone with 20 in a morning, and seen only two perhaps come home with the man at night. Then girls will have bad language among them-selves, though the man might wish to stop it, but there are so many together, 20 or 30 perhaps, that he can't keep them quiet. I have worked in gangs many years. Sometimes the poor children are very ill-used by the gang-master. One has used them horribly, kicking them, hitting them with fork handles, hurdle sticks, &c., and even knocking them down. These are not things to hit a child with. My own children have been dropped into across the loins and dropped right down, and if they don't know how to get up he has kicked them. I have many a time seen my own and other

children knocked about by him in this way. It was not from
drink ; he was quite sober.   Sometimes, too, they cannot work
properly because their hands are cut all across and blistered where
they twist the stalk round to pull up the root.  Of course he don't
knock the big ones ; it is the little ones he takes advantage of.   I
have heard him use to a child most awful words for a girl to hear.
My boy, when about 10 or 11, had a white swelling on his knee,
and lay suffering nearly six years before he had his leg and thigh
taken off, all but about as long as a finger.  He came back one
day and said he had a thorn, but others told me about the man
kicking him.  He was a very quiet boy, and was for peace.  The
doctor said it was from ill-usage, a fall or kick ; there was no
thorn."

In the next place, I request the attention of your Lordships
to the sixth report of the medical officer of the Privy Council,
because he there points out how serious is the effect produced on
the mortality of the children by work such as that to which I am
referring.  The report states—

"That in some entirely rural marsh districts the habitual
mortality of young children is almost as great as in the most
infanticidal of our manufacturing towns; that Wisbeach, for
instance, is within a fraction as bad as Manchester; and that
generally in the registration districts (18 others, which include
several in which the gang system prevails) the death-rate of
infants under one year of age is from two and a quarter to nearly
three times as high as in the 16 districts of England which have
the lowest infantile mortality.  The result of this new inquiry,
however, has been to show that the monstrous infantine rate of
the examined agricultural districts depends only on the fact that
there has been introduced into these districts the influence which
has already been recognized as enormously fatal to the infants of
manufacturing populations—the influence of the employment of
adult women."

It goes on to say the effect of the gang system is to increase the
employment of females, adult as well as young.  The consequences
are thus described :—

"The opinions of about 70 medical practitioners, with those of
other gentlemen acquainted with the condition of the poor, were
obtained.  With wonderful accord the cause of the mortality was
traced by nearly all these well-qualified witnesses to the bringing
of the land under tillage—that is, to the cause which has banished
malaria, and has substituted a fertile though unsightly garden for
the winter marshes and summer pastures of 50 and 100 years ago.
It was very generally thought that the infants no longer received

any injury from soil, climate, or malarious influence, but that a
more fatal enemy had been introduced by the employment of
mothers in the field."

It is unnecessary to multiply instances of the evil consequences
of this system, but I think I must give you the results of the
employment of women in this way, as stated by the Rev. H.
Mackenzie, rector of Tydd St. Mary's, who says :

"The causes of the gang system are the comparative cheapness
of female and child labour. The effects of the employment of
women in field-work are :—1. Loss of self-respect, and dirty
and degraded habits. 2. Slovenly and slatternly households.
3. Alienation of husbands by the discomforts of home. 4. Neglect of the education of children. 5. Drinking habits among the
men, and opium consumption among the women. The effects of
the employment of girls in gang field-work are :—1. Boldness.
2. Ignorance. 3. Unchastity. 4. Want of cleanliness in work
and person. 5. Incompetence in sewing, mending, cooking, and
all that pertains to household economy. 6. Indifference to
parental control. 7. Unwillingness to apply themselves to any
regular mode of gaining a livelihood. Girls who have up to a
certain time made good progress at school are materially injured
in morals, discipline, knowledge, and regularity by going for two
or three weeks to work in the fields. It will be a blessing to this
neighbourhood if field-work for girls under age can be prohibited.
This in a few years would abolish field-work for women altogether."

There is only one other extract with which I shall trouble your
Lordships, showing how totally unnecessary it is to employ females
in this manner, and that it is merely by indulgence in an old
habit that the system is persevered in. This, my Lords, is described as the state of things at Eye, with a population of 2430
persons, and on the property of Sir Edward Kerrison :—

"It will be seen that no females are employed on the gang
system here. This is owing to the interest taken in it by Sir
Edward Kerrison, who is owner of the greater part of the parish
of Eye. It was entirely by his desire that girls were not employed in these gangs. The demoralizing effects were seen to be
so great that for some years past only males have constituted the
gang, and it certainly has worked admirably, for a distinct moral
control is at the same time exercised over these lads by the instruction given to the master to check all obscene language and
unbecoming behaviour, not only in their work, but if they are so
ill-behaved either by language or manner when not in their work
it is checked by special observation to the proper quarter, and the

individual is admonished so as to let him know that he is not un-observed, and most probably he will find it much more to his own interest to behave in such a manner as may warrant those who have the power and influence to help him in after-life. And all these poor people well know from practical experience that they have the kindest friends in Sir Edward and Lady Caroline Kerrison. Year after year young lads and young girls are looked after and helped out in their start in life, and assistance given in clothing and travelling expenses, where the parents require the help. This has an immense moral effect on the poor of the place and neighbourhood, coupled with the fact that the large land-owner is a resident, and taking personal interest in the welfare of the people."

Here, then, is ample proof that the employment of females in these gangs is wholly unnecessary; and that if their labour of this kind can be dispensed with in a district like Eye, it can be dispensed with anywhere. Such, my Lords, in a very few words, is an outline of this system as described in the report of the Com-missioners; and a remedy may be easily and speedily applied to it. In a recent debate in another place it was alleged that no legisla-tion on the subject can be effectual. This is the old argument; always urged, and always exploded by experience. I hold that when such a frightful state of things as this is found to exist it is incumbent on us to strive to correct it. I am myself disposed to undertake, immediately after the Easter recess, a motion that your Lordships should adopt a Bill containing provisions which are almost certain to meet the requirements of the case. In the first place, I would proceed on the principles of the Factory and Colliery Acts. When in 1842 I introduced a Bill in the House of Commons to remove women from employment in the collieries of the United Kingdom, I was told that I should do no end of mis-chief by depriving women of their means of subsistence. Never-theless, I persisted, the Legislature adopted my proposal, and nothing but good has come out of it. From that hour to this the condition of the colliery districts has been greatly improved in consequence of the non-employment of women in that disgusting and unsuitable labour. I shall propose by my Bill, immediately it passes, to exclude from these public gangs all women whatever under 18 years of age. If I were to exclude women altogether, even above that age, I might be thought to be asking too much, as old habits cannot be got rid of all at once, and a little time might be necessary to find some substitute for the labour of women. But by removing all women under 18 from these public gangs you would at once set at liberty 1478 girls out of a population of 7000. I speak now only of the public gangs. The private gangs are, it is true, the most numerous; but I should reach them in another way, by clauses which would affect the whole agricultural population, it being perfectly manifest that some measure relating to this matter must be brought in which will touch the whole class. The particular machinery of the Factory and Colliery Acts would be wholly inapplicable to agricultural industry; but, as I have said, I should propose to proceed upon the principles of those Acts. The main outlines, then, of the Bill which I desire to introduce would be as follows:—1. That no female under 18 years of age shall be employed in any public gang of agricultural labourers. 2. That no child under 8 years of age shall be employed for hire in field labour at all. 3. That after the 1st of January, 1869, no female under 11 years of age (I should like to say up to 13), shall be employed for hire in any field labour whatever. This will affect not only the private gangs, but the entire agricultural population of every county; exceptions, of course, being allowed for the time of harvest. I maintain that physically, morally, and economically, such a provision as this will be most beneficial in its effects. Certainly the extensive employment of women and girls in field work has tended more to degrade women and lower the rate of agricultural wages than the operation of almost any other causes whatsoever. I should next provide that no child between the ages of 8 and 13 shall be employed for hire, in field labour, without producing to its employer, at times to be appointed, a certificate of its having attended school during the preceding intervals, for a certain number of hours, calculated according to the most convenient arrangements, whether by half time, alternate days, or by the system under the Print Works Act, of so many hours collectively, of education, in any assigned period, regard being had to the seasons of the year.

My Lords, in attempting to grapple with this evil I hope your Lordships will kindly aid me by your sympathy and support. In this way you will give the crowning stroke to the various efforts made for many years past to bring all the industrial occupations of the young and the defenceless under the protection of the law; and that, whether they are employed in trade, in manufactures, or in any handicraft whatever, every child under a certain age may be subject only to a limited amount of labour, and be certain to receive an adequate amount of education. All that remains for your Lordships now to do, as representing the landowners of the kingdom, is to embrace within the scope of your beneficent legislation the whole mass of the agricultural population. Then, I believe, we shall be enabled to say that no country upon earth surpasses us in the care we take of the physical, the moral, and the educational well-being of the myriads of our humbler fellow-creatures. My Lords, the object you have in view is one well worthy of all the time, the anxiety, the zeal, and the talents which can be bestowed upon it; and I am satisfied that your Lordships will earnestly desire to see it accomplished.

---

NOTE.—A bill was introduced and read a second time, the House thereby affirming the principle. Further progress was, however, delayed until after another report from the Commissioners.

*Representation of the People Bill.*

## HOUSE OF LORDS,

JULY 23, 1867.

On the Second Reading of the Representation of the People Bill,

THE Earl of Shaftesbury said: My Lords, it is somewhat difficult to argue against a Bill which we do not wish to reject,
and which it seems next to impossible that we can amend. It
seems useless, moreover, to complain of a measure when, by so
doing, we have no prospect of any favourable result. Nevertheless, the members of a constituent branch of the Legislature are
bound, I think, to express their opinions upon this Bill, the
opinions which they sincerely and conscientiously feel, and not
to allow ourselves to be reduced to the condition of a mere office
of registration.

I was very anxious to hear from my noble friend, who propounded this measure, some statement of his views, not only as to
its causes, but as to its consequences. I was anxious that he
should do something to allay the fears that exist, to calm the
troubles which prevail, and to give us some assurance that, in his
conviction at least, great and manifold benefits are to result to
the country from the passing of this great act of legislation. I
heard, however, nothing of the kind from him; I heard only the
one stout assertion that this measure was so conservative as to
leave no grounds for apprehension. Now, that assertion was,
I must say, alike comforting and astounding. But when I listened
to the speeches of other members of the Government, who, I
hoped, would supply the deficiencies of the noble earl, I heard
not a syllable of comfort. Indeed, the greater part of the debate
consisted, with some exceptions, in the endeavour to set up one
Bill against another, one Cabinet against another, one Minister
against another, all which had no bearing on the great question
before us—namely, the Bill which we have to consider, and all the

mighty consequences that are to accrue from it to the present and to future generations. Now, I maintain we are bound to look this question fully in the face. The opinions I hold may, no doubt, seem to some exaggerated; but I am sure that those opinions are shared by many thoughtful and intelligent men, and all I can venture to say is, that they are the result of much thought and long experience : that they are conscientiously and honestly entertained; and that I think they ought to be fully stated, and as fully confuted.

My Lords, this Bill comes to us under very peculiar circumstances. It comes to us from the House of Commons without a division upon the second reading—without a division on the main principles, the household suffrage and the lodger franchise—without a division upon the re-distribution clauses—without a division on the third reading. It is, therefore, in appearance, whatever it be in reality, the unanimous expression of the will of the House of Commons, and as such entitled to homage and respect. It was elaborated in that assembly during a period of six months; but to us will be allowed for its consideration about six days. It is impossible, therefore, to discuss the principle of the Bill in its full extent. We cannot consider all the various plans of reform, and then select the one best adapted to the necessities of the country. We are shut up to the four corners of this Bill, to say whether it be good or bad; and I should not have ventured to trespass upon your Lordships' attention had I not felt—though this, perhaps, is one of the exaggerated opinions which I may hold—that this is one of the last opportunities we shall have of expressing our opinions in a free and independent Parliament, uncontrolled by the presence of a powerful democratic representation.

Now, my Lords, I do not entertain any hostility to reform—very far from it. I have long been of opinion that some reform, though not necessary for good government, had become indispensable ; indeed, inevitable. It is not necessary to enter into the various causes which have made it so; but I readily admit that some measure of reform could not much longer be postponed. I should have wished, however, to proceed more carefully and gradually. I should have wished to hold up the suffrage as a great object of ambition to the working man; I should have wished to hold it up as the reward of thrift, honesty, and industry. We have examples before us of what, in this respect, may be done by the labouring classes. If we turn to the Potteries, we there see a large body of intelligent men, who, by their own act, by their own diligence and economy, have raised themselves to the possession of the suffrage. There are in that district about 9000 potters; men in the receipt of high wages; and I am told that very nearly 3000 of these by their own toil and care have purchased their own freehold, and are now living in their own houses. These 3000 working men by their own act have done that which almost every working man in the receipt of good wages might have done had he been so inclined. That is, to a considerable extent, my notion of reform; but I would have gone further. I would not have kept the suffrage at 10*l*. I would have taken it as low as the Bill of last year proposed; namely, to 7*l*., and on this ground—that though working men are able, in many instances, by their own efforts to reach the line of 10*l*., we must recollect that there are differences of position. A man with a family earning 2*l*. a week is not in the same position as a man without any family with the same weekly wages. To meet that difference I should have been glad to bring down the limit to 7*l*.; and surely the addition of thousands of such men elevated by such means, would be an honour and a security to the kingdom. In this respect I have always been a very considerable radical. Such a radical I am now, and a radical I shall be to the end of my days. The thing of all others which I most rejoice in is to see the working man rising by his own industry and character from the lowest point in the scale of society to the very highest point; and if a man whom I had known as originally a chimney-sweeper filled the office of Prime Minister of this country, I should see in that issue one of the noblest proofs of the freedom and generosity of our institutions, and of their possessing a breadth and expansion that we ought, in the face of all contradiction, to assert and maintain as an equal benefit for all—but to proceed, as is done by this Bill, to lift by the sudden jerk of an Act of Parliament the whole residuum of society up to the level of the honest, thrifty, working man, is, I am sure, perilous to the state, and, I believe, distasteful to the working men themselves. I am sure it dishonours the suffrage, and that you are throwing the franchise broadcast over the heads of men who will accept it, but who will misuse it.

But let us not say anything now in the spirit of recrimination—God forbid that I should speak in that spirit when our nearest and dearest interests are at stake—I have no charge to make against one side or the other. It may have been perfectly right for the late Government to introduce a measure of the character I have mentioned into the House of Commons; it may have been perfectly right for the present Government to oppose it by every means in their power, to turn out that Government, to take their offices, and then to bring in a measure ten times more sweeping; it may have been perfectly right in the present Opposition in the House of Commons to declare that measure to be too extreme, and yet by every means in their power to prevent any limitation to it. I do not pretend to give any judgment—but thus much may be said, that the measure proposed by Mr. Gladstone would, at least, have had this one beneficial effect—it would have been a gradual change; it would have given us something like breathing time; it would have given us a little leisure to accommodate the people to the change and the change to the people. The transition might not have been agreeable, yet it would have been comparatively easy. But this measure proceeds in a rough-and-ready way to carry us to the edge of the Tarpeian rock,—it topples us over like criminals, and future generations will have to estimate, by the magnitude of the fragments, what were once the dimensions and the glory of the British Empire.

My Lords, we are brought to household suffrage as near as possible pure and simple, because the payment annexed to it is the very smallest payment that could well be imposed. We are told that the Government came to household suffrage because they were quite sure to come to it at last. Now, there can be no doubt about that. No thinking man conversant with the state of things in this country, no man seeing the progress of opinion, and seeing how the notions of social and political equality are rapidly developing themselves, could have had any doubt whatever that in the course of a short time we must have come to the point at which we have now arrived. But why are we to jump out of the window when we can go, with comparative safety, downstairs? Why are we to take all at once, as was remarked by Lord Chesterfield, that peck of dirt which should be diffused over our whole life? We could have arrived securely at the same end with equal contentment to the people. I believe the measure proposed by Mr. Gladstone, however extreme it might have been according to the notions of that time, would have been accepted by the country, and that they would have been for a while contented with it. Now, the present measure will be accepted, it is true, but not with contentment; and this conclusion will afford a convincing proof that no party should undertake to carry those measures which they have long and persistently opposed. That party should leave it, even with the surrender of office, to their opponents, who have long, ardently, and conscientiously maintained them; and in this way alone, I am sure, can confidence be given to those for whose benefit a measure is intended.

But then, we are told that household suffrage is the only de-

finite and permanent resting-place.   A resting-place, indeed, I
would ask, in what sense ?   I agree with my noble friend (the
Duke of Marlborough) that there can be no finality.   We are not
now contemplating a final measure, but only a short period of
repose.   Now, I hold that this is no resting-place whatever.   The
suffrage is not an end, it is only a means to an end; and whenever
you read the periodicals of the day, or listen to the speeches
delivered on the platform, in every instance you hear that the
suffrage now obtained must be used for definite purposes which
are described—purposes that cannot be reached under the existing
system.   Look, my Lords, to what happened when the last Reform
Bill was passed.   Was the suffrage of 1832 a resting-place?   Was
it not used for the purpose of obtaining the great remedial
measures which have been passed since that time ?   Far be it
from me to say that the legislation between 1832 and the present
day has not been of the noblest, the most beneficial character.
Ten thousand encumbrances and obstacles have been swept away,
and the country is deeply indebted to that Bill for what has been
done.   But the suffrage henceforward will be employed on very
different matters.   Between 1832 and the present time almost
every commercial and political impediment and difficulty has been
removed.   There remain now none but organic and social changes,
the distribution of property and the incidence of taxation.   These
are the serious matters that deeply and intimately affect the feelings of the great mass of the people of this country.

Now, my Lords, I wish to say that this household suffrage is
not a resting-place even for the suffrage itself, not merely in the
sense of finality, but even in the sense of repose.   The measure
before you goes a very great way indeed ; but the arguments by
which all the parts of it have been sustained go a great deal
further.   In the first place, I must recall to your Lordships' recollection a famous declaration made by Mr. Gladstone, when Chancellor of the Exchequer.   Two years ago, I think, Mr. Gladstone
made a great declaration—that every man of mature age, and not
tainted by crime, had a moral right to the suffrage.   [Earl
RUSSELL indicated dissent.]   Of course, I shall withdraw the
statement if incorrect, but such was the impression upon my
mind.   [Lord LYTTELTON : Without political danger.]   Without
political danger.   Yes; well, that comes very near the point; for
none, it seems, are, in his view, politically dangerous unless they
are actually criminal.   But last year, I think, there was a still
more decided declaration from the same eminent person, that
flesh and blood was entitled to a vote, and this year the Chancellor of the Exchequer confirms the whole by saying that the

present Bill is for the purpose of restoring to the people the rights that have been violently taken from them.

Now, my Lords, I must say that the result of all this has been to infuse into the minds of the people—and, be assured, you will never disabuse them of it whatever you may say or do—the notion that the elective franchise is a right and not a trust. I shrink from openly asserting to what an extent the issues of that notion may be pushed. That the elective franchise was a trust, was a doctrine of an elevating character; now that you say it is a right of all, I cannot see how it is possible for us to remain within the four corners of the Bill which you have now propounded.

I heard last night a remark which comes very much in aid of that view. My noble friend went thus far; he said that the Bill was introduced in order that there might be no class left in England dissatisfied with the suffrage—that one great object of going so low was that no condition of people might have ground to complain of the state of things. Well, my Lords, having laid down this principle, that the suffrage is a right, and that universal satisfaction is your object, I hold that you have also laid down the great principle of universal suffrage; it is even clearer, when you come to the lodger franchise, for see how that enactment will work upon the whole system. The lodger franchise assumes this principle; it contemplates the voter simply as a man, and not as a man in connection with the duties of a citizen. It contemplates the voter as a man who, having a certain income, is disposed to spend a portion in a certain way —that is to say, 10*l.* a year for a room in which to lodge. That man, as a lodger, has none of the duties of a citizen to fulfil. He is not under the necessity of paying rates, he has not to serve as a juror, or discharge any of the functions which fall to the lot of the householder or ratepayer. Just see how this will operate. Take it in the first place in the capital and the great towns. You can as yet form no notion whatever of the numbers that will be added to the register in London and the great towns by the lodger clause. You are going to build in the dark; you are laying down a principle of the most expansive character, so expansive that there is no human force that will be able to control it. I am not going to trouble your Lordships with numerous statistics, but to give merely a few simple facts. There is a district which I know containing 144 houses; it now furnishes fifteen voters to the register. By this lodger franchise there will be furnished ninety-seven—that is, more than six times the present number of voters upon 144 houses.

The EARL OF DERBY: I beg my noble Friend's pardon; do I

understand him to say that in these 144 houses there are 97 persons who permanently occupy these lodgings from year to year, and will therefore be entitled to be put on the register under the Bill?

THE EARL OF SHAFTESBURY: I wish that my noble Friend would wait a while—I was going to state what is the condition of London and the great towns in this respect. I was going to say that you will find in London many single houses filled by a class far lower, and far more needy than anything that has come within your contemplation, and containing many lodgers all fulfilling the conditions of paying at least 10*l.* a year. Yet no calculation can at present be formed of the numbers that will be put upon the register under the terms of the lodger clause. These persons are generally married men with families, who occupy one or two rooms. But when you come to the other class, the great mass of unmarried men, who are lodgers, you will see how wide the principle is, and how necessary it will be that you should expand it so as to admit the large body of men who are not paying 10*l.* a year. Bear this in mind, that a great number of the young unmarried men, many of them in the prime of life, active, intelligent, and earning wages of from 25*s.* to 40*s.*, and even 50*s.* a week, will not come under the category of those who rent a single room at 10*l.* A large number of foremen and superintendents are in that condition, but few others. Now, I am ready to allow that the lodger franchise will be very useful in London, because it will admit to the register a number of highly competent persons—bankers' clerks, literary and scientific persons, many who pass their days at clubs, and others in a similar position. But, numerically, they will be infinitely below the others that must eventually be admitted. Now, of the young men that I have referred to, many live two or three in one room, paying each his quota for it of 1*s.* 6*d.* or 2*s.* a week. And can you suppose when the register comes to be filled up, and the time arrives for the claim to be made, that these young men, finding themselves excluded when others not one hair's breadth above them in social and financial position, and in many cases in the lowest condition as regards education, are put on the register merely because they occupy an entire room to themselves —do you suppose, I say, that these young men will not feèl the greatest possible dissatisfaction and discontent? Believe me, my Lords, there will be no end to the agitation that will be excited by them and their friends to have the amount of the qualification reduced. The Reform League has said that unless you reduce the qualification to 2*s.* 6*d.* a week you will exclude the very

pith and marrow of the country,—I believe this in many respects
to be true, and that you will exclude the young unmarried men to
whom I have referred, though in the prime of life, intelligent, and
in the receipt of excellent wages;—it will become perfectly impossible, I am convinced, to resist the claim that will soon be made on
their behalf. But if you reduce the qualification to 2s. 6d. for those
that will not pay more, you reduce it at the same time to 2s. 6d. for
those that cannot pay more. You will thus flood the towns with a
number of voters totally different in character and position from
the class you have selected. I know it is the fashion to say that this
lodger system is almost peculiar to London. There is no doubt that
it prevails more in London than in any other town. In the great
manufacturing towns of Lancashire and Yorkshire married people
live much more in houses of their own; but the unmarried there
far exceed the number of the married, and many of them live in
lodgings, particularly those of the poorer sort. I will go even
further, and say that statements have been made to me from
country and provincial towns which show that the number of
lodgers, even in such localities, is far greater than is supposed,
and that you will never know the whole number with which you
will have to deal until the lists are formed and the registers completed. The career upon which you have entered in adopting
this lodger franchise is far wider than your calculations; yet,
both that and household suffrage having been adopted, they are
absolutely beyond your recall, and I believe beyond your control.
The decree once passed must be carried into effect, however uncertain the prospect, and however great the danger.

In my opinion, my Lords, this bears us far on towards universal
suffrage, and a great many people share that opinion. You see
this fear by all the efforts and contrivances resorted to, in order,
if possible, to prevent the preponderance of one class over another.
If one thing was emphatically promised to us, it was that nothing
should be done which should in the least degree give one class a
predominance; but, assuredly, you will soon find that a predominant voice has now been given. Argue as you will you cannot
disprove this fact except by figures, and the more you examine
into figures the more clearly you will see that in every instance
the number of additional voters called into existence by the Bill
will be equal to that which exists already, while in a great many
boroughs the number will be increased three, four, and even five-
fold. Surely such an increase as this brings us into the presence
of the democratic influence, and will give to one class so overwhelming a weight in the House of Commons, that the voice of
the minority there will be almost extinguished.

Now, it was to avoid such a result that an attempt was made to introduce cumulative voting and unicorn boroughs—that Mr. Stuart Mill addressed to the other House his able but unintelligible argument upon the representation of minorities—all this shows a strong impression that democratic views will ultimately preponderate, and that something must be done, however experimental and feeble, for the purpose of resisting that mighty power. It may be that democracy will prevail; well, my Lords, if so, we must submit to it. It has its advantages. All forms of government have their virtues as well as their evils. But our business is now to consider, not what are the virtues, but what are the evils of democracy. Now I venture to assert that the suffrage we are about to give, will produce such effects as those which I shall endeavour to lay before your Lordships. I cannot but think that the democratic influence in the House of Commons, and the preponderance given to the representatives of that class of men, will speedily act in a most dangerous way against the old-established and organized institutions of the country. It will act prejudicially to the Church of England. I cannot believe that the representatives of those who are in a great measure so unacquainted with the Church of England and with its benefits will have any friendly feeling towards the Establishment itself. When we come to look at the House in which I have now the honour to address your Lordships, I ask how it will be affected by this great democratic change? So long as the other house of Parliament was elected upon a restricted principle, I can understand that it would submit to a check from such a House as this. But in the presence of this mighty democratic power, and the advance of this great democratic wave, which is rolling on even in spite of itself—for I believe its rapid advance is against the wishes even of many of those who give to it a considerable amount of its impetus—in such a presence it passes my comprehension to understand how an hereditary House like this can hold its own. It might be possible for this House, in one instance, to withstand a measure sent up for our acceptance, if it were violent, unjust, and coercive; but I do not believe that the democracy would permit the repetition of such an offence. It would be said, by action, as is now daily said in words, " The people must govern, and not a set of hereditary peers never chosen by the people." Why, is not what I am now saying very much in accordance with your Lordships' own observation? Are we not living in a time in which nothing is taken for granted? Everything must be ripped up to its first principles, and in vain you argue that a thing is good; your adversary admits it, but says that a change will make it better.

What human institutions can stand such tests? Thus it is that we are going on at the present day; and thus we are continually manifesting that we have in a great measure outgrown our institutions. There is an expansive force among the people. The advance of wealth, the increase of education, the capacity, or at least the ambition, that every man now feels to occupy a higher station than that in which he has been placed by Providence—all these things tend to make men dissatisfied with the institutions of the country, because they fancy themselves cribbed, cabined, and confined by the restrictions which those institutions impose. I am not afraid of direct democratic violence; I believe that the changes which we should all deprecate will rather be brought about by the stealthy progress of legislation. Probably, this very House will be put out not by any sudden and turbulent acts, but with all the gradation and elegance of a dissolving view. The country may have a respect for its old constitutional arrangements, but there the feeling ends. There is no longer any deep spirit remaining to defend its institutions at any cost of safety, or of peace.

Behind this, however, there lurk other questions of greater and more serious importance, as far as the country at large is concerned. There are many social questions to which minds of the new holders of the suffrage will be directed—questions in respect of Free Trade and protection; of money and labour; of wages and the relations between employers and employed; of claims now made by thousands to have a much larger share than at present falls to them of the profits of their toil and of the capital which they help to accumulate, with all the various notions of the distribution of property. Wherever you go you cannot but hear these remarks. You hear them in the various speeches made to the working men; you find them in the discussions of the working classes themselves. Let me confirm this by reading a passage which will show your Lordships the feeling that is growing up in America, and if in America, why not here? In *The Times* of July 11, there was an able letter " From our own Correspondent " in the United States, and in that letter I read this very remarkable narrative—

" Mr. Wade, President of the Senate, has been making a tour west, in the course of which he indulged himself in some extraordinary speeches. In Kansas, he said that, the slavery question being disposed of, that of labour and capital would next demand the attention of the country. ' Property,' he said, ' was not equally divided, and a more equal distribution of capital must be wrought out. That Congress, which had done so much for the slave, cannot quietly regard the terrible distinction which exists between the man that labours and him that does not.' He went on to argue that the Almighty 'never intended' that one man should work while another feasted in idleness. The position (the writer goes on to say), which Mr. Wade holds in the Radical party gives these opinions a weighty significance, and they are a striking commentary on the perverse statements of the philosophers abroad who contend that this is the country of universal content, and that jealousies of class are unknown. We may have a ' Re-distribution of Property' party before many years are over."—*(Vide Note at end.)*

I am specially desirous to call the particular attention of your Lordships to this document, because it is a man of eminence in the United States who lays down these principles. With the strong resemblance between the two countries, the frequent inter-course and interchange of ideas, and the fraternization which takes place between the two peoples, may we not expect that what is going on in America will be imitated here, and that we shall come in this country to the assertion of similar principles, and the agitation of similar questions? Let me observe that such opinions may be expressed and acted on by large masses of the working people—and here I am speaking of what I know—in no spirit of spoliation. I am sure that a large proportion of the work-ing classes have a deep and solemn conviction—and I have found it among working people of religious views—that property is not distributed as property ought to be; that some checks ought to be kept upon the accumulation of property in single hands; that to take away by a legislative enactment that which is in excess, with a view to bestow it on those who have insufficient means, is not a breach of any law, human or divine. It is certain that many entertain these opinions. It is certain also that in times of distress and difficulty, these opinions, urged upon the people by any great demagogue, or by any person of power or influence among them, would take possession of their minds and sink deeply into their hearts; and if they had power through their re-presentatives to give expression to those principles, they would do so speedily and emphatically.

But this measure, my Lords, will lead to other and certain evils. It is curious to find an honourable gentleman in the House of Commons, who, until lately, had no strong opinion in favour of the ballot, now declaring that he should support it by every means in his power because it will henceforward be necessary to protect mob against mob, people against people; so, then, there is no longer any fear of intimidation from rich manufacturers, rich capitalists, rich lawyers, rich landowners, or rich anybody else;

the danger to the people is from themselves, and from themselves they must be protected. I fear, too, that, among other things, we shall soon arrive at the institution of triennial Parliaments, and with them we shall have all the various evils of frequent elections; we shall lead as in America an election-life, and thus, with frequent changes of members, and frequent changes of policy to suit the fickleness of the multitude, we shall be deluged with crude opinions, pernicious theories, and inexperienced representatives, and thus give a deadly stroke to the contemplated perfection of the House of Commons.

But as a counterpoise to all this action we are promised a certain amount of securities, some of them in the shape of enactments, and some in the shape of hopes. We are told, in the first place, that this is essentially the same Bill that was first introduced into the House of Commons. Doubtless it is true that if you take a man and divest him of shoes, stockings, pantaloons, coat, and shirt, he is essentially the same man; but by so doing you have deprived him of everything which gave him decency and protection. In a great measure such is the case with this Bill. Now, the first provision is that the householder, to be entitled to vote, shall have paid the rates levied for the relief of the poor, and shall have resided twelve months. With regard to the personal payment of rates, I think the argument of my noble friend (Earl Grey) last evening, that personal payment could not be universally insisted upon, was quite unanswerable. I am certain, from what I know and have heard, that if you insist upon personal payment of the rate, you will exclude so very many from the suffrage, that you will hardly increase appreciably the constituency, at least, in London. Abolish the payment of rates, and you will flood the register with such a mass of abject poverty that the boldest will be appalled at the result. Residence, if insisted upon, is, in many instances, a guarantee of respectability to a certain extent; but it is not so in every case; and I know many instances to the contrary, many in which a tenant has resided a year simply and solely because he has not paid his rent, and because the landlord would not turn him out, fearing that, if he did so, he would lose his rent altogether and not get a better tenant. Nevertheless, residence, no doubt, to a certain extent, is a test of respectability; but, at the same time, I will undertake to say that the 80 out of 97 persons living in the houses I have spoken of, and here is the answer to my noble friend, will be put upon the register if they chose, having resided in them for more than a year; and yet they will not be more than a hair's breadth above the condition of paupers. It is said, too, by way of comfort to us, that men must demand to be put upon the register, and it appears, for a moment, to be in some measure a security; but I doubt very much whether it is one. The sending in of claims will be attended to by caucuses and agents, if it is in the interest of any party that it should be done. If any one is interested in securing the honour of representing a constituency he will take good care that due preparation is made for the election; and, whether demands have been made or not, that those who are qualified shall be placed on the register if they will subserve his interests.

These are pretty nearly the legislative securities given us by this Bill; but we have a number of other securities in the form of hopes. I heard from the opposite side of the House last night, and I have often heard it in private conversation, that this is a most conservative measure. I have heard it said that the middle classes are not conservative, but that if you go deeper you get into a vein of gold, and encounter the presence of a highly conservative feeling. In the first place, I ask is that so? And in the second place, what do you mean by the term Conservative? Do you mean to say that this large mass that they call the "residuum," of which, am I presumptuous if I say that, from various circumstances, few men living have more knowledge than I have, is conservative of your Lordships' titles and estates? Not a bit; they know little about them and care less. Will you venture to say that they are conservative of the interests of the Established Church? Certainly they are not. Thousands upon thousands living in this vast City of London do not know the name of the parish in which they reside nor the name of the minister in charge of it. They are, however, very conservative indeed of their own sense of right and wrong. They are living from hand to mouth, and, in consequence, they are very conservative of what they consider to be their own interests. They are affectionate, grateful, and open to sympathy. If there were to go among them two persons, one a lord and the other a plebeian, they would, without adopting the lord's opinion, prefer, in many instances, the lord because they would think he would have more power to forward their views. Their own interests, as is natural, take the lead. They have no wanton desire for plunder or spoliation; but they have rights and wrongs of their own conception, which they will insist upon maintaining or redressing. They have known me long, but were I to go to a meeting of a thousand, take a different view of their interests from that which they had taken, and try to persuade them to adopt my view, I am sure that 995 out of the 1000 would vote against me, and would take good care to look out for some one who would better serve what they considered their just purposes.

1 cannot understand, my Lords, upon what ground this is proved to be a conservative measure. I have heard it argued, that to obtain that issue we must rely a good deal upon social influences. I can perfectly comprehend how social influences can prevail where a landlord and his tenants live in mutual acquaintance and reciprocity of kindness; but a totally different state of things is found in London and other large towns. The people live together in vast masses far removed from the influences you speak of, and I cannot give a better proof of it than in this statement not long ago from an excellent clergyman of the Church of England. He told me that in the whole of his district, containing 6000 people, there was not a single family that kept a housemaid. Where were the social influences here? and yet that is only a sample of the general condition. Look, too, at what is going on among all the vast aggregations of the people. Persons of property, and even tradesmen, are leaving the towns for country residences. In the neighbourhood of this House there is a remarkable congregation. Twenty-five years ago it was so rich that the minister could find agents and money for any object. The other day he informed me that the wealthy were deserting the district in such numbers that the necessary agencies could hardly be maintained. It is the same in the manufacturing towns—in Manchester, Huddersfield, and others I could name. The same complaint is made everywhere—that the people of property and station are leaving the towns and are removing themselves from the working classes, and that a "hard and fast line" is being drawn between employer and employed, between persons of influence and those who ought to be the subject of it. Be assured, my Lords, that to trust to social influences under existing circumstances such as these, is to trust to the greatest of all chimeras.

Another hope held out is that of education. I am sure I shall not be misunderstood when I say that the hope from education is one of the most fallacious that could be entertained for the present exigency. If you would give us ten years of preparation education might do a great deal; but what you are going to do is this, to give the franchise before you give education, whereas you should have given education before the franchise. It will take ten years to bring up the residuum by education; but it will not take six months for them, through their representatives, to destroy everything that comes in their way. I cannot but say, when I look at the state of this vast population, when I know what they are, how easily they are deluded, how impressible and open they are to bad influences, that this gift of the suffrage is one of the most fatal gifts ever bestowed upon an unprepared people. In the interest of the people you ought to have withheld it for some years, or conferred it by gradations. Do not shut your eyes to the danger; there will be no lack of rich, unscrupulous candidates, desirous, at any cost, of social position as Members of Parliament, who will find the new voters purchasable as a flock of sheep. I am certain you will learn hereafter, to your great regret, that by this measure, instead of promoting purity, you have unwittingly extended the worst political corruption.

Again, it is said that we should throw our whole confidence on the people. Yes, my Lords, I say so too, for if they are left to follow their natural instincts it will be seen that they have no desire in themselves to make any aggressive movement on the institutions of the country. But they are easily excited, easily open to misrepresentation; a skilful and adroit orator may bring them to almost any conviction he pleases, and then say, my Lords, in what state we shall be. The nation is by no means in the same position in which it was some twenty years ago. A certain moral electric telegraph now runs through the whole of the people of this country. Anything said or done in London is felt simultaneously at John o'Groat's House and the Land's End. The people act together rightly or wrongly by one simultaneous movement. They have common affections and common action; and if in a time of distress and difficulty designing, skilful demagogues should bring their influence to bear upon the public excitement, they would, in the plenitude of their strength, assail almost every existing institution—

"Malé judicavit populus, at judicavit; non debuit, sed potuit."

They would possess the power, and, defying all right, would exercise it in their passion. I know that in the generosity of their hearts many would afterwards be grieved, but they would then have done that of which they would have to repent unavailingly in sackcloth and ashes.

Again, many are entertaining sanguine hopes that after the dissolution of 1869 there will be large returns on the Conservative side. For my own part I cannot venture to say how that will be. But, certainly, if that time be a time of distress in the land, if there be a lack of employment and a lowering of wages, or anything which touches the deepest interests of the people, there will be no such result; but a movement which will lead to very rapid changes. This, my Lords, I believe to be the real state of the case in regard to the great mass of the population, by which I mean that preponderating class which will shape the whole character of the representation, which will have the greatest influence in the House of Commons, and which will determine the future destinies of this great empire.

As to re-distribution, I can only remark that it seems, as was stated last night, to be a question which must be re-opened altogether. And I cannot blame the Government for that event, for I am convinced that, upon the principles laid down, if even an angel from heaven had drawn the clauses he could not possibly have given satisfaction. If you lay down the principle that representation must follow wealth and population, the representation will travel, as it is travelling now, rapidly to the north, where new towns are springing up every day, and demanding a position in the Parliament. Already I have seen a list of several which are dissatisfied, and which will in the new Parliament assert their right. You cannot avoid a new Reform Bill at every census, and things are quickly approaching to one great consummation—that great consummation announced by Mr. Cobden, that " the towns must govern."

Surely, my Lords, all these movements are tending to Republican issues! If we have any doubt upon that point, we may refer to the authority of Mr. Bright, who stated broadly in his speech that whatever might be the outward form, the principle of the Government must hereafter be Republican or Democratic; and, perhaps, one of the heaviest charges which can be brought against this Bill is that it is accelerating our already too rapid progress. Rapid indeed it is, for what is new one day becomes antiquated the next. The Reform Act of 1832 gave us a pause of 30 years. But what will be given by the Reform Bill of 1867? My Lords, I do not believe it will give us the pause of a single session. Everything at the present day is swift and gigantic. We have gigantic wars, gigantic ships, gigantic speculations, gigantic frauds, gigantic crimes, a gigantic Reform Bill, and I much fear that we shall have a gigantic downfall. Our position is, indeed, full of misgivings and fears—we are bringing, suddenly and roughly, old England into collision with young England; ancient and venerable institutions to be tried, without notice or preparation, by poverty, levity, and ignorance; and by many who, being neither poor, nor vain, nor ignorant, are yet too full of hot blood, effervescing youth, and burning ambition, to be calm, dispassionate and just.

But, after all this, there will arise the many great and social questions. From all which I have seen and heard I fully conclude that there will spring up in this country, and speedily, too, a revival of that hazardous and angry feud instituted long ago between the House of Want and the House of Have. Then you will have new schemes, new agencies, new conditions, new problems, and new fears; and to such an extent, that those who have been foremost in urging the passing of this measure will be among the very first to lament and condemn it.

But, my Lords, if all this were necessary for the real advancement of the human race, if it were necessary for the interests of England, I am quite sure your Lordships would be the first to accede to it. Institutions must be expanded to suit men, but men are not to be dwarfed or cramped to suit institutions. Yet, my Lords, I should have thought that statesmen of high minds and patriotic hearts might have devised a scheme by which these discordant elements might have been brought into union, so that, for a time at least, all that appears jarring and difficult might have been reconciled in some one safe and harmonious movement.

But, my Lords, however dark and dismal may be the future of England, it is our duty to fight for our country, into whatever hands the Government may fall. England, though not so great and happy, may yet be a great and happy land. Whether monarchical, republican, or democratic, she will be England still; and let us beguile our fears by indulging our imagination, and by picturing to ourselves that which can never be realized—that out of this hecatomb of British traditions, and British institutions, there will arise the great and glorious Phœnix of a Conservative Democracy.

———————

[NOTE. Our own Correspondent, United States, *Times*, August 26, 1867. " I see the quotations made in the House of Lords from Mr. Wade's agrarian speech gave rise to the publication in England of a contradiction purporting to come from Mr. Wade. The fact that the President of the Senate *did* make a speech of the character described to you is of so much importance that I venture to trouble you with a short statement with regard to it.

"Mr. Wade, in the statement to which I have referred, states that no stenographer was present when he made his speech. This has been proved to be an error. A reporter of the *New York Times* (one of the most trusted of its staff) was on the spot, and took notes of all that Mr. Wade said in shorthand. For this fact the editor of the *New York Times* has vouched to the public; and to give weight to this statement he made known the name of his reporter, which appears to be well known in the journalist world. This gentleman has assured his chief of the strict accuracy of his report, and affirms that Mr. Wade really said every word attributed to him. In this he is confirmed by the evidence of other persons present on the occasion; and the editor of the *New York Times*, having made searching inquiries into all the circumstances, gave the assurance to the public that the report was accurate in every particular, Mr. Wade's denial notwithstanding.

" The truth is, that when Mr. Wade returned from Kansas he found his speech had made a great commotion.   What he had said pleased the Kansas people very much, and Mr. Wade thought he had made a success ; but he discovered that he had failed to take into account the sentiment of the great cities and populations of the North.   He saw, in short, that he had gone too far, and his friends begged him to make some explanation.   Yielding to their advice, he attempted to explain away his imprudent speech, after the manner of approved precedents elsewhere.

" The question for the public to decide, and the one which they have decided here long ago, is whether the notes of a reporter, acting in the impartial exercise of his profession, are to be taken as the truth, or the denial of a gentleman who is told by his political associates that he has damaged himself with the public ?   Mr. Wade is at best a very impassioned and hasty speaker, and if he *believed* (as he evidently did) that no reporter was present in Kansas, he would be very likely to say more than he would be prepared to stand by in his cooler moments at Boston, Washington, or New York.   Moreover, there is this important circumstance to consider.   Mr. Wade, while denying the accuracy of the report, has never disclaimed the sentiments conveyed in it.   This has been pointed out to him by the public journals here, but still Mr. Wade has held his peace.   Upon the whole, the people in this country believe that he made the speech, and will hold him responsible for it."]

THE END.

LONDON: PRINTED BY WILLIAM CLOWES AND SONS, STAMFORD STREET AND CHARING CROSS.